Political Crises, Social Conflict and Economic Development

Political Crises, Social Conflict and Economic Development

The Political Economy of the Andean Region

Edited by

Andrés Solimano

Edward Elgar

Cheltenham, UK • Northampton, MA, USA

Published by
Edward Elgar Publishing Limited
Glensanda House
Montpellier Parade
Cheltenham
Glos GL50 1UA
UK

Edward Elgar Publishing, Inc.
136 West Street
Suite 202
Northampton
Massachusetts 01060
USA

A catalogue record for this book
is available from the British Library

ISBN 1 84542 196 5

Printed and bound in Great Britain by MPG Books Ltd, Bodmin, Cornwall

Contents

PART II COUNTRY STUDIES

List of figures

List of tables

Contributors

Gustavo Arteta
Director of Research, Corporation for Economic Development Studies (CORDES), Quito, Ecuador

Gonzalo Chávez
Director of the Masters Program in Economic Development Studies, Bolivian Catholic University (UCB), La Paz, Bolivia

Enzo Del Bufalo
Professor of Economics, Department of Economics, Central University of Venezuela, Caracas, Venezuela

Amanda Glassman
Specialist in Social Development, Inter-American Development Bank, Washington, DC, United States

George Gray Molina
Executive Director, Economic and Social Policy Analysis Unit (UDAPE), Ministry of the Presidency, La Paz, Bolivia

Sudhanshu Handa
Associate Professor, Department of Public Policy, University of North Carolina-Chapel Hill, United States

Osvaldo Hurtado
Former President of Ecuador and President of Corporation for Economic Development Studies (CORDES), Quito, Ecuador

Miguel Jaramillo
Senior Researcher, Group for the Analysis of Development (GRADE), Lima, Peru

José Antonio Ocampo
Former Minister of Finance of Colombia and Under-Secretary General for Economic and Social Affairs, United Nations, New York, United States

Jaime Saavedra
Senior Researcher, Group for the Analysis of Economic Development (GRADE), Lima, Peru

Andrés Solimano
Regional Advisor, Economic Commission for Latin America and the Caribbean (ECLAC), United Nations, Santiago, Chile

Acknowledgements

This book is the fruit of a project supported by a grant (# 1010–0586) from Ford Foundation in New York. The project was administered by the Inter-American Dialogue in Washington, DC. It also had the substantive collaboration of the Economic Commission for Latin America and the Caribbean of the United Nations in Santiago, Chile. Special thanks for the support throughout this project go to: Manuel Montes from the Ford Foundation; to Peter Hakim, President of the Inter-American Dialogue for continuous support; to José Antonio Ocampo, former Executive Secretary of ECLAC and author of one of the country studies in this book and, in the initial stage of the project, to Barbara Stallings, former head of the Economic Development Division at ECLAC.

An international conference to present the different chapters that led to the book was held at the New School University in New York City in May 2003. Chapter 2 was also presented in seminars held at the World Bank, the Inter-American Development Bank and the University of Paris, III, Sorbonne La Nouvelle.

I am also very grateful to Claudio Aravena who provided excellent assistance for the development of the whole project. Ximena Sánchez and Maritza Agar from the Economic Development Division of ECLAC participated in the organization of the workshops for the project. Claudia Allendes provided effective editorial support and coordination with the various contributors for the preparation of this book.

Finally, we would like to mention that the content of this book represents the views of the authors and not necessarily the institutions to which they belong.

1. Introduction and synthesis

Andrés Solimano

Economic growth and the process of development do not evolve in a political and institutional vacuum. Economic choices depend on rules, institutions and social constraints that are mediated by a political process. A governance environment characterized by stability, the rule of law, and social cooperation will foster wealth creation provided good economic opportunities are in place. However, in many societies – including the Andean countries – the political process is often messy, institutions are far from being the ideal set of rules that minimize transactions costs and social relations are characterized by conflict and even violence. Ultimately, underdevelopment is not only a problem of lack of economic resources but it is largely associated also with volatile politics, dysfunctional institutions and highly differentiated social structures.

The subject of this book is to understand the main characteristics of political systems, institutions and social structures in the Andean region of Latin America and their impact on and interplay with their economic performance. The Andean region is comprised of Bolivia, Colombia, Ecuador, Peru and Venezuela.[1] These economies have a per capita income of around US$2000. They are rich in natural resources such as oil, mining, forestry, biodiversity, fishery, and so on. In the Andean region we find a high frequency of political crises in recent decades. In some countries there is also a high turnover of ministers and other authorities. Constitutions have been reformed in the five Andean countries in the last 15 years. International rankings of quality of institutions as measured by indices of rule of law, effectiveness of regulation, control of corruption and others place the Andean group in a relatively low place of the rankings. Their social structure is characterized by considerable poverty, inequality of income and wealth and social exclusion of certain social groups. In Bolivia, Ecuador and Peru a significant share of the population is of indigenous origin but this is not the case in Colombia and Venezuela. Economic growth has been moderate and volatile in the last two to three decades and some countries, such as Venezuela, have suffered a protracted growth slowdown in the last quarter century. The Andean economies also have had their fair share of economic crises associated with terms of trade shocks, changes in capital flows and, at different junctures, internal destabilization.

1.1 MAIN QUESTIONS

This book includes comparative cross-country studies along with political economy country papers for each Andean country. The country studies cover at least the 1990s and early 2000s although some of them go even further back and include previous decades as a background to understand current political economy developments in these countries. The volume tries to address the following questions:

a. What are the main characteristics of the political system and the stability of democracy in the Andean countries?
b. What is the frequency of episodes of systemic breakdown (coup d' état, authoritarian regimes, major social upheavals) and collapse of democracy in recent decades in the Andean nations?
c. Are social contracts – as embedded in the constitutions – stable over time? Conversely, what is the frequency of constitutional change in the Andean region?
d. How common are presidential crises and turnover of ministers and other authorities in the Andean countries, reflecting continuous political change and instability in these countries? How can we measure political instability and institutional fragility?
e. What is the interplay between economic and political crises? Is the causality running from political crises to economic crises or from economic crises to political crises? Does one type of crises necessarily lead to the other?
f. What is the quality of institutions in the Andean region as measured by historical indicators and by subjective indices of rule of law, control of corruption, effectiveness of regulations, degree of violence?
g. What are the main political and economic effects of income and wealth inequality in the Andean region? Does inequality worsen governance? Does inequality hamper economic growth?
h. How have the abundance of natural resources and the existence of illegal activities (for example drug traffic) affected the economy and governance conditions in the Andean region?
i. What are the main economic effects of political instability and the quality of institutions on the rate of economic growth and other dimensions of economic development?

1.2 MAIN FINDINGS

The main findings of this book can be summarized as follows:

Political Systems, Constitutions and Crises

A theme underscored in this book is that *formal* political systems do not always guarantee strong presidencies and stable democracies. We document a high incidence of presidential crises in the Andean countries. Recent examples are Bolivia in 2003, Ecuador and Peru in 2000, Venezuela in 2001. Traditionally a response to recurrent instability in the Andean countries has been trying to strengthen the presidential system. However, this reform may not, per se, avoid political crises. We are not advocating parliamentary systems either. The point is that strong presidencies may take more than having a presidential system written into the constitution.

In the 1990–2003 period, Colombia, Ecuador, Peru, Bolivia and Venezuela – all five Andean countries – reformed, in major ways, their constitutions as a way to solve their chronic political and economic problems. Historically, say during the 20th century, the frequency of constitutional reform in the Andean region was high. If we interpret (major) constitutional reforms as an attempt to redraw existing social contracts, we find that social contracts are not very stable in the Andean countries. Again we have to distinguish between formal social contracts – as expressed in constitutions – and actual (or 'informal' social contracts), that embed other considerations such as political culture, history and social norms that are certainly more difficult to change than the constitutions. The specific consequences of the last round of constitutional reforms undertaken since the 1990s in the Andean countries merit their own analysis but are beyond the scope of this book. Still the experiences of the last ten or 15 years suggest that changing the constitution is not an overnight fix for the political, economic and social problems of these countries. In addition, new constitutions in some cases may create new problems that probably were not envisaged by the reformers. A sensitive issue, for example, is the expansion of economic rights (and devolution of powers to sub-national levels) sanctioned by some of the new constitutions without concomitant increases in wealth and income to finance the new mandates of the reformed constitutions. This could be relevant for Colombia following the constitution of 1991 and in Venezuela after the constitutional reform of 1999–2000. Other new rules that have proved complex are provisos on the number of political parties, re-election rules, decentralization and others.

Interplay between Economic and Political Crises

The Andean countries, some more than others, suffered a number of economic crises in recent decades. From a political economy perspective, the question arises whether these economic crises are always followed by political crises? Of course, we may also have a reverse causality in which political instability leads to economic crises. The answer to the first question is mixed. The Bolivian presidential crisis of 2003 that led to the departure of former President Sánchez de Lozada, who flew to Miami after resigning, came at a time when the incomes of coca growers and poor peasants sharply declined following the policy of coca eradication initiated earlier. So although there were economic and social causes behind the departure of President Sánchez de Lozada, such as the above mentioned squeeze of the incomes of coca growers, it was not a case of a political crisis that follows a macroeconomic crisis (defined as high inflation, continuous currency devaluation, massive decline in GDP, and so on). In contrast, in Ecuador in the last 1990s, the country indeed suffered a severe macroeconomic and financial crisis in 1998–99 characterized by accelerated currency depreciation, inflation, a crisis in the banking system and a decline in gross domestic product of over 9 per cent in 1999. Against this background of economic crisis, President Mahuad was deposed in an indigenous-military uprising in January of 2000. The Ecuadorian political crisis of early 2000 was a clear case in which economic crises preceded a presidential crisis. Of course, these are not purely mechanical relationships and there were also political factors (the management by the President of various conflicts between the sierra and the coast, the relationship with parliament, etc.) behind the collapse of President Mahuad's administration. Anyhow, it is clear that the serious economic crises of 1998–99, intertwined with various political factors, created a climate conducive to a presidential crisis.

Other presidential crises have a different origin. Some of them are related to corruption scandals associated with lack of transparency and weak mechanisms of checks and balances. The departure of Peruvian President Fujimori in 2000, triggered by a bribery scandal involving Chief of Security Vladimiro Montesinos, is a case in point of a corruption-led crisis. In addition, the neo-authoritarian style of government of Fujimori in the 1990s certainly generated increasing levels of social resistance and delegitimization at domestic and international levels that led to such a crisis. Regarding the interplay between economic and political crises, it is apparent that no open, large-scale economic crises happened to occur before or after the departure of Fujimori. In sum, various recent experiences in the Andean region suggest that economic and political crises are not always closely related with each other. Crises in each realm seem to have a certain degree of 'autonomy'. One type of crisis (political or economic) is not necessarily preceded or followed by the other.

Stability and Quality of Democracy

The cross-country analysis and individual country cases in this book show that historically, and recently, democracy has followed cycles (alternating with authoritarianism) in some Andean countries. In the 1960s and 1970s, there were frequent regime changes in which military regimes alternated with democracy in Bolivia, Peru and Ecuador. This underscores the fragility of democracy in these countries. In contrast, in the last four decades democracy has been more stable in Colombia and Venezuela, although these countries have been also affected by chronic internal armed conflict (Colombia) and political polarization (Venezuela).

The Andean countries' experience suggests that the dichotomy between democracy and authoritarianism has to be qualified. This brings us to the complex issue of quality of democracy. At a broad level we may associate the quality of democracy with the efficacy with which political institutions mediate and aggregate the interests, voice and preferences of different individuals, political parties and social groups to produce results that are deemed to be socially desirable (including creating an environment conducive to economic prosperity and stability). Also democracies are incomplete when civic and political rights are not respected and enforced for everyone.

In the context of the Andean countries, the demands by certain social and ethnic groups for an increased voice and political representation are an important test of the quality of democracy. Exclusion and lack of representation of these groups show that democracy is incomplete. Recently we have seen the increasing demands of indigenous groups in Bolivia, Ecuador, and Peru for a greater voice and representation (and eventually autonomy). Traditionally these groups have been largely excluded from the political system although in the 1990s that situation started to be reversed.

Another issue pertaining to the quality and stability of democracy is how democracy manages violence. Colombia is the country with the highest incidence of political violence in the Andean group and in Latin America. The country has suffered for more than four decades an armed conflict that started in the 1960s with socioeconomic and political demands by armed peasants' organizations but that later on became linked to drug-trafficking, changing the original nature of the conflict. Peru also suffered from heightened violence by Sendero Luminoso in the 1980s and early 1990s. Persistent political violence reflects a failure of the democratic system that cannot impose the rule of law and maintain the monopoly of the use of force by the institutions of the state. The economic consequences of violence are bound to be severe as it often destroys human lives and valuable economic assets and creates an environment that penalizes the accumulation of capital.

The Nature and Quality of Institutions

Economic theories of institutions stress that they are created to minimize transaction costs and facilitate economic exchange. However, recent political economy theories take a different approach and envisage institutions as instruments that are designed and maintained to protect the economic and political interests of certain elites which are not necessarily coincident with the interests and general welfare of society. In fact, we may find several historical and recent examples of countries in the world in which dysfunctional institutions can bring stagnation, economic retardation and misery to the population.

The country studies in this volume assess the effectiveness of institutions using both historical and recent indicators of institutional change as well as a set of indices of quality of institutions compiled by the World Bank and the World Economic Forum for a large sample of countries. This allows us to put the institutions of the Andean countries in international comparative perspective. The World Bank-World Economic Forum indices are based on surveys applied to users of these institutions such as individuals, domestic companies and foreign investors. These are subjective indices in the sense of being based on people's opinions of how institutions work. Although there are differences within the Andean group in general these countries rate below some other Latin American countries and the OECD in terms of quality of institutions.

Natural Resources, External Vulnerability and Illegal Activities

Political institutions interact with economic structures and international conditions in generating certain economic outcomes. Several Andean countries depend on natural resources as their main source of foreign exchange and fiscal revenues. This is the case of oil in Venezuela and Ecuador, of hydrocarbon in Bolivia, copper in Peru, and so on. This dependence on natural resources makes these economies vulnerable to international volatility in commodity prices. Commodity price shocks often create internal cycles of boom and bust in Latin American countries and the Andean group is not an exception in that regard. These cycles occur, in part, because mechanisms of 'financing' the shocks (when they are considered as transitory) are limited given the incomplete nature of domestic and international capital markets. Commodity stabilization funds have been set up in several Andean countries with various degrees of success (or failure) in avoiding macroeconomic fluctuations. This dependence on natural resources not only create problems of macroeconomic management (that is, how much to save or spend of a positive shock) but also raise political economy dilemmas, chief among them to decide how and in which sectors to spend revenue windfalls when they occur. Moreover, managing the revenues of natural resources in a transparent way – avoiding rent seeking and corruption – is also a political challenge.

Another issue related to 'natural' resources is the importance of illegal activity such as drug trafficking based in the cultivation of coca leaf and poppies. This has been especially serious in Colombia since the 1960s and 1970s where the revenues of the drug traffic provide resources to rebel groups fueling and perpetuating internal conflict. Also Bolivia and Peru have been affected by drug trafficking problems at least since the 1980s. Also money from illegal activity can have a corrupting effect on institutions debilitating the democratic system and altering economic priorities away from development.

Social Structure, Institutions and Growth

The social structure of the Andean countries is very complex. It comprises poverty and economic inequality and exclusion of certain social groups. Traditionally, the urban and rural economic elites (landowners, industrialists, bankers, renters) have a disproportionate influence in society. This is in contrast with the limited political and economic influence of low-income groups, including the working class, the unemployed or underemployed, poor peasants and part of the middle class. This social structure generates distributive conflicts over the shares of national income accruing to each group and conflict over access to and use of political power.

A very important role of political institutions is to mediate this latent (or open) social conflict in such ways that society remains reasonably stable and in which the capital accumulation and growth process can develop. When institutions fail to mediate this conflict, for example after a negative shock has occurred, the result is likely to be a combination of both political instability and lower growth. Institutions and governance conditions affect economic growth through factor accumulation and productivity growth. The combination of weak institutions and social conflict creates uncertainty over policies and rules, deteriorates the quality of labor–employer relations and worsens the general business climate in the country. In the external dimension, they can deter international investors and capital inflows also affecting growth. This book examines at country level how these mechanisms operate in practice identifying the channels through which social and governance factors affect economic outcomes. The empirical growth literature has ample evidence showing the negative effects of weak governance conditions on economic growth. The country studies included in this volume examine in rich institutional and historical detail the interactions between politics and institutions on the one hand and economic performance and growth on the other.

Geopolitical Considerations

This book focuses, mainly, on the internal political-economy factors that affect economic performance. Still, we should not neglect the importance of international politics and geopolitical factors. The Andean region is under the direct influence of the United States, its foreign policy and its international financial policies. The influence of Latin American and European governments is also relevant.

The Andean region is affected by the decisions of international financial institutions such as the IMF, the World Bank and the regional development banks. Stabilization plans supported by the Bretton Woods institutions have been critically important at times in affecting the economic and political outcomes in these countries. For example the withholding of a large loan by the IMF to Ecuador in 1999 has been credited with a decisive effect on the eventual demise of President Mahuad in early 2000. Also Plan Colombia actively supported by the United States and some European countries has been instrumental in trying to affect the course of the four-decades-old internal armed conflict in Colombia. The US policy towards drugs in Bolivia and Peru affected the actual patterns of geographical location of drug production in the Andean region and outside it. As already mentioned, policies of coca eradication in Bolivia, encouraged from abroad, altered the fragile social and political balances of the country.

1.3 ORGANIZATION OF THE BOOK

This book is organized in two parts besides this introduction. Part I includes two essays, Chapters 2 and 3, that consider the Andean group in international comparative perspective. Chapter 2, 'Governance crises and the Andean region: a political economy analysis' by Andrés Solimano provides a conceptual framework to study governance patterns distinguishing between (a) the political regimes and the constitution, (b) the quality of institutions and (c) the patterns of social conflict and cooperation. The chapter then undertakes an empirical analysis for the Andean region that combines historical and recent data on political crises, changes of constitutions for the 20th century along with subjective indices of quality of institutions published by the World Bank and the World Economic Forum. The chapter also illustrates the linkages between governance, inequality and growth performance. Chapter 3, 'Poverty, inequality and governance in the Andean region' by Amanda Glassman and Ashu Handa analyses the main trends in poverty and inequality in the Andean countries. The chapter explores the role of the level and volatility of economic growth, the incidence of recessions and crises, inflation, labor market dynamics and governance factors in terms of their impact on poverty and inequality. The chapter also highlights options for social policy and reform that make compatible growth with social equity and inclusion.

Part II of the book is devoted to five political economy country studies written by well-known economists and political economists of each Andean country. These studies distinguish between institutional and governance factors and economic and social outcomes, exploring the interfaces between both sets of variables. The country studies provide rich institutional detail and place the country experiences in the proper historical and contemporaneous context of each country. Chapter 4, 'The political economy of the crisis in the Andean region: the case of Bolivia' written by George Gray Molina and Gonzalo Chávez make a distinction between a 'governance block' and an 'economic block'. The study covers from 1982 to 2002. The governance block identifies political fragmentation, corruption, ethnic fragmentation and drug trafficking as important governance issues in Bolivia. The economic block documents the stabilization of hyperinflation in the mid-1980s and the successive economic and social reforms undertaken in the 1990s and early 2000s. The authors warn of some critical contradictions of Bolivian society; particularly the fact that the modernizing economic reforms of the 1990s were unable, to a large extent, to tackle a variety of fundamental problems of Bolivia such as its economic dependence on non-renewable natural resources, the sizeable coca sector that provides the inputs for drug processing, a fragmented political system, a high level of poverty and inequality and a history of exclusion of indigenous groups. These factors have been important in explaining the crises that shook Bolivia in 2003 (and previous crises as well). Chapter 5, 'The economy, conflict and governance in Colombia' by José Antonio Ocampo examines the evolution of governance conditions and economic developments in Colombia in the 1990s and early 2000s. The chapter also provides some discussion of historical trends and data when relevant. The author relates the four-decades-old internal armed conflict of Colombia started in the 1960s to colonization, the geographical fragmentation of power, intensified by the effects of drug trafficking and its degenerative effects on the rebel groups and society at large. In the economic area Ocampo analyses the impact of incomplete adjustment to trade liberalization and the vulnerability of the Colombian economy to external financial cycles. He also notes the tensions between economic openness and an increased role of the state sanctioned by the constitution of 1991. Ocampo characterizes Colombia as a relatively stable democracy (in terms of duration and continuity since the 1950s) although it coexists with a violent, gang-controlled system largely related to drug trafficking activity and armed conflict.

Chapter 6, 'Political economy of Ecuador: the quandary of governance and economic development' by Gustavo Arteta and Osvaldo Hurtado analyzes the political and economic performance of Ecuador in the 1990s and early 2000s. The authors highlight the fact that Ecuador was the first country in Latin America to begin the transition to democracy in 1977–79 after successive authoritarian regimes. Ecuadorian democracy, however, has been characterized by political instability, a high turnover of presidents and ministers, volatility of laws and reforms, fragmented and conflictive politics, regional divides, influential corporate interests and weak executives. Ecuador grew very rapidly in the 1970s following the oil price boom but the 1980s and 1990s were two decades of low and unstable growth, inflation, recurrent currency devaluations, external vulnerability to commodity price shocks and volatile capital flows. The authors highlight two important political and economic reforms oriented to restoring good governance and economic stability in Ecuador: the constitutional reform of 1998 and the adoption of official dollarization in 2000.

Chapter 7, 'Governance and economic performance in Peru in the 1990s' by Miguel Jaramillo and Jaime Saavedra examines the main politico-institutional and economic developments in Peru up to 2000. The authors document that in the late 1980s, before the Fujimori administration, Peru was affected by economic collapse and social turbulence and violence led by the Maoist group Sendero Luminoso. The chapter highlights, however, that the new Fujimori administration combined free market policies with neo-authoritarian political methods. The Fujimori administration's economic program comprised macroeconomic stabilization, liberalization, and privatization. However, Fujimori also showed social concern and an active effort at providing social infrastructure in rural and urban areas was launched. For almost a decade, these policies maintained a certain legitimacy. However, the contradictory mix of social market economics and authoritarian politics in any incomplete democracy proved ultimately explosive when the Montesinos corruption and Mafia-like scandal erupted forcing the departure from the country of President Fujimori who sent his resignation from Japan in mid-2000 where he stayed afterwards in self-imposed exile.

Chapter 8, 'Venezuela: from stability to turmoil' by Enzo Del Bufalo provides an interpretative essay on the events and factors that led to the government of President Hugo Chávez in the late 1990s and the economic and political polarization of the early to mid-2000s in Venezuela. The author discusses several features of Venezuelan society during the second half of the 20th century and before: the heavy economic reliance on oil (the 'oil rental' model, *el modelo rentista*), a political system dominated by two traditional political parties (ADECO and COPEI), a varied 'human geography', the influence of the international economy and global politics. This model led to persistent economic decline from the late 1970s, followed by political instability and attempts at either partial reform of the system or to more radicalized alternatives oriented to shattering the prevailing system along neopopulist lines. The author also looks at economic performance in Venezuela and discusses the interplay between governance and economics in the early part of the Chávez administration.

NOTE

1. The criterion for including the five countries in the definition of 'Andean region' is their membership of CAN (Andean Community of Nations), an economic integration and political agreement that has a governing council, a parliament and forms a customs union. Chile is also an 'Andean country' in a geographical sense but it is not a member of CAN.

PART I

Analytical overview and cross-country analysis

2. Political instability, institutional quality and social conflict in the Andes

Andrés Solimano*

2.1 INTRODUCTION

The Andean region of Latin America has experienced governance and economic difficulties that have compounded its structural problems of poverty, slow growth, inequality and financial volatility. Governance difficulties are reflected in a high turnover of authorities, low rankings in international indices of institutional effectiveness, recurrent political crises, violence (particularly acute in Colombia) and potentially fragile democracies.[1] All these governance problems put clear obstacles to steady economic growth besides affecting the quality of democracy.

The last few years have been marked by considerable political instability in the Andean region. Recently, in October of 2003, the Bolivian President Sánchez de Lozada was forced to resign following a sequence of social protests directed by groups of indigenous peoples and peasants. In April of 2002, for example, a failed coup d'état took place in which Venezuelan President Hugo Chávez was temporarily ousted from power only to regain the presidency a day later in a confusing set of events that involved the military and some leaders of the main business association. In Ecuador in January of 2000, the democratically elected President Jamil Mahuad was deposed by the military following an indigenous uprising in which a short lived military-indigenous junta took power for a few hours, only to eventually, under strong foreign pressure, turn power over to Vice President Gustavo Noboa. In 2000, Peru's President Alberto Fujimori fled the country after a scandal of corruption and political intimidation that involved his Chief of Security, Vladimiro Montesinos, stripped the Fujimori administration of all its remaining credibility.

The economies of the Andean countries have also been affected by governance and instability problems. In the last ten years the average rate of economic growth for the five Andean countries[2] (Bolivia, Colombia, Ecuador, Peru and Venezuela) was lower than the average growth rate in the Latin American region as a whole. Colombia has seen its historically stable economy give way to slow growth and financial vulnerability. Ecuador, in turn, suffered a severe economic and financial crisis in 1998–99 and has experienced recurrent currency depreciation and escalating inflation that was further complicated by a severe banking system crisis.[3] Ecuador's answer to this instability was to radically change the currency regime and adopt the US dollar as its official currency in early 2000. Official dollarization, supportive fiscal and financial policies, and better external conditions helped Ecuador to, albeit gradually, restore domestic confidence, reduce inflation, and resume economic growth in the last two years; although external imbalances developed in 2002. In Peru the political turbulence associated with the demise of the Fujimori regime affected output growth in 2001 though it recovered in 2002 and 2003. Venezuela has experienced a volatile growth record that followed the fluctuations in international oil prices. Gross domestic product in Venezuela declined substantially in 2002 and 2003 (accumulating a drop of 22 per cent) associated with a cut in investment and output following domestic political polarization and strikes. Although Bolivia's growth rate increased during the 1990s, Bolivia's economy has also been affected by the regional slowdown and by internal social unrest in the early 2000s.

This chapter underscores the critical importance of governance conditions in affecting economic development. The purpose of this chapter is to characterize political and constitutional regimes, the quality of institutions, social inequality, and ethnic diversity in the Andean region. To that end, a conceptual framework is developed (Section 2.2) that distinguishes the specific roles of political regimes, constitutional rules, the quality of institutions, and patterns of social conflict in generating governance patterns that, in turn, affect economic outcomes. The focus of the chapter is mainly on how to characterize and understand governance rather than on providing a detailed analysis of the channels through which governance conditions affect economic growth. This will be the subject of a subsequent chapter. The empirical analysis of the chapter (Section 2.3) combines long-run evidence on the frequency of constitutional reforms, presidential crises, and political regimes of the Andean region in the 20th century along with more recent indicators of governance and institutional quality in the 1990s and early 2000s prepared independently by the World Bank and the World Economic Forum in conjunction with Harvard University. Indicators of social inequality, ethnic diversity, and economic performance for each of the five Andean countries are also provided in this section. Section 2.4 gives an interpretation of the governance and economic record of the Andean region countries and Section 2.5 presents our conclusions.

2.2 POLITICAL REGIMES, INSTITUTIONS AND SOCIAL CONFLICT: A CONCEPTUAL FRAMEWORK

The conceptual framework adopted in this chapter sees governance conditions as the result of the interaction of three sets of variables:

a. the nature and stability of the political regime and the constitution;
b. the quality of state institutions;
c. the pattern of social conflict and cooperation related to inequality and ethnic diversity;
d. other factors affecting governance.

The political regime and constitutional rules constitute the highest echelon in the hierarchy of institutions.[4] The judiciary, the regulatory bodies, the ministries, the budgetary process are part of the second level in the hierarchy of institutions. This chapter identifies complex agent–principal problems, rent seeking, corruption, and violence as important factors that weaken state institutions and create serious governance problems. The third set of variables goes beyond formal institutions and focuses on patterns of social behavior such as cooperation and conflict, largely related to inequality of income and wealth and to ethnic diversity. This framework highlights the impact of each of these three sets of variables (and the effects of their interaction) on the governance and economic performance of the Andean countries.

(a) Political Regimes and Constitutions

Constitutional theory has a long history going back to Montesquieu (1748), Hamilton and the Founding Fathers of the US Constitution, Hayek (1960), Buchanan and Tullock (1962), with more recent treatments given by Cooter (2000) and Aghion, Alesina and Trebbi (2002).

The *public choice school* or *contractarian approach*[6] championed by Nobel Prize Winner James Buchanan focuses on a social contract, such as the constitution, that defines the overall political framework under which society evolves. Buchanan (1988) distinguishes between the process of writing up a constitution – setting up the basic rules of the game in society – and the specific policymaking process that unfolds under the rules established by that constitution. In the words of game theory, the constitution is the first stage establishing the rules of the game: the second stage is playing the game. A normative analysis would enter into the first stage (writing the constitution and creating the basic institutions). The positive analysis, in turn, would focus on playing the game.[6] Under ideal conditions, constitutions are assumed to have been written under the 'veil of ignorance' regarding initial resources and interests and such that the writers of the constitution did not end up in a better or worse position in society as a result. This assumption has been criticized as unrealistic because the framers of constitutions do often consider their own interests in the process of writing the constitution.[7]

An important tradition in political theory focuses on the design of the main political institutions of the state. This institutional design includes electoral rules, division of powers, and checks and balances among different branches of the state. The constitution is the main legal charter that establishes the basic rights and responsibilities of individuals and the workings of the political system. The major types of democracies are the *parliamentary* and *presidential* systems with *semi-presidential* regimes (for example France) that mix elements of both systems. In presidential systems (for example like in the United States), presidents are elected either by a direct vote or by an electoral college, have fixed terms in office, and often have legislative initiative. In fact, presidents are often endowed with considerable powers to present legislation to congress and to administer the executive branch of government and cannot be removed from office before the expiration of their official term, except in cases of impeachment or resignation. Presidential regimes do not require legislative majorities. In contrast, in parliamentary regimes, heads of government or prime ministers are the leaders of the majority party in parliament. They can be removed through a vote of no-confidence in cases of political crisis and the head of government (that is the prime minister) needs a parliamentary majority to sustain their government.

Basic criteria with which to compare presidential and parliamentary systems include how each system contributes to the continuity and stability of democracy and how the system forestalls 'regime breakdowns' in the event of a major political crisis. Authors such as Juan Linz and Arturo Valenzuela (1994) argue that the 'dual legitimacy' between the president and parliament, the alleged tendency towards a 'winner-take-all' system in presidential regimes, the role of outsiders in bidding for the presidency, and the rigidity of terms make presidential regimes more prone to generate political crises than parliamentary regimes.[8] From an economic viewpoint the choice of political regime and, even more importantly, its stability over time are important factors that affect the degree of political stability in a country, a variable that influences both investment and the rate of economic growth.

(b) Institutions of the State: Strengths, Weaknesses and Factors that Affect Quality

Once the basic political framework of a country has been defined by its constitution, there is a vast array of political and economic institutions (for example ministries, central banks, customs, public investment agencies, the judiciary) whose quality of performance is critical for ensuring appropriate governance and, ultimately, good economic outcomes. Positive political economy (PPE) applies economic principles of individualism, incentives, rationality and constraints to the analysis of institutions and of their impact on economic performance.[9] In this view, institutions are formed to reduce transaction costs both in the economic and political realms.[10] A political-economy approach that has gained considerable attention in recent years is the theory of *transaction costs politics* (TCP) developed by North (1990) and Dixit (1996, 2001a, 2001b). This approach evaluates how different political governance structures (constitutions, government agencies, laws) cope with 'transaction costs'. In an analogy with transaction cost economics (TCE), transaction cost politics uses the contract as a unit of analysis. While in economics a contract is a verifiable process (for example renting a house or lending to a firm), in politics contracts are more complex. The definition of a 'political contract' is often ambiguous: a president or senator may be elected on a platform that is vague, making it difficult to monitor the fulfillment of the initial promises. Besides, there are incentives to change policies along the way, dismissing initial commitments (for example the phenomenon known as 'time inconsistency').[11] These agency problems are further complicated by the existence of several principals (the general public, voters, specific interest groups); these multiple principals lead agents (the government, parliament, public agencies) to face several mandates that are often inconsistent. The enforcement of 'political contracts' is difficult because the institutional mechanisms of enforcement (elections, the supreme court, referendums) cannot be activated at every small deviation from initial commitments. In recognition of all these difficulties, modern political economy theories have devised new concepts such as reputation, commitments, rules, and delegation (using independent central banks, for example, to conduct non-inflationary monetary policy). This literature sees these institutional mechanisms as a way to cope with incentives for non-compliance by agents that face incentives to be inconsistent, conflicting mandates, and a system with limited accountability. These complex principal–agent problems make clear the need for appropriate institutions that can deal with governance problems.

Rent-seeking, corruption, and violence as factors that weaken institutions
Under ideal conditions, institutions and organizations must have clear goals, be properly funded, have a sound financial and human resource base, and be free of undue political interference. At a 'general equilibrium level' they must be part of an institutional architecture that is based on adequate governance principles that ensure a proper working of institutions for among other things fostering economic prosperity. In the previous subsection we identified several reasons related to the agent–principal problems that are particularly serious in the case of political transactions as regards why institutions fail to function properly. Here we identify three phenomena that tend to weaken the institutions of the state. These three factors are:

a. rent-seeking behavior;
b. corruption;
c. violence.

Rent seeking The rent seeking approach[12] in political economy sees society as formed by individuals organized in special interest groups (or acting alone) that are motivated by their particular interests rather than by the general interest of society. Common examples include: farmers seeking price support schemes, industrialists wanting import protection, bankers pressing for protective regulation and less competition from new intermediaries. From this perspective, the state is seen as institutional machinery that, among other things, dispenses economic favors and transfers income among groups in exchange for political support.

Rent seeking behavior leads some groups to attempt the *capture* of key state institutions such as customs, tax administration authorities, public contracts agencies, where they can extract rents.

Corruption These rents can be obtained by lobbying (rent seeking) or simply by illegally appropriating public assets for personal benefit. In this latter case we are referring to corruption. In some cases, groups may attempt to capture the whole state apparatus and corruption becomes the norm for the predatory groups (for example the kleptocracy) that have captured the state. Corruption and the stealing of state assets (like the 'spontaneous privatization' in post-Soviet Russia) tend to flourish in weak states where mechanisms that make government officials accountable to the public, parliament, and the courts work very poorly and curtail the rule of law. Corruption and rent seeking clearly undermine the strength of state institutions. Moreover, intense rent seeking can lead to corruption.

Violence In a world of voluntary exchange and compliance with the rule of law, there is no role for violence. Less so for internal armed conflict entailing different armed groups from the official army. An important feature of several contemporary societies[13] and relevant for some of the Andean countries, however, is pervasive violence and internal conflict that severely weaken the state and can lead to its collapse. In these cases, the state loses its monopoly on the use of force and the rule of law becomes severely limited or simply non-existent. In the case of armed conflicts, it is interesting to analyse the different motivations of rebel groups. They may be a mix of political motives (rebellion as justice seeking) and quasi-criminal motives (rebellion as crime).[14] The view of rebellion as driven by greed considerations emphasizes the quasi-criminal features of rebel organizations and the motivations that those organization have in common with criminal organizations.[15] The scale of rebellion and armed conflict is much larger than that of crime, even including organized crime.[16]

The view of rebellion as 'justice seeking' emphasizes 'grievance factors' such as income inequality, ethnic and religious divisions, and political motivations as the most important driving factors of the groups engaged in internal conflict.

Rebel groups with a mix of both political and quasi-criminal motives consistently behave in a way oriented to *weakening* and even *destroying* the state, so as to pursue their goals more easily, and with impunity. It is interesting to note that in many cases, rebel organizations do not want victory against the government (that is the seizure of power). They are often interested in preserving a very weak state and profiting from that situation. In these conditions, an armed conflict becomes an 'equilibrium' or at least a stable situation that can last for a long time (see Collier 2000).[17] Interestingly, this model can be used to explain the long duration of certain internal conflicts such as the one in Colombia.

(c) Social Cooperation and Conflict, Inequality and Ethnic Fragmentation

Beyond formal institutions, social cooperation and social conflict also play an important role in generating actual governance and economic outcomes. Individuals, groups and social classes each have different economic interests and motivations. Society, in turn, is an arena in which conflict and cooperation coexist with a political system that mediates the various demands and claims from different social groups.[18] Social conflict can vary in nature: one type is distributive conflict, in which groups (or economic classes) fight over their shares of the national income.[19] In a situation of distributive conflict, inflation can be seen as the result of the conflict over real income in which each group manages a price (wages, markups, and so on), which combines with an accommodative monetary policy to generate inflation. Other points of distributive conflict are taxes, transfers, and spending, with low-income groups pressing for higher taxation to finance social spending and income transfers. In contrast, the upper middle class and the wealthy tend to favor lower taxation of income, financial assets and productive wealth. In practice, conflict and cooperation alternate; the approval of tax and spending laws, for example, has different distributive implications and requires some degree of cooperation and consensus in parliament.

The endogenous growth theory investigates the role of inequality in economic growth and finds that more unequal societies such as countries with more income and wealth inequality among their members tend to generate more social polarization and political conflict than more egalitarian societies. Thus economic growth, controlling for development levels, would be higher in more egalitarian societies than in unequal and polarized ones, as in the latter the pressures for higher taxation tend to be higher and the quality of labor–capital relations tends to be lower than in the more egalitarian societies.[20] Recent literature on the origins of institutions (Acemoglu 2002) relates them to social and distributive conflict, and argues that inefficient policies and institutions are functional to the interests of politicians and social groups holding power to the detriment of society at large. In this view institutions can be socially inefficient. The only and overriding motivation to create institutions is not to reduce transaction costs: they are often set up and maintained to help keep power for certain groups and individuals.

Another dimension of social differentiation that is especially relevant for Bolivia, Peru and Ecuador is ethnic diversity. The question arises whether multiethnic societies have more difficulties in reaching consensus than ethnically homogeneous societies. Empirical studies of the impact of ethnolinguistic fractionalization on economic performance (growth) suggest different answers to this question. On the one hand, authors such as Easterly and Levine (1997) attach a central role to ethnolinguistic fractionalization in explaining the poor growth performance of multiethnic Africa. In contrast, other analysts such as Collier (2001) find that ethnically differentiated societies do not necessarily have either worse economic performance or greater risk of civil conflict than more ethnically homogeneous societies. For Collier, the political regime and the degree of ethnic dominance are more important than simple ethnic diversity in explaining growth performance in Africa.

(d) Other Factors Affecting Governance

The previous set of variables affecting governance does not exhaust the factors that explain the type and quality of governance. A variable emphasized by Max Weber, for example, is the quality of leadership. A forceful leader (for example a president) can be important in steering a country in a certain direction and help it to avoid political conflict, ensuring stability.[21] However, that leader can also be authoritarian, therefore their behavior could be inconsistent with democracy. Moreover the economic ideas of the leader may be inconsistent with economic policies that bring prosperity.

This discussion underscores the fact that the type of leader, their personality, ideas, political abilities, and so on, can have an important influence in creating good or bad governance in a country. Other governance variables that can be important are ideology, the type of legal system (Anglo-Saxon, Napoleonic, and so on), and the degree of professionalism (or politization) of the armed forces and others.

2.3 EMPIRICAL ANALYSIS

In this section, we empirically investigate the effects that political regimes, constitutional change, the quality of institutions and social conflict have on governance and economics in the Andean countries.

(a) Frequency of Constitutional Reforms, Presidential Crises and Political Regime Change

We start our analysis of governance in the Andean countries by looking first at the stability of the constitutional framework. To examine this, we investigate the frequency of major changes in the constitution that led to the approval of a new constitution in each of the countries during the 20th century (see Table 2.1). This is an important indicator of the frequency of changes in the basic rules of the game in society and therefore a crucial indicator of instability in rulemaking institutions. This is, certainly, a 'low frequency' indicator of instability, but still of a great importance. The Andean country that experienced the highest number of new constitutions in the period running from 1900 to 2000 is Venezuela with eight constitutions approved in that period (six out of those eight constitutions were approved between 1901 and 1953, Table 2.1). It is followed by Ecuador with seven constitutions (three approved since 1967); Bolivia (five constitutions), Peru (four constitutions) and Colombia (just one new constitution approved in 1991). Table 2.2 also shows the number of new 20th century constitutions in

Table 2.1 Constitutional reforms, presidential crises and political regimes, Andean countries, 1900–2003

Countries	Number of constitutions [a] 1900–2000		Presidential crises [b] 1950–2003			
	Year	Number of constitutional reforms in the 20th century	Crisis year and president	Presidential period until crisis	Number of presidential crises in the period 1950–2003	Prevailing political regime before presidential crisis
Bolivia	1938		1951(Mamerto Urriolagoitia)	1949–1951		Democracy
	1945	5	1952 (Gral. Hugo Ballivián)	1951–1952	17	Authoritarian, military
	1960		1964 (Víctor Paz)	1960–1964		Democracy
	1967		1969 (Gral. René Barrientos) [d]	1966–1969		Authoritarian, military
	1994		1969 (Luis Siles)	1969		Authoritarian, civilian
			1970 (Gral. Alfredo Ovando)	1969–1970		Authoritarian, military
			1971 (Gral. Juan José Torres)	1970–1971		Authoritarian, military
			1978 (Gral. Juan Pereda)	1978		Authoritarian, military
			1979 (Walter Guevara)	1979		Democracy
			1979 (Gral. Alberto Natusch)	1979		Authoritarian, military
			1980 (Lidia Gueilier)	1979–1980		Democracy
			1981 (Gral. Luis García)	1908–1981		Authoritarian, military
			1982 (Gral. Celso Torrelio)	1981–1982		Authoritarian, military
			1982 (Gral. Guido Vildoso)	1982		Authoritarian, military
			1985 (Hernán Siles)	1982–1985		Democracy
			2001(Hugo Banzer) [c]	1997–2002		Democracy
			2003 (Gonzalo Sánchez de Lozada) [b]	2002–2003		Democracy
Colombia	1991	1	1953 (Laureano Gómez)	1953	2	Democracy
			1957 (Gustavo Rojas)	1953–1958		Authoritarian, military

Ecuador	1929		1961 (José María Velasco)	1960–1961		Democracy
	1938	7	1963 (Carlos Arosemena)	1961–1963	10	Democracy
	1945		1970 (José María Velasco) [e]	1968–1970		Democracy
	1946		1972 (José María Velasco)	1970–1972		Authoritarian, civilian
	1967		1976 (Gral. Guillermo Rodriguez)	1972–1976		Authoritarian, military
	1979		1981 (Jaime Roldás) [e]	1979–1981		Democracy
	1998		1997 (Abdalá Bucaram)	1996–1997		Democracy
			1997 (Rosalía Arteaga)	1997		Democracy
			2000 (Jamil Mahuad)	1998–2000		Democracy
			2000 (Solórzeno, Mendoza, Vargas)	2000		Democracy
Peru	1920		1962 (Manuel Prado)	1956–1962		Democracy
	1933	4	1963 (Ricardo Pérez)	1962–1962	6	Authoritarian, military
	1979		1968 (Fernando Belaude)	1963–1968		Democracy
	1993		1975 (Juan Velasco)	1968–1975		Authoritarian, military
			1992 (Alberto Fujimori) [e]	1990–1992		Democracy
			2001 (Alberto Fujimori)	1995–2000		Democracy
Venezuela	1901		1950 (Carlos Delgado) [d]	1948–1950		Authoritarian, military
	1909	8	1958 (Marcos Pérez)	1952–1958	4	Authoritarian, military
	1931		1993 (Carlos Andrés Pérez)	1989–1993		Democracy
	1945		2002 (Hugo Chávez) [f]	1999–		Democracy
	1947					
	1953					
	1961					
	1999					

Notes:
[a] New constitution approved
[b] Presidents that did not complete their constitutional periods by coups, resignation and non-voluntary removals
[c] By illness of the president
[d] Death of the president
[e] Self-coup
[f] Failed coup

Sources: http://geocities.yahoo.com.br/escritoriorbm/historia/index_b.html
http://es.geocities.com/datalia2002/colombia.htm
www.explored.com.ec/ecuador/1960.htm, http://www.tierra-inca.com/presidents/index_es.html, http://www.aldeaeducativa.com

Table 2.2 Constitutional reforms, presidential crises and turnover of prime minister, selected countries, 1900–2002

Regime	Country	Number of constitutions [a] 1900–2000		Presidential crises [b] 1950–2002			Prevailing political regime before presidential crisis
		Year	Number of constitutional reforms in the 20th century	Crisis year and president	Presidential period until crisis	Number of presidential crises in the period 1950–2002	
Presidential	Chile	1925	2	1973 (Salvador Allende)	1970–1973	1	Democracy
		1980					
	Costa Rica	1949	1			0	
	Uruguay	1918		1976 (Juan M. Bordaberry)	1972–1976		Democracy
		1934	5	1976 (Alberto Demichelli)	1976	2	Authoritarian, civilian
		1942					
		1952					
		1967					
	USA		0	1963 (John F. Kennedy)	1961–1963	2	Democracy
				1974 (Richard Nixon)	1969–1974		Democracy
		Year	Number of constitutional reforms in the 20th century			Turnover of prime minister	
Parliamentary	Germany	1919	2			5	Democracy
		1949					
	Italy	1948	1			58	Democracy
	United Kingdom		0			12	Democracy

Notes:
[a] New constitution approved. [b] Presidents that did not complete their constitutional periods by coups, resignation and non-voluntary removals.

Sources: http://icarito.tercera.cl
www.observa.com.uy/eluruguay/historia/1presidentes.html
www.guiascostarica.com/h02.htm#republica
www.inter-nationes.de/d/frames/presse/sonder/s/brjabre-s-11.html
www.fmmeducacion.com.ar/historia/notas/prestadosunidos.htm
www.bbc.co.uk/portuguesa/noticias/2001/01/010509-italiatempo.shtml
http://es.geocities.com/datalia2002/inglaterra.htm

the three countries that are often considered the most politically stable countries in Latin America: Costa Rica, Chile, and Uruguay. A similar computation is done for four OECD countries: the United States, Germany, Great Britain, and Italy. All the Latin American countries analysed, as well as the US, had presidential regimes during the period of analysis. In contrast, Germany, the UK, and Italy have parliamentary regimes.

The five Andean countries had an average of five new constitutions in the 20th century, a high number when considered from an international perspective. In the same time period, the average number of new constitutions for Costa Rica, Chile, and Uruguay was 2.5.[22] In turn, the average number of constitutional reforms in the US, UK, Italy and Germany in the 20th century was 0.8. Neither the United States nor the United Kingdom has had new constitutions approved in the last century. Germany, on the other hand, approved one new constitution in 1919 and then another in 1949, after World War I and II, respectively.

Another measure of political instability is the frequency of presidential crises (turnover). By 'presidential crisis' we refer to a situation in which a head of state (the president) does not complete his/her constitutional term for various reasons: forced removals by a coup d'état, resignation, and so on. Table 2.1 provides the number of such presidential crises in the five Andean countries in the period 1950–2003.

The country with the highest number of presidential crises in this period is Bolivia, with 17 crises between 1950 and 2002. Most of those crises (11) took place in the period 1969–82. Clearly the 1970s (and surrounding years) were a period of high political instability for Bolivia. Another country with a high frequency of presidential crises is Ecuador, with ten such crises, mostly concentrated both in the 1970s and in the 1990s. In contrast, Colombia registered only two presidential crises in the last half century, both in the 1950s. Interestingly, Colombia displays a remarkable degree of democratic continuity (as demonstrated by low frequency of presidential crises) in spite of its internal armed conflicts. This is certainly a paradoxical situation (see Chapter 5, 'The Economy, Conflict and Governance in Colombia' in this volume).

The last column of Table 2.1 shows the prevailing political regime (democratic, authoritarian) at the time of the presidential crises in each of the five Andean countries. There seems to be no clear correlation between the nature of the political regime and the frequency of presidential crises although the nature of the relationship varies across countries. In fact, in Bolivia, most of the presidential crises took place in the 1970s within non-elected military regimes, in a pattern of generals-turned-presidents replacing other generals-turned-presidents. In contrast, Ecuador, the second highest frequency country in terms of presidential crises, had several presidential crises in a period of democracy, mostly in the 1990s (that is Abdalah Bucaram and Jamil Mahuad were two presidents who were democratically elected and then ousted from office before the expiration of their constitutional mandates). Another important dimension of a political regime is the distinction between presidential and parliamentary regimes.[23] As mentioned before, Linz and Valenzuela (1994) have argued that presidential regimes are more prone to generate political crises and regime breakdowns than parliamentary systems. We have noted that the frequency of presidential crises has been very high in Ecuador and Bolivia, low to moderate in Peru and Venezuela, and low in Colombia.

An interesting case of a country, outside the Latin American region, with high turnover of prime ministers (a different concept to that of presidential crisis) is Italy, which has had 58 prime ministers in the last 52 years of the 20th century (on average more than one prime minister per year). The Italian case suggests the perplexing conclusion that an exceedingly high frequency of change in prime ministers can take place without constitutional and economic crisis in a parliamentary regime.

In the Andean region, the degree of continuity of democracy (defined as an absence of constitutional breakdowns) in the last 40 years has been much higher in Colombia and in Venezuela than in Peru, Bolivia, and Ecuador. In fact, while these countries had several military interventions in the 1960s and 1970s, Colombia and Venezuela have managed to avoid military regimes since the 1950s. This is not to say, however, that these two countries have had complete political stability in the years following their military regimes. In fact, Venezuela had a presidential crisis with Carlos Andrés Perez in 1993 and a coup attempt against Chávez in 2002; this turbulence, however, has not led to a collapse of democracy (at least so far).[24]

(b) Subjective Indicators of Quality of Institutions and Governance: the World Bank Indices

We will now turn to the empirical assessment of institutions in the five Andean countries in comparative perspective. Drawing from a data set of over 150 countries, Kaufmann, Kraay, and Zoido-Lobatón (1999, 2002) of the World Bank provide six governance indicators for each Andean country in two years: 1998 and 2001. Using the indices of Kaufmann et al., Table 2.3 provides the values of these indices for Costa Rica, Chile, and Uruguay, and the average of Latin American and OECD countries. These governance indicators are based on qualitative response surveys taken of citizens, investors, and users of public services and comprise the following dimensions:[25]

- voice and accountability;
- political instability and violence;
- government effectiveness;
- regulatory quality;
- rule of law;
- control of corruption.

These variables reflect several aspects of 'good governance'.[26] Voice and accountability, for example, are an important feedback mechanism between users and providers of public services, or between principals (voters) and agents (government, politicians) regarding compliance with public mandates. The existence of political instability and violence are indicative of governance problems and are also correlated with poor economic performance.[27] The other variables listed above are also identified by the literature as indicators of qualities both of government and of the stability of institutions. From a development perspective, there is a growing literature that finds a positive correlation between economic performance and quality of government and institutions (see Knack and Keefer 1995; Mauro 1995; Barro 1996 and others).

Table 2.3 shows that the Andean group as a whole ranks lower on different governance measures (in the sense of lower institutional performance) than the Latin American and Caribbean average. This is clear in the indices of voice and accountability, the degree of political instability and violence, government effectiveness, rule of law, and control of corruption. Their rankings are lower when compared with Chile, Costa Rica, Uruguay, and the OECD. Within the Andean countries there are also cross-country differences in the value of the indices. Bolivia, for example, has a level of regulatory burdens that is closer to OECD levels than that of the other Andean countries. There are, however, some changes in the rankings between 1998 and 2001, such as the way that voice and accountability improves in Peru in 2001 compared to 1998 (this is probably associated with greater government accountability after the demise of the Fujimori administration). Voice and accountability worsens, however, in Colombia, Ecuador, and Venezuela between 1998 and 2001. Political instability and violence increases (lowering a country's place in the rankings) in Bolivia, Colombia, and Venezuela but improves in Peru. The control of corruption improved in Colombia, Peru, and Venezuela in 2001 compared to 1998.

World Economic Forum-Harvard University indices

Another set of governance indices that include the five Andean countries is the *Global Competitiveness Report* prepared jointly by the World Economic Forum and Harvard University. This Report computes a 'Growth

Table 2.3 Ranking of governance indicators, Andean countries

Countries	Voice and accountability		Political instability and violence		Government effectiveness		Regulatory quality		Rule of law		Control of corruption	
Year	1998	2001	1998	2001	1998	2001	1998	2001	1998	2001	1998	2001
Number of countries	170	173	152	161	153	159	163	168	167	169	152	160
Bolivia	63	67	87	122	83	101	22	39	97	100	95	119
Colombia	91	112	140	149	74	95	69	93	128	132	102	89
Ecuador	66	92	108	131	110	129	61	95	121	130	123	140
Peru	124	70	111	95	54	93	37	61	110	109	73	72
Venezuela, RB	68	106	92	100	131	124	91	115	117	136	114	107
Andean Countries	82	89	108	119	90	108	56	81	115	121	101	105
Top Latin American												
Chile	54	52	51	30	23	23	18	13	24	24	25	17
Costa Rica	21	16	30	24	42	37	16	26	48	50	37	32
Uruguay	46	32	58	25	37	44	13	22	61	48	45	37
Latin America	83	81	83	91	92	83	79	61	105	101	91	89
OECD	24	23	28	26	24	25	28	29	27	27	25	23

Source: Kaufmann et al. (1999, 2002).

Competitiveness Index' for 75 countries including developed nations, transition economies, and developing countries. This index assesses the medium-term potential of sustained economic growth for a given country as a function of three sets of sub-indices: (i) technology index, (ii) quality of public institutions index and (iii) macroeconomic environment index.

The growth competitiveness index[28] for 2000–01 is calculated for a group of 18 'core economies' that includes countries with higher levels of income per capita, and a more advanced level of technological capabilities (measured by number of patents per million population). The index also includes a group of 'non-core economies' of low to intermediate income per capita levels and less advanced technological development. For the group of non-core economies, among which we find the Andean group, the index is computed by giving equal weights (one third each) to technology, quality of public institutions, and macroeconomic environment sub-indices. In the core group, the technology sub-index has a higher share, 40 per cent versus 33 per cent, reflecting the higher contribution of technological improvements to output growth in higher per capita income economies. In order to highlight the links between growth potential and quality of institutions, Table 2.4 presents the rankings of the Growth Competitiveness Index, and the public institutions sub-index. This latter sub-index is composed of (i) a contracts and law sub-index and (ii) a corruption sub-index. These two sub-indices are based entirely on survey questions and measure the average scores given to judicial independence, government procurement practices, law enforcement, and costs related to organized crime. The corruption sub-index measures the pervasiveness of bribery in three key public services areas: import and export agencies, public utilities, and tax collection. Table 2.4 shows that on average for the five Andean countries there is a close association between their ranking in the Growth Competitiveness Index (ranking 63 out of 75 nations) and their ranking in the public institutions sub-index (59 out of 75), suggesting a direct positive correlation between medium-term growth potential and the quality of public institutions. The Andean countries on average occupy 67th place in the ranking for contracts and law sub-index and 50th in the corruption sub-index. Cross-country differences among Andean countries are not very large except for the corruption sub-index, in which Peru has the best ranking and Ecuador has the worst (in 2000–01).

Finally, another aspect of governance lies in citizens' attitudes towards democracy. Latin Barometer, a survey conducted on an annual basis in several Latin American countries, provides a measure of such public attitudes. Table 2.5 shows that, on average, the degree of public support for democracy has been declining since 1997, with a sharper decline in 2001. In 2001, within the Andean group, the country with the lowest public support for democracy is Colombia (30 per cent), a country that has suffered severe violence; the highest degree of support for democracy, on the other hand, is found in Peru (62 per cent). The degree of support for the democratic system was also low in Ecuador in the late 1990s and early 2000s. It is interesting to note that the lower support for democracy after 1997 coincides with the post-1997 worsening of economic conditions in these countries that was associated with the Asian crisis and other internal economic developments.

Table 2.4 Competitiveness and governance indicators rankings, Andean countries 2001–02

Countries	Growth Competitiveness Index rank	Public institutions sub-index rank	Contracts and law sub-index rank	Corruption sub-index rank
Number of countries	75	75	75	75
Peru	55	45	60	30
Venezuela	62	65	71	61
Colombia	65	57	67	40
Bolivia	67	62	62	56
Ecuador	68	68	73	63
Andean countries	63	59	67	50
Top Latin American				
Chile	27	21	26	13
Costa Rica	35	37	35	43
Uruguay	46	31	27	38
Latin America	56	55	57	51
OECD	20	21	21	23

Note: Growth Competitiveness Index = one third technology index + one third public institutions sub-index + one third macroeconomic environment sub-index. Public institutions sub-index = one half contracts and law sub-index + one half corruption sub-index. The rank is of 75 countries.

Source: Porter et al. (2002).

Social Inequality and Ethnic Diversity

The Andean countries have stratified social structures characterized by high inequality and large incidences of poverty. This social situation is bound to affect patterns of social conflict and cooperation in society. Another important element of their social structure that is more relevant in Bolivia, Ecuador and Peru is ethnic diversity.[29] In fact, the share of indigenous population in total population for Bolivia, Ecuador and Peru in the early 1990s (last census available) is 44 per cent (see Table 2.6). In contrast, the average share of indigenous population in Colombia and Venezuela is very low, less than 1 per cent. Ethnic diversity often comes along with a linguistic and cultural variety among different ethnic groups within the same state. Ethnic diversity has some important implications for the capacity of the political system to articulate a social consensus. The ability to reach consensus depends on a range of factors, such as the levels of political participation of the different groups, their rights, their organization, the quality of their leadership and others.

Table 2.5 Democracy is preferable to any other political regime (per cent of public support)

Countries	1996	1997	1998	2000	2001
Bolivia	64	66	55	62	54
Colombia	60	69	55	50	36
Ecuador	52	41	57	54	40
Peru	63	60	63	64	62
Venezuela	62	64	60	61	57
Andean countries	60.2	60.0	58.0	58.2	49.8
Latin America	60.6	62.8	61.6	59.8	47.4

Source: Latinobarómetro.

Table 2.6 Indigenous population in the Andean countries (per cent of total population)

Countries	Year	Total population	Indigenous population	%
Bolivia	1992	5 183 403	3 058 208	59.0
Colombia	1985	29 719 875	237 759	0.8
Ecuador	1992	11 078 717	3 800 000	34.3
Peru*	1992	22 500 000	9 000 000	40.0
Venezuela	1992	34 974 667	314 772	0.9

(*) Estimate.

Source: Based on last censuses, CELADE.

Returning to the social indicators, Table 2.7 provides poverty levels, the values of Gini coefficients measuring inequality, and the ratio between the top and bottom quintiles in the income distribution for selected years in the 1980s and 1990s. These social indicators show a significant incidence of poverty in the Andean countries, over 40 per cent in recent years (above the average poverty levels for Latin America). The highest incidences of poverty are found in Ecuador and Bolivia. Moreover, poverty is on the rise in Venezuela, a country that in the past had relatively lower poverty rates within the Andean region. The Gini coefficients are higher in Colombia, Bolivia and rising in Venezuela, than they are in the other Andean countries, although the Gini coefficients are generally high in all five Andean countries.

Table 2.7 Poverty and inequality in the Andean countries 1990–97

Countries	Year	% households below the poverty line	Gini coefficient	Ratio Q5/Q1
Bolivia [a]	1989	49	0.484	0.062
	1994	46	0.435	0.104
	1997	47	0.455	0.088
Colombia	1980	39	0.518	0.058
	1991	50	0.403	0.117
	1994	47	0.505	0.104
	1997	45	0.477	0.088
Ecuador [a]	1990	56	0.381	0.128
	1994	52	0.397	0.108
	1997	50	0.388	0.125
Peru	1979	46		
	1986	52		
	1990		0.438 [a]	
	1991		0.370 [a]	
	1994		0.350 [a]	
	1995	41		
	1997	37		
Venezuela	1981	22	0.306	0.184
	1990	34	0.378	0.127
	1994	42	0.387	0.132
	1997	42	0.425	0.101
Latin America	1980	35		
	1990	41		
	1994	38		
	1997	36		

Notes:
[a] Urban zones.
Q5/Q1 = Ratio of the poorest quintile to the richest quintile.

Sources: Economic Commission for Latin America and the Caribbean and The World Bank

(d) Economic Performance

In the second half of the 20th century (1950–2000), the five Andean countries grew at an average rate of 3.9 per cent per year, a bit below the average rate of growth of 4.2 per cent for the whole Latin American and Caribbean region in the same period (ECLAC, statistical data base).

In the 1990s, the economic growth performance in the Andean group was moderate, although important economic reforms were undertaken in several of them. Average annual growth for the five Andean countries declined from 4.1 per cent in 1950–90 to 2.9 per cent in 1990–99 and 1.5 per cent in 2000–03. The countries that experienced the largest deceleration in growth rates were Colombia and Ecuador (see Table 2.8).[30] While Ecuador managed to grow at an annual rate of 5.2 per cent in the period 1950–90, its annual growth rate of the 1990s was only 1.9 per cent. Colombia's average growth rate decelerated from 4.7 per cent in 1950–90 to 2.9 per cent in 1990–99 and 2.2 in 2000–03.[31] In contrast, Bolivia's growth rate accelerated, albeit moderately, in the 1990s (4 per cent per year versus 2.5 per cent in the 1950–90 period).[32] The average per capita income level of the Andean group is around U$2000 (period 2000–03, see Table 2.9), below the average in Latin America of near $3900 for the same period. There is no doubt that the modest governance and political instability already documented is correlated with this economic growth performance. Although we will not enter here into the transmission mechanisms between governance and growth, the literature has highlighted the impact of institutions on private investment and productivity growth.

Table 2.8 Economic growth in the Andean countries 1950–2003

Countries	1950–00	1950–90	1990–95	1995–99	1990–99	2000–03[a]
Bolivia	2.8	2.5	4.2	3.9	4.0	2.3
Colombia	4.3	4.7	4.5	1.4	2.9	2.2
Ecuador	4.5	5.2	3.4	0.2	1.9	3.1
Peru	3.6	3.5	3.9	3.6	3.3	3.0
Venezuela	4.1	4.6	4.0	0.9	2.4	2.8
Andean countries	3.9	4.1	4.0	2.0	2.9	1.5
Latin America	4.2	4.5	2.6	2.5	2.7	1.3

Note: [a] 2003 preliminary estimates.

Source: Economic Commission for Latin America and the Caribbean.

Table 2.9 GDP per capita in the Andean countries 1970–2003 (US$ at 1995 price/number of persons)

Countries	1970–89	1990–95	1995–99	1990–99	2000–03 [a]
Bolivia	934.0	868.0	940.6	900.5	937.1
Colombia	1815.5	2229.9	2382.6	2289.2	2285.3
Ecuador	1367.4	1530.1	1538.4	1530.7	1740.5
Peru	2734.3	2199.5	2579.4	2351.4	2355.0
Venezuela	3523.0	3258.8	3179.6	3227.1	2856.0
Andean countries	2074.8	2017.2	2124.1	2059.8	2034.8
Latin America	3325.2	3455.0	3708.7	3570.1	3846.1

Note: [a] 2003 Preliminary estimates.

Sources: Economic Commission for Latin America and the Caribbean and CELADE.

2.4 INTERPRETING ANDEAN COUNTRIES' GOVERNANCE PERFORMANCE

Along with the conceptual framework of Section 2.2 and the empirical analysis in Section 2.3, we can highlight three main factors that are important to explain governance patterns observed in the Andean region:

a. characteristics of the political system;
b. weaknesses of the state;
c. the impact of high inequality and the ethnic makeup.

(a) The Political System

One hypothesis is that at the root of the governance problems of the Andean region lies the nature of its political system. An important dimension of the political system is the presidential regime that governs all the Andean countries. As mentioned before, it is argued that presidential systems, with their rigidity of fixed presidential terms, their tendency to produce a winner-take-all situation, and their dual legitimacy with legislatures and executives, tend to be associated with more frequent presidential crises that in some cases can lead to 'regime breakdowns', that is, the collapse of democracy and the disruption of constitutional rule. While this argument has validity, it needs to be qualified. All Andean countries have presidential regimes but not all of them have the same high frequency of presidential crises that has been observed in the recent histories of Bolivia, Ecuador and Peru, nor the same record of regime breakdowns. With respect to regime breakdowns, however, the potential fragility of democracy can be a real problem even for Colombia and Venezuela, two countries that have avoided the disruption of democratic rule in the past four decades. Current polarization between the Chávez administration and the opposition is indicative that Venezuela is far from immune to destabilizing pressures on democracy.

Another important indicator of problems in the political system is the relatively high frequency of constitutional reforms (higher than other Latin American and OECD countries) that has been observed in several Andean countries during the last century (already documented in Section 2.3). This frequent constitutional reform is indicative of a certain instability in the core rules of the political game in Andean countries. Regarding the perception of the presidential system, it is worth noting that in their last two new constitutions, both Ecuador in 1998 and Venezuela in 1999 reinforced the authority of the president ('more presidentialism'). New constitutions addressed other issues as well, like the indigenous population problem by increasing indigenous political and economic rights. In fact, the Colombian and Ecuadorian more recent constitutions encouraged decentralization and a greater access to social services, such as education and health services, by excluded groups. The Venezuelan constitution that was approved in 1999, besides strengthening the presidency, also had an explicit redistributive objective pursued through an increase in social rights and entitlements (see Chapter 8, 'Venezuela: from stability to turmoil' in this volume). Also the constitution of 1991 in Colombia that expanded the economic entitlements and fostered decentralization led to an important increase in public spending as a share of GDP in the 1990s (see Chapter 5, 'The economy, conflict and governance in Colombia' in this volume).

Another feature of the political system in some Andean countries is the fragmentation and weakening of political parties. Ecuador, for example, has more than 12 political parties; there was an attempt to change this situation in the constitution of 1998 by putting a minimum vote requirement (5 per cent) on forming and legally maintaining a political party. The large number of parties in Ecuador, some reflecting strong regional interests, makes it difficult to reach a parliamentary consensus and, in other instances, fractionalizes national politics (see Arteta and Hurtado 2002). In contrast, in Colombia and Venezuela the political systems have traditionally gravitated around two large parties: liberals and conservatives in Colombia and ADECO and COPEI in Venezuela – although in recent years even these parties have been severely weakened. In Colombia, internal factions undermine the strength of the conservative and liberal umbrella groups. In Venezuela, the Chávez administration presided over the virtual disintegration of ADECO and COPEI that left a political vacuum in the place of strong parties or movements. In Peru, the traditional APRA party suffered a considerable loss of influence in the early 1990s after the government of Alan García in the late 1980s (García made a strong return a decade later in the presidential election of 2001).

(b) The Weak State Hypothesis

The state must be able to provide public goods such as law and order, infrastructure, contract enforcement, control of the territory. A 'weak state' is one that fails to provide the required amounts of these public goods with the consequence that individual security becomes precarious, that the rule of law is partial and incomplete, and that respect for civil rights and property rights is limited. Physical and institutional infrastructures, in turn, become weak and economic prosperity fails to develop.

Colombia is an interesting case in this regard. On the one hand, it has high levels of violence (political and criminal), an ongoing internal conflict that has lasted for more than four decades, and an important illegal drug industry. On the other hand, Colombia in the last 40 years has maintained normal and regular elections, presidents complete their constitutional terms, and democratic institutions operate with apparent normalcy. The state is 'weak' in some governance dimensions, for example lack of maintenance of law and order in the whole territory, but relatively 'strong' in others (elections are maintained regularly, civil freedoms are preserved).

Our empirical analysis of quality of institutions based on survey indices suggests several problems of governance and institutional weaknesses already discussed that fit the description of a weak state; although the concept has its nuances that are important to keep in mind.

(c) Social Inequality and Ethnic Structure

A third hypothesis that helps explain the governance problems of the Andean nations is their high levels of income and wealth inequality and, in three out of five countries, their significant ethnic diversity. During the first three to four decades of the 20th century, these countries were predominantly rural societies with a concentrated structure of land ownership and a wide income differential between landowners, small landholders, and peasants. Inequality was predominantly a rural phenomenon associated largely with the prevailing land tenure patterns.[33] Following the development of local manufacturing, the expansion of the state sector, and the adoption of import substitution policies, rural-urban migration took on a greater intensity around the mid 20th century and a middle class formed (varying across countries in size and importance) that helped to stabilize societies. In this new setting, social inequalities remained, but revolved around the ownership of productive capital, access to credit, access to educational opportunities, and access to political decisionmaking. As mentioned before, various strands of social theory, including recent endogenous growth models, predict that countries with high inequality will tend to have higher levels of social conflict, polarization, and political instability than more egalitarian countries.[34]

To income and wealth inequality, we must add the significant ethnic diversity in Bolivia, Ecuador, and Peru. As Table 2.9 shows, between 34 and 59 per cent of the population in all three countries is indigenous. Gray Molina and Chávez (Chapter 4 in this volume) show that only 58 per cent of the population of Bolivia speaks Spanish, followed by Quechua (22.9 per cent), Aymara (15.7 per cent) and other languages.[35] In Bolivia, the pattern of indigenous population participation in national civic life went from exclusion and marginalization to active demands for ethnic rights and nationalistic claims such as Aymara Nationalism. The presidential candidates that were supported by several indigenous groups also obtained a high number of votes in the recent presidential election. In 2003 the pressure of the indigenous movement was ultimately decisive in the resignation of President Sánchez de Losada.

The indigenous movement also became an important political actor in Ecuador in 1998 and 1999, during the Mahuad administration. The CONAIE, the largest Ecuadorian confederation of indigenous people, organized several mass protests in 1999, culminating in January of 2000 with an indigenous uprising that was joined by colonels of the army and that eventually led to the ousting of President Mahuad. The main point here is that indigenous groups have become an important political force in some Andean countries. These indigenous movements demand economic and civic rights and entertain, at times, a nationalistic agenda.

2.5 CONCLUDING REMARKS

The Andean countries, which form a region with an abundance of natural resources and other valuable assets, exhibit a variety of governance problems that hinder their potential for social peace, stability, and economic prosperity. Their governance records, past and present, vary from country to country but have generally been characterized by political instability, frequent constitutional reforms, presidential crises, volatility of democratic institutions, and violence. The empirical evidence of the quality of institutions puts the Andean region in a low place in international rankings of (survey-based) indices of voice and accountability, rule of law, regulatory burden, control of corruption, political instability, and violence, although improvements in some of these governance dimensions have also been observed.

This chapter highlights the way that governance problems can be decomposed at three levels: the political-constitutional regime, the working of intermediate level institutions, and the patterns of social conflict, inequality, and ethnic diversity. Important features of the political regime in Andean countries need further scrutiny for any broad agenda of institutional reform. These features comprise the scope and limits of presidential regimes to handle political crises, the workings of the party system and other constitutional provisions. At the level of intermediate institutions, complex principal–agent problems combine with the chronic problems of rent seeking, corruption, and violence that governments have tried to tackle but that continue to severely hinder institutional effectiveness. Organizational principles of goal clarity, adequate resources, and freedom from undue political interference must be reinforced. Income and wealth inequality, although not new phenomena in the Andean region or in Latin America, need to be addressed as high inequality is often correlated with social conflict, political polarization, and slow economic growth. Although radical redistribution of existing assets can be destabilizing and can slow growth, policies that foster a more egalitarian access to capital, credit, education, and political representation can have good medium-term payoffs in terms of enhanced stability and more rapid economic growth. Ethnic diversity is another important social feature in countries such as Bolivia, Ecuador, and Peru that needs to be addressed through creative political and economic reforms with an ethnically inclusive component. This analysis suggests that for the Andean region to realize its economic potential, it must adequately tackle its complex political, social and institutional problems.

NOTES

* Regional Advisor, United Nations Economic Commission for Latin America and the Caribbean. Paper presented at the conference 'Political Crises and Development Alternatives in the Andean Region' at New School University, New York, 8–9 May 2003. The very efficient research assistance and comments by Claudio Aravena are much appreciated. Comments made on an earlier version of the paper at seminars held at the World Bank and the Inter-American Development Bank are appreciated. The paper is part of a multicountry project on the political economy of the Andean region coexecuted by ECLAC and the Inter-American Dialogue with the financial support of the Ford Foundation. Individual comments by Enrique Garcia, Carol Graham, Peter Hakim, Fidel Jaramillo and José Antonio Ocampo are acknowledged.

1. The definition of 'Andean countries' comprises Bolivia, Colombia, Ecuador, Peru and Venezuela, which are the member countries of the Community of Andean Nations, CAN.

2. By 'Andean countries' we refer to the countries that are currently members of the CAN (Andean Community of Nations).
3. See Beckerman and Solimano (2002).
4. See Tommasi (2002) for a discussion of the concept of 'hierarchy of institutions'.
5. See Buchanan and Tullock (1962) and Buchanan (1988).
6. Dixit (1996) stresses that, in practice, the distinction between rulemaking and actions is more a continuum rather than a discrete choice binary category. Specific policies can have long-run permanent effects comparable to the impacts of rulemaking decisions.
7. See Dixit (2003).
8. See Linz and Valenzuela (1994) and Mainwaring and Scully (1997) for alternative views on presidentialism and parliamentarianism.
9. See North (1991).
10. An alternative view of the origin of institutions is provided by Olsen (2000) who puts forward a theory of power and compulsory compliance to explain the origin of the state and institutions. In Olsen's framework institutions are not necessarily created for efficiency reasons to reduce transaction costs but for purposes of redistributing resources towards those in power. In this vein institutions can be dysfunctional and consistent with bad social outcomes such as economic decline and recurrent crisis.
11. See Drazen (2000).
12. See Krueger (1974).
13. Currently around 40 countries, included Colombia, are experiencing some sort of internal conflict, civil war, or significant rebellions within their own territories.
14. Collier and Hoeffler (2002), using data for 78 large civil conflicts between 1960 and 1999 find econometric evidence that the risk (probability) that a civil war will start during a five-year period is better explained by a set of determinants known as greed factors than by 'grievance' factors.
15. In general the determinants of crime are not the same determinants of rebellions and civil wars, although crime and rebellion often intertwine in complex ways.
16. Empirically the literature identifies a civil war as a conflict involving at least 1000 battle deaths per year, with deaths taking place in a context of violence between a government and an identifiable organized group; moreover, at least 5 per cent of the deaths must be on each side. In turn, while criminal organizations, gangs and mafias, typically range from around 20 to 500 members, rebel organizations have 500 to 5000 or more combatants.
17. Rebel movements may have several sources of funding: (i) criminal activities such as kidnapping, extortion and ransom to raise revenues to finance their activities along with alliances or taxes on criminal organizations (for example it is found that guerrilla groups in Colombia derive an important part of their income from taxes to drug cartels); (ii) predation of natural resources that they control; (iii) funding coming from foreign governments hostile to the adversaries of those rebel groups; (iv) funding from diasporas (often living in developed economies) formed by nationals that left their home countries because of civil wars or extended conflict and send financial contributions to support rebel groups they identified for historical reasons with their exit.
18. Marxian theory puts considerable emphasis on the conflicting nature of capitalist development, although its main channel is conflict between capital and labor. Other theories identify other actors and channels of social conflict that go beyond the simple capital–labor dichotomy.
19. See Taylor (1991).
20. See Solimano (1998).
21. Conversely the formal leader can be weak, politically inept and unable to manage conflict.
22. Uruguay had the highest number of constitutional reforms of the three most 'stable' countries in Latin America.
23. All the Andean countries have presidential regimes like most Latin American and Caribbean countries.
24. See Hartlyn (1994) and Coppedge (1994) for analysis of presidentialism in Venezuela.

25. Studies of the relationship between institutional quality and growth performance are Barro (1996), Mauro (1995), Knack and Keefer (1995). A useful survey of this literature is Aron (2000).
26. See La Porta et al. (1998) for an interesting discussion of 'quality of government' and its determinants.
27. See Serven and Solimano (1993) and Pindyck and Solimano (1993) for analytical discussion and empirical evidence of the adverse effects of (mainly economic) instability on private capital formation, an important determinant of the rate of economic growth. Studies of the effects of political instability on growth are Alesina and Rodrik (1994), Barro (1991), Alesina et al. (1996).
28. Porter et al. (2002), Chapter 1.
29. An analysis of ethnicity and governance for Latin America and Andean countries is De Gregori (1998).
30. See Beckerman and Solimano (2002) and Solimano (2000).
31. See Ocampo (2002) for an analysis of the economic performance of Colombia in recent years.
32. The individual country story of the evolution of the economy of each Andean countries is told in the country papers of the Political Economy of the Andean Region's project.
33. See Thorpe (2000).
34. See Solimano (1998), Alesina and Rodrik (1994), Persson and Tabellini (2000).
35. According to the last published national population census of population (1992).

REFERENCES

Acemoglu, D. (2002), 'Why not a political cause theorem? Social conflict, commitment and politics', *NBER Working Paper*, 9377.

Aghion, P., A. Alesina and F. Trebbi (2002), 'Endogenous political institutions', *NBER Working Paper*, 9006.

Alesina, A. and D. Rodrik (1994), 'Distributive politics and economic growth', *Quarterly Journal of Economics*, **109** (May), 465–90.

Alesina, A., S. Ozler, N. Roubini and S. Swagel (1996), 'Political instability and economic growth', *Journal of Economic Growth*, **1** (2), 189–211.

Aron, J. (2000), 'Growth and institutions: a review of the evidence', *The World Bank Research Observer*, **15** (1), 99–135.

Arteta, G. and O. Hurtado (2002), 'Political economy of Ecuador', mimeo, *Project Political Economy of the Andean Region*, ECLAC.

Barro, R. (1991), 'Economic growth in cross section of countries', *Quarterly Journal of Economics*, **106** (2), 407–43.

Barro, R. (1996), 'Democracy and growth', *Journal of Economic Growth*, **1** (1), 1–27.

Beckerman, P. and A. Solimano (eds) (2002), *Crisis, Dollarization and Social Impact. The Case of Ecuador*, Directions in Development, The World Bank.

Buchanan, J.M. (1988), 'Contractarian political economy and constitutional interpretation', *American Economic Review*, **78** (2), (Papers and Proceedings), 135–9.

Buchanan, J.M. and G. Tullock (1962), *The Calculus of Consent: Logical Foundation for Constitutional Democracy*, Ann Arbor, MI: University of Michigan Press.

Collier, P. (2000), 'Rebellion as a quasi-criminal activity', *Journal of Conflict Resolution*, **44** (6), 839–53.

Collier, P. (2001), 'Ethnic diversity: an economic analysis', *Economic Policy*, **32** (April), 129–66.

Collier, P. and A. Hoeffler (2002), 'Greed and grievance in civil war', *Working Paper Series 2002–01*, Centre for the Study of African Economies, Oxford, UK. Available at www.csac.ox.ac.uk.

Cooter, R.D., (2000), *The Strategic Constitution*, Princeton, NJ: Princeton University Press.

Coppedge, M. (1994), 'Venezuela: democratic despite presidentialism', in J. Linz and A. Valenzuela (eds), *The Failure of Presidential Democracy*, Johns Hopkins University Press.

De Gregori, I. (1998), 'Ethnicity and democratic governability in Latin America: reflections from two Central Andean countries', in F. Aguero and J. Stark (eds), *Fault Lines of Democracy in Post-Transition Latin America*, North South Center Press.

Dixit, A. (1996), *The Making of Economic Policy. A Transaction Costs Politics Perspective*, MIT Press.

Dixit, A. (2001a), 'Some lessons from transaction costs politics for less- developed countries', mimeo, Princeton University.

Dixit, A. (2001b), 'On modes of economic governance', mimeo, Princeton University.

Dixit, A. (2003), 'Some lessons from transaction-cost politics for less-developed countries', *Economics and Politics*, **15** (2), July, 107–33.

Drazen, A. (2000), *Political Economy in Macroeconomics*, Princeton, NJ: Princeton University Press.

Easterly, W. and R. Levine (1997), 'Africa's growth tragedy: policies and ethnic divisions', *Quarterly Journal of Economics*, **112** (4), 1203–50.

Hartlyn, J. (1994), 'Presidentialism and Colombian politics', in J. Linz and A. Valenzuela (eds), *The Failure of Presidential Democracy*, Johns Hopkins University Press.

Hayek, F. (1960), *The Constitution of Liberty*, Chicago: University of Chicago Press.

Kaufmann, D., A. Kraay and P. Zoido-Lobatón (1999), 'Governance matters', *Policy Research Working Paper*, 2196, The World Bank.

Kaufmann, D., A. Kraay and P. Zoido-Lobatón (2002), 'Governance matters II', *Policy Research Working Paper*, 2772, The World Bank.

Knack, S. and P. Keefer (1995), 'Institutions and economic performance: cross country tests using alternative institutional measures', *Economics and Politics*, **7** (3), 207–27.

Krueger, A. (1974), 'The political economy of the rent seeking society', *American Economic Review*, **64**, 291–303.

La Porta, R., F. López de Silanes, A. Schleifer and R. Vishny (1998), 'The quality of government', *National Bureau of Economic Research Working Paper Series*, 6727.

Linz, J. and A. Valenzuela (eds) (1994), *The Failure of Presidential Democracies: The Case of Latin America*, Johns Hopkins University Press.

Mainwaring, S. and T. Scully (1997), *La Construcción de Instituciones Democráticas. Sistema de Partidos Políticos en América Latina*, CIEPLAN, Santiago, Chile.

Mauro, P. (1995), 'Corruption and economic growth', *Quarterly Journal of Economics*, **110** (3), 681–712.

Montesquieu, C. (1748), *The Spirit of the Laws*, Paris.

North, D. (1990), 'A transaction costs theory of politics', *Journal of Theoretical Politics*, **2** (4): 355–67.

North, D. (1991), *Institutions, Institutional Change and Economic Performance*, Cambridge University Press.

Ocampo, José Antonio (2002), 'Política Económica y Economía Política en Colombia en la década de los Noventa', mimeo, *Project Political Economy of the Andean Region*, ECLAC.

Olsen, M. (2000), *Power and Prosperity, Outgrowing Communist and Capitalist Dictatorships*, Basic Books.

Persson, T. and G. Tabellini (2000), *Political Economics. Explainging Economic Policy*, MIT Press.

Pindyck, R. and A. Solimano (1993), 'Economic instability and aggregate investment', in O. Blanchard and S. Fischer (eds), *NBNER Macroeconomic Annual 1993*, MIT Press.

Porter, M., J. Sachs, P. Cornelius, J. McArthur and K. Schwab (2002), *The Global Competitiveness Report 2001–2002*, World Economic Forum and Harvard University.

Serven, L. and A. Solimano (eds) (1993), *Striving for Growth After Adjustment. The Role of Capital Formation*, The World Bank Regional and Sectoral Studies.

Solimano, A. (ed.) (1998), *Social Inequality. Growth, Values and the State*, Ann Arbor, MI: University of Michigan Press.

Solimano, A. (ed.) (2000), *Colombia. Essays on Conflict, Peace and Development*, The World Bank.

Taylor, L. (1991), *Income Distribution, Inflation and Growth: Lectures on Structuralist Macroeconomic Theory*, MIT Press.

Thorpe, R. (2000), *An Economic History of Latin America in the 20th Century*, Inter-American Development Bank.

Tommasi, M. (2002), 'Crisis, political institutions and policy reform', paper presented at the 4th World Bank ABCDE Conference held in Oslo, Norway, 24–26 June 2002.

3. Poverty, inequality and public policy in the Andean region: a comparative perspective

Amanda Glassman and Sudhansu Handa*

INTRODUCTION

Using a comparative perspective, this chapter describes trends in poverty and inequality in the Andean countries, and examines the relationships between these factors and economic growth, growth volatility, labor markets, human capital formation, governance and political economy issues. A second brief section reviews patterns in public social spending and programs intended to deal with some of the effects of poverty and inequality. Finally, a concluding section summarizes the stylized facts and sets out unanswered questions and policy issues. The chapter is not intended to exhaustively review the literature in each area, which is significant, but rather seeks to present key stylized facts important to understanding the country case studies included in the rest of the volume.

3.1 POVERTY AND INEQUALITY

Poverty

In 2000, approximately 35 per cent of the Latin America region[1] lived in poverty, defined as less than $2 per day.[2,3] While showing great dispersion within the Andean subregion and within nations, the Andean countries display a slighly higher ratio than the regional average, with nearly 38 per cent of the population under the $2 per day poverty line (see Figure 3.1). In absolute terms, of total world poor, 1.5 per cent live in the Andean region, which represents approximately 20 per cent of the total poor in the Latin American region.

At the regional level, the IDB estimates that the incidence of poverty has stagnated during the 1990s (see Annex 3.1 to this chapter). While the

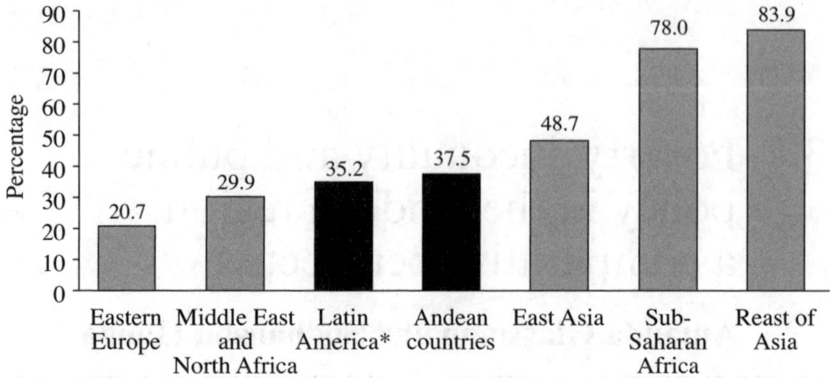

Source: IDB (Székely and Hilgert).

Figure 3.1 Percentage of population living on less than two US dollars a day (PPP 1985) by region, 1998

first half of the 1990s led to poverty reduction, the second half led to poverty increase, resulting in little change over the period. Results in the Andean region are generally consistent with these regional patterns. In Ecuador, Colombia and Bolivia poverty decreased marginally between 1990 and 2000. In Peru, poverty incidence increased slightly. The exception has been Venezuela, where a 64 per cent increase in poverty incidence has been recorded. The poverty gap increased slightly during the 1990s as well, with Venezuela as a clear outlier where the poverty gap has increased 76 per cent. Andean exceptions are Colombia and Ecuador, though the magnitude of the decline is marginal.

Disparities within countries are well-known. Rural areas tend to display higher levels of incidence; regionally, rural poverty incidence is double the urban figure. Certain Andean countries display this same relationship but of a more significant order of magnitude. In Peru, for example, poverty incidences in the Rural Jungle (79.6 per cent) and the Rural Highlands (79.5 per cent) are more than five times that in the Metropolitan Area of Lima (14.6 per cent). The incidence of poverty by ethnicity or mother tongue is also high when compared to respondents who classify themselves as white or Spanish speakers (see Figure 3.2).

Other determinants of poverty in both Latin America and the Andean subregion include the occupation of the household head (those working in agriculture tend to be worst off), educational attainment (lower levels of attainment are most significant predictors of poverty) and family size (larger family sizes are related to poverty incidence). These factors will be

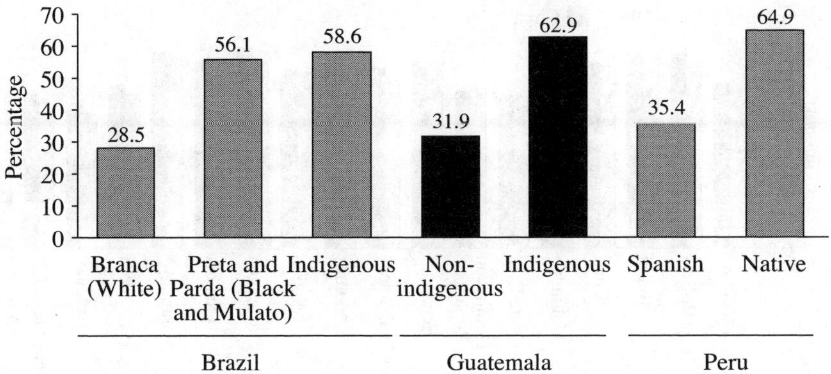

Source: IDB MECOVI Household Survey, calculated by the Poverty Unit, IDB.

Figure 3.2 Incidence of poverty by race or mother tongue, circa 2000 (two US dollars a day PPP 1985)

explored in more detail in the section on human capital endowment, poverty and inequality. At the regional level, in urban settings, poverty is higher amongst female heads of household (FHH) (30.4 per cent) than their male counterparts (25 per cent).[4] The evidence in Andean countries is mixed; urban Colombian FHH (World Bank 2002) are disproportionately poorer than other households while Peruvian FHH (Bouillon and Montes 2001) show no clear patterns over time.

Inequality

As is well known, Latin America is the most unequal region in the world; more than 31 per cent of national income is earned by the wealthiest 5 per cent of the population. The bottom 30 per cent earns only 7.5 per cent of total income. In the Andean subregion, 28.5 per cent of the national income is earned by the wealthiest 5 per cent of the population. In the non-Andean Latin American nations, this share is 31.9 per cent, indicating that while highly unequal, the Andean subregion is not much more unequal than the rest of the Latin America region. Circa 2000, the Gini index in the Andean subregion ranges from a low of 0.47 in Venezuela to a high of 0.60 in Bolivia (see Annex 3.1 for a table on income distribution and poverty in the 1990s and Figures 3.3A and 3.3B).

Inequality, as measured by the Gini, has increased substantially in Bolivia over the past decade (more than 10 per cent), while in the remaining Andean countries the index has remained more or less unchanged. In the longer-

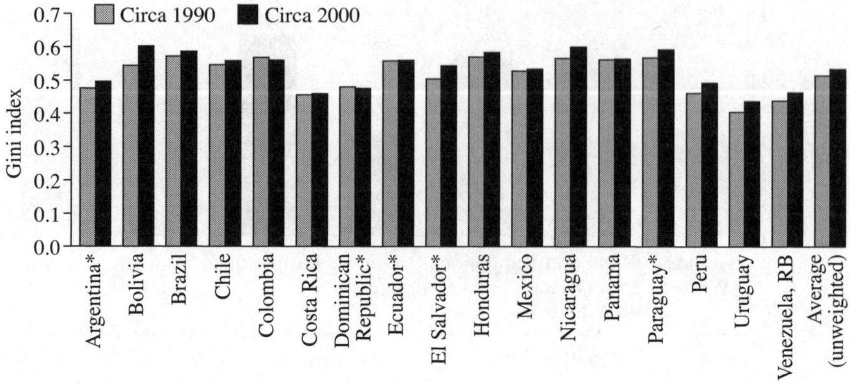

Source: Poverty Unit, Inter American Development Bank (see Annex 3.1).

Figure 3.3A Changes in the Gini index in Latin America during the 1990s

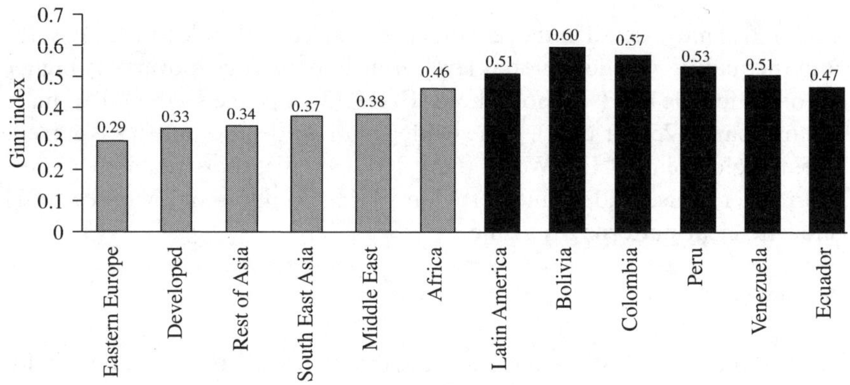

Figure 3.3B Income inequality by regions (Gini index), 1990s

term perspective, however, inequality appears to be increasing. In Colombia, for example, the Gini coefficient increased 4 per centage points during the last two decades, and simultaneously, the income share of the top quintile relative to the share of the poorest 20 per cent increased from 17 to 20 times as high (World Bank 2002).

Growth, Poverty and Inequality

Rising per worker wage differentials have not automatically translated into simultaneous increases in inequality and poverty in terms of per capita household income. In a recent book on the topic, Vos et al. (2002) analyse 17 Latin American nations[5] and 47 economic periods to assess trends in growth, poverty and inequality. In this analysis, Ecuador (national data, 95–99) and Peru (national data, 85–91) are the subregional cases where poverty and inequality increased together,[6] while the remainder of the subregional episodes fall into the falling poverty/rising inequality category. (This analysis, however, omits the post-1997 effects of the recession in Colombia, where poverty and inequality have increased jointly.)

Where poverty reduction did occur, economic growth was a clear contributor in the subregion (see Figure 3.4 and Table 3.1), and this effect is more pronounced in the Andean subregion than in non-Andean nations. While most countries in the Latin America region achieved moderate growth rates in the 1990s, it is difficult to speak of a strong and sustained recovery from the dismal performance of the 1980s. In the countries of the subregion, this recovery was extremely modest, with Peru showing the greatest gains. In large part, this disappointing performance is attributable to a tapering off of growth towards the end of the 1990s due to emerging domestic financial crises (Ecuador), natural disasters (Ecuador, Colombia) or external events such as plummeting commodity prices and international financial crises (Colombia).

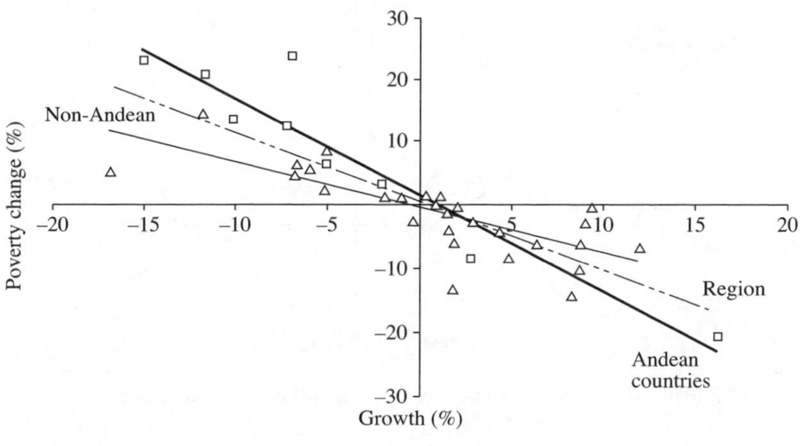

Source: IDB MECOVI household surveys data bank, authors' calculations.

Figure 3.4 Changes in poverty and growth during the 1990s, regional, Andean and non-Andean countries

Economic growth is also a major determinant of inequality reduction, particularly for the Andean subregion (See Figure 3.5). In the non-Andean

Latin American countries, the relationship between changes in inequality and growth is flat, that is, changes in growth are seemingly unrelated to changes in inequality. In the Andean subregion, however, the slope of this relationship is quite steep, primarily due to Ecuador's performance in the 1997–99 period.

Table 3.1 Per capita GDP growth in Latin America (per cent)

Country	1960s	1970s	1980s	1990s
Bolivia	0.7	1.7	–2.5	1.8
Colombia	2.0	3.3	1.2	0.6
Ecuador	1.0	5.8	–0.3	–0.3
Peru	2.2	1.1	–2.4	1.9
Venezuela	1.2	0.4	–2.8	–0.2
Andean mean	1.4	2.5	–1.4	0.8

Source: De Ferranti et al. (2000).

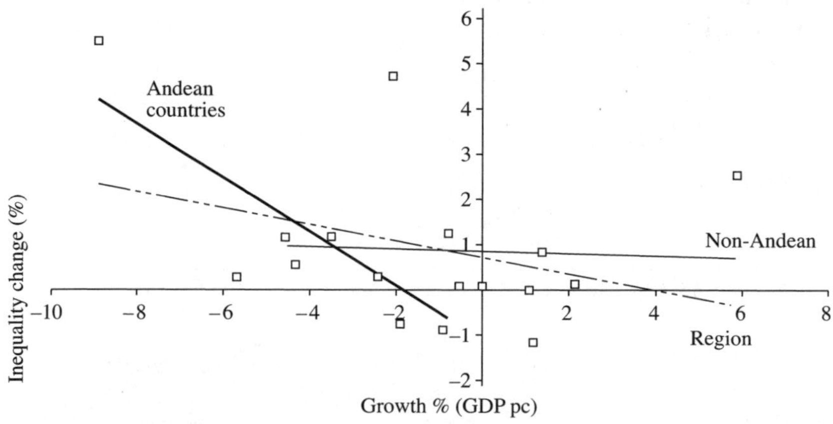

Source: IDB MECOVI household surveys data bank, authors' calculations.

Figure 3.5[7] *Changes in inequality and growth during the 1990s, regional, Andean and non-Andean countries*

Growth Volatility and its Impact on Poverty and Inequality

While the Latin America region has high levels of growth volatility relative to industrialized countries between 1970 and 2000, there is evidence of a decline in GDP growth volatility that affected most countries in the region. The variability of GDP growth remained roughly stable until the late 1970s, and then rose sharply in the 1980s, due principally to the debt crisis and associated macroeconomic and financial effects. In the 1990s, however, the rising trend in aggregate volatility in Latin America was reversed. GDP data up to 1999 shows that the variability of real GDP growth declined substantially across the region, approximately to levels experienced in the 1960s and 1970s (De Ferranti et al. 2000).[8] The evidence ultimately is mixed, however, on whether volatility has become higher today than it was in the relatively normal 1970s, because the 1980s are viewed as an unusually turbulent decade. And when taking into account the most recent data from 2001–02 (Solimano and Soto 2003), volatility appears to be increasing.

The Andean experience is mixed. Growth volatility, as measured by standard deviations of growth rates by decade, increased in Colombia (substantially) and Venezuela (marginally) since the 1960s, while decreasing in Bolivia, Ecuador and Peru during the same time period (De Ferranti et al. 2000). Wage or earnings volatility captures a central dimension of income volatility. The cycle of rise and fall in wage volatility tracks closely that found in the macroeconomic aggregates. Nevertheless, since the 1970s, real wage growth volatility has declined substantially in the Andes with the exception of Venezuela. However, although volatility at the macro level (GDP growth, consumption growth) decreased during the 1990s, microeconomic volatility (expressed in turnover rates, Saavedra (2003)) has increased in several countries in part due to the flexibility required to compete in world markets. This is the case in the subregion.

It has been amply documented that recessions and economic instability intensify wage inequality. Over the past 20 years, the subregion has weathered a succession of macroeconomic crises, which, apart from armed conflict and natural disasters, have been the chief cause of the surge in poverty and in many cases have also increased inequality. Panel data from Peru show how significant movements in and out of poverty can occur during recessive periods (Bouillon and Montes 2001). Such upheavals can cause setbacks in human capital accumulation, particularly in the poorest households, when family members display malnutrition or have to cut short their schooling. De Janvry and Sadoulet (2001) analysing income growth and inequality for the 1970–94 period show that crises create ratchet effects on inequality that growth cannot erase. The effects of recessions mean, for instance, that a 1 per cent decline in income cancels the poverty reduction effects of more than 0 per cent of income growth.

Volatility and inflation also exacerbate inequality (Lustig 2001; Birdsall and Székeley 2003). Inflation hurts the poor more than the upper income brackets, since their meager financial holdings are undiversified and cash-heavy. Likewise, the poor are more likely to be dependent upon government cash transfers, subsidies or pensions that are not adjusted for inflation.

Labor Market Dynamics, Poverty and Inequality

As total household income is more dependent on labor earnings than in other regions of the world, most recent poverty increases in the region are due to decreases in labor income. In contrast to Central America where unemployment rates declined or increased only moderately, the 1990s have been characterized by rising unemployment rates in the Andean subregion, with the exception of Bolivia (Duryea et al. 2003). In Colombia, unemployment rates increased from 7.1 per cent in the early nineties to 16.7 at the end of the decade. In Venezuela, unemployment rose from 4.8 to 10.3 per cent during this same period. Participation rates of women and youth also increased substantially during the decade of the 1990s. In the Andean subregion, unemployment rates also increased sharply for youth at ages 15–18, but as the share of youth unemployment of total unemployment has dropped due to demographic trends (not increased schooling), this phenomenon does not explain increases in the unemployment rate. A similar pattern has emerged for females.

Average wages (measured in PPP-adjusted $) remained constant or declined throughout the region during the 1990s (Duryea et al. 2003). The decline was very pronounced in Colombia and Venezuela. In Bolivia and Peru, however, wages in dollars have not changed much relative to their values at the beginning of the decade. The gender gap in wages, controlling for educational attainment, experience and sector of employment, has been steadily declining in the Andean countries. However, the quality of jobs is poor overall. In an exercise to estimate the percentage of workers earning 'poverty wages', defined as individual hourly earnings of one PPP-adjusted US dollar or less, Duryea et al. (2003) estimate that 48 per cent of Colombian workers earned poverty wages while in Bolivia, this figure was more than 70 per cent of the workforce. The remainder of the Andean countries fell in between these two figures. Women tend to be concentrated in poverty wage employment.

Labor market segmentation and both occupational and wage discrimination are also important contributors to inequality. Controlling for education, experience and hours worked, rural workers make nearly 30 per cent less than urban workers; urban formal workers make about 20 per cent more than their informal counterparts (IDB 1999). Occupational and wage discrimination, along with stigma, is common and affects women, indigenous people, Afro descendants and other excluded workers. For instance, in urban Peru, after controlling for a number of variables, predominantly white individuals have better jobs (in the service sector) and earn higher wages than predominantly indigenous workers (Saavedra et al. 2002). Further, with no exceptions in the Andean region, the proportion of persons in low paying jobs is higher among women than men.

Child labor is also a significant feature of labor markets in the Andean subregion. Figure 3.6[9] illustrates the magnitude of this phenomenon. Ecuador presents the most dramatic case. At age 15, more than half of children in the bottom two quintiles of the income distribution are in the labor market, perhaps due to a combination of extremely low secondary school supply, poverty and significant earnings opportunities in the market.

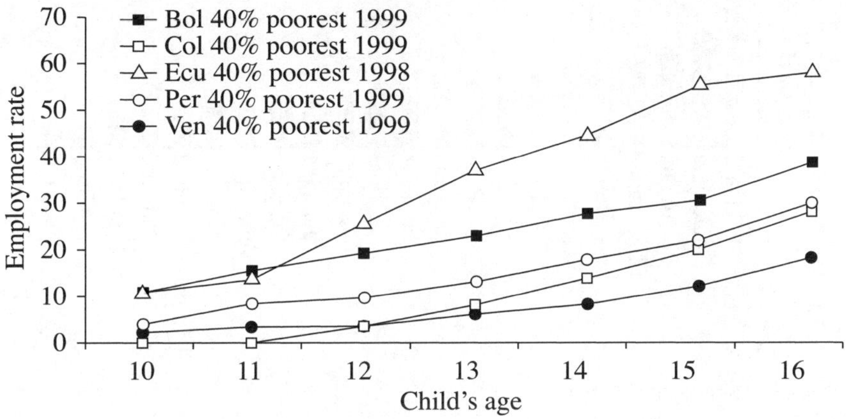

Source: Social Indicators Information Service, Research Department, IDB 2001

Figure 3.6 Employment rates for children by age and income level, 1998–99

Human Capital Endowment, Poverty and Inequality

Despite the growing inequality of incomes and limited poverty reduction, the region did make important progress in improving social indicators during the past decade. For example, taking the UNDP's Human Development Index (HDI), which measures a combination of life expectancy at birth, adult literacy (over 15 years), enrollment in primary, secondary and post-secondary education, and GDP per capita, rose from 0.69 in the 1980s to 0.74 in the 1990s. The HDI for Latin America and the Caribbean is exceeded only by the overall average for developed countries, and the gap between these two groups has narrowed over time. The Andean HDI is close to the regional average, though somewhat above it, and shows an improvement over time.

The UNDP's human poverty index (HPI), which measures human poverty or capacity poverty, summarizes three different aspects of poverty in a single index: the probability of premature death, the absence of basic education (illiteracy) and lack of access to public services, such as health and potable water, as well as the percentage of underweight children under five years old. The HPI ranges more broadly within the Andean group, with Peru showing the worst results and Colombia the best (see Figure 3.7).

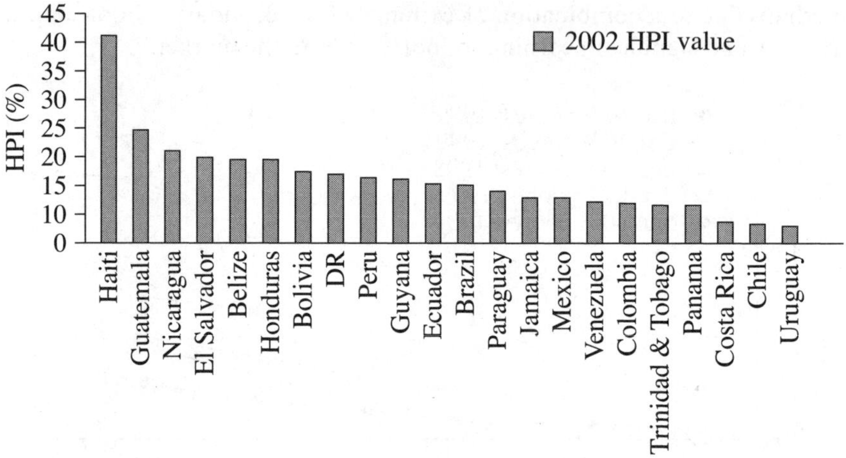

Source: UNDP (2001).

Figure 3.7 Human poverty index in Latin America, 1999

This improvement can also be seen in the progress that the region has been making in human development, particularly in education and health. Primary school enrolment is near 90 per cent, while secondary is 70 per cent on average (Ecuador is a notable exception to this record, with only 51 per cent of the eligible population attending secondary school). Infant mortality (IMR) has declined dramatically in the Andes and is now below the regional average; 26.1 per 1000 live births versus 28.5 in the non-Andean nations. Bolivia remains an important exception, with an IMR of 61 per 1000 live births. Fertility rates, however, remain higher than the non-Andean nations and above the regional average; this is a key factor as family size is a crucial determinant of poverty (see Figures 3.8 and 3.9).

However, the relatively positive performance of the subregion in human development must also be analysed from the perspective of inequality. The discriminatory power of human capital endowments has been increasing over the past two decades, with recessions accentuating the value of higher

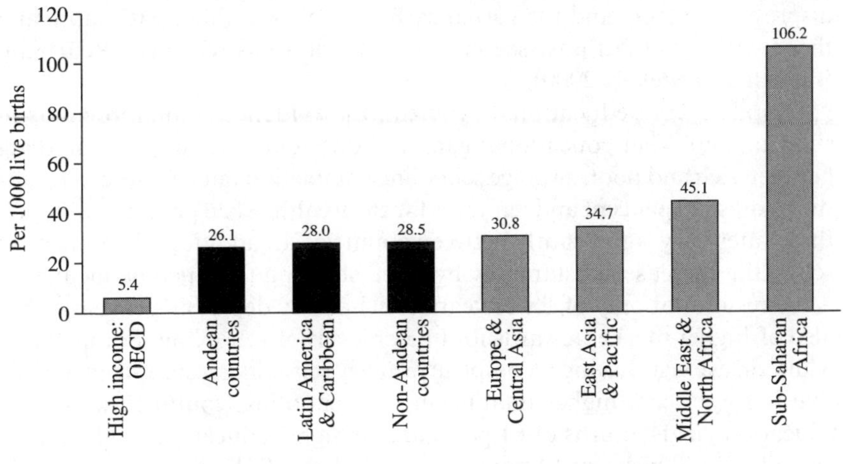

Figure 3.8 Infant mortality rates, circa 2000 (per 1000 live births)

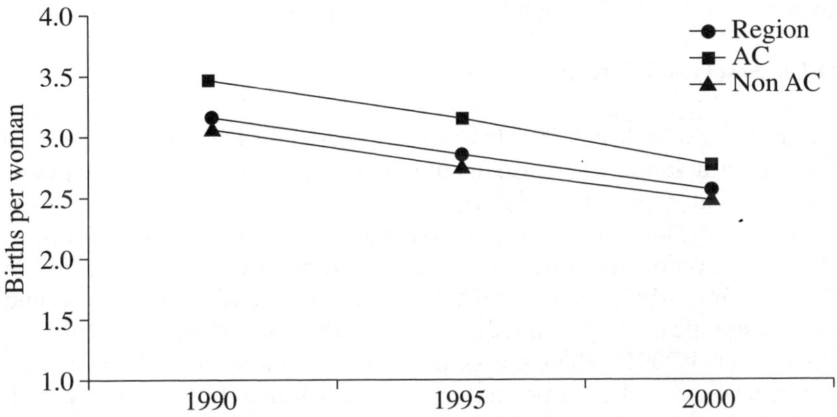

Figure 3.9 Fertility rates in the region, 1990–2000, circa 2000 (births per woman)

education. Across the subregion, decreasing wage returns to secondary education and increasing returns to tertiary have been recorded (Duryea and Pagés 2001), which has a clear impact on income inequality. In Colombia, for example, on average, individuals with post-secondary education receive 4.3 times the labor earnings of individuals with incomplete primary education (World Bank 2002). Globalization-related growth and recent market reforms have reinforced wage inequality, due to the higher premia that they have placed on skills. Returns to post-secondary education have been rewarded disproportionately and the gap in earnings between those with more and those with less than post-secondary education has widened (Behrman, Birdsall and Székely 2000).

Despite recent educational progress, the evidence is unambiguous in showing persistent educational gaps and differential returns to schooling between rich and poor. Average schooling completion rates are four years for the poorest 20 per cent and ten years for the wealthiest 20 per cent, although these rates vary significantly between countries. In addition, the returns to schooling increase substantially by level, showing that income inequality is the result, not only of fewer years of schooling depressing earnings, but also of higher market rewards for higher levels of schooling. For instance, while, on average, having incomplete primary schooling results in an income that is 18 per cent higher than having no schooling, complete secondary education yields returns of 61 per cent and higher education yields returns as high as 152 per cent (Attanasio and Székely 2001). Duryea and Pagés (2003) demonstrate that, using a fixed-effect regression method, returns to secondary are falling slightly in the subregion while returns to tertiary education are rising, though Peru is the exception to this phenomenon.

Other Assets and Poverty

Attanasio and Székely (2001) have demonstrated the key role that access to assets (credit, land ownership), including public assets such as basic public services (water, sewerage, electricity), play in the generation of poverty. Level of assets and the changes in returns on them are as important as the possession of assets in the determination of poverty. Case studies on Bolivia (Gray-Molina et al. 2001), where access to social capital was found to be a significant factor in reducing the probability of poverty, and Peru (Escobal et al. 2001), where access to assets, particularly in the form of basic public services, had an important effect on the probability of poverty, both confirm the importance of non-human capital assets for poverty reduction in the subregion.

Governance, Poverty and Inequality

The region has been characterized by weak social contracts between governments and citizens and little societal consensus on and enforcement of the principles of fairness and solidarity, precluding domestic support for and sustainability of redistributive policies (Graham 2001; Birdsall 2003). Solimano (2003), following on Kaufmann et al. (1999), highlights the important role that governance variables may play in the production of development outcomes and the relatively low levels of achievement in governance among the Andean countries vis-a-vis the rest of the region. Using the same framework, an analysis of the relationship between governance indicators, growth and poverty confirms that the Andean countries follow the regional mean in all cases. Better governance translates into higher growth rates and, by extension, lower poverty, and this effect is more pronounced in the Andean subregion (see Figures 3.10 to 3.13).

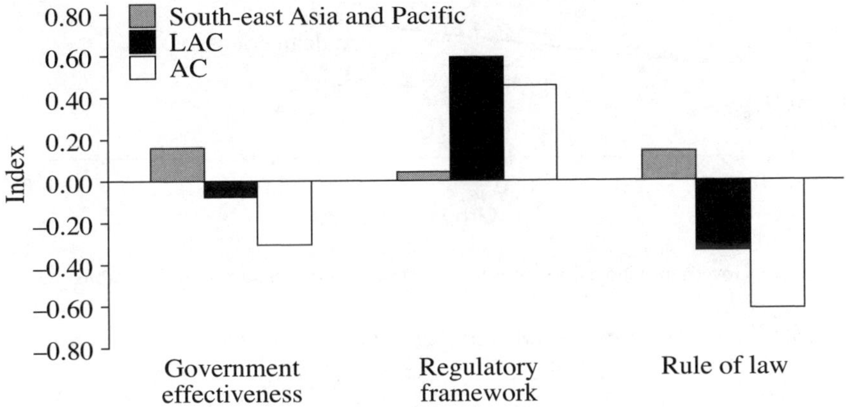

Source: Governance indicators from Kaufmann et al. (1999), authors' calculations

Figure 3.10 Governance indicators

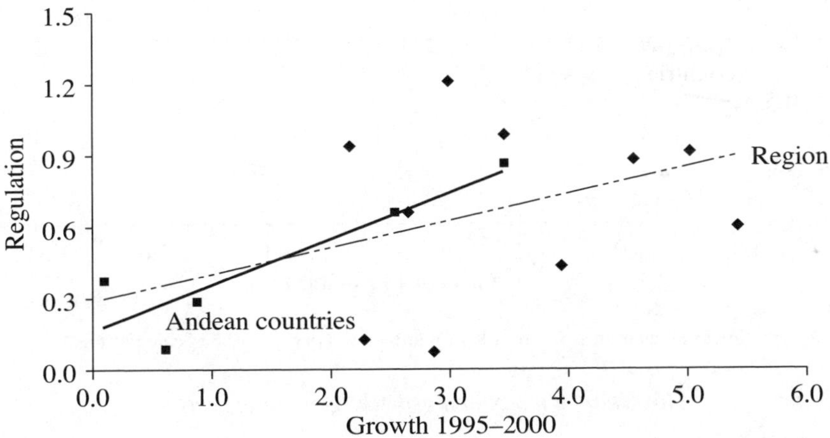

Source: Governance indicators from Kaufmann et al. (1999), authors' calculations

Figure 3.11 Governance index and growth: regulation

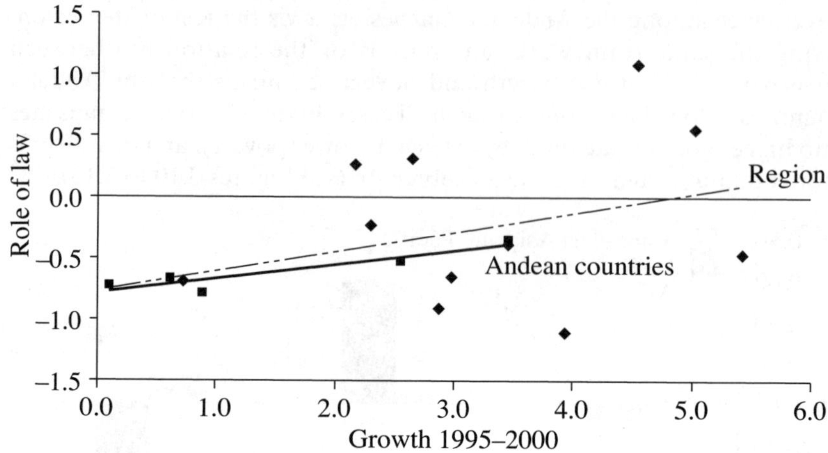

Source: Governance indicators from Kaufmann et al. (1999), authors' calculations

Figure 3.12 Governance index and growth: rule of law

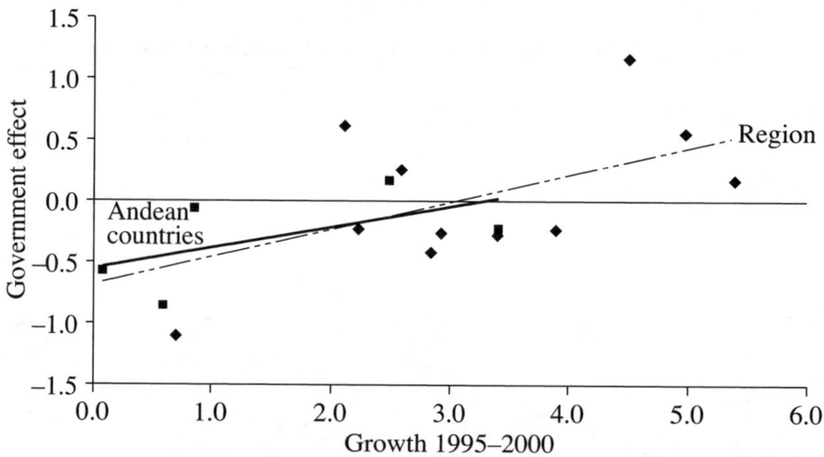

Source: Governance indicators from Kaufmann et al. (1999), authors' calculations

Figure 3.13 Governance index and growth: government effect

Hall and Jones (1999) and Duryea and Pagés (2002) find these same governance variables to be highly associated with productivity per worker and earnings. While some of this association may be due to reverse causation

– richer countries can afford better institutions – there is some evidence of causality running from institutions to earnings. Therefore, efforts to improve the quality of the institutional environment may help to reduce poverty. Duryea and Pagés (2002), for example, report that improving the quality of Peruvian institutions to the level achieved in Chile would achieve a reduction in poverty equivalent to the one attained with 2.71 extra years of tertiary education or 4.3 additional years of secondary education on average.

Social Exclusion, Poverty and Inequality

Inequality and exclusion can also dampen countries' growth potential by the social and political consequences that result from their direct negative impacts on individual and group welfare. The social problems that increasingly are linked to inequality and exclusion – crime and violence, substance abuse and other dysfunctional behavior – can trap the poor and exact high economic costs that block a country's growth prospects. The subregion's particularly high rates of crime and violence are strongly associated with its high levels of inequality, though the association with poverty is not significant in the research to date (see Fanjzylber 1997).

Inequality and social exclusion have been linked, in Latin America as well as in other world regions, with social upheaval and threats to public safety, especially in countries with high ethnic or racial diversity, and in environments where social injustice and discrimination pervade. The democratic process is undermined as a result, thus affecting a country's chances for growth. Distributional conflicts can beget inefficient political practices (inefficient tax systems, unproductive spending, and corruption) that weaken capital accumulation incentives and lead to suboptimal investment equilibria (Alesina and Rodrik 1994; Persson and Tabellini 1994). Accordingly, a lack of direct attention to problems of inequality and social exclusion may translate into social and political instability and low growth. Inequality and exclusion are closely associated, in vicious cycles, with each other and with increased poverty, reduced growth, and social and political disruptions. Disentangling causes and consequences, therefore, is not easy, particularly in the Andean region.

Political Economy, Poverty and Inequality

While quantitative data provides some level of explanatory information on poverty and inequality dynamics, recent research has focused on perceptions (Latinobarómetro surveys) and local level experiences (focus groups, stakeholder interviews) as a means to explain the quantitative phenomenon observed. This research can also provide insight into the political economy issues 'behind' aggregate phenomenon. Although poverty and inequality has stagnated in the subregion during the decade, gains in human development have been exceptionally positive. Why then has political upheaval remained at high levels in the subregion? Recent work by Carol Graham, using Latinobarómetro and panel survey data in Lima, shows that there is a large discrepancy in Peru between perceptions of quality of life improvements and actual improvements. This research found that those whose quality of life, as measured by increases in income and assets over time, had improved most relative to other groups were precisely those who felt most frustrated and dissatisfied with their (and the country's) progress to date. These findings may partially explain the low level of political attention given to date to the dramatic advancements in human poverty reduction in the Andean region. Other work in Colombia (McIlwaine and Moser 2001) has focused on the role of social capital, both 'productive' (generating institutional change and favoring growth) and 'perverse' (social networks that encourage rent seeking behavior), in generating social fragmentation and low levels of development. This qualitative study found that problems linked with a lack of social capital, related to the effects of political, street and domestic violence, lack of trust in government institutions, and a general atmosphere of fear, were identified by focus group participants much more frequently than those relating to a lack of human capital. While these studies are small-scale and so difficult to generalize, their results may illustrate a political economic context where important advances in the reduction of human poverty have been made in the presence of stagnating poverty and inequality, accompanied by high levels of frustration among the relatively better off and low levels of social capital in society in general. It is perhaps the latter factors that have most affected the subregion.

3.2 ADDRESSING POVERTY AND INEQUALITY IN THE ANDEAN REGION: SOCIAL POLICY AND PROGRAMS

Many government-financed actions might be taken to address poverty and inequality through facilitating access to human, financial and physical capital for the poor. This chapter, however, will focus on a subset of activities generally titled social policy and programs which seek to promote human capital accumulation and poverty reduction. These activites include social security (pensions, health, unemployment insurance), public health, nutrition, education, social infrastructure, training, housing, safety net/ poverty reduction, and water and sanitation.

Social expenditure in the Andean countries is significantly lower than in countries of comparative levels of economic development and with respect to the non-Andean nations. Further, although social expenditure increased in the subregion in the first half of the 1990s (in Colombia and Peru, there was a 100 per cent increase), from 1995 onwards social expenditure remained flat. Venezuela is the exception, as social expenditure declined over the decade (See Figures 3.14A and 3.14B).

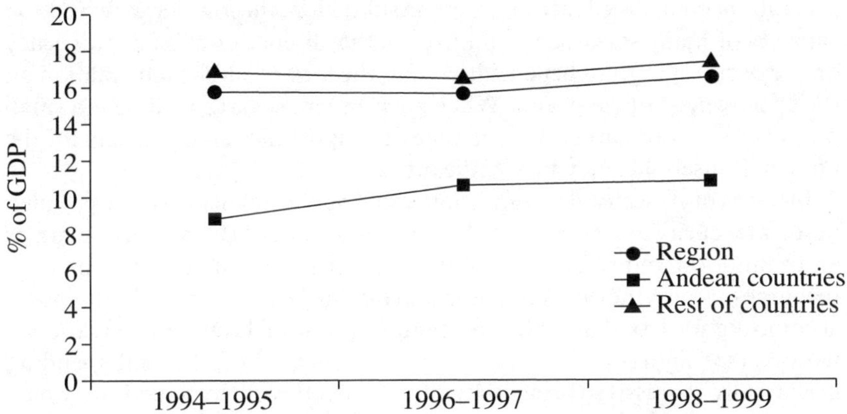

Figure 3.14A *Latin America: total social public expenditures as a percentage of GDP (millions, constant 1995 US$)*

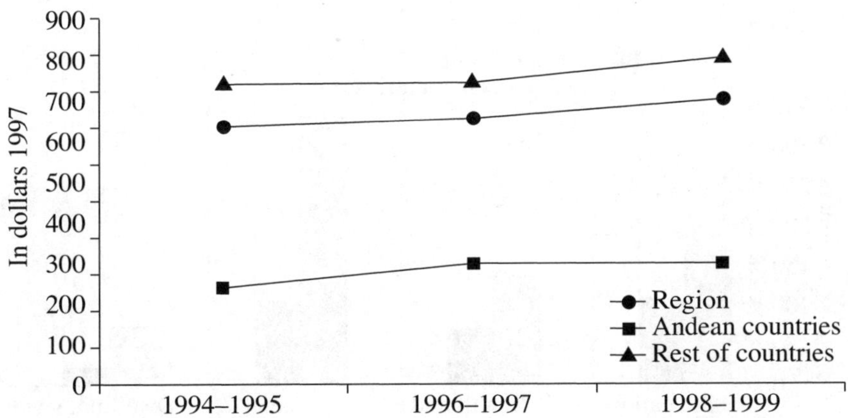

Figure 3.14B *Latin America: public social expenditure per capita, 1994–99*

Since the post-1995 era included many negative shocks with a resulting increase in poverty, it is clear that social expenditure is not anticyclical. Other studies have demonstrated this effect: total social spending in the Andean subregion is in fact procyclical with economic growth (CEPAL 2000, for Colombia CRECE 2001), thus accentuating the effects of economic downturns on the national economy and households. This effect is attributable to the flexible nature of certain kinds of social expenditure (such as social assistance transfers) during periods of fiscal adjustment that have generally accompanied recessions in the subregion, the low budget execution capacity of many social sector ministries, the absence of effective advocacy on the part of program beneficiaries, and the lack of public information on the effectiveness of programs. While government social spending is a small proportion of total household income, its importance at the margin for the poorest households may be significant.

In terms of its sectoral composition, most public financing is concentrated in social security and education. Non-social security health, housing, water and sanitation and safety net programs receive very small shares of total resources. Safety net programs, in particular, are very poorly financed, accounting for less than half a percentage point of GDP in most Andean nations (see figure 3.15). The benefit incidence of total social spending is generally regressive (principally due to social security spending, which is concentrated among formal sector employees and the relatively well off[10]), the exception being Peru where total social spending is moderately progressive (World Bank and IDB 2002).

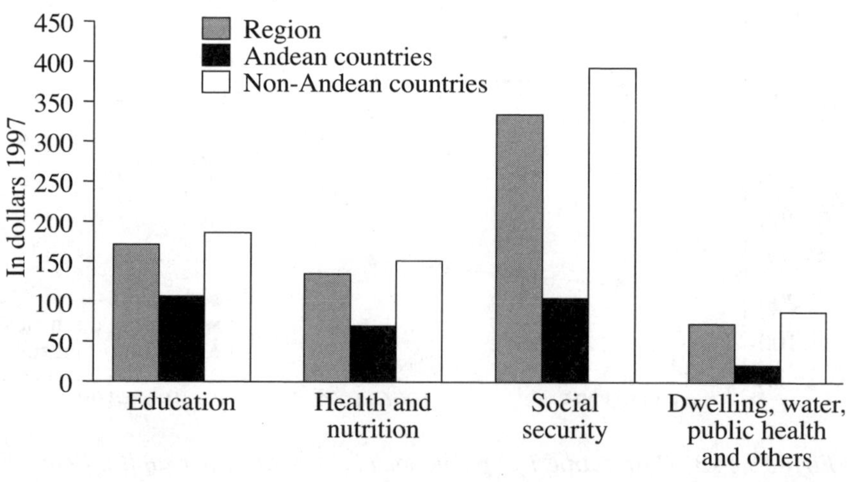

Figure 3.15 Social expenditure per capita by sector and region, 1998–99

3.3 CONCLUSIONS

The decade of the 1990s may be considered a 'lost decade' for the Andean countries in terms of poverty and inequality reduction. Initial improvements in poverty and inequality during the first half of the decade were essentially eliminated during the second half, resulting in virtually no net gain over the period. While the HPI and HDI did show significant improvements over the period, this did not translate into lower overall income poverty because these gains were made over a low base, and within a context of deep and persistent inequality as manifested by the continued exclusion of the 'hard-core' structural poor coupled with increasing dispersion in wages driven by higher rates of return at higher schooling levels.

Poverty and inequality are sensitive to economic growth, and this relationship is stronger in the Andean countries than in the Latin American region as a whole. This relationship is good news-bad news; in the presence of slow growth, as in the 1990s, poverty and inequality remain unabated. Conversely, in periods of stable and rapid growth, poverty and inequality decline. Governance also matters – the indicators of governance presented above show a fairly strong (positive) correlation with economic growth, and by extension, to poverty and inequality. And while the Andean countries rank below the region in these indicators, this means that some progress on poverty can be made through improvements along the governance dimension.

A major area of public policy concern is economic volatility and exposure to shocks. The number and magnitude of shocks increased significantly over the decade as countries became more open and participated in the world economy. Aggregate shocks have a disproportionate effect on the poor and vulnerable, and can eliminate years of poverty reduction in a very short period of time (Colombia late 1990s).

After a decade of economic frustration, civil society and governments in the region have become increasingly critical and apprehensive about the so-called Washington Consensus (WC) reform agenda. The antiglobalization sentiment has been unprecedented in the last three years, with demonstrations and protests now a normal part of the landscape of the World Bank/International Monetary Fund and World Trade Organization meetings. On the other hand, the actual reform record is mixed at best. A recent paper by Lora and Panizza (2002)[11] shows that the pace of these reforms came to a virtual standstill in the second half of the 1990s after significant progress in the first half. In terms of areas of reform, trade and financial sector reform saw the most progress, with very little (if any) progress in the area of taxes and labor market regulations. The one exception to the timing of the reform process is privatizations, which showed a significant increase in the second half of the decade, although this might be related to the need to raise funds to counter persistent fiscal deficits.

Given the economic performance over the last decade and the increasing pessimism towards WC reforms, a key public policy issue is how governments and civil society will approach the poverty reduction (and overall Millennium Development Goal) agenda in this decade. Leaders critical of the WC have been elected in Venezuela and Ecuador, and Peru's president has criticized WC policies while at the same time commiting himself to market-friendly policies. In the current environment, efficiency and growth cannot be the overriding driving force behind policy decisions; issues of equity and social inclusion must be addressed directly – getting the right balance will be the key challenge for policymakers. An important side issue is the role that markets will play in the eventual policies that are employed given the level of distrust in market institutions that has been generated over the previous decade.

One specific area of reform that has been relatively untouched is the labor market. The existence of entrenched groups from the upper income brackets who stand to lose significant benefits makes reform in this area the most controversial of all. Yet at the same time wages are the most important source of income among poor households, indicating that macroeconomic stability coupled with labor market reforms that allow the poor access to more and better-paying jobs will likely have the most impact on poverty and inequality in the long term. Actions such as improving job–worker matching processes, insuring workers against the risk of job churning, enhancing opportunities for workers through training and adult education, and improving and enforcing labor market regulations, may help to improve competitivity and attract jobs to the struggling Andean nations. However, the political economic difficulties associated with changes in labor market legislation are likely the greatest barriers to sustained poverty reduction in the region and require a social contract which does not seem likely in the near future.

A key stylized fact among the Andean countries is the relatively low level of social spending per capita or per GDP. This spending is heavily weighted towards wages and salaries, and towards social security and pensions which disproportionately favor urban and formal sector employees. In addition, social safety net expenditures are highly procyclical, meaning that they contract during economic downturns when they are needed the most. The low level and destination of spending is a key concern in the Andean countries. But simply raising spending is not the answer; the efficiency of this spending can be improved significantly through the fusion of programs with similar objectives and overlapping target groups, while the direct impact on poverty and inequality can be raised by addressing issues of leakage and undercoverage. A more complicated issue is the need to construct systems to ensure countercyclical expansion in the social safety net. A social stabilization fund was recently created in Colombia, for example, with rules to allow for savings during boom periods and dissaving to finance poverty alleviation programs during recessions. In general, the high level of fiscal inflexibility due to earmarked expenditures makes it very difficult for governments in the region to respond during recessions and crises in order to smooth consumption for the poor – this should be a key policy issue on the agenda in the next few years. Aside from more fiscal flexibility, well-managed and targeted programs should be created which can easily be expanded during periods of crises in order to provide a true safety net for the transitory poor.

Finally, the deep structural poverty among traditionally excluded groups continues to be a pressing area of concern in the region. While innovative and culturally appropriate approaches are clearly needed, even more important is the political commitment to address the historic inequities and underdevelopment. One of the key failings of past economic and social policy has been their inattention to excluded populations for reasons of gender, race and ethnicity, migration status or other features that marginalize groups. While pioneer policy initiatives can be traced back to the late 1980s to the early 1990s, for instance the 1991 Colombian Constitution which recognized ethnic and cultural diversity as a fundamental principle of the state, the use of the term in the social policy discourse and a flurry of government activity promoting social inclusion have taken place only in the last three to five years. Noted examples, among others, are Peru's 1997 law to outlaw racial discrimination and a few comprehensive development projects targeted specifically to address the constraints faced by excluded populations, for instance, Afro descendants on the Pacific coast of Colombia, among others.

NOTES

* The authors appreciate the valuable contribution of José Luis Montes in the preparation of this chapter. Ethel Muhlstein provided useful editorial assistance. Opinions expressed are those of the authors and do not reflect the opinions, policies or programs of the Inter American Development Bank.

1. Unless otherwise specified, when the chapter refers to the Latin America region, it is referring to the nations of Argentina, Bolivia, Brazil, Chile, Colombia, Costa Rica, Dominican Republic, Ecuador, El Salvador, Guatemala, Honduras, Mexico, Nicaragua, Panama, Paraguay, Peru, Uruguay and Venezuela.
2. Estimated from household surveys in the region by the IDB (SDS/POV), adjusted for underreporting and following a protocol described in Székely and Hilgert (2001) for treatment of missing values and zeros. The US$2 purchasing power parity (PPP) daily income cutoff is considered to be an adequate basis for poverty comparisons among the

countries of the region, given their relative development level. The base year is 1985. The region's poverty profile has been constructed using this poverty line. Note that both the US$1 and US$2 PPP per day thresholds are being used to track the Millennium Development Goals.

3. The Economic Commission on Latin America and the Caribbean has published data in the 2002 Panorama Social showing that 44 per cent of the region lived in poverty, using the same income cutoff definitions. However, this publication does not describe how these estimates were obtained, nor what procedures were used to adjust for underreporting and other errors.
4. Aggregate figures do not consider possible gender inequalities in the distribution of income or consumption within the household.
5. Of the Andean subregion, only Venezuela is not included.
6. Mexico (84–94) and Argentina (94–98) are other countries that fall into the rising poverty, rising inequality group.
7. Figure 3.5 reflects changes in the Gini and GDP per capita during the 1997–99 period. Each data point represents the per cent change in inequality contrasted with the per cent change in GDP per capita. The Andean countries included are Bolivia, Colombia, Ecuador, Peru and Venezuela.
8. According to these authors, the reported decline in volatility is not a result of the breakdown of the period of analysis into subperiods (decades) used here, and the same pattern arises with alternative period definitions, and even if annual rather than decade-based measures of volatility are used.
9. Prepared by Suzanne Duryea of the Inter American Development Bank (Research Department).
10. As these are contributory systems, many without a solidarity component, there may be an argument for excluding this type of expenditure from an overall analysis of public expenditure, as there is little scope for reallocation of this spending within the social sector.
11. In their reform index, they report that in the decade of the 1990s, Peru was the one of the best reformers, and Ecuador and Venezuela were in the group of worst reformers.

REFERENCES

Alesina, A. and D. Rodrik (1994), 'Distributive politics and economic growth 1994', *Quarterly Journal of Economics*, **108**, 465–90, Working Paper, Center for Global Development, Washington, DC.

Attanasio, O. and M. Székely (2001), *Portrait of the Poor: An Assets-Based Approach*, Washington, DC: Inter American Development Bank.

Behrman, J., N. Birdsall and M. Székely (2000), *Intergenerational Mobility in Latin America: Deeper Markets and Better Schools Make a Difference,* in Nancy Birdsall and Carol Graham (eds), *New Markets, New Opportunities? Economic and Social Mobility in a Changing World*, Washington, DC: Brookings Institution Press and the Carnegie Endowment for International Peace.

Birdsall, N. (2003), 'Global economic governance and representation of developing countries: some issues and the IDB example', *Working Paper*, **22**, Washington, DC: Center for Global Development, January.

Birdsall, N. and M. Székely (2003), 'Bootstraps not Band-Aids: poverty, equity and social policy in Latin America', *Working Paper*, **24**, Washington, DC: Center for Global Development, February.

Bouillon, C.P. and J. Montes (2001), 'Pobreza y desigualdad en el Perú durante la década de los noventa: lecciones aprendidas', *Technical Paper*, Washington, DC: Inter American Development Bank.

Comisión Económica para América Latina y el Caribe (CEPAL) (2000), *Panorama Social de América Latina 1999–2000*, Santiago de Chile: CEPAL.

CRECE (2001), *Análisis de la prociclicidad del gasto público social en Colombia*, Informe preparado para el BID.

De Ferranti, D., G.E. Perry, I.S. Gill and L. Servén with F.H.G. Ferreira, N. Ilahi, W.F. Maloney and M. Rama (2000), *Securing Our Future in a Global Economy*, Washington, DC: The World Bank.

De Janvry, A. and E. Sadoulet (2001), *Has Aggregate Income Growth Been Effective in Reducing Poverty and Inequality in Latin America?*, in Nora Lustig (ed.), *Shielding the Poor: Social Protection in the Developing World*, Washington, DC: Inter American Development Bank.

Duryea, S., O. Jaramillo and C. Pagés (2003), *Latin American Labor Markets in the 1990s: Deciphering the Decade*, Washington, DC: Inter American Development Bank, May.

Duryea, S. and C. Pagés (2003), *Human Capital Policies: What They Can and Cannot Do for Productivity and Poverty Reduction in Latin America*, in *Latin American Democracies in the New Global Economy*, Miami, USA: North South Press.

Duryea, S. and C. Pagés (2002), 'Achieving high labor productivity in Latin America: is education enough?', *Research Department Working Paper*, **468**, Washington, DC: Inter American Development Bank.

Escobal, J., J. Saavedra and M. Torero (2001), 'Distribution, access and complementarity: capital of the poor in Peru', in Orazio Attanasio and Miguel Székely (eds), *Portrait of the Poor: An Assets-Based Approach*, Washington, DC: Inter American Development Bank.

Fajnzylber, P. (1997), *What Causes Crime and Violence?*, Washington, DC: World Bank, Office of the Chief Economist, Latin America and the Caribbean.

Graham, C. (2001), 'Stemming the backlash against globalization', *Policy Brief*, **78**, Washington, DC: Brookings Institution, April.

Gray Molina, G., W. Jiménez, E. Pérez de Rada and E. Yáñez (2001), 'Poverty and assets in Bolivia: what role does social capital play?', in Orazio Attanasio and Miguel Székely (eds), *Portrait of the Poor: An Assets-Based Approach*, Washington, DC: Inter American Development Bank.

Inter American Development Bank (1999), *IPES 1998/1999: Facing Up to Inequality in Latin America*, Washington, DC: IDB, September.

Hall, R. and C. Jones (1999), 'Why do some countries produce so much more output per worker than others?', *The Quarterly Journal of Economics*, **CXIV**(1), 83–116, February.

Kaufmann, D., K. Aart and P. Zoido-Lobatón (1999), *Governance Matters*, Washington, DC: The World Bank, October.

Lora, E. and U. Panizza (2002), 'Structural reforms in Latin America under scrutiny', *Research Dept Working Paper*, **WP 470**, Washington, DC: Inter American Development Bank, March.

Lustig, N. (ed.) (2001), *Shielding the Poor: Social Protection in the Developing World*, Washington, DC: Inter American Development Bank.

McIlwaine, C. and C.O.N. Moser (2001), 'Violence and social capital in urban poor communities: perspectives from Colombia and Guatemala', *Journal of International Development*, **13**, 965–84.

Persson, T. and G. Tabellini (1994), 'Is inequality harmful for growth?', Working Paper, *American Economic Review*, **84**, 600–21, Washington, DC: Center for Global Development.
Saavedra, J. (2003), 'Labor markets during the 1990s', in Pedro-Pablo Kuczynski and John Williamson (eds), *After the Washington Consensus: Restarting Growth and Reform in Latin America*, Washington, DC: Institute for International Economics.
Saavedra, J., M. Torero and H. Ñopo (2002), 'Ethnicity and earnings in urban Peru', *GRADE Working Paper*, Lima: GRADE.
Solimano, A. (2003), 'Governance crisis and the Andean region: a political economy analysis', paper prepared for Conference on Political Crises and Development Alternatives in the Andes, New School University, 8–9 May.
Solimano, A. and R. Soto (2003), 'Latin American economic growth in the late 20th century: evidence and interpretation', paper prepared for the seminar 'Latin American Growth: Why So Slow?', 4–5 December.
Székely, M. and M. Hilgert (2001), 'The 1990s in Latin America: another decade of persistent inequality, but with less poverty', *Technical Paper*, Washington, DC: Inter American Development Bank Research Department.
United Nations Development Program (UNDP) (2001), *Human Development Report 2001*, New York: UNDP.
Vos, R., L. Taylor and R. Paes de Barros (2002), *Economic Liberalization, Distribution and Poverty: Latin America in the 1990s*, Cheltenham, UK and Northampton, MA: Edward Elgar and the United Nations Development Programme.
World Bank (2002), *Colombia Poverty Report*, Washington, DC: The World Bank, November.
World Bank and Inter American Development Bank (2002), *Peru: Restoring Fiscal Discipline for Poverty Reduction. A Public Expenditure Review*, Washington, DC: World Bank and Inter American Development Bank, 24 October.

Annex 3.1 Income distribution and poverty in Latin America and the Caribbean in the 1990s

Country	Per capita GDP growth ratee (1990–2000 yearly average)[a]	Gini[b] Circa 1990	Circa 2000	% change	Ho[b] Circa 1990	Circa 2000	% change	Gap[b] Circa 1990	Circa 2000	% change	FGT2[b] Circa 1990	Circa 2000	% chang
Argentina*	4.28	0.48	0.49	3.44	18.40	17.90	–2.72	4.55	4.47	–1.76	2.27	2.26	–0.44
Bolivia	4.02	0.54	0.60	10.37	65.63	61.36	–6.51	32.78	36.91	12.60	20.19	27.40	35.71
Brazil	1.82	0.57	0.58	2.08	48.26	41.26	–14.50	23.80	18.65	–21.64	15.03	11.11	–26.08
Chile	6.37	0.55	0.56	2.14	32.37	16.11	–50.23	11.96	5.31	–55.60	6.12	2.60	–57.52
Colombia	2.86	0.57	0.56	–0.88	42.39	39.37	–7.12	18.32	17.23	–5.95	10.73	10.14	–5.50
Costa Rica	5.36	0.46	0.46	0.30	34.23	30.47	–10.98	14.18	11.18	–21.16	8.07	5.88	–27.14
Dominican Republic*	4.62	0.48	0.48	–0.67	38.13	34.56	–9.36	15.05	11.64	–22.66	8.05	5.32	–33.91
Ecuador*	2.24	0.56	0.56	0.29	49.53	47.98	–3.13	25.47	23.69	–6.99	17.15	15.41	–10.15
El Salvador*	4.9	0.51	0.55	7.98	58.60	63.98	9.18	26.40	33.42	26.59	14.54	21.29	46.42
Honduras	2.76	0.57	0.58	2.45	77.20	75.25	–2.53	46.22	47.42	2.60	32.25	35.42	9.83
Mexico	3.37	0.53	0.54	1.28	19.74	21.17	7.24	6.67	7.99	19.79	3.28	4.15	26.52
Nicaragua	2.87	0.57	0.60	6.26	70.67	72.68	2.84	41.16	40.94	–0.53	28.88	28.14	–2.56
Panama	5.07	0.56	0.56	0.11	47.75	36.61	–23.33	24.97	17.18	–31.20	17.04	10.80	–36.62
Paraguay*	2.33	0.57	0.59	4.25	52.09	61.12	17.34	27.29	33.84	24.00	17.96	23.28	29.62
Peru	3.46	0.46	0.49	6.25	41.86	42.43	1.36	18.11	19.61	8.28	10.33	12.22	18.30
Uruguay	3.29	0.41	0.44	7.97	23.15	13.59	–41.30	6.46	3.95	–38.85	2.70	1.78	–34.07
Venezuela, RB	2.46	0.44	0.47	6.35	12.55	20.63	64.38	4.31	7.57	75.64	2.13	4.08	91.55
Average (unweighted)	3.65	0.52	0.54	3.42	43.09	40.97	–4.93	20.45	20.06	–1.93	12.75	13.02	2.10

*Circa 1995–2000.

Sources:
(a) International Monetary Fund, World Economic Outlook.
(b) Székely and Hilgert (2001).
Prepared by the Poverty and Inequality Unit, Inter American Development Bank, 2003.

PART II

Country studies

4. The political economy of the crisis in the Andean region: the case of Bolivia

George Gray Molina and Gonzalo Chávez

4.1 INTRODUCTION

The fragility of the economic and political achievements of the Andean region in recent years has revived an interest in using a political economy approach to explain the shifts in economic policy and in democratic strength. Bolivia initially appears to have had a successful experience of stabilization and structural adjustment (1985–89), and of political and institutional reform (1993–97). The implementation of reforms has, however, revealed the significant difficulties of the process and suggests the necessity of amending any analysis of the 'success' of these reforms with an analysis of the 'viability' of the conditions that facilitate or impede the implementation of any public policy of magnitude. In the last two years, social violence, road blocks, strikes, and the rise of antisystem movements suggests that the 'democratic transition' as much as the 'structural adjustment' of the last 80 years is still incomplete. Instead of extending the first and second generations of reform, there exists the perception in Bolivia that the country has only gone back to where it started from (see Graham and Pettinato 2001; Lora and Panizza 2002).[1]

In this chapter, we propose to (i) formulate an interpretive framework of the political economy to understand the success and the crisis behind the process of economic and political reform in the last two decades: (ii) analyse the determinants of governance, understood here as the political conditions that make the development of a representative democracy possible and the reform of public policy viable, and (iii) analyse the determinants of economic development, with a particular emphasis on determinants of economic stability, sustained growth, and the struggle against poverty. From a practical point of view, we ask why the reforms' 'success' did not become a 'success' in terms of growth rates, reduced poverty, and decreased inequality.

From an analytical point of view, the study approaches the paradoxical trajectory of the reforms: why didn't economic and political success coincide instead of diverging and thereby weakening the chances of further political and institutional reform?

The analysis of economic policy reform could be approached from two critical 'moments': the first being the foundation of the initial rules of the game (the political moment) and the second being the clarification of economic policies in those rules (the policy moment). The more stable the rules of the game are, the lower the transaction costs are of making public policy. The more unstable the rules of the game are, the higher the transaction costs are and, therefore, the larger is the disparity between economic and political cycles. When the rules of the game are not stable, discontent with a public policy reflects not only a disapproval of the policy itself, but also a disapproval of the rules, institutions, and actors that produced the policy. The rejection of one policy can produce a crisis of legitimacy and force the government to go through a costly process of political reaffirmation to strengthen legitimacy. In the Bolivian experience, the problems of political credibility continue to return in an iterative way, persistently eroding the political and bureaucratic system. Rather than reduce transaction costs of reforms, many political pacts that are constructed simply indefinitely postpone solving the problem.

An Interpretive Framework

How to approach the different time frames of the political and economic moments in Bolivian experience? We suggest an interpretive framework that complements the model of 'policy transaction costs', proposed by Avinash Dixit (Dixit 1996, 2000), to discover the effects of these distinct time frames and create a new understanding of Bolivia's case. In the literature of 'policy transaction costs' initiated by Douglas North (1990) and expanded upon by Avinash Dixit, economic policy is understood to be the result of a political process of negotiation. This process is also marked by multiple failures of information in the political market – negotiations occur with asymmetries of information in a market that, in the absence of credible external sanctions, depends upon self-enforcement of rules. The increase in the transaction costs of the negotiation process frequently determines the viability of an economic policy. One way of decreasing transaction costs is creating arbitrating institutions with high credibility (superintendent offices, offices that control public spending, public prosecutor offices, courts of justice), that enforce obedience to the law in an impartial way. Another way is to decrease transaction costs is to align interest groups to maintain checks and balances during the construction of arbitrating institutions.

The focus of 'policy transaction cost' requires an entrance into the 'black box' of the political process of negotiations to identify the sources of stability or instability in the construction of credibility (see Graham et al. 1999; Grindle 2000). In Bolivia, the three factors that characterize the social and historical conditions of negotiation policy also help explain some of the most important restrictions on the political process.

First, in Bolivian political negotiations there is a serious clash between formal and informal institutions. The formal rules discussed in Gamarra (1997), Gray Molina et al. (1999), emphasize the hybrid aspect of the formal system of the political coalitions that generate a political space in the legislature to make reforms viable with the president's support. The stability of the democratic system observed during the last four presidential elections has made a set of political and economic reforms viable in recent years. The informal rules discussed by Calderón and Smukler (2000), however, suggest that parallel to the 'coalition politics' are 'street politics' that burst into the careful order created by the political rules, and push multiple negotiations and concessions to pressuring groups, social movements, and regional organizations in the country. The nature of reducing transaction costs frequently favors partial negotiations that make reform viable but push vital issues of institutional credibility towards a distant future.

Second, it is clear that formal channels of negotiation currently work through highly fragmented political parties and a political clientele that provides a fragile base for political governance. In recent years, the weakening of the traditional parties of the Bolivian democracy – MNR, AND, MIR – has made the system of political pacts and agreements more unstable than they were when a credible political infrastructure existed. Local and partial leaderships have multiplied the possible scenarios in political negotiation, both inside and outside of the formal system of political mediation. The presidential elections of 2002 had 19 political parties registered and another 13 that had requests at the election registry. The political analysts predicted that not one party would get more than 25 per cent of the votes and that the total vote for the traditional parties would not exceed 50 per cent of the total votes. The political fragmentation evident here makes it more difficult to create stable coalitions that can govern.

Third, even informal mechanisms of political negotiation and mediation are also fragmented. After more than a decade from the disbanding of the Central Workers of Bolivia (COB), the social movements of April and September 2000 marked an inflection point in the relations between the state and popular organizations. A leadership of colleges – the Coordination of Water – propped up the War of Water and Cochabamba and the personal leadership – Felipe Quispe Huanca, the Mallku – led the confrontation between the farmers and soldiers on the Northern plateau. These two actors were incorporated in a sporadic way into the leadership of the movement of the coca growers in Chapare, but in recent months there has been a clear splintering apart of the 2000 social movements. The 'new fragmentation' of traditional social actors has been accompanied by the proliferation of actors that announce their displeasure with the formal political system and the market economy.

We will adapt the analytical framework described by Solimano (2001), with the approach that 'transaction costs' explain two aspects of the crisis in the Andean region: (i) a crisis of governance, defined in terms of decreasing support and satisfaction with democracy, worsening of the quality of political and bureaucratic institutions, the presence of high levels of corruption, and the presence of growing social violence; (ii) an economic crisis, defined by the indicators of growth, inflation, employment creation, and poverty reduction. For both issues, we have created hypotheses about the course of the crises and the more structural factors of the crisis in the Andean region. Among the determinants of governance that we analyse are the effect of the weak presence of the state, the effect of political fragmentation and volatility, ethnic fragmentation, and the increasing levels of inequality. Among the determinants of the economic crisis that we analyse are the effects of the context of macroeconomic policies, the macroeconomic environment, the productivity rate of the economy, the effects of geography, and the effects of distribution. Finally, we incorporate governance variables to explain the path of the political and economic crises from a political economy approach.

4.2 GOVERNANCE BLOCK

We will use the definition of 'governance' of Kaufmann, Kraay and Zoido-Lobatón (1999), 'as a set of traditions and institutions that determine how authority is wielded in the country'. Governance defined this way is made up of three interrelated processes: (i) the process of selection and substitution of governments; (ii) the capacity of the government to design and implement public policies in an efficient way, and (iii) respect on the part of the citizens for the institutions that govern their economic and social relations. The central hypothesis of the following analysis is that the success and failure of Bolivia's governance in the last decade turns on the effectiveness of the 'coalition politics' that create the political space to govern. Coalition politics encompass three important aspects: (i) the selection of the president, that depends on (ii) the design and implementation of public policy and (iii) the political mediation between formal and informal systems of political action, that reflects the processes identified by Kaufmann et al. in their analysis of governance.

The analysis is divided into three parts. In the first subsection, we will consider the four periods of governance that cover the period 1982–2002. In the second subsection, we will consider a few problems of Bolivian governance, including perceptions about democracy, the quality of political and bureaucratic institutions, indices of perceptions of corruption and measurement indices of strikes and social mobilizations. In the third subsection, we will analyse a few determinants of governance, including the weakness of the state apparatus, the fragmentation and the volatility of the system of political parties, ethnic fragmentation, and growing levels of poverty and inequality in the last decade.

Five Periods of Governance

Hyperinflation and crisis (1982–85)

The difficult democratic transition in Bolivia and the crisis that resulted in the resignation of the President Hernán Siles Suazo were as documented in economic literature (Sachs and Morales 1986) as they were in journals of political science (Whitehead 1986, Mally and Gamarra 1987). After the failed elections, the election of 1980 favored the Unidad Democrática y Popular (UDP), an alliance of leftist political parties that included the MNR-I, the MIR, and the PCB, and that won with 38.7 per cent of the popular vote. Siles Suazo immediately felt under pressure from the members of his coalition and from the Bolivian Workers Center (COB) that would eventually lead the calls for his resignation. From its beginning, the administration was characterized by a pattern of social conflict, packages of economic reform, and then more street protests. Siles Suazo presided over more than 80 ministers in three years and suffered the abandonment of one of the most important parties of his coalition in the midst of his attempts to manage the crisis (Gamarra 1997: p. 371).

Siles Suazo saw himself besieged by growing pressures from the COB, civic committees, the confederation of businesses, and other social and political organizations. An unsustainable monetary and fiscal situation resulted in an uncontrolled hyperinflation that reached 22 per cent annually in 1984–85. The ambivalent role of the International Monetary Fund and the risk of a new military coup added layers of instability that finally drove a negotiation between opposition parties, the COB, and what was left of the administration coalition. In 1985, Siles Suazo called an election and, in August of that year, the first transition between two civil governments of the democratic era occurred.

Stabilization and structural adjustment (1985–93)

But even the 1985 elections lacked the presence of a clear presidential mandate. Acción Nacionalista Democrática (AND) got 32.8 per cent of the vote, followed by the Movimiento Nacionalista Revolucionario (MNR) with 30.4 per cent of the vote. After the political negotiations in Congress, a new political pact, 'pact for democracy', was created between the MNR and the AND that set a precedent for later post-election agreements and alliances. The pact for democracy ushered in the presidency of Victor Paz Estenssoro, three-time president of Bolivia and 78 years old. The agreement generated enough political space for Paz Estenssoro to prepare an aggressive package to combat inflation, announced as Decree 21 060 of stabilization and structural adjustment.

The new economic policy (NPE) developed in Decree 21 060 included three central pillars: (i) control of the fiscal deficit and the freezing of prices and salaries; (ii) the liberalization of the economy, (iii) a progressive role for the private sector. In one year, the new economic policy had reduced inflation to less than 10 per cent, but began to struggle with the important external shock that resulted in the collapse of the price of tin. In 1986, with the restructuring of COMIBOL, the Company of Bolivian Miners that had sustained the Bolivian economy during the previous three decades, thousands of miners were left without work. As a response to the mining crisis, and in the face of growing unemployment in both rural and urban areas in the country, the Paz Estenssoro administration created an Emergency Social Fund (FSE) to provide employment and increase public investment during the crisis period. The FSE functioned successfully until 1989, when it was institutionalized as an investment and development fund.

The Paz Estenssoro administration represented an inflection point, as much for Bolivia's political path as for the economic policy of the country. It brought about both a system of democratic alternatives and a gradual economic reactivation. The high social cost of the economic adjustment became a central part of the presidential campaign of 1989, but the issue always stayed within the framework of democratic politics.

Administration of the adjustment (1989–93)

The presidential elections of 1989 resulted in a 'triple tie' between the MNR (25.6 per cent), the AND (25.2 per cent), and the MIR (21.8 per cent). The breakup of the pact for democracy and the intense confrontation between the MNR and the AND during the elections gave the votes to Jaime Paz Zamora, the third candidate for president of the republic in a second congressional round. A new agreement, 'the patriotic agreement', was forged between the AND and the MIR and created a new space for governance and for the administration of structural adjustment. With the MNR as the opposition, the patriotic agreement gave rise to an administration from the political coalition that did little in the realm of public policy. Towards the end of Paz Zamora's term, he pushed through the third population and housing census of the century and put social policy and the struggle against poverty at the top of his agenda.

Reform of the state (1993–97)

The presidential election of 1993 was dominated by the MNR and its presidential candidate, Gonzalo Sánchez de Lozada, an architect of the new economic policy of Victor Paz Estenssoro in 1985–89. Sánchez de Lozada won 34.6 per cent of the popular vote and created a new agreement, the 'Pact for Governance' with the neopopulist Unión Cívica Solidaridad (UCS) and the center-left Movimiento Bolivia Libre (MBL). During the campaign Sánchez de Lozada detailed a government program, the 'Plan for All', that would guide the actions of the new coalition. The Sánchez de Lozada administration is characterized by the beginning of a series of ambitious institutional and economic reforms, including the capitalization of public businesses (1993), pension reform (1996), the construction of the regulatory system (1996) for privatized businesses, the reforms of popular participation (1994), administrative decentralization (1995), education reform (1993), and reform of the land administration and possession system, INRA (1996).

Throughout his administration, Sánchez de Lozada portrayed himself as a technocrat and created broad areas of reforms, particularly of the office of president. The coalition that supported the administration stayed intact during Sánchez de Lozada's term in office and passed a range of laws, including the Reform of the Political Constitution of the State Law in 1994. The reforms begun in this period were not free of opposition. Protests against the privatization of businesses, pension reform, and the reform of the INRA law marked the beginning of the end of the ambiguity that had characterized public sentiment over the reform of the state. Towards the end of his term in office, Sánchez de Lozada had exhausted all of his political capital and found himself with approval ratings that hovered in the single digits. The 1997 elections were dominated by two ex-presidents: Hugo Banzer Suárez and Jaime Paz Zamora, who capitalized on the discontent to apply second generation reforms.

Stagnation and crisis (1997–2002)

Hugo Banzer Suárez won the election with 22.3 per cent of the popular vote. He constructed a new pact, known as 'Megacoalition', with the MIR, UCS, NFR, and CONDEPA, which gave him an absolute majority in Congress. The megacoalition exemplified many of the problems of political negotiation between multiple parties under conditions of political benefits and clientelism. Some 19 years after leaving the presidency de facto in 1978, Banzer Suárez had returned to the presidency as the constitutional president. The ascent of the new government coincided with the end of the Asian economic crisis and the beginning of the Brazilian devaluation that acted as a macroeconomic shock to undermine Bolivian prospects for growth. After growing more than 5 per cent in 1997 and 1998, beginning in 1999, the economy entered a profound recession that would continue to stagnate for three years.

Banzer's term was characterized by a clear agenda of coca leaf eradication and the construction of a strategy to reduce poverty under the HIPC initiative. He confronted two of the less serious social crises of the democratic period with the Water War in April of 2000 and the farmers' blockades in September of that same year. Between April of 2000 and April of 2001, 54 people would lose their lives in 12 confrontations between the police or military authorities and farmers or public organizers. In August of 2001, Hugo Banzer Suárez resigned for health reasons and Vice President Jorge Quiroga Ramirez assumed the presidency. The Quiroga administration was distinguished by an aggressive anticrisis plan and continuous negotiations about the future of natural gas exports that would become, as of 2001, the country's most important export.

Problems of Governance

Perceptions of democracy

The most reliable numbers available for people's perceptions of political and economic institutions come from the Latinobarómetro surveys that have been performed throughout the region since 1996. We will concentrate our analysis on the important indicators from the surveys: support for democracy and satisfaction with democracy. The first indicator tries to gauge the level of support for democracy as a government regime, comparing it with authoritarian regimes of the government. (The question in the survey asks: 'With which of the following responses do you most identify? (i) Democracy is better than any other system of government; (ii) in some circumstances, an authoritarian government is better than a democracy, or (iii) it doesn't matter to people like me whether we have a democratic government.') The second indicator tries to measure the level of satisfaction with the democratic performance on a progressive scale of agreement with the question: 'Are you… "very satisfied" or "satisfied" with the democracy of your country?'

Table 4.1 compares levels of democratic support between 1996, 1998, and 2000 and a few noticeable patterns emerge. First, Bolivia is the country with the second highest level of volatility in its democratic support, with a fall of 10 percentage points over the course of the previous five years. Second, there seems to have been a clear drop in support for democracy throughout this time. The major point of disillusionment is registered in 2001, months after the social mobilizations of September 2000 and in the midst of a cycle of recession. Third, at the regional level, the Andean countries show lower levels of support for democracy, compared to the average levels in Latin America. The exceptions are Peru and Venezuela, which have support levels as high as the rest of the countries in Latin America.

Table 4.1 *Support for democracy*

	1996		1998		2002		2003		2004	
	Dem%	Aut%	Dem%	Aut%	Dem%	Aut%	Dem%	Aut%	Dem%	Aut%
Bolivia	64	17	55	22	56	20	50	22	45	19
Ecuador	52	18	57	19	49	18	46	34	46	30
Peru	63	13	63	12	57	16	52	20	45	20
Colombia	60	20	55	17	39	11	46	14	46	12
Venezuela	62	19	60	25	75	12	67	15	74	11

Source: Latinobarómetro 1996–2004

Table 4.2 compares indicators of satisfaction with democracy in 1996, 1998, and 2001. There are two interesting aspects: first, Bolivia is one of the countries with the lowest level of satisfaction in the Latin American region, and has an average level of satisfaction in comparison with the other Andean countries. Second, the level of satisfaction drops significantly (18 percentage points) between 1998 and 2001. As well as a relatively weak level of support for the democratic regime, Bolivia demonstrates dissatisfaction with the economic and social returns of democracy. Bolivia is going through a period of serious questioning of both the democratic model and the economic model that took root in 1985.

Table 4.2 *Satisfaction with democracy*

	1996 %	1998 %	2001 %	2002 %	2003 %	2004 %
Bolivia	25	34	16	24	25	16
Ecuador	34	33	15	19	23	14
Peru	28	17	16	17	11	7
Colombia	16	24	7	12	22	30
Venezuela	30	35	41	40	38	42

Question: 'Are you … "very satisfied" or "satisfied" with the democracy in your country?'

Source: Latinobarómetro 1996–2004

Quality of political and bureaucratic institutions

The most consistent indicators of government quality come from the database of information compiled by Kaufmann, Kraay and Zoido-Lobatón (1999 and 2002). Kaufmann et al. analyse six types of indicators of government quality on the basis of public opinion surveys and surveys of experts: (i) voice and accountability; (ii) political stability and the absence of social violence; (iii) government effectiveness; (iv) regulatory quality; (v) the domination of the state or the rule of law, and (vi) control of corruption. Kaufmann et. al.'s indicators constitute a primary source of comparable indicators between countries and times.

Table 4.3 shows indicators of government quality in Bolivia 2000–01. The column of 'percentile rank' shows where Bolivia falls at the international level. The column 'average regional percentage' shows Bolivia's place in relation to the other Latin American countries. Three important characteristics emerge from these columns. First, at an international level, Bolivia is distinguished by two types of indicators, voice and accountability and regulatory quality, where it ranks among the top third of the countries surveyed. Second, at a regional level, Bolivia is at the average level in terms of government quality. Figure 4.1 compares the indicators of quality between 1997–98 and 2000–01. There was a clear fall in all of the indicators of government quality, particularly political stability and control of corruption, during the period 1997–2001.

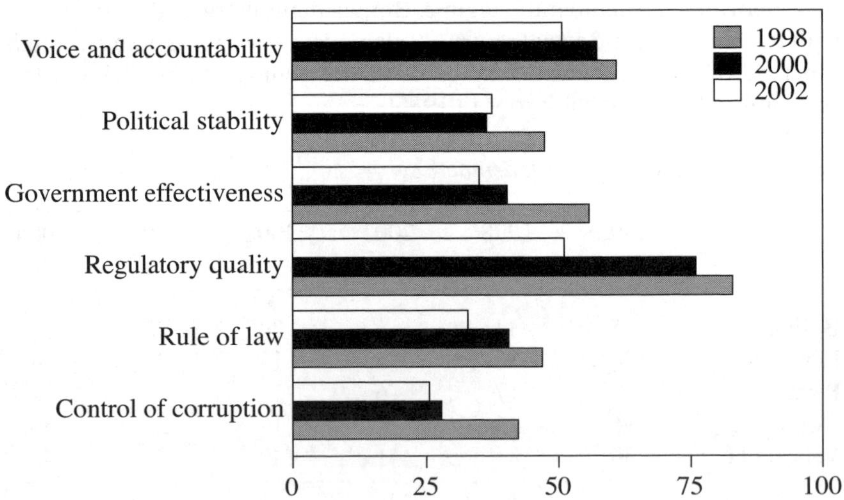

Source: Kaufmann et al. (2002)

Figure 4.1 Quality of institutions

Table 4.3 Quality of institutions in Bolivia

Indicator	Year	Percentile rank (0–100) in %	Estimation (–2.5 to +2.5)	Standard deviation	Number of surveys	Average regional percentage
Voice and accountability	2000	56.5	0.23	0.22	6	60.4
	2002	50	0.01	0.18	9	61.2
Political stability	2000	35.8	–0.42	0.27	7	51.2
	2002	36.8	–0.2	0.22	7	51.2
Government effectiveness	2000	39.7	–0.35	0.22	7	50.4
	2002	34.5	–0.53	0.17	7	53.3
Regulatory quality	2000	75.1	0.65	0.29	6	59.4
	2002	50.5	–0.11	0.18	7	58.4
Rule of law	2000	40	–0.51	0.16	11	51.4
	2002	32.5	–0.6	0.14	10	53.2
Control of corruption	2000	27.7	–0.68	0.17	9	51.3
	2002	25.3	–0.82	0.16	8	54.9

Source: Governance Research Indicators, World Bank.

Perception of corruption

To measure the perception of corruption, we will use the data collected by Transparency International between 1996 and 2001. Transparency structures its indices on the basis of weighted indices of public opinion surveys and surveys of experts. In the case of Bolivia, the source of information has changed over the course of recent years, but today the indices are based on the 1999 and 2000 *World Competitiveness Reports*, the services of the Economist Intelligence Unit, and the University of Syracuse's Political Risk Service. In general terms, Bolivia is among the countries with the strongest perceptions of corruption in the country. It is consistently found in the bottom fifth of the countries surveyed. Table 4.4 shows the evolution of perceptions of corruption from 1996 to 2001 in the Andean countries.

There are two interesting patterns in the comparison of the region's numbers. First, throughout the time measured, Bolivia continues to be one of the countries with greatest perceptions of corruption in the Andean region. The only comparable case in this period is Ecuador, which showed a sustained fall from the levels registered in 1996. Second, there is a slight oscillating tendency in the perceptions of corruption: in the best year (1996) Bolivia reached 3.4 points, whereas in the worst year (2001), it scored a 2.0. Despite the data collected by Transparency, Bolivian public opinion seems to have grown less tolerant of corruption in recent years. The convergence of the political crisis and distrust in traditional political actors in 2002 made the issue of corruption a pivotal one in the year's presidential elections.

Strikes, slowdowns, and social violence

In looking at this variable, we will use some comparative data on strikes and slowdowns collected by the Ministry of Labor for the period of 1982–2000. The data registers episodes of strikes or slowdowns on the basis of information from newspapers with greater national circulation and is therefore susceptible to a publicity slant, especially in relation to the strikes and slowdowns that occurred in capital cities. Nevertheless, the data is a proxy for social discontent with the policies of the state or with the political actors of different time periods. Figure 4.2 organizes the episodes of strikes and slowdowns according to the administration in which they occurred. There are two important tendencies in the registered information. First, the episodes with the most social protest occurred during the government of Hernán Siles Suazo (1982–85) and that of Hugo Banzer Suárez (1997–2001). There were 959 registered episodes in the former period, compared to 822 in the latter. Second, the administrations of Paz Zamora (1989–93) and Sánchez de Lozada (1993–97) showed only moderate levels of protest, despite the fact that both governments instituted states of emergency that suspended civil liberties.

Table 4.4 Corruption perception index

Country	1996 (54 countries)	1997 (52 countries)	1998 (85 countries)	1999 (99 countries)	2000 (90 countries)	2001 (91 countries)	2002 (102 countries)	2003 (133 countries)
Bolivia								
Index	3.40	2.05	2.8	2.5	2.7	2.0	2.2	2.3
Ranking	36	51	69	81	71	85	89	106
Ecuador								
Index	3.19	(s.d.)	2.3	2.4	2.6	2.3	2.2	2.2
Ranking	39	(s.d.)	77	82	74	79	91	114
Peru								
Index	(s.d.)	(s.d.)	4.5	4.5	4.4	4.1	4.0	3.7
Ranking	(s.d.)	(s.d.)	41	40	41	44	48	62
Colombia								
Index	2.73	2.23	2.2	2.9	3.2	3.8	3.6	3.7
Ranking	42	50	79	72	60	50	57	59
Venezuela								
Index	2.50	2.77	2.3	2.6	2.7	2.8	2.5	2.4
Ranking	46	44	78	78	73	69	84	104

Source: Transparency International, 1996–2003.

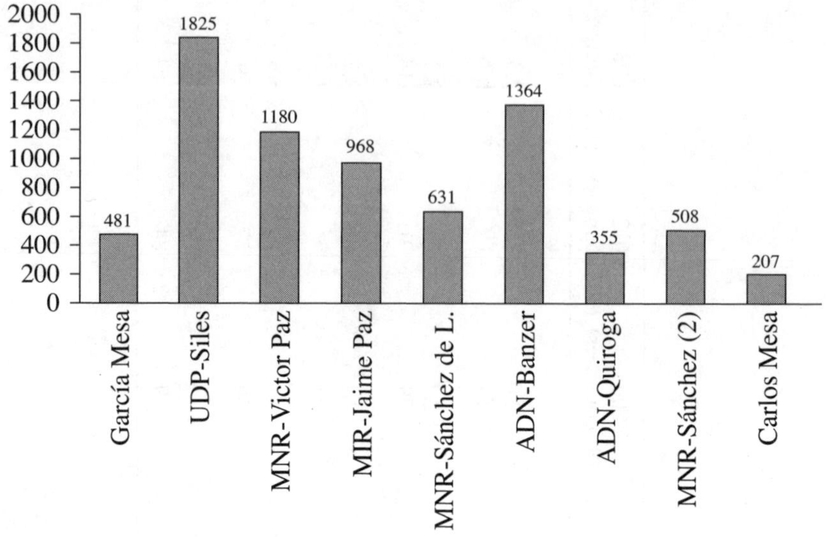

Source: CERES (2004).

Figure 4.2 Slowdowns and strikes 1982–2000

The high degree of social polarization registered during the administration of Hugo Banzer Suárez is due as much to transitional factors as to structural ones: Within the structural factors there emerges a change in the pattern of social and political intermediation. The progressive fragmentation of corporate negotiations between workers' unions (COB), farmers' unions (CSUTCB) and the government in the 1980s and the 1990s undermined any capacity to govern during times of crisis. There was a simultaneous rise of multiple sources of social discontent (about conflicts over water, land, transportation, urban and rural teaching, regional power, and problems related to universities). The second structural factor is the wearing away of the legitimacy of the institutions and democratic actors – such as traditional parties – that, after 15 years of political rotation, existed with a growing loss of credibility. Within the transitional factors, a combination of adverse macroeconomic shocks (natural disasters, reduced coca-cocaine, the struggle against illegal products) stand out, as does the general incapacity of the government to anticipate, prevent or resolve foreseeable social conflicts.

Determinants of Governance

We will analyse four of the key determinants of the political crisis and recovery: (i) the structural weakness of the Bolivian state, reflected in its sporadic bureaucratic/territorial presence and weak authority in the exercise of rule of law: (ii) the growing political fragmentation observed over the previous decade, that accentuated the fragile nature of the political coalitions in the country; (iii) the growing ethnic divisions, exemplified in the rise of nationalist/ethnic voices within social movements, and (iv) an ever growing increase in the absolute number of poor people and homes, as well as an increase in levels of inequality as registered in the surveys of homes.

In their indication of the profound weakness in the Bolivian democracy in recent years, these determinants are fundamentally reflecting a crisis of governance. The weakness of the principle mechanism of political and social governance has immediate consequences on public opinion about the executive's capacity to design and implement social and economic reform. Many of the determinants of governance analysed in this subsection show that in the medium and long runs there are serious restrictions on the government's ability to create areas of governance in Bolivia. As ethnic divisions and social and economic inequality increase, so, too, does the propensity towards political fragmentation in the party system. This propensity itself causes difficulties in the construction of governable coalitions both inside and outside the formal political system.

State weakness

Guillermo O'Donnell (1993 and 1996) notes three types of weaknesses in the configuration of Latin American states undergoing democratic transitions, including Bolivia. The first type of weakness comes from the irregular bureaucratic extension of the state in certain geographic areas of the country – rural and *periurbana* areas – and for certain groups of the population – indigenous and poor people. This means that the bureaucratic and legal workings of the state are based neither in institutions nor in the political culture of the society. Second, the irregular extension of the state is made up of a particular set of institutions – clientilism, nepotism, local boss-rule (*caciquismo*) – that produce a dynamic hybrid of political intermediation between 'formal' and 'informal' actors in civil and political society. Third, the irregular extension has the later effect of weakening the construction of a shared political culture – the ideological dimension and the national cohesion of the state.

This weak legal bureaucracy and political culture manifests itself in some of the perverse patterns of political development that were explained in the first part of the governance analysis. The continuous pendulum of political negotiations between formal and informal actors – coalition politics and street politics – generates high transaction costs for the design and implementation of public policy reform. The additional effort of sustaining viable coalitions inside of a formal system – made more difficult by the high level of political fragmentation – or even of sustaining viable coalitions inside of an informal system of intermediation – made more difficult by the strong social and ethnic divisions – describes a centripetal dynamic that creates incentives to continuously negotiate rather than work to forge a lasting consensus. The structural weakness of the Bolivian state, therefore, plays a critical role in transitional policies, particularly during crisis periods.

Political fragmentation

The Latin American literature on the politics of representation underlines the presence of unstructured (inchoate), fragmented, and volatile systems that hinder the construction of stable systems of government (see Mainwaring and Shugart 1997). The quintessential example of the paradigm of unstructured, fragmented, and volatile systems is Bolivia that in the last 20 years has shown growing levels of multipartisanship and political disintegration. In the last five elections, for example, more than 20 different political parties participated, and yet the maximum level of popular support was never more than 35 per cent. Figure 4.3 has the

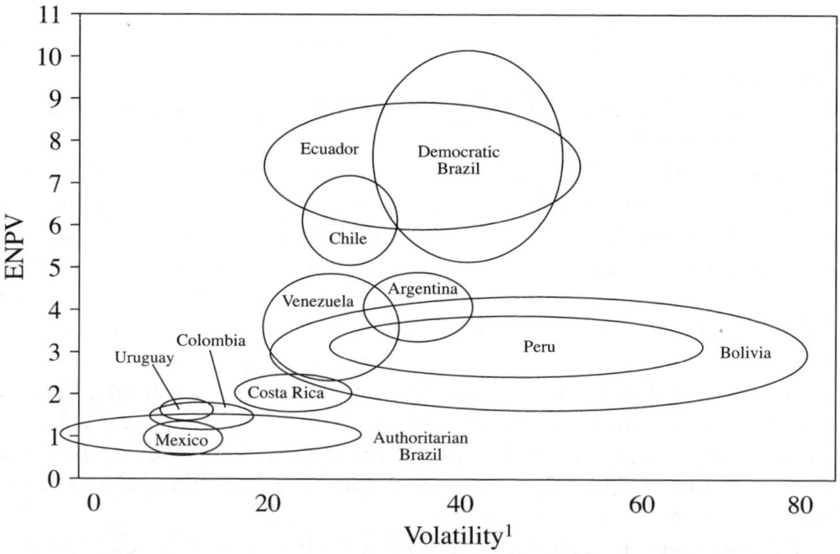

Note: (ENPV is the Laakso-Taagepera Index of the Effective Number of Parties, based on votes).

Source: Coppedge (1998).

Figure 4.3 Political fragmentation: Bolivia and Latin America, 1979–97, the dynamic diversity of Latin American party systems, 95% confidence intervals

effective number of parties on the vertical axis and the volatility of the popular vote of these parties during the previous 19 years (1979–97) on the horizontal axis. Bolivia's pattern forms an ellipse with a wide base at an average level of multipartisanship for the region. It also shows high levels of fragmentation and political volatility in recent years

In the 2002 elections, 19 political parties were registered and 13 more were trying to be recognized by the National Election Court. Although public opinion has baptized many of these new political movements 'antisystem', the information suggests a systemic process of political fragmentation within the system. One of the central ingredients that contribute to the disintegration of the system is the existence of hereditary or personal parties with a particular platform (Gamarra 1997). In a system that does not act according to ideological directives, hereditary parties function within coalition politics through a strict discipline that is maintained by the party leader/party boss. In the previous five elections, only one of the traditional parties had experienced a change in leadership (the MNR). Two others experienced the death of their founding leader (the UCS and the CONDEPA) that caused the gradual splintering of both parties.

Ethnic fragmentation

One important cause of the political fragmentation in Bolivia lies in the social and ethnic divisions of civil society. Bolivia is, in this respect, one of the countries with the most ethnic fragmentation of the region. Table 4.5 shows the proportion of the population that speaks a native language, according to the 1992 National Census of Population and Housing. Of the total population of Bolivia, 60 per cent speak Quechua, Aymara or Guaraní, among other indigenous languages. An interesting statistic from the housing survey MECOVI suggests that the proportion of individuals that see themselves as indigenous has grown in recent years and is higher today than the proportion that speak a native language in their home. According to the 1999 survey, 32 per cent of the population speak a native language in their home, but 57 per cent see themselves as belonging to an indigenous group.

An important consequence of the growing significance of ethnic fragmentation is the politicization of ethnicity within social movements in recent years. 'Aymara nationalism', that was led by the executive secretary of the Union Confederation of Bolivian Farm Workers (CSUTCB), emerged from the crises in April and September of 2000 that ended in long roadblocks, violent confrontations between farmers and the army, and the restoration of a state of emergency. Aymara nationalism distinguishes itself from other indigenous movements that reclaim their ethnic rights, in that it maintains an ambivalent position of inclusion/exclusion of the political system and the Bolivian state. The 2002 presidential elections were anticipated to both incorporate one or more candidates from an indigenous party and also reap the condemnation of the traditional political parties from movements and unions of farmers and indigenous people outside of the formal system.

Table 4.5 Ethnic fragmentation

Most–spoken language (> 6 years old)	1992	%	2001	%
Spanish	4 594 110	58.3	6 097 122	60.8
Aymara	1 237 658	15.7	1 462 286	14.6
Quechua	1 805 843	22.9	2 124 040	21.2
Guaraní	49 618	0.6	57 218	0.6
Other native languages	29 582	0.4	43 953	0.4
Foreign language	161 056	2.0	241 417	2.4

Source: National Institute of Statistics, National Census of Population and Housing, 1992–2001.

Poverty and inequality

A determining factor in the actual disenchantment with political and economic institutions is the increase in the concentration of assets and income. Gray Molina's recent study (2001) estimates an increase in the absolute number of impoverished people – 30 000 people between 1990 and 2000 – despite both the 4 per cent growth throughout the decade and a decline of about approximately 7 percentage points in the relative incidence of poverty. The factors that contribute to the paradoxical result are as much about the increase in the concentration of income as they are about the high rate of population growth, especially in poor homes. Between 1990 and 1999, the rate of income concentration, measured by the gini coefficient, increased from 0.42 in 1990 to 0.51 in 1999 (World Bank 2002). In the last three years at the time of writing, it is estimated that there will be a temporary increase in the incidence of poverty as an effect of the economic recession that affects the particular way the informal urban and agrarian sectors, that make up the majority of the people in poverty in Bolivia.

The 2000–01 recession also provided evidence of the fragile nature of the productive business base. The actual structure of the productive base accentuates this fragility and creates some problems in the medium and long-term for the poverty reduction agenda. The majority of GDP is produced by large businesses and the majority of employment is created by micro-businesses. Small and medium-sized companies are almost non-existent.

While micro and big businesses contribute together more than 90 per cent of GDP, small and medium-sized businesses – the center of enterprise distribution – only contribute a little more than 6 per cent of GDP. The microbusinesses contribute 25 per cent of GDP but provide employment to more than 83 per cent of the economically active population (PEA). From the opposite point of view, big business contributes 65 per cent of GDP, but employs only 9 per cent of the PEA. In the pyramid, the unequal distribution of economic resources becomes patently obvious.

Table 4.6 shows the distribution of moderate and extreme poverty, arranged by urban and rural areas and by primary language spoken. Three characteristics are particularly notable. First, there is a significant

Table 4.6 Poverty according to ethnicity and urban/rural geography

Area/ethnicity	Poverty indices	Extreme poverty indices
Urban area		
Quechua	55.87	28.04
Aymara	61.45	36.08
Spanish	48.86	21.08
Guaraní and other native language	92.90	69.05
Foreigner	11.44	3.02
None of the above	64.90	31.05
Urban population	51.50	23.63
Rural area		
Quechua	87.50	68.67
Aymara	89.08	70.43
Spanish	65.84	35.20
Guaraní and other native language	78.85	49.12
Foreigner	50.00	0.00
None of the above	86.62	65.23
Rural population	81.58	59.06
Total		
Quechua	80.19	59.28
Aymara	78.29	57.02
Spanish	51.80	23.53
Guaraní and other native language	83.84	56.19
Foreigner	13.32	2.87
None of the above	74.67	46.43
Population	62.64	36.76

Source: National Institute of Statistics, MECOVI 1999

gap between incidences of rural and urban poverty. Although today there are more people living in urban poverty in absolute numbers, there is still a gap of more than 30 percentage points in the incidence of poverty between rural and urban areas. Second, the significant gap between people who speak native languages and those that speak Spanish is as prevalent in urban areas as it is in rural areas. Between 78 per cent and 80 per cent of the population that speaks Aymara and Quechua live in poverty, compared to 51 per cent of the people that speak Spanish. Third, it is clear that the gap between language and geographic location is most severe for indigenous people living in rural areas.

4.3 ECONOMIC BLOCK

The five periods of government from 1982, when the democratic period began, had three basic economic policy objectives: Between 1982 and 1993, controlling inflation dominated the public policy scene. Three governments were determined to implement and consolidate monetary-financial stability (Siles Suazo, Paz Estenssoro, and Paz Zamora). After 1993, the recovery and sustainability of economic growth became an axis of economic policy, although near the end of the 1990s the struggle against poverty also became an important point on the agenda. Sánchez de Lozada, Banzer and Quiroga all tried to push through these policies. It is important to clarify at this point that this does not mean that other issues were not relevant during the indicated periods, but the aforementioned objectives were without question the goals that dominated the public agenda.

The Hyperinflation Crisis

Throughout almost all of the 1980s, the Bolivian economy went through intense fiscal and monetary imbalances whose more evident manifestations were the process of hyperinflation, the drastic reduction in growth, and the powerful deterioration in the terms of trade. At the beginning of the 1980s, it was possible to identify the first symptoms of exhaustion of the economic growth model, as could be seen in the gradual contraction of the global supply of goods and services and the imbalance of the principle macroprices. The type of exchange rate had stayed fixed and overvalued and the public tariffs and prices were artificially low. Wages had been systematically controlled by the military regime of General Banzer. During almost the entire decade of the 1970s, the union movement had been unable to recover the loss in wages. The struggle to distribute income and wealth had been systematically repressed.

At the beginning of 1982, the Bolivian peso devalued by 43 per cent and a double exchange rate was introduced. In a context of high levels of political uncertainty, the actions of economic agents diminished, generating defensive and speculative attitudes in the establishment of prices and returns, and this process rapidly produced an inflationary mentality in the Bolivian economy that drove the economic community to informally adopt diverse mechanisms of indexing to protect real income. The inflation initially passed the index of the price of gasoline and finally even the exchange rate of the parallel market.

When Siles Suazo assumed the presidency in October of 1982, he found himself faced with an economy in a process of accelerated inflation and serious fiscal imbalances, in a context of exhaustion of the economic growth model.[2] The principle challenges of the political economy of the incoming government were price stabilization and the maintenance of the democracy, but in the meantime the six programs that had been implemented to further these goals were ineffective and actually accelerated inflation. During the Siles Suazo administration, the salary-price run concentrated around decreasing public sector resources; the non-cooperative game of restructuring salaries and establishment of speculation with wider margins of profit was validated by an accommodating monetary policy and a wage policy that attempted to improve the wages of workers. Both types of policy contributed to a rapid informal indexing of the Bolivian economy. Siles Suazo's own political structure prevented him from doing anything but moderating the distribution conflict by expanding the monetary base; the alternative was to permit a greater contraction of GDP.

The stabilization packages were basically made up of relatively slight price adjustments, including the exchange rate, the prices of fuel, public tariffs, and wage compensations, and were accompanied by a freezing of partial or general prices. The strategies that were adopted had internal contradictions that made them fail, because they repressed an inflation (trying to freeze it) that they were themselves accelerating through the relative price shocks mentioned above and through the creation of higher expectations of inflation. The relative prices shocks and the intense distribution struggle, amplified both by growing mechanisms of indexing and a strong monetary expansion drove the Bolivian economy into hyperinflation.

The New Political Economy (NPE)

The stabilization program implemented by the Victor Paz Estenssoro administration, also known as the NPE, was based on three fundamentals: an anti-inflationary shock, internal and external economic liberalization, and the restructuring and downsizing of the public sector. The most important anti-inflationary measure was the stabilization of the exchange rate, which was the principle index (*indexador*) of the informal inflationary process, supported by intense fiscal policies and contractive monetary policies.

The stabilization program consistently combined contractive fiscal and monetary policy, accompanied by a strong devaluation and, later, by a stabilization of the exchange rate. It also simultaneously promoted the liberalization of internal and external markets. The program strongly reflected the regime's message of a change in economic policy and relied on the administration's credibility.

Among the most important fiscal measures was a strict control of public spending. Wages in the public sector were frozen and a process of dismissals was initiated in a majority of the state firms. The most extreme action taken was the closing of the Mining Corporation of Bolivia (COMIBOL), an administrator of various state mines, which implied the dismissal of nearly 21 000 mineworkers. In terms of spending, the government eliminated the Central Bank's internal credit and imposed a rigid control of the bank's operations by the General Treasury of the Nation.

To recover some revenue, the government introduced significant changes in the prices and tariffs of public sector goods and services. The most notable increase was in the price of gasoline, which was readjusted nearly 800 per cent. A new system was also created to transfer the YPFB to the TGN (Tesoro General de la Nación – Treasury), equivalent to 65 per cent of its revenues from foreign sales.

The fiscal shock policy was successful because it reduced the public deficit in relation to GDP to single digit levels (2.7 per cent), after previous years when it had been around 20 per cent. The stabilization plan allowed monetary policy to recover its independence from fiscal management. The liberalization of the interest rate and the acceptance that the government could make contracts and operations in foreign currencies were key in the stabilization of the exchange rate.

Nevertheless, it is clear that the stability achieved was the result not only of the stabilization program, but also, and more importantly, of the dynamic itself of the hyperinflationary process which, on provoking the dollarization of the economy, gave rise to a stable new relative price structure in a foreign currency. As high inflation became hyperinflation, the prices of goods and services stabilized, creating the illusion of an abrupt end to Bolivia's inflation. The efficiency of the orthodox shock also had other benefits in the inflationary process (Chávez 1989).

Structural Reforms and Stabilization

Along with the stabilization measures, the Paz Estenssoro administration also initiated a series of structural reforms destined primarily to contribute to the control of inflation and to create better market conditions. The most important of these reforms include tributary reform, commercial and financial liberalization, and changes in the structure of the state.

First generation reforms

Tax reform The hyperinflationary process that passed through the Bolivian economy in the middle of the period was the result of an intense distributive struggle that degenerated into a fiscal crisis. Excessive spending based on the emission of currency without the support of real resources, the drastic reduction of revenue due to the collapse of the tax system, and the negative effect of inflation on tax collection,[3] all contributed to the collapse of the Bolivian public sector.

One of the pillars of the stabilization program in August of 1985 was the fiscal adjustment that was based on the drastic rationalization of public spending and the rapid increase in revenue. In 1986, to consolidate stability and to balance the public accounts, the National Congress passed Law 843 of Tax Reform. The law created a tax structure of eight primarily indirect taxes on consumption and some on the wealth of businesses and people.[4] The tax reform also established a system of coparticipation in tax collection that established that 75 per cent of the revenue would go to the Central Government, that 20 per cent would go to municipalities, and that 15 per cent would go to public universities. Until the end of the 1980s, the reform did not have a significant effect. Government revenue continued to depend on the sale of goods and services of state-owned businesses, especially in the oil sector. The spending framework remained relatively stable, thanks to better access to external financing. In the 1990s, tax reform began to finally bear fruit. Tax revenue increased from 7.2 per cent of GDP in 1990 to 14.5 per cent of GDP in 1998.

On the spending side, the government implemented administrative changes that helped improve the execution of public investment, for which they created a budget system organized by programs. The results of these institutional reforms were not encouraging at the time of writing.

Commercial liberalization The NPE eliminated the dispersion of tariffs that varied between 0 per cent and 150 per cent, and established single uniform tariff of 20 per cent, to be applied to all imports. They also abolished all the institutional and administrative distortions that hindered foreign consumption.

There were no clear guidelines on the issue of exports and, in the beginning, the NPE opted for policies that would guarantee a certain tax neutrality. The diverse mechanisms of compensation that were applied[5] were harmed by the lack of liquidity of the TGN and by administrative difficulties. In 1987, the government also established price and tariff subsidies for hydrocarbons, railroad transportation, electric energy, and air transportation with which it hoped to increase productivity of the export sectors. These instruments were eliminated as they began to put the fiscal balance at risk. Another reform that sought to promote exports began with the creation of an institution of export support, first in the form of the National Institute of Exports (INPEX) and then later with the Center of Bolivian Promotion (CEPROBOL).

Financial liberalization This began in 1985 with the NPE and, in its first stage, tried to eliminate the repression of the financial sector and promote better financial intermediation. To achieve these objectives, the government freed interest rates, opened the capital account of the balance of payments, authorized the opening of the accounts to foreign currencies, and, last but not least, reduced the use of internal credit for the financing of the public sector. As part of the financial reform, the public commercial bank was closed.[6]

The financial system also went through profound legal and institutional transformations that were aimed at developing and strengthening the supervision and financial regulation and included the creation of the Bank Superintendent and then later the independence of the Central Bank. The achievements of the stabilization programs were as important as the first generation structural reforms. Inflation was controlled, the public deficit was reduced, and the economy started to slowly recover, as is observed in Table 4.7.

Table 4.7 Macroeconomic indicators 1985–90

Indicator	1985	1986	1987	1988	1989	1990
Inflation rate (%)	8170.5	66.0	10.7	21.5	16.6	18.8
GDP growth (%)	–1.7	–2.6	2.5	2.9	3.8	4.6
Public balance	–9.8	–2.7	–7.7	–6.3	–5.5	–4.4
Net international reserves (millions $)	136.2	246.6	168.4	160.9	18.6	132.3
Lending rates $ (%)	21.6	22.6	29.6	25.7	24.3	23.0
Saving rates US$ (%)	10.8	14	17.8	16.7	15.7	14.7
Debt (% PIB)	106.1	96.0	99.3	88.5	73.9	77.5
Terms of trade	174.4	149.0	132.0	123.7	116.7	100.0

Source: UDAPE and National Institute of Statistics.

The Search for Growth

Second generation reforms

In the 1990s, the government tried to consolidate macroeconomic stability and give a new push towards economic growth through reforms that tried to reshape the role of the state, restructure and open the public services markets, and create the legal and institutional conditions to attract private investment. Among the most important measures of the second generation reforms are capitalization, pension reform, education reform, popular participation, administrative decentralization.

Among the most important reforms to create better conditions for investment and the promotion of development are: the Law of Investment, passed in September of 1990, that granted a series of guarantees to foreign investment and strengthened definitions in reference to a free market, the convertibility of currency, and the free circulation of merchandise, services, and capital.

Capitalization and pension reform One of the objectives of the second generation structural reforms was to substantially increase the growth rate of the country, based on private investment and efficient state actions. To reach this goal after having consolidated monetary-financial stability, the administration implemented changes in the diverse markets of public services, created a new regulatory framework, and capitalization of the principle public businesses in electricity, telecommunications, transportation, railway, and hydrocarbon sectors.

Capitalization emerged as an alternative to privatization. The objective of capitalization was to maximize the efficiency and production of public businesses. The strategy of capitalization allowed the transfer of 50 per cent of the ownership of the state businesses to strategic partners (private investors), in exchange for which the partners were committed to injecting fresh capital into the business. The strategic partners also got control over 100 per cent of the administration of the newly capitalized businesses. The rest of the 50 per cent of the ownership was distributed among Bolivian citizens older than 21 years in December of 1995. The Bolivian citizens' assets were managed by pension funds through a trust account.

The capitalization process of the major state-owned businesses,[7] which also included a restructuring of the industries and the deregulation of prices,[8] was one of the most controversial reforms. Among the issues that are still debated from the reforms are its fiscal impact (especially in the capitalization of the YPFB), the challenges of the new corporate heads of the businesses, alternative uses of the financial revenue going to Bolivian citizens, and the destiny of the pension system.

Before its reform in 1997, the pension system in Bolivia was based on a simple distribution system (the PAYGO system). The system broke down as a consequence of the contraction of the public production apparatus. In 1993, the *cotizante* relation for retired people went from three to one. The system was also badly administered and tolerated rampant corruption. The pension reform sought to resolve the financial crisis and the deficit of the pay-as-you-go system; it also tried both to increase the coverage of a pension system that only included 10 per cent of the economically active population and to stimulate internal savings. With part of the assets that belonged to Bolivian citizens from the capitalized businesses, the government created individual pension accounts for citizens and established resources to pay the BONSOL (see below).

The reform had an important fiscal impact. The government took charge of the pension payments to retired people and compensations for the eventual retirement of still-active workers who had contributed in the past. Part of the financing of this reforms was achieved with an increase in public debt.

BONSOL, BOLIVIDA, and popular actions The capitalizations were connected with the pension reform that transferred the non-contributive fund with the assets of Bolivians from the capitalizations (collective capitalization fund) and another fund constructed by contributions to long-term social security (individual capitalization fund) to private administration.

With the profits from the collective capitalization fund, the government created the Solidarity Bond (BONSOL), an annual transfer of money to be distributed to all Bolivians that had reached 21 years of age by 31 December 1995, beginning when they turn 65 and continuing for the rest of their life. The Paz Zamora administration changed the benefit mechanism by making the recipient's age younger (50 years old) and naming it BOLIVIDA. Popular Action (the name of the property from the capitalized companies) was distributed to all of the remaining beneficiaries between 21 and 50 years old.

The systems of regulation The sector system of regulation (SIRSE) was created with the Law of the Republic to regulate, control, and supervise the activities of the telecommunications, electricity, hydrocarbons, water, and transportation sectors.

The laws of the SIRSE and the laws of the sectors[9] had new economic and institutional rules that sought to promote competition and to correct the failings of the market arising from natural monopolies. Specifically the legal frameworks have different incentive systems such as: the fixing and approval of tariffs, the mechanisms for granting concessions and licenses, the promotion of competition, the supervision of services, attention to complaints and controversy, the proposition of norms, regulations, and other techno-administrative rules.

As a result of the process of deregulating the public service markets, and the capitalization and privatization of state-owned businesses, the industrial structures of the hydrocarbon, telecommunications, electricity, transportation, and water sectors have all been modified in Bolivia. Table 4.8 presents the major characteristics of the post-reform markets.

The SIRESE is a regulatory agency with very particular characteristics in part because it is a multisector entity that simultaneously deals with the industries from hydrocarbons, telecommunications, electricity, transportation, and water sectors, and also in part because it is a system that regulates each industry in a specific way through sector superintendents (unisector). The hybrid character of the SIRESE allows it a lot of flexibility and offers it the chance to create conditions of regulatory governance through mechanisms of agreement.

The SIRESE in an agency with multiple objectives. Through the sector superintendents, it must carry out tasks of regulation, promotion of competition, supervision of services, and of the creation of new rules. The general superintendent coordinates, fiscalizes, and meets the appeals from the actors in the regulation process. From a more administrative point of view, the general superintendent performs the functions of appeal, fiscalization, and coordination of, in this case, the superintendent of electricity.

In terms of the environment and natural resources, the government created a system of regulation of renewable natural resources with the objectives of regulating and supervising the sustainable use of non-renewable resources. Another important change came with the establishment of a legal framework (the INRA Law) to guarantee the ownership and use of the land. Some of these changes in Bolivian agriculture are controversial and have caused intense social conflict.

This second stage of reform was also trying to modernize the public administration, but produced few significant results. At various points the composition of the executive branch changed with a constant putting in and taking out of various ministries. There were also various failed attempts at creating a public bureaucracy through a program of civil service. Only in 2001 was the Statute of Civil Service created to institutionalize a career path in the public sector. At the beginning of the 1990s, mechanisms for the administration and control of public resources were created through the Law of Systems of Administration, Fiscalization, and Government Control (the SAFCO Law).

Table 4.8 *Structure of the markets, post-reform*

Sector	Monopoly services	Competitive services	Potentially competitive services
Water	Drinkable water		Production of fresh water
	Sanitary sewage system		
Electricity	Distribution	Generation	Transmission*
	Transmission		Non-regulated consumers (large consumers)
	Integration of isolated systems		
Hydrocarbons	Transport through ducts	Commercialization	Transportation through ducts*
	Natural gas distribution through mains		
Telecommunications	Local telephone	Radio	
		Television	
		Long distance telephone**	
		Cellular phones	
Transportation	Airports	Air navigation	
	Railways	Railroads ***	

Notes:
*   In the Bolivian case, given rights are nonexclusive.
**   Until 2001, this activity was done by a monopoly established by law.
***   In the sectors where means of land transport exists.

Source: General Superintendent (1999).

Education reform This reform focused on the elementary school teaching and acknowledged the multicultural and multiethnic character of Bolivia, which means that cultural and regional diversity was taken into account in new educational curriculums. The reform also incorporated qualitative changes, like a new curriculum design, bilingual education, better teachers, and also improved delivery of equipment, school supplies, and of a new infrastructure. The financing of fiscal education in all stages is handled by the General Treasury of the Nation and by local governments. This was one of the reforms that exerted the most pressure on public resources. The education reform creates a strong incentive for community participation, especially for fathers, in the process of educating children.

Despite the important advances made by this reform, two challenges are still looming ahead. First: better operation of the decentralization and participation is needed, especially in the poorest communities. Second: absenteeism must be reduced both in primary and secondary education. This would represent action in response to the demand for basic education.

Popular participation and administrative decentralization Both measures ended the centralized state. The first outlined the transfer of the physical infrastructure (health, education, local roads, and micro-irrigation) to local governments. The national government increased local government resources so that they would be able to carry out their new functions, distributing 20 per cent of the internal tax and customs collection under the principle of per capita distribution.

The administrative decentralization law transferred the achievements of national works of infrastructure (construction and maintenance of roads, rural electrification, infrastructure of irrigation, and support of production) to the regions. The public resources that finance regional action come in large measure from the departmental exemptions in the production of minerals and hydrocarbons. Popular participation changed the direction of public investment in an important way. After 1996, public investment reached over 50 per cent when until recently it had barely reached 20 per cent.

The Achievements of the Reforms

The results of both the first and second generation reforms show important advances on the issues of monetary-financial balance, important but still incomplete institutional changes, and a better functioning of some markets. After 1990, economic growth was high, with an annual average of 4.5 per cent, single digit inflation, and a substantial improvement in the financial indicators, with the exception of deteriorating terms of trade, as can be seen in Table 4.9.

Table 4.9 Macroeconomic indicators 1991–2001

	1991	1992	1993	1994	1995	1996	1997	1998	1999	2000	2001	2002	2003
Inflation rate (%)	14.52	10.46	9.31	8.52	12.57	7.95	6.73	4.39	3.13	3.41	0.92	2.45	3.94
GDP growth (%)	5.27	1.65	4.27	4.67	4.68	4.36	4.95	5.03	0.43	2.28	1.51	2.75	2.45
Public balance (% PIB)	–4.2	–4.4	–6.1	–3.0	–1.8	–1.9	–3.3	–4.7	–3.5	–3.7	–6.9	–9	–8.1
Net international reserves (US$ millions)	200.3	258	370.9	502.4	650.2	950.9	1066	1063.7	1113.6	1084.8	1077.4	853.8	975.8
Lending rate US$ (%)	21.5	19.1	18.5	16.3	17.0	17.6	16.3	15.6	15.8	18.0	13.7	–	–
Saving rate US$ (%)	12.9	11.4	11.2	9.9	10.5	9.9	8.2	8.0	6.5	7.8	2.3	–	–
Debt (% PIB)	68	67.1	69.9	75	71.4	62.9	56.6	54.8	55.3	53.2	55.1	55.2	64
Terms of trade	87.14	76.34	67.26	68.86	69.01	67.51	67.47	63.73	60.62	62.49	59.87	60.1	63.89

Sources: UDAPE and National Institute of Statistics.

The structural reforms, however, did not have the same positive impact in the social sphere that they had in the economic sphere. While there were some important advances, the indices of poverty and social exclusion are still very high and, in large measure, have been the origin of political and social instability in recent years. Table 4.10 presents a summary of the social situation in Bolivia.

Table 4.10 Bolivia: selected social indicators

Position index of human development	104
Poverty index	63.2%
Urban	51.5%
Rural	81.6%
Extreme poverty	36.5%
Adult illiteracy	15%
Life expectancy at birth	62.92
Infant mortality 5 years, per 1000	67.0%
Health	
Physicians per 10 000 population	3614
Health centers per 10 000 population	3
Distribution cities' revenue	
Perecentage of revenue received	
By richest 20% of households	54%
By poorest 20% of households	4%
Gini coefficient	0.51

Source: IMF Bolivia Statistical Annex, 2001.

The economic model effective in Bolivia since 1985 has done little to advance the understanding and resolving of the microeconomic restrictions on issues like productivity in rural areas, technological development, competition in exports, quality and use of manual labor, the lack of road infrastructure, integral institutional development, and the development of the small and micro business, to mention a few of the most relevant themes. Many of these restrictions significantly compromise economic growth and, even worse, deepen the social exclusion that lies at the heart of a vicious cycle of poverty and low growth.

Historically, as Birdsall et al. (1998) indicates, in Bolivia, like the rest of Latin America, unequal access for the poor to assets that generate revenue has created a political and economic context that limits even further the opportunities of the poor. Without education and without any kind of productive activity, the poor are condemned to low-productivity jobs and low income, and this excludes them from economic systems, reduces their political participation, seriously restricts their ability to choose, and limits their use of freedom. This social exclusion in turn limits access to education, productive jobs, and basic liberties, and ultimately the employment of their civil rights.

According to the figures from the Interamerican Development Bank, if the per capita GDP (an indicator of income) grows at the same rate as it did in the1990s, 1.43 per cent (the equivalent of a 4.5 per cent growth in production), it would take Bolivia 49 years to double its wealth and 139 years to reach the per capita income of Argentina. With its current production profile, levels of social exclusion and poverty, stock in human capital, and productivity, Bolivia is condemned, in the best-case scenario, to a growth of around 4 per cent – not high enough to lift nearly 37 per cent of the population out of poverty.

Challenges of Growth

The central question of economic policy in recent years is why, if it has implemented structural reforms, has adequate macroeconomic management, and has a very open economy compared to the rest of the region, Bolivia is not growing enough to be able to attack its problems of poverty. We will go through four explanations of the insufficient growth in Bolivia: (1) The shortage of savings and investment; (2) a production apparatus that is too dependent on the export of natural resources and that is therefore very vulnerable to external shocks; (3) a complicated geography, and, last but not least; (4) a very fragile institutionalization that is rife with problems of corruption.

Savings and investment

The stabilization and structural reform period have helped both savings and investment recover, although their average rates are still low compared to other countries in the region. Between 1986 and 1990 the internal savings rate represented 8.6 per cent of GDP. In the 1990s, it rose to 11.1 per cent, as can be seen in Table 4.11.

It is also worth noting that the composition of savings changed; the private sector has acquired more importance as public savings have recovered. External savings have also increased in large measure because of the capitalization process of the state-owned businesses and have been intensely concentrated in the hydrocarbon sector. The investment rate also increased, passing 10 per cent of GDP between 1981 and 1985 to reach close to 17 per cent in the 1990s (see Table 4.11). Macroeconomic stability, more stable legal and economic rules, and a more competitive tax system, all largely explain the economic recovery.

Table 4.11 Savings and investment in Bolivia averaged by time period (per cent of GDP)

Factor	1981–85	1986–90	1991–2000
Savings	10.4	12.0	16.6
Private	16.1	6.7	6.3
Public	–10.8	1.9	4.8
Foreign	5.1	3.4	5.5
Investment	10.4	12.0	16.6
Private	5.4	4.8	8.3
Public	5.0	7.2	8.4
GDP growth rate	–1.4	2.2	4.5

Sources: UDAPE and Vice-Ministry of Investment.

Nevertheless, it is worth mentioning that the lack of dynamism in investment is explained by the problems of governance described earlier in this chapter. Problems of the reforms' incomplete credibility and social and political uncertainty have worked to decelerate private investment. In summary, while the structural reforms have allowed levels of savings and investment to improve, they are clearly insufficient. Both the savings rate and the investment rate are still low compared to other countries in Latin America.

Foreign resources and vulnerability

The growth rate of the economy once it had recovered was being maintained until 1998, but then the crisis that began in 1999 showed the vulnerability of the Bolivian economy to external shocks. This quality originates in a structure of production in the Bolivian economy that continued to be concentrated in agriculture, natural resources (mining and oil), manufacturing (industrial agriculture, textiles, and oil refineries), and commerce. The production of coca-cocaine and the natural gas sector have a particular importance in that they generate problems of illness.

Between 1990 and 1998, one of the sectors with the most vitality was the production of coca and its byproducts which grew more than 12 per cent, as can be seen in Table 4.12 and Figure 4.4. The growth in the construction sector was one direct effect of this vitality and is explained by the theory of Dutch illness. At the end of the 1990s, the Bolivian government pushed through a successful program of coca leaf eradication that had important recessive effects on the economy. In this time period, the sector contracted by 25 per cent and dragged down the construction sector with it (see Table 4.12). The internal policy conflict shows how vulnerable the economy is as a result of its little diversity.

Table 4.12 Bolivia: growth by sector

Average annual rates	1990–98	1999–2000	Var.[1]
Not transferable			
Construction and public works	8.78	–8.34	–17.12
Housing property	1.6	1.67	0.07
Government services	2.16	2.78	0.62
Personal services	3.98	4.18	0.2
Transferable			
Food, beverages, and tobacco	4.88	2.8	–2.08
Others industries	3.75	2.33	–1.43
Seasonal exports			
Industrial agricultural products	13.1	–0.43	–13.52
Cocaine	12.69	–24.84	–37.53
Metal and non-metal minerals	3.34	–2.48	–5.82
Gas	6.04	4.96	–1.08

Note: [1] in percentage points.

Source: National Institute of Statistics.

In the 1990s, investments in the natural gas sector and its exports were hugely impacted by economic growth. The average value of natural gas in sales first to Argentina and then to Brazil was 93 million dollars a year (see Figure 4.5).

The future economy and wellbeing of the Bolivian population is newly invested in a non-renewable natural resource, as it has been in silver and tin in the past. There is a large potential for the use of gas in Bolivia. The level of established reserves is up to 47 trillion cubic feet, and while natural gas exports are and will, without a doubt, continue to be an engine for growth in Bolivia's economy, it is important to mention the collateral effects that concentrating expectations around natural gas could have.

The international experience teaches us that countries that based their development on only natural resources experienced a short-term euphoria and then grew less in the long term than did other economies that didn't have oil or minerals.

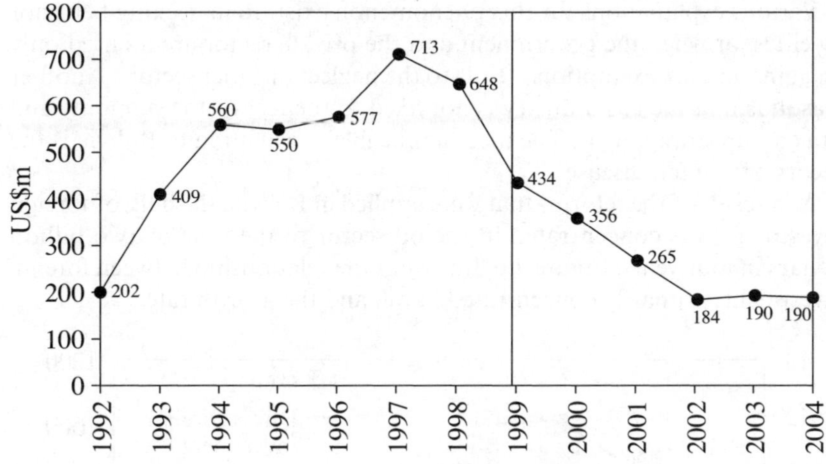

Source: Nogales and Eduardo (2000).

Figure 4.4 The impact of drug traffic (narcotraffic in millions of US$)

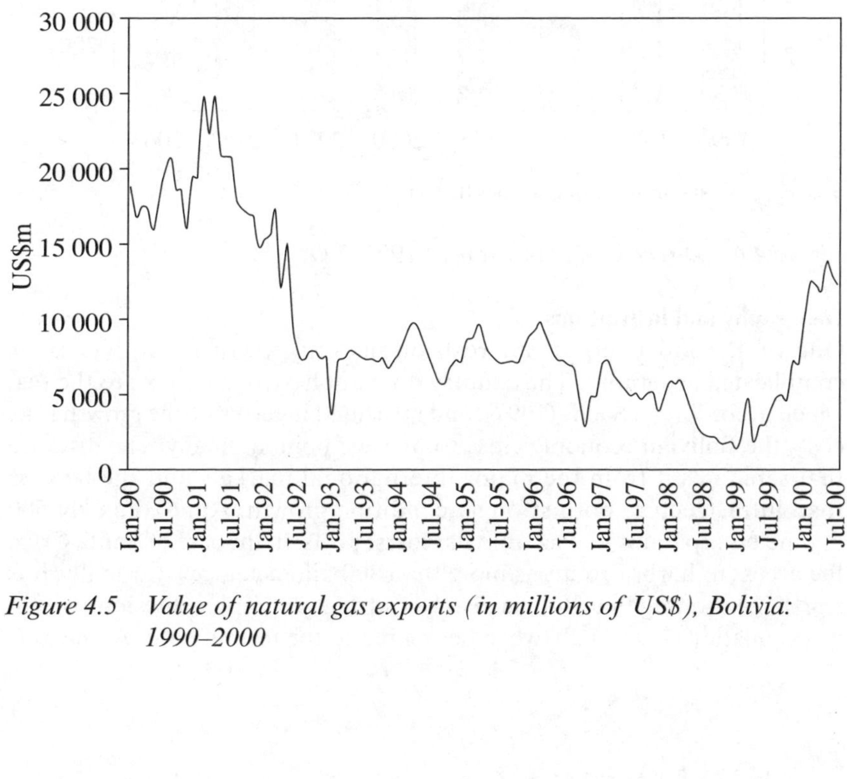

Figure 4.5 Value of natural gas exports (in millions of US$), Bolivia: 1990–2000

Various explanations for this phenomenon exist. Rent-seeking behavior by elites, or when the government and the private sector are focused only on gains and tax exemptions, leads to the neglect of other sectors. Another reason is that the gas industry is not fixed to the rest of the economy and can end up strangling it. The most applicable explanation to Bolivia is the theory of 'Dutch disease'.

As a result of the reforms that were applied in Bolivia, the bulk of foreign investment was concentrated in the oil sector to the tune of two billion dollars in four years. Figure 4.6 illustrates the relationship between foreign investment, primarily concentrated in oil, and the growth rate.

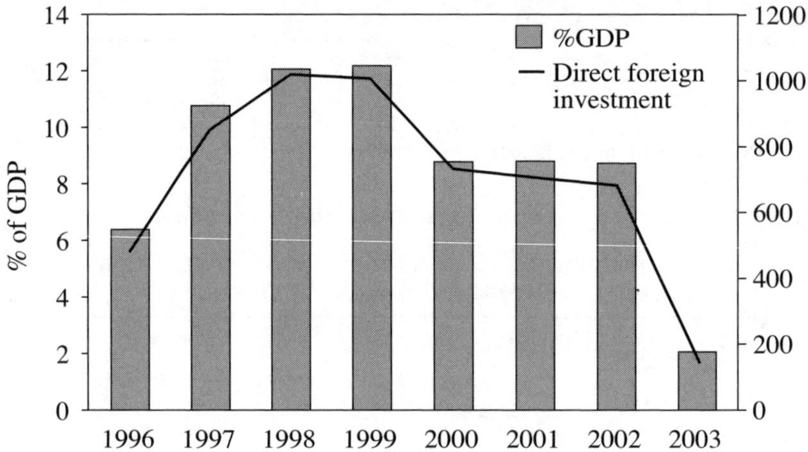

Source: National Institute of Statistics Bolivia.

Figure 4.6 Direct foreign investment 1996–2001

Geography and institutions

One of the most important restrictions on growth in Bolivia is its complicated geography. The country does not have open access to the sea, which according to Sachs (1997), and measured in terms of the growth rate, costs the Bolivian economy close to one age point annually. The distance that separates it from the major international markets and the lack of road infrastructure both strongly condition growth. Approximately 500 kilometers separates La Paz from its closest ports. In the case of Santa Cruz, the access to harbor routes is more than 800 kilometers away. Finally, it is worth mentioning that Bolivia also has strong geographic divisions within its population – especially when compared to the rest of Latin America.

In terms of institutional and legal development, although Bolivia advanced significantly in ways already described, much development in these areas is still lacking, especially relating to the control of corruption. In Bolivia, the judicial system is still very weak and has many holes, and the provision of public services (electricity, water, roads, and security) is, despite the fact that some services are under the control of the private sector, overall very poor. In respect of the regulatory framework, it is being constructed with serious limitations on financial resources and human capital.

But the more complicated institutional weakness is corruption, which, as appears in Figure 4.7, is what most concerns businessmen. Corruption reduces levels of foreign and domestic investment. The lack of transparency tends to attract investors with suspicious reputations. Corruption also distorts and often encourages the development of an informal economy, reducing the resources that go to the state and provoking the slow death of dozens of small businessmen who are trying to survive in a business world without clear rules. This kind of corruption also expands public spending and public investment.

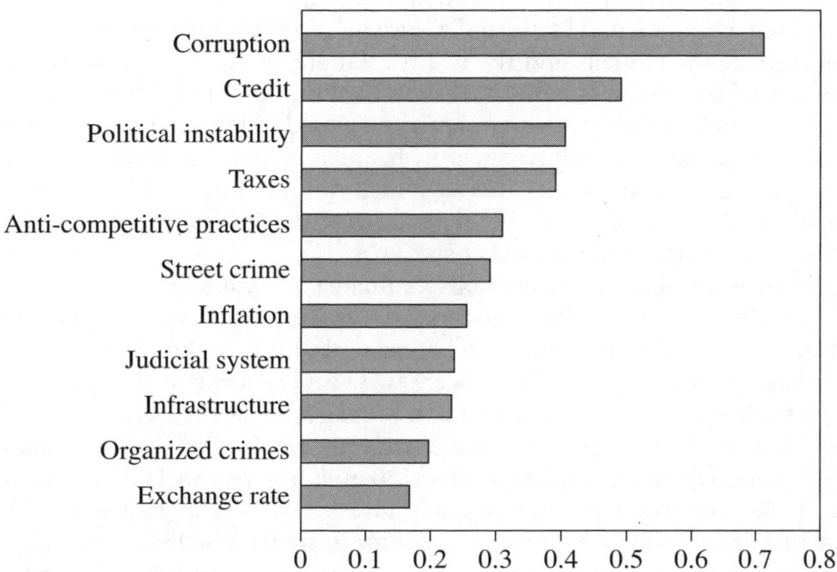

Source: World Bank (2000).

Figure 4.7 What most worries Bolivian businessmen is corruption. Bolivia: obstacles to the growth of business

Bribery decreases the government's income and limits and impoverishes state-provided public goods and services. Businesses that keep double accounts to evade taxes, elevated levels of fiscal evasion, and little tax consciousness are at least a few examples of weak public finances that translate into a very poor supply of roads, schools, and hospitals.

4.4 CONCLUSIONS

The Bolivian experience in the last 15 years, like that of other countries in the region, demonstrates a political economy affected by relatively volatile changes, exposed to external macroeconomic shocks, and vulnerable to internal political and social shocks. Among the particular characteristics of the Bolivian case are: a fragile system of political governance that depends on coalition politics and a highly volatile economy that is subject to price shocks of non-renewable resources and of the coca-cocaine cycle in both the formal and informal economy. In this conclusion, we return to the paradox presented in the introduction to this chapter: How to explain the apparent contradiction between the 'success' of the economic institutional policies of the reforms and the relative 'failure' of the reforms to spark sustained economic growth, poverty reduction, and fewer inequalities? How are political cycles that are open and closed to reform different from economic cycles of stabilization, growth, and recession? In this chapter, we considered determinants of this asymmetry in the short and long terms, distinguishing between transitional and structural factors that explain the current economic and political crisis.

In the short term, three factors accentuate the asymmetry of economic and political cycles in Bolivia. First, the space for governance, and the system of coalition politics itself depends on a highly discretional system of redistribution. There were two visible shocks to the inherited system triggered by the capitalization processes of public businesses and administrative decentralization that did the *prebendal* cycle out of more than 500 million dollars annually (around 200 million a year in TGN revenues and 300 million dollars a year in public investment). The immediate effects of this drain on the government's resources were the visible weakening of the system of coalition politics, and its total collapse during the 1997–2002 administration, along with the growing disenchantment and disillusion of public opinion about the effective political and economic model.

Second, a weak system of social protection and of buffering economic shocks exacerbates social polarization in times of economic crisis. The bipolar structure of job creation – microbusinesses that generate 83 per cent of employment but only contribute 25 per cent of GDP and big businesses that only generate 9 per cent of the employment and contribute 65 per cent of GDP – guarantees that there is no buffer of small and medium-sized businesses to cushion the impact of recessive shocks and economic deceleration. The high costs of formalization, the multiple obstacles to capital markets access, the adoption of technology, and commercial incorporation, all perpetuate a system of family microbusinesses that does not grow. This assets and revenue distribution structure also perpetuates a cycle of 'growing impoverishment', as can be seen in the experience of the 1990s. Despite having an average growth rate of 4 per cent between 1999 and 2000, the Bolivian economy saw an increase in the absolute number of people in poverty of about 30 000 individuals per year.

Third, a heavy dependence on non-renewable natural resources – first on tin, then on the coca leaf, and, most recently, on natural gas – conditions the possibilities for the development of the rest of the economy. In the future, the magnitude of exports related to natural gas will have foreseeable effects on the overvaluation of the exchange rate and the decrease in competition of exports from other sectors of the economy. In one way, this has been the historical pattern of the Bolivian economy in the last century. Measures attempting to buffer the new effects of Dutch disease include plans to create stabilization funds and other measures that would neutralize the exchange rate and inflationary pressures.

In the long term, the most important determinants of the iterative cycles of economic reform and social discontent would seem to point to three key structural factors. First, Bolivia has a history of unequal access to assets that generate revenue (including human capital, property, and financial market assets). Bolivia lived through a cycle of major redistribution around the middle of the last century with the agrarian reform of 1953. The redistribution of land assets had the long-term effect of creating conditions for urbanization and migration to lower lands in the 1960s and 1970s. After 50 years in the cycle of redistribution, nevertheless, the coefficient of income concentration, as measured by the MECOVI surveys, suggests that today Bolivia is among the most unequal countries in the region (Gini of 0.51). Paired with the empirical evidence is the public perception of pronounced social and economic inequality.

Second, there is a growing ethnic fragmentation that signifies the political disintegration of the country. The ethnic and cultural diversity has a long history and, nevertheless, has been recently politicized in the course of the primary and secondary generation reforms, The rise of a 'nationalist' Aymara movement suggests an inflection point in ethnic self-perception and in the consequences for a highly divided and volatile political system. A reading of history implies that the politicization of ethnicity occurs in moments of transition from one mechanism of social and political inclusion to another. The collapse of the farm and party corporatism in the 1960s and 1970s created one of these crises and simultaneously gave rise to a *katarismo* within Bolivian union politics. In recent years the disenchantment with the 'political class' has manifested with a new ethnic political movement: the rise of the Movimiento Indígena Rachacuti, organized by the Aymara leader Felipe Quispe.

Third, Bolivia's geography plays a determining role in prospects for economic development and in the construction of a realized state. The transportation costs that come from the accidental geography and the Bolivian *mediterraneidad* (land-locked situation) weigh on the competitiveness of the export sector and on the capacity to attract foreign direct investment. The geography also has a dissuasive effect on the consolidation of an effective state that guarantees its presence throughout the country's territory. The weak and intermittent presence of the state increases the transaction costs in the resolution of social and political disputes, as well as on the presence of effective rule of law. The institutional reforms that were begun in the 1990s focused on the backbone of the state as much as on the physical backbone of the country in its attempts to reduce transportation costs.

In this study, we considered two types of determinants of the political and economic crisis cycles. Among the short-term determinants, there are a few that buffer shocks, particularly those that weaken or support the system of coalition politics; among the long-term determinants, some of the factors that affect governance emerge, including patterns of inequality, ethnic fragmentation, and the geographic fragmentation of the country. Bolivia must still confront formidable challenges in the construction of political spaces to consolidate current reforms and to implement new economic and state reforms. The growing disenchantment with the economic model, social violence, and political polarization condition the government's capacity to respond to economic and political crises by sustaining a basis for redistributive growth in the future. The transitional fragility seems to match the fragile nature of the long-term economic and political situation in Bolivia, and seems to foreshadow still another period of social turbulence after the transitional recession.

NOTES

1. The opinion polls taken by the Latinobarómetro show that, despite a sustained 'support for democracy' in the 1990s, Bolivians show less 'democratic satisfaction', particularly related to economic achievements during the democratic period. See Latinobarómetro (2001).
2. Morales (1987, 1988, 1989) and Sachs (1986) did an in-depth study of the characteristics of the Bolivian inflationary process with an emphasis on the fiscal problems.

3. When high inflation rates were registered and the tributary base was eroded, the government's real revenue contracted. This phenomenon is known as the Olivera-Tanzi effect.
4. The principle taxes created were: Value Added Tax (VAT), Complementary Regime to the VAT (CR-VAT), Transaction Tax (IT), Consolidated Tariff Burden (GAC), Tax on Presumed Rent of Business (IRPE), Tax on Specific Consumption (ICE), applied to the sale of alcoholic drinks, cigarettes, and jewelry, among others.
5. The most commonly used mechanisms of compensation were: Certificate of Tariff Drawback (CRA), Certificates of Negotiable Lines of Credit (CENOCREN), Redeemable Treasury Bonds (BTRs), and Drawbacks and Certificates of Tax Returns (CEDEIM).
6. The following public banks were sold: Banco del Estado, Banco Minero and Banco Agrícola.
7. State-owned field (YPFB), National Company of Electricity (ENDE), National Company of Telecommunications (ENTEL), National Company of Railroads (ENFE) and Lloyd Aero Boliviano (LAB), represented 90 per cent of the state businesses.
8. The exception was ENTEL that was capitalized as a monopoly.
9. When we talk about the laws of sectors we are referring to the laws of hydrocarbons, electricity, and telecommunications that were approved. The laws of transportation, hydro resources, and basic sanitation are part of this analysis. The Bolivian legal regulatory framework also includes the regulation that complements the aforementioned norms.

REFERENCES

Birdsall, N., C. Graham and R.H. Sabot (eds) (1998), *Beyond Tradeoffs: Market Reforms and Equitable Growth in Latin America*, Brookings Institution Press and Inter-American Develoment Bank, Washington DC.

Calděron, F. and A. Szmukler (2000), *La política en las calles*, Plural UASB (ed.), CERES, La Paz, Bolivia.

Chávez, G. (1989) *Alta inflación, hiperinflación y variabilidad de los precios relativos: el caso boliviano*, Universidad Católica – IISEC, La Paz, Bolivia.

Coppedge, M. (1998), 'The dynamics diversity of Latin American party systems', *Party Politics*, **4**(4), 547–68, October.

Dixit A. (1996), *The Making of Economic Policy: A Transaction Cost Perspective*, Cambridge, MA: MIT Press.

Dixit A. (2000), 'Some lessons from transaction cost politics for less-developed countries', Princeton Working Paper, Princeton, NJ: Princeton University Press.

Gamarra, E. (1997), 'Hybrid presidentialism and democratization: the case of Bolivia', in S. Mainwaring and M.S. Shugart, *Residentialism and Democracy in Latin America*, Cambridge: Cambridge University Press, pp. 363–93.

Gamarra, E. and J. Malloy (1990), 'Bolivia: revolution and reaction', in Howard J. Wiarda and Harvey F. Kline (eds), *Latin American Politics and Development*, 3rd edition.

General Superadent (1999), www.sirese.gov.bo

Graham, C. and S. Pettinato (2001), *Happiness and Hardship: Opportunities and Insecurity in New Market Economies*, Washington, DC: Brookings Institution.

Graham, C., M. Grindle, J. Seddon and E. Lora (1999), *Improving the Odds: Political Strategies for Institutional Reform in Latin America*, Washington, DC: Inter American Development Bank.

Gray Molina, G. (2001), 'Un puente entre el corto y largo plazo: pobreza, desigualdad y política social en Bolivia', Documento de Trabajo, La Paz: Maestrías para el Desarrollo, Universidad Católica Boliviana.
Gray Molina, G., E. Perez de Rada and E. Yañez (1999), 'Economía política de reformas institucionales en Bolivia', Documento de Trabajo, R-350, Washington, DC: Banco Interamericano de Desarrollo.
Grindle, M. (2000), *Audacious Reforms: Invention and Democracy in Latin America*, Baltimore, MD: Johns Hopkins University Press.
Kaufmann, D., A. Kraay and P. Zoido-Lobatón (2002), *Governance Matters II: Updated Governance Indicators for 2000–2001*, Washington, DC: World Bank.
Kaufmann, K. and P. Zoido-Lobatón (1999), *Governance Matters: Updated Governance Indicators*, Washington, DC: World Bank.
Latinobarómetro (2001), *Corporación Latinobarómetro*, Santiago, Chile.
Lora, E. and U. Panizza (2002), *Structural Reforms in Latin America Under Scrutiny*, Washington, DC: Inter American Development Bank.
Mainwaring, S. and M. Soberg Shugart (eds) (1997), *Presidentialism and Democracy in Latin America*, Cambridge: Cambridge University Press.
Morales, J.A. (1987), 'Inflation stabilization in Bolivia', in *Inflation Stabilization: the Experience of Israel, Argentina, Brazil, Bolivia and Mexico*, Cambridge, MA: MIT Press.
Morales, J.A. (1988), 'The end of the Bolivian hyperinflation', *Viertejahres Berichte* 114 Boon.
Morales, J.A. (1989), 'La transición de la estabilidad al crecimiento sostenido en Bolivia', in CIEPLAN – HACHETE (eds), *Inflación rebelde en América Latina*, Santiago, Chile.
Nogales, X. and P. Eduardo (2000), *Aduana nacional: el contrabando en Bolivia*, La Paz, Bolivia.
North, D. (1990), 'A transaction cost theory of politics', *Journal of Theoretical Politics*, **2**(4), 355–67.
O'Donnell, G. (1993), 'Illusions about consolidation', *Journal of Democracy*, **7**(2), 34–51.
O'Donnell, G. (1996), 'On the state, democratization and some conceptual problems: a Latin American view glances at some postcommunist countries', *World Development*, **21**(8), 1355–69.
Sachs, J. (1986), 'A new approach for managing the debt crisis', *Columbia Journal of World Business*, **XXI** (3).
Sachs, J. and J. Luke Gallup (1997), CAER II Discussion Paper 39, Harvard Institute for International Development, Cambridge, MA.
Sachs, J. and J.A. Morales (1989), 'Bolivia's economic crisis' in Jeffrey Sachs (ed.), *Developing Country Debt and the World Economy*, Chicago: Chicago University Press.
Solimano, A. (2001), *Can Reforming Global Institutions Help Developing Countries Share More in the Benefits from Globalization*? World Bank, Country Economics Department.
Whitehead, L. (1986), 'Bolivia's failed democratization: 1977–1980', in Guillermo O'Donnell, Phillipe C. Schmitter and Lawrence Whitehead (eds), *Transitions from Authoritarian Rule: Latin America*, Baltimore, MD: John Hopkins University Press, pp. 221–36.
World Bank (2000), *The World Business Environment Survey*, (WBES).
World Bank (2002), *Sustained Macroeconomic Reforms, Tepid Growth: a Governance Puzzle in Bolivia?* Daniel Kaufman, Massimo Mastruzzi and Diego Zaraleta.

5. The economy, conflict and governance in Colombia

José Antonio Ocampo*

5.1 INTRODUCTION

Colombia crossed the threshold into the twenty-first century in the midst of a two-pronged crisis. One facet of this crisis stems from the serious problems of governance generated, in large part, by the irregular armed conflict that continues to trouble the country. The other derives from the lingering effects of the worst economic recession in the country's modern history, which has resulted in the loss of a full half-decade of potential economic growth and in the deterioration of social conditions.

The country's internal conflict bears some resemblance to other episodes in its history, particularly in terms of the important role played by the zones open to colonization which, due to the peculiar features of its geography, are located throughout its territory. The country's traditional fragmentation of power is another historical feature that has acted as a contributing factor. Nonetheless, the extent and intensity of this conflict is associated with an entirely new phenomenon: the magnitude of the existing drug traffic and the overwhelmingly degenerative effect it has had in terms of the scale of violence and its impact on Colombian society as a whole.

The second facet of this crisis, the economic recession, involves elements that are new to a country which, until not long ago, was moving forward with its economic development, albeit at a somewhat measured pace but avoiding the sharp business cycles that have troubled Latin America since the mid-1970s. Thus, unlike its predecessors, the most recent crisis has various elements in common with those experienced by other Latin American countries. One of those shared features is, in particular, the economy's incomplete adjustment to trade liberalization and its excessive vulnerability to external financial cycles. Other elements are more specific to Colombia, such as the critical situation that arose when, in an effort to resolve the internal conflict in the country, an attempt was made to combine the opening of the economy[1] with an expansion of the state's spheres of action.

These two histories – the history of the internal conflict and the history of the economic crisis – are intertwined at some points, but they have primarily proceeded in parallel to one another. Their separation is a reflection of structural features of Colombian society. In fact, Colombia's recent history can only be understood if it is viewed as the conjunction of two dynamic systems that have existed side by side for many years. On the one hand, there is a relatively successful 'formal' economic, social and political system which is, nonetheless, subject to weaknesses and periodic crises much like those experienced by other Latin American or developing countries. On the other, there is a violent, even gang-controlled 'informal' system which has at times risen to a position of dominance in different segments of Colombia's complex geography and social structure.

The existence of this structural dualism and its intractability are in themselves a problem. The former system has held sway throughout most of the country's history, but the latter's expansion has threatened its hegemony at two critical junctures: during what came to be known as simply 'The Violence', which broke out in the mid-twentieth century, and again during the closing decade of the twentieth century and dawning years of the twenty-first. At various stages, the informal system has performed a functional role for its formal counterpart – as, for example, when it has been used by large-scale rural landholders or by political groups to ensure their dominance in certain parts of the country's territory – but this does not mean that the latter exists by virtue of the functions it provides to the former. In fact, it would be more accurate to say that, on the whole, the informal system is dysfunctional in terms of the formal system. This has only been evidenced, however, in extreme circumstances (as during the violence that erupted in the mid-twentieth century and in its closing years), due to the formal system's tendency towards a deconcentration of power and avoidance of open conflict, both within its own confines and in its relationship with the informal system.

In terms of the dual crisis being discussed here, this separation between the two systems is manifested in a number of dimensions. First of all, although the internal conflict has indeed undermined economic growth in various ways, it cannot be convincingly argued that it is the main cause of the recent economic crisis. By the same token, and as indicated by the voluminous literature on the causes of the violence, nor are there grounds for identifying internal inequalities or deepening poverty – features clearly exhibited by the 'formal' system – as the fundamental causes of the recent outbreaks of violence.

Nor should we look for the underlying causes of these problems of governance in the various characteristics that Colombia shares with other developing countries, such as a lack of civic awareness or institutional failings in the operation of the political and judicial systems. In fact, in many of these areas, Colombia is better off than other Latin American countries, thanks to such attributes as its strong republican tradition and the stability of its party system, which set it apart in the regional and even global context. It is therefore not in the more 'Latin American' traits but rather in the more specifically Colombian characteristics – such as the impact of drug trafficking, the country's open geography and its tradition of fragmented power – that we should look for the causes of the country's recent problems of violence and poor governance.

Nor can it be credibly argued that Colombian society has been remiss in striving to overcome its problems in the area of governance. The decision to replace its century-old constitution with a new political charter in 1991 was the culmination of a determined effort to find political solutions for the internal conflict. The peace processes undertaken by five presidents of the republic, which succeeded in demobilizing a number of guerrilla groups, provide further evidence of this effort. One of the explicit objectives of the new political charter was, furthermore, to increase public social expenditure in order to help resolve the internal conflict. Other signs of the efforts being made in this direction are the government's political commitment to international conventions on human rights (which, unfortunately, has not been fully rewarded by the results), court rulings that have helped thwart drug traffickers' attempts to penetrate the political system and the frontal attacks launched against this activity during the last three administrations.

In fact, viewed from this vantage point, the 1990s can be seen as an attempt to confront the country's economic and political problems based on a combination of measures designed to put the economy in step with the globalization process, steps to ensure that social services will reach a larger portion of the population and efforts to consolidate democracy. This was a bold experiment which also sought to meet the central challenge facing all contemporary societies: to reconcile economic modernization with social equity and democracy. Like other countries, however, Colombia has had great difficulty in achieving these objectives.

This chapter will analyse this dual crisis of the late twentieth and early twenty-first centuries. It is divided into four sections, the first of which is this introduction. The second looks at aspects of the economic crisis that are similar to those experienced by other Latin American countries, namely, the difficulties associated with trade liberalization and macroeconomic volatility. The third focuses on the critical situation created by the growth of the state and the contradictory social outcomes seen in the final decade of the twentieth century. The fourth analyses problems that are more specifically associated with governance and the internal conflict.

5.2 OPENNESS AND MACROECONOMIC VOLATILITY

The record of the Colombian economy's performance since the implementation of measures aimed at opening up the economy in 1990 are not encouraging. In fact, the only area in which progress has clearly been made is in bringing inflation under control. The economy began the 1990s with a legacy of over 15 years of moderate but highly inertial inflation. What is more, the rate of inflation was then trending upward and was starting to reach levels that were higher than those regarded in earlier decades as being manageable. The international community's experience has been that, when inflation is moderate and inertial, turning it around can be very difficult.[2] Having closed out the decade with single-digit inflation is, therefore, a noteworthy achievement.

In terms of economic growth, however, the results have been very disappointing (see Figure 5.1). Actually, the rate of economic growth had been slowing down since the mid-1970s, primarily because the long-lasting industrial boom that had underpinned the country's growth since the 1930s was running out of steam. The economic authorities had hoped that by opening up the economy, they could reverse this slowdown, but this expectation was not fulfilled.[3] Between 1990 and 1997, the expansion of economic activity was much the same as it had been in 1975–90, but activity in both the agricultural and manufacturing sectors fell off sharply, leaving

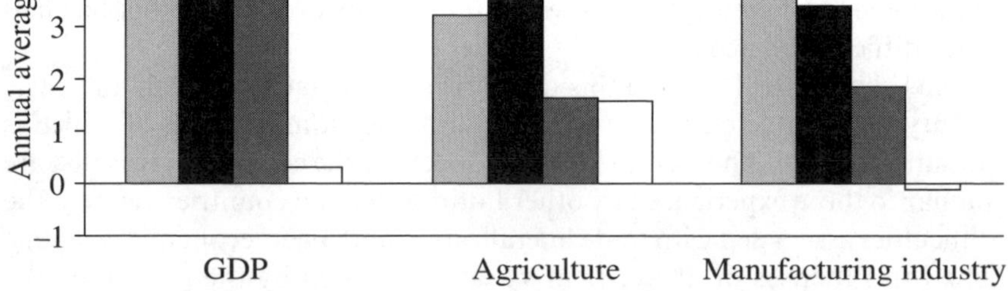

Source: Calculations of the author, based on data from DANE and the Banco de la República.

Figure 5.1 Long-term economic growth

the services sector as virtually the sole mainstay of economic growth. This indicates that, far from galvanizing tradables sectors, the liberalization of trade shifted the responsibility for maintaining growth to non-tradables, which were buoyed by an ultimately unsustainable boom in aggregate domestic demand. This was followed by a 'lost half-decade' (1998–2002) in terms of economic growth, with per capita GDP shrinking by 7 per cent – the most serious contraction ever recorded.

A Slow and Costly Adjustment to an Open Economy

Advocates of the move to open up the economy in Colombia, as in the rest of Latin America, argued that the import-substitution model had become an obstacle to economic development because it promoted a type of development that was based on the extraction of economic rents generated by protection and other advantages granted by the state, rather than the development of competitive economic activities. This was a one-sided and rather inaccurate version of the country's economic history, however. Colombia had, after all, succeeded in growing at a moderate but stable rate for six decades (from the 1930s to the 1980s) while avoiding any major crises or uncontrollable inflationary spirals. In order to accomplish this, it had combined its tradition of macroeconomic pragmatism, which was marked by a mixture of fiscal discipline (although with some lapses in this respect) with strong interventionism in monetary, exchange-rate and trade policy, and an active strategy for diversifying production.[4]

In the 1930s, this strategy had enabled the country to make a fairly smooth transition from an economic model based on the expansion of coffee exports to a model based on manufacturing activities catering to the domestic market. Later, it allowed the country to make a transition from the classic import-substitution model to a mixed model that combined import substitution with the explicit objective of export diversification. This second transition was made relatively early on, starting with the coffee crisis of the mid-1950s, and then gathered steam with the implementation of the 1967 economic reforms.[5] Import substitution, as an objective to work towards, was explicitly abandoned in the early 1970s. In fact, every development plan introduced since President Pastrana Borrero unveiled his 'Four Strategies' plan in the early 1970s has taken a critical view of import substitution. Consequently, stating that 'import substitution' was the predominant model prior to the opening of the economy is a glaring anachronism. It should be noted, however, that the abandonment of import substitution did not mean that the economy's protectionist structure was dismantled, although a gradual rationalization of this structure was undertaken during the 1970s and again since the mid-1980s.[6]

In economic terms, the mixed model used by the country before it opened up its economy yielded exceptional results. Colombia's industrial development process avoided lapsing into a bias towards branches of heavy industry in which it had little chance of becoming competitive, and a rapid modernization and expansion of non-coffee agricultural activities began in the 1950s. Many new export activities arose in agricultural and manufacturing industries that had gone through an earlier productive and technological learning process while shielded by protective measures. Non-coffee exports grew swiftly when the exchange rate was competitive (especially in 1967–74 and 1985–91). High levels of protection did not interfere with this expansion, thanks to the existence of special mechanisms that gave export sectors access to duty-free imported inputs, preferential access to credit and tax incentives. By the early 1990s, as shown in Figure 5.2, the country's exports had been growing rapidly for over five years. This upswing allowed it to finally break free of its dependence on coffee exports, an accomplishment that, although certainly late in coming, was nonetheless an outstanding one in historical terms. There were, of course, inefficient activities, protectionist excesses, and an anti-export and anti-agriculture bias, but by international – and, especially, Latin American – standards, the development pattern could hardly be regarded as inefficient.[7]

By the early 1990s, however, it was evident that, given the sweeping changes taking place in the world economy, government decisionmakers and entrepreneurs should direct their energies towards achieving fuller integration into the international economy. This is the reality that the move to a more open economy acknowledged. This change in direction called for a rationalization of protection mechanisms, which had, in any case, ceased to perform a useful function as an incentive for new economic activities.

Before 1990, the controversy regarding the need for trade reform revolved around different variations on the theme of gradualism. Moreover, given the reactivation of economic growth based on the traditional mixed model which began in the mid-1980s, there was little reason to advocate a sharp break with that tradition. Viewed from this standpoint, the move to open up the economy arose, in its most radical form, out of the 'demonstration effect' of developments in other Latin American countries more than it did out of a debate within the country.

The preference for gradualism was also based on four sets of circumstances that were identified in the course of the internal debate of the 1980s and early 1990s. The first was that production sectors needed time to adapt; sectors that competed against imports needed time to modernize, and those that were capable of developing an export capacity needed time not only to modernize but also to conquer new markets. The second was that a competitive exchange rate was the best guarantee of export success, as

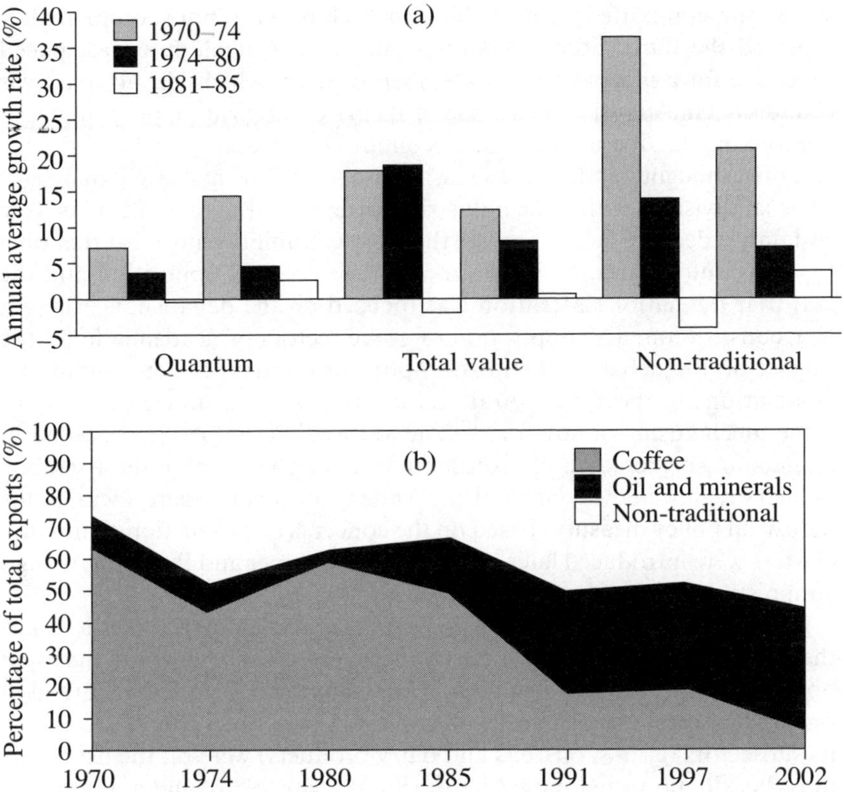

Source: Calculations of the author based on data from the Banco de la República, ECLAC and DANE.

Figure 5.2 Export growth (a) and export diversification (b)

demonstrated by the growth of the country's non-traditional exports. The third consideration was that, in order to compete successfully, supplementary elements were needed, particularly a technology development strategy and suitable infrastructure. Finally, although the world had been moving in the direction of free trade, there were some notable exceptions, where protectionism was still the rule. These exceptions included such sectors as agriculture, textiles and wearing apparel, and the automobile industry.

In line with the gradualism and pragmatism typical of Colombian economic policy in the past, the plan for opening the economy to trade was announced by the Barco administration, in February 1990, as a gradual strategy. The Gaviria administration, which took office in August of that same year, committed itself to this approach initially, but soon thereafter replaced the Barco administration's plan with a much more fast-paced timetable for a more radical trade liberalization, which, for all that, was abandoned in August 1991 as part of its price stabilization programme.

From the standpoint of political economy, the reasons why the gradualist school of thought was defeated so easily have not been exhaustively analysed.[8] Internal divisions within the industrial entrepreneurial organizations were certainly a decisive factor, as were the great credibility enjoyed at that time by President Gaviria, the absence of a true political opposition and the fact that the nation's attention was focused on the debate concerning a new constitution. The opposition of some sectors of academia had little impact on the debate.[9] The most important opponents were employers' associations in the agricultural sector, and their resistance gave rise to some mechanisms of support.[10] The automobile industry succeeded in maintaining higher levels of protection, including a variant of the assembly-industry regime in the context of the Andean automotive agreement. Some industrial policy measures based on the concepts of production chains and clusters were introduced later on, during the Samper and Pastrana Arango administrations.

The poor performance of the agricultural and industrial sectors since the early 1990s shows just how costly these sectors' adjustment to the rapid opening of the economy has been. The Colombian farm sector turned in one of the worst performances of any Latin American country; some of its subsectors (grains, oilseeds and dairy products) were on the list of the most heavily protected industries during the late 1980s, and a number of them, as well as various export sectors (including, most particularly, coffee), were faced with adverse price conditions on international markets. Various manufacturing industries were confronted with the same problem, although in their case the most severe shock came from the contraction of domestic demand in the second half of the decade. The crisis in the agricultural and manufacturing sectors was reflected very clearly in employment, with these sectors going from accounting for 43 per cent of national employment in 1991 to 36.8 per cent in 1997.

Contrary to the expectations of the advocates of this course of action, the growth of exports slowed in comparison to its pace in 1985–91, especially in the case of non-traditional exports (see Figure 5.2). The only two dynamic components of the export sector were petroleum and sales to other Latin American countries, especially the Andean nations. The slump in oil prices, first of all, and the reduction in the output of crude and in exports that followed, together with the ups and downs of the Andean countries' trade performance since 1998, were therefore particularly unfortunate, since they hurt the only dynamic components of the export sector. The rapid growth of imports was thus not matched by similar progress in the country's export performance. In the vocabulary of the Colombian debate on the issue, the fact that the process of 'inward-looking' liberalization was more forceful than its 'outward-looking' counterpart eventually led to a deterioration in the balance-of-payments current account and generated a net recessionary effect.

Obviously, one of the decisive factors in this outcome was real exchange rate appreciation. The heated controversy about the causes of this phenomenon focused on three main determinants, to which different authors ascribed varying degrees of importance during the debate:[11] (a) the avalanche of capital inflows and the boom in private and public spending that accompanied it; (b) the increase in public expenditure and the resulting fiscal deficit; and (c) the exchange-rate policy's bias towards revaluation. There is a compelling reason for thinking that the first of these factors was the most decisive one. After all, the largest real appreciation took place between 1991 and 1994, which were the years when total (public and private) expenditure rose the most. The rate of real revaluation started to slow somewhat in 1995, despite further increases in public expenditure and a deepening fiscal deficit. In addition, the currency experienced a real devaluation when the flow of external finance began to dwindle, even though the adjustment in public spending was moderate and the fiscal deficit grew. Obviously, Banco de la República's exchange-rate policy determined the exact timing of the real appreciations and devaluations of the peso.

Capital Flows and Macroeconomic Instability

The economy's growth rate was also much more unstable in the 1990s. In this respect too, there was a break with Colombia's traditional gradualism and pragmatism. The cyclical swings in aggregate domestic demand were particularly intense. As shown in Figure 5.3, nothing like the 1992–94 spending boom or the 1998–99 bust had ever been seen before in Colombia. The great expectations sparked by the discovery of the Cusiana oil deposits and the opening of the economy at the start of the decade, as well as by the flood of capital that started to pour into Latin America at that time, set the stage for the boom in spending that occurred in the early 1990s.

As is demonstrated by the abundant literature on the subject, the international community's experience shows that booms and busts are interrelated. The 'speculative bubbles' generated during booms in external finance eventually burst, giving way to economic adjustments whose severity is in direct proportion to the size of the bubble. Colombia had partly avoided being drawn into this pattern in the late 1970s and early 1980s,[12] but fell victim to it in the 1990s.[13] Both the crisis of the early 1980s and the bust

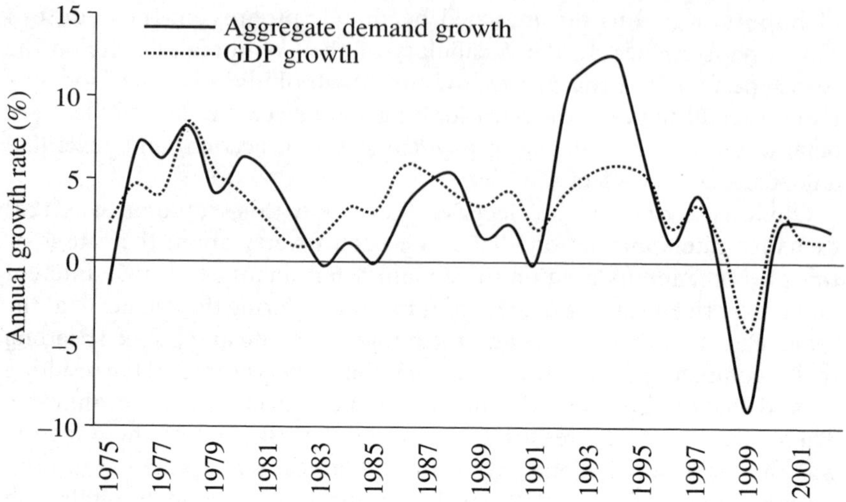

Source: DANE

Figure 5.3 Growth and domestic demand volatility

of the late 1990s were preceded (with a lag in relation to Latin American patterns in the first case) by an expansion in internal and external borrowing which had financed a sharp upswing in public and private spending. In addition, in both cases there was a real appreciation of the peso and an accompanying balance-of-payments current account deficit. The relative severity of the problems faced by the public and private sectors differed in the two cases, however. This difference did not have as much to do with the behaviour of public expenditure as it did with the problems confronting the private sector. As will be discussed later on, in the 1990s public spending expanded in similar magnitudes as it did in the late 1970s and early 1980s, and the fiscal deficit was lower than it had been during that earlier period. On the other hand, the problems associated with private spending and the private sector deficit were much more severe during the more recent crisis.

A comparison of the external debt statistics leaves no doubt about the nature of the situation. Colombia's external debt swelled by $14.7 billion between 1991 and 1997, and $13.4 billion, or 90 per cent, of that amount was private debt, which increased sevenfold during that period. On the other hand, in 1979–83, the private sector accounted for less than one third of the increase in external indebtedness. What is more, the private sector's total (domestic and external) debt rose by the equivalent of 24.7 points of GDP between 1991 and 1997, or almost twice as much as in 1979–83 (see Figure 5.4). The country's spending spree (1992–95) also occurred during the same time that the private sector's surplus, which it had maintained since 1975, turned into a deficit, as private saving dropped below the level needed to finance private investment.[14] This was the major difference between the two crises: whereas the private sector had always run a surplus for more than a decade prior to the crisis of the early 1980s, 1998 was the sixth consecutive year in which it posted a deficit.

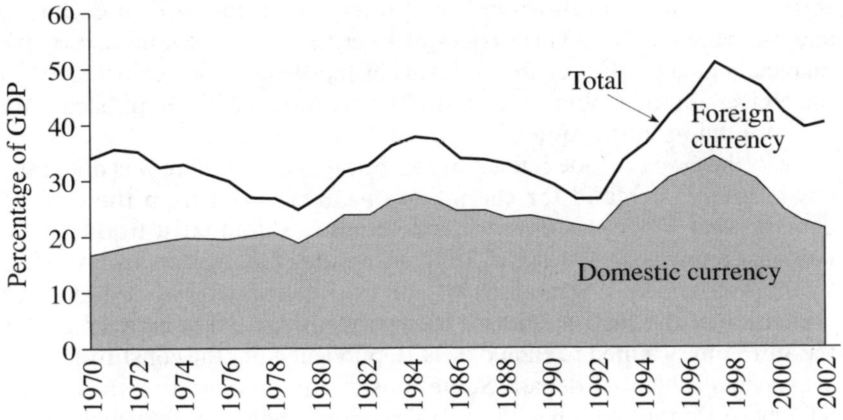

Source: Calculations of the author based on data from the Banco de la República.

Figure 5.4 Private indebtedness

Thus, the reason why the crisis of the late 1990s was more severe than the crisis of the early 1980s was not so much because of its fiscal dimension (although this also played a role, as will be discussed later) but because it took place at a time when the private sector was financially fragile. The domestic and external debt overhang made the economy extremely sensitive to interest-rate increases and to devaluations. Eventually, both of these things occurred. This did serious harm to the private sector's equity position and thus led to a sharp adjustment in private spending. The domestic financial crises during these two episodes were similar in scale, in both cases being equivalent to a cost of 5–6 per cent of GDP. However, in the first, failings in terms of prudential regulation and banking practices were a relatively more important factor, while in the second the deterioration in the private sector's equity position was the determining element.

There are, of course, two additional factors underlying macroeconomic instability in the 1990s. The first is the political economy dynamics that makes it difficult to implement restrictive macroeconomic measures at times when external financing is in abundant supply. The second, which arose with the creation of an autonomous central bank under the 1991 constitution, is the difficulty of coordinating monetary and exchange-rate policy, which is managed by Banco de la República, with fiscal policy, which is the responsibility of the government.

Colombia's relatively successful record in terms of macroeconomic stability indicates that it was able to manage the first of these factors before this institutional duality arose, but doing so required a complex apparatus through which the authorities could intervene in the foreign-exchange and financial markets. This system of intervention was eliminated by the financial and foreign-exchange reforms of the 1990s, which coincided with the conversion of Colombia's central bank, Banco de la República, into an autonomous institution.

As in the case of trade reform, it can be argued that there was not really any authentic demand for change in this area, apart from the type of demand that was in keeping with the country's gradualist tradition. In fact, just a few years earlier, in 1987, when the exchange controls created by the well-known Decree-Law 444 of 1967 celebrated two decades, the evaluation of this instrument had been very positive.[15] The actual scope of the autonomy granted to Banco de la República under the constitution has also been a subject of debate. Some constituents contend that the explicit reference to 'coordination with general economic policy' in the article of the constitution that grants autonomy to Banco de la República is an express acknowledgement of the limits placed on its independence and, in some measure, even a subordination to the government, which determines general economic policy.[16] What is more, in response to the polemics surrounding Banco de la República's management of monetary and exchange-rate policy during its early years, in a 1999 ruling the Constitutional Court[17] determined that central bank autonomy is limited, since management of monetary, credit and exchange rate policy must be done subject to the way Congress legally regulates the constitutional provisions, and in coordination with the general economic policy that the national government determines. It also emphatically determined that, although curbing inflation was the central objective of exchange-rate policy, Banco de la República should also pay heed to the impact its policies have on the real economic variables, particularly on economic activity and employment.

It should be recalled, however, that as part of its tradition of control and gradualism, the Banco de la República itself maintained exchange controls when it established new foreign-exchange regulations in 1993 (the requirement that most foreign exchange had to be channelled through the regulated market and the possibility of returning to a fully regulated market if circumstances so warranted) and adopted a Chilean-style system for regulating capital flows. The reserve requirement for external borrowings was strictly applied during some periods – especially 1994–95 and 1997

– and proved to be fairly effective.[18] In any event, in line with the political economy dynamics mentioned earlier, the Colombian financial sector opposed measures aimed at constraining the credit boom and especially the lending caps established in 1994, whose effectiveness was limited.

The problems encountered in coordinating the policies of the country's two macroeconomic authorities were clearly reflected in the management of exchange-rate policy throughout the 1990s. Banco de la República's appreciation bias became evident in late 1991 and again when it revalued the currency band in December 1994. On the other hand, when the market exerted downward pressure on the peso in 1998–99, Banco de la República opted instead for a drastic increase in interest rates to defend the band and waited as long as it could before finally adjusting it. The costs of this decision were considerable. Given the sharp increase in domestic credit that occurred between 1991 and 1997, the interest-rate hikes undermined borrowers' financial standing and had a contractionary effect on the non-financial private sector to an extent not experienced before in the country.[19]

Banco de la República was afraid that an early devaluation would jeopardize the gains that had been made in reducing inflation, since these accomplishments had been quite precarious before the crisis broke out (1997 was the first year in which Banco de la República's inflation target had been met). The fear that a devaluation would fuel inflation may have been unfounded, since the rapid expansion of demand had abated in 1996 (see Figure 5.3), and, in the end, this actually did prove to be the case, but at the time most economists shared Banco de la República's views. Once the crisis erupted, it was also feared that if the exchange rate were freed, it would spiral out of control, as it had initially in various Asian countries in 1997. In Banco de la República's favour, it can be said that the real devaluation was carried out in an orderly fashion without disrupting the downward trend of inflation and without sacrificing its high level of international reserves.

The recession that was triggered, in large measure, by the deterioration of the private sector's equity position and the external financial crisis was followed by a slow recovery. The steep decrease in inflation and the strong performance of the flexible exchange-rate system introduced in 1999 allowed Banco de la República to abandon its procyclical policy bias that had marked it in its early years as an autonomous institution and adopt a countercyclical approach in the first years of the current decade.

5.3 AN ACTIVE SOCIAL POLICY AND INCONCLUSIVE SOCIAL RESULTS

If the move to open up the economy was the villain of the 1990s in the eyes of the economic reforms' critics, for their defenders the fundamental cause of all the economy's problems was the increase in public expenditure. The expansion of public spending was certainly rapid and disorderly, and it led to a crisis caused by the excessive growth of the state, which was reflected in fiscal disequilibria and the explosive growth of the public debt. These effects have continued to influence macroeconomic behaviour years after the first fiscal adjustment efforts were launched. This expansion also adversely affected coordination between the government and Banco de la República and, in the latter's view, justified, first, a policy stance in favour of revaluation and, later, a contractionary one.

An outright condemnation of the increase in the public debt, however, overlooks the fact that it was part of a strategy which blended economic modernization with a more active social policy and enhanced democracy. In point of fact, the decision to increase public expenditure adopted by the 1991 constitution was based on two different justifications, about which there was a broad consensus at the time: the need to address the serious social lags that marked the country then and continue to do so today; and the importance of consolidating democracy by delegating more functions and assigning more resources to departmental and municipal governments.

An Active Social Policy and the Upsizing of the State

Given the heated controversy surrounding the expansion of public expenditure, it is odd that there are such strikingly different calculations of the size of that increase during the 1990s. A report prepared by the National Planning Department (DNP 2000, Table 26) cites a figure for the increase in public spending, based on data from the National Department of Statistics (DANE), of slightly less than 6 percentage points of GDP between 1990 and 1998 (as the net result of higher spending in some sectors and lower spending in sectors where firms were privatized). IMF data give a somewhat higher figure for the increase in the primary expenditure of the consolidated public sector (10 percentage points of GDP during the same period, according to Table 5.1). The largest increases in central national government expenditure occurred between 1991 and 1996. The austerity measures adopted in 1997 halted the increase in the central government's primary expenditure, but the public sector's rate of expansion held steady that year owing to the growth of social security expenditure and spending by local governments. Social security was the only item of public expenditure in which steady growth continued to be seen in later years. In any case, the fiscal adjustment measures adopted since 1997 became permanent features of the economy, but they did not translate into a downsizing of the state. The sharp increase in debt service (and particularly that of the central national government) also has to be considered, however, since these payments have

Table 5.1 Public finances

	1990	1991	1992	1993	1994	1995	1996	1997	1998	1999	2000	2001	2002
Primary non-financial public-sector spending	17.3	17.6	18.7	20.7	22.2	23.9	26.6	28.8	27.5	29.5	27.3	28.0	29.2
Primary central government spending	8.3	8.8	9.6	10.7	11.4	12.1	14.9	14.4	15.3	16.8	15.4	16.0	17.1
Non-financial public-sector balance	–0.5	0.4	–0.1	0.2	0.1	–0.8	–2.4	–3.9	–4.6	–6.5	–3.5	–3.5	–4.4
Central government balance	–0.8	–0.2	–1.7	–0.7	–1.4	–2.2	–4.5	–3.4	–5.4	–7.4	–5.8	–5.8	–6.5
(Primary deficit)	0.3	1.0	–0.6	0.4	–0.2	–1.0	–3.4	–2.2	–3.5	–5.3	–2.8	–2.3	–3.1
(Interest payments)	1.1	1.2	1.0	1.1	1.2	1.2	1.1	1.2	1.9	2.1	3.0	3.5	3.4
Gross public-sector debt	45.2	39.8	33.7	33.8	27.2	29.2	30.3	34.2	39.2	49.4			
Net public-sector debt[1]								27.3	29.8	37.2	42.3	45.8	50.2

Note: [1] Excludes debt held by other public-sector entities.

Sources: Colombian Government and IMF.

climbed from slightly over 1 per cent of GDP in the years leading up to 1997 to over 3 per cent in recent years.

Interestingly enough, and contrary to what is often claimed in national debates, the extent of the increase in public expenditure during the 1990s was not very different from what it was in the late 1970s and early 1980s, when it rose by 9 percentage points of GDP, according to data published by DANE. The difference is that, in the 1990s, the increase was concentrated in government administration rather than in public-sector enterprises and, in particular, in the central national government's transfers to departmental and municipal governments for social spending and to the social security system for the payment of public-sector pensions, as well as in the rising self-financed expenditure of the public social security system. In addition, the increase in spending was financed much better in the 1990s than it was in the earlier episode. This is because a conscious effort was made to cover the upturn in expenditure through a series of tax reforms, an increase in social security contributions and a suitable management of the prices charged by public sector enterprises. Thus, although, as it turned out, the revenues generated by these efforts fell short of the mark, the Gaviria and Samper administrations did not set out to increase the fiscal deficit; their objective was to bring about an orderly upsizing of the state.[20] Consequently, it would be inaccurate to say that this episode was an instance of 'macroeconomic populism' in the sense that the term is used by Dornbusch and Edwards (1989).

Thanks to these increased revenues, the fiscal deficit was substantially lower prior to the 1998 crisis than it had been before the outbreak of the 1984 fiscal crisis. In the five years leading up to 1984, the cumulative fiscal deficit amounted to 23.5 per cent of GDP; during the three years prior to the 1998 crisis, it was a mere 7.1 per cent (and had been quite similar – 7.2 per cent – for the five years prior to the crisis). As a result, while public-sector borrowing climbed sharply prior to the crisis of the 1980s, the national public sector debt was much smaller in 1997 than it was in 1990 (see Table 5.1). Obviously, privatizations helped to curb the increase in the national public debt in the 1990s. Nevertheless, government transfers of the profits on Banco de la República's special exchange account had had a similar (or even greater) effect in the 1980s, as had the low interest rates that the government negotiated with the central bank as the holder of a large portion of the domestic public debt (a practice which came to an end when Banco de la República became autonomous).[21] In fact, in the more recent episode, the fiscal deficit and the public debt did not skyrocket until 1998–99, once the adjustment process was already in full swing and the upswing in expenditure had come to a halt. The recession's effects on public-sector revenues and the explosive growth of the debt service that was triggered by high interest rates and the devaluation, taken together, account for this outcome.

As foreseen in the constitution, the steeper increase in public expenditure was concentrated in the social sector. The National Planning Dcpartment data quoted earlier indicate that social spending had risen from 8.2 per cent of GDP in 1990 to 14.4 per cent by 1998, or by 6.2 percentage points, which is slightly higher than the figure for the increase in total public expenditure given by the same source. Colombia's upturn in social spending was actually one of the steepest in Latin America. As a result, the country went from having a level of social expenditure below the Latin American average in the early 1990s to having an above-average level (ECLAC 2001). There were, of course, increases in expenditure on other items as well, some of which turned out to be permanent (defence and the justice system) and others which did not (the road system, science and technology), but there were also cuts in some areas (sectors where privatizations were undertaken). It is interesting to note, however, that despite this increase in public spending, Colombia has continued to have one of the lowest levels of public-sector employment in Latin America (9.5 per cent of urban employment versus the regional average of 13.7 per cent in 1998). What is more, this ratio actually fell during the 1990s (from 11.6 per cent in 1991 to the 9.5 per cent mark posted for 1998) (ECLAC 2000b).

It has repeatedly been claimed that the increase in transfers to departmental and municipal governments was not accompanied by spending cuts by the central government in the corresponding areas. This allegation is unfounded. In the areas that have been decentralized, especially in education and health, the items of direct expenditure that became the responsibility of departmental and municipal governments were taken off the national government's budget altogether, although they are funded, in large part, by central government transfers. There are, however, specific items within these sectors that remain the responsibility of the national government (university education and national health campaigns, for example). What proved to be a much more serious problem were the wage hikes given to all public employees during the boom years in public-sector spending. This was a very disorderly process. It began with a very expensive 'wage realignment' in defence that was passed by Congress in 1992. This was accompanied by steep salary hikes in the judiciary and for senior posts in the executive and legislative branches. These increases created imbalances in the relative wage scales which, in turn, led to a chain reaction of wage demands in the rest of the public sector – particularly in education and health care – in subsequent years.

The increase in public social expenditure achieved its objective of broadening social service coverage. Educational (especially secondary education) coverage and health care coverage under the social security system expanded rapidly between 1993 and 1997, rising from 48 per cent to 61 per cent in the first case and from 23.9 per cent to 57.1 per cent in the second (see Table 5.2). The coverage of public utilities also increased and, as a result, the sector of the population with unmet basic needs shrank considerably, from 37.2 per cent to 25.9 per cent, which meant that as much progress was made in this respect in those four years as had been made in the eight years before that. Since this process coincided with a phase of economic growth, the human development index also improved markedly. Furthermore, as indicated in a recent DNP/UNDP study, although the progress made in terms of human development at the start of the 1990s was produced by improved economic conditions, the inroads made in 1993–97 were directly attributable to the country's social policy (DNP/UNDP 2003). In all of these cases, greater advances were made in rural areas that in urban zones.[22]

Table 5.2 Social indicators

	1985	1991	1993	1997	2001
Human development index					
Urban	0.763	0.774	0.779	0.811	0.794
Rural	0.567	0.658	0.654	0.69	0.698
Total	0.699	0.728	0.739	0.776	0.771
Combined scholarity	0.52	0.60	0.62	0.72	0.68
	1985	**1991**	**1993**	**1997**	**2000**
Unsatisfied basic needs					
Total	45.0		37.2	25.9	23.0
Urban	32.3		26.7	17.8	16.4
Rural	71.8		59.4	46.5	40.0
Net scholarity coverage					
Primary	61.6		75.2	83.5	83.6
Secondary	32.8		47.8	61.1	62.7
Income poverty line					
% of population below poverty line		53.8	51.7	50.3	59.8
Social security health coverage					
% of population insured			23.9	57.1	52.6

Sources: DNP and UNDP.

The targeting of social expenditure for the poorest segment of the population also improved thanks, among other reasons, to the concentration of spending increases in redistributive items, the allocation of transfers to municipalities where the proportion of unmet basic needs is the greatest and the implementation of the Beneficiary Identification System (SISBEN). This combination of increased social expenditure and improved targeting resulted in a significant redistribution of income (based on estimates of the income-equivalent of the social services received by households) (Sánchez and Núñez 1999). In fact, social expenditure's contribution to the effective income of the poorest 40 per cent of Colombia's population now exceeds the Latin American average (ECLAC 2000a, Chapter 7).

The Social Effects of Economic Change

When the 1990s began, trends in the labour market were favorable. Since 1987, the steep rise in open urban unemployment that had occurred in the first half of the 1980s had been reversed. In 1992, as trade liberalization was completed, the trend shifted again, reflecting the severe blow that it generated on agricultural and manufacturing employment. Although urban employment was buoyed for some time by a boom in other sectors (construction and some services), it weakened overall from 1992. The interruption of the upward trend in the labour participation rate prevented the sluggish employment situation from being reflected in unemployment for several years. In fact, the jobless rate for urban areas in 1993–95 averaged 8.7 per cent, the lowest since the start of the 1980s.

The deterioration in the labour market started to become evident in the mid-1990s, when the structural effects of economic openness on agricultural and manufacturing employment were compounded by a renewed upturn in the labour force participation rate and by the effects, first, of slackening aggregate domestic demand and, later, of an outright recession. Open urban unemployment jumped in 1996 as economic growth slowed and then began to shoot up even more steeply in 1998, rising to record-breaking figures for the country and to one of the highest levels of Latin America in 1999–2002. Informal employment had been declining quite rapidly until 1996, but that trend also came to a stop and was followed by a sharp upswing from 1998 on.

The progress that the country had been making in terms of income distribution since the 1970s – which was more rapid, in any event, during that decade than in the 1980s – came to an end in the late 1980s (that is, before economic reforms, as such) and gave way to a deterioration in income distribution during the 1990s.[23] The most important element in this process was the massive redistribution of income between the city and the countryside, with the big winners being high-income sectors in urban areas and the big losers being high-income sectors in rural areas. The moderate deterioration in income inequality coefficient that occurred at the national level during the decade was thus the net result of opposing trends in the urban and rural zones. In urban areas, distribution worsened significantly, primarily because of the increase in the relative labour income of the most skilled workers, while in rural areas, the crisis in agriculture brought about a 'downward levelling' of incomes which translated into a reduction in income concentration, but amidst an escalation in poverty.

A number of studies have linked the widening of the urban wage-income gap to a relative increase in the demand for skilled labour as a result of trade liberalization and technical change, higher wages for civil servants and a relative expansion of the private services sector, where, as in government, skilled jobs account for a large proportion of total employment. Even though income distribution worsened, poverty declined substantially in urban areas between 1991 and 1997 – from 47.3 per cent to 39.1 per cent, according to data from the National Planning Department, but this improvement was not matched in rural areas. Instead, as a result of the severe agrarian crisis of those years, rural income poverty increased. The reduction in urban poverty was associated not only with the economic growth but also with a sizeable decrease in the cost of the food basket, which obviously had opposite impacts on income levels in urban and rural areas.

The crisis that broke out in 1998 clearly led to setbacks in various areas (see Table 5.2). The expansion of social services coverage ceased both because of cutbacks in social public spending and as a consequence of the growing economic needs of the population (as, for example, when young people drop out of school in order to contribute to household income). As a result of this and the reduction in real income, Colombia's human development index declined in 1997–99 and showed no progress for the crisis period as a whole (up to 2001), in contrast with the strong improvement posted between 1991 and 1997.

The most obvious setback was the increase in the percentage of the urban population falling below the poverty line, which in just two years reversed the gains of the previous six. The quality of life index for the poorest 40 per cent of the population also worsened (DNP 2000). These trends were closely linked to the dramatic surge in open unemployment discussed above. The 1996 slump had added almost 400 000 persons to the ranks of the unemployed, while the 1998–99 recession caused unemployment figures to swell by another 1.4 million persons. Informal employment, which had run counter to the overall pattern in Latin America by shrinking during the boom years, soared during the recent crisis, thereby reversing the gains of an entire decade.

Viewed in terms of Colombia's history, these opposing results suggest that there are three prerequisites for sustained social progress: (a) an active social policy; (b) stable economic growth, and (c) a reduction in the dualism of production structures leading to a fall in the productivity and income gaps separating different activities and economic agents. Until the 1950s, Colombia had fulfilled only the second of these requirements, and social progress was slow; income distribution worsened and poverty remained at very high levels. In the 1960s, thanks to the consensus reached during the National Front (1958–74), state social services were expanded and the modernization of rural areas proceeded more rapidly, and urban/rural productivity differentials began to narrow as a result. The combination of these three factors accounts for the improvement in income distribution and the significant decline in poverty levels achieved in the 1970s. The inroads made in all of these areas were less noteworthy in the 1980s, and the improvement in social indicators consequently lost momentum. In the 1990s, social services coverage expanded a great deal, but the significant widening of the urban/rural divide, uneven progress in the modernization of urban areas (in which certain sectors and workers with university education have emerged as the main winners), and the crisis that began in 1998 combined to create a mixed social situation. These factors partially blocked the results expected from the political consensus that shaped the 1991 constitution, which had led to an active social policy.

The expectation that an active social policy would help reverse the escalation of conflict indicators was not borne out either, largely because the root causes of this conflict are of a different sort, as will be seen in the following section. Instead, and contrary to initial expectations, some of the social effects of economic changes may have actually exacerbated the country's violence indicators. Effects of this sort that may have had a particularly strong influence include the decline in rural income levels seen throughout the 1990s and the more widespread deterioration in social conditions that occurred during the recent lost half-decade.

5.4 VIOLENCE AND THE GOVERNANCE CRISIS

In addition to the uneven progress made in terms of social indicators, Colombia has been witnessing a deterioration in social cohesion and is facing difficulties in turning its political system into an effective mechanism for social articulation. The phenomena occurring in this and many other sociopolitical dimensions are, however, quite similar to those being experienced by other Latin American nations. In fact, in some of these spheres, Colombia has undeniable advantages over other countries of Latin

America, thanks to its strong republican tradition and the stability of its party system. Its extremely high levels of violence, on the other hand, are a more specifically Colombian problem. It is, in part, associated with long-standing conflicts, but in recent decades drug trafficking has had a stronger impact in this regard. Another factor is the country's entrenched tendency towards negotiation and the fragmentation of power, which is deeply rooted in its history of regional heterogeneity.

Colombia in the Light of Selected Comparative Indicators of Governance

Table 5.3 shows Colombia's relative position as measured by the World Bank's governance index (Kaufmann, Kraay and Zoido-Lobatón 2002). This information highlights two fundamental aspects. One is the serious deterioration of all these indicators in the last few years, with the sole exception of that for perceived corruption. This fact can be interpreted in various ways, but perhaps it is best to regard it, in the light of recent Colombian debates, as the outcome of a combination of the economic crisis, a feeling that the problem of public order is slipping out of control because of the failure of the Pastrana Arango (1998–2002) administration's peace initiative and the decline in the political influence wielded by the traditional parties (more in the case of the Conservative Party than in that of the Liberal Party, judging by voting patterns), coupled with the failure of other political forces to emerge that could offer stable alternatives to the country's traditional two-party structure.

Table 5.3 World Bank governance indicators

	1997–98	2000–01
Voice and accountability	46.5	35.5
Political instability and violence	9.1	7.5
Government effectiveness	52.9	40.5
Regulatory quality	58.8	44.9
Rule of law	22.4	22.0
Control of corruption	33.8	44.7

Sources: Kaufmann, Kraay and Zoido-Lobatón (2002).

Data provided by the Latinobarómetro survey, which are shown in Figure 5.5, back up this interpretation. Even in 1997, when the controversy about the illegal funding of President Samper's election campaign was in full swing, Colombia continued to exhibit levels of trust in democracy and satisfaction with its results that were similar to or higher than the Latin American average. The same can be said about Colombians' perception of their country's future. One peculiarity of Colombia in this regard was the disparity between the respondents' perception of their personal outlook for the future (much higher than the average for Latin America) and their feeling about their country's future prospects (similar to the results for other countries).[24] The worsening of these indicators, in some of which Colombia now ranks below the averages for Latin America, is therefore a very recent phenomenon. The 2003 survey results may show major changes in these areas, however, since President Andrés Pastrana Arango, whose popularity ratings in the polls were very low for the last three years of his administration, finished his term in office in 2002, and his successor, President Álvaro Uribe, is held in very high esteem.

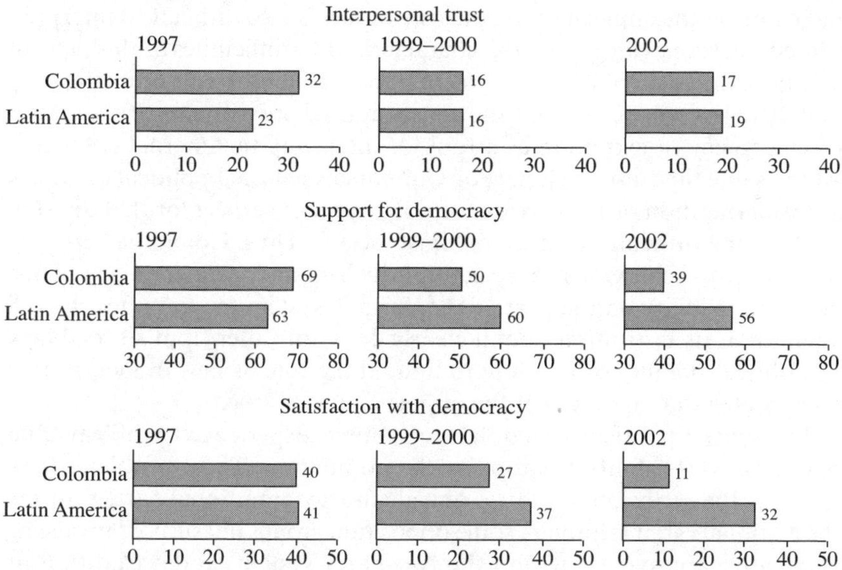

Source: Latinobarómetro.

Figure 5.5 Latinobarómetro comparative results

Table 5.3 also shows that even as far back as 1997–98, Colombia ranked poorly in the international indices for political stability and violence and for the maintenance of the rule of law. This was also the case for perceived corruption, but, as noted earlier, considerable progress has been made in this regard. It is difficult to interpret these data accurately because of the structural dualism of Colombian society. On the one hand, both indicators clearly reflect the extremely high levels of violence found in Colombia. They also show that in areas where the violence is intense, basic human rights violations are occurring. This includes violations of the most basic right of all – the right to life – which the state has been incapable of safeguarding. On the other hand, it is difficult to argue convincingly that violence in Colombia is a general problem of political instability or of a limited application of the rule of law.

By contrast, Colombia has excellent indices of political stability, and this includes the stability of its party system (Colombia and Uruguay are the only two countries that have maintained the same party system that they had in the nineteenth century), its constitutional framework, its strong electoral tradition and elections-based system of alternation in power (which was interrupted for a total of only five years during the twentieth century).[25] The indicator on the application of the rule of law is also difficult to interpret. The conflict zones are, of course, characterized by difficulties of this type. In addition, the country's judicial system suffers from problems of inefficiency and there is a tendency to use the constitutional provision regarding states of emergency or exception as a tool for managing the internal conflict.[26] At the same time, however, part of Colombia's national political culture is a strong tradition of the division of power and of respect for that division even during difficult political circumstances.[27] Thus, Colombia certainly has problems with violence, structural dualism and, as a corollary of the latter, an inability on the part of the 'formal' system to guarantee the full strength of its institutions, but it clearly does not suffer from a broad lack of political stability or a failure to uphold the rule of law. In fact, from a comparative standpoint, just the opposite may be true.

The formal political system has, of course, experienced problems that have limited its ability to mobilize the population. These problems have included the exclusion of groups outside the two traditional parties during the National Front (although some opposition groups did succeed in voicing alternative approaches within the two-party system) and a tradition of power sharing between the two parties that arose during that period and survived in various forms after the Front's disappearance. This created a political system in which formal opposition has often been non-existent or has surfaced only in preparation for the formation of two-party (or now, perhaps, broader) governing alliances that include dissenting groups. In addition, the absence of a broader spectrum of political competition has curbed certain forms of political mobilization (programmatic and ideological confrontations) and maximized others (patronage). This problem may have grown more serious in the 1990s because of the centrifugal forces exerted on the traditional parties as a consequence of electoral rules and practices that create powerful incentives for individual rather than party-based congressional representation ('electoral microenterprises', to use the Colombian expression).

Although, judging from their results, the attempts made in Colombia to remedy these problems through political reform have certainly fallen short of the mark, they have been undertaken in earnest and have been more ambitious than those seen in other Latin American countries, especially because they have built upon a much sturdier republican tradition. Manifestations of the nation's political institutional soundness and, hence, of its political stability and the applicability of the rule of law include: the revitalization of local politics and affairs since the mid-1980s; the robust balance of power, which the 1991 constitution reinforced, including more control by the Constitutional Court over the use of states of emergency; the creation of new machinery for political participation within the framework of participatory democracy (a deeply rooted concept in the country's political vocabulary) as a means of complementing its representative democracy; the creation of a powerful constitutional instrument – the right of *amparo* (refuge) – to safeguard basic human rights; the judicial system's demonstrated ability to initiate proceedings to combat political corruption and to bring them to completion; and the country's success in dealing with the political turbulence of the 1990s without disrupting its institutional structure.

The formal system's inability to safeguard its institutions has, of course, taken a heavy toll. What is more, at certain points in time and certain locations, some segments of the formal system have, either implicitly or explicitly, forged alliances with segments of the informal system which have proven to be extremely costly. The massacre of leaders of the Patriotic Union[28] – the group formed by the Revolutionary Armed Forces of Colombia (usually known by the Spanish-language acronym, FARC) to prepare the way for its re-entry into politics during the peace negotiations with the Betancur Administration (1982–86) – perpetrated by paramilitary groups[29] has not only impaired the country's democracy but has also reduced the chances of holding successful negotiations with the major guerrilla group in the country. The use of assassinations as a means of suppressing the expression of certain types of political views also impacted other political parties. This tactic reached its height during the 1990 presidential campaign, when three candidates for president (including Luis Carlos Galán, who would probably have won the election) were assassinated and attempts were made on the lives of various other political leaders, including a future president (Ernesto Samper). The murder of numerous union leaders has greatly weakened this form of social mobilization and organization. Alliances formed by segments of the economic, political and military power structure with drug traffickers and paramilitary groups have left a trail of weakened institutions and human rights violations in their wake. These processes have also tarnished the country's international image. Nonetheless, although their response was delayed somewhat, formal institutions have moved to suppress these alliances and illicit activities and have staunchly upheld their commitment to human rights, even though, unfortunately, their efforts have thus far not had the hoped-for results.

In addition to the foregoing considerations, it should be noted that some well-known interpretations of the situation in Colombia have characterized the country's main problem as being a lack of civic awareness, which is in turn an outgrowth of a private rationale's predominance over a public rationale.[30] This is no doubt true, and it points to the absence and, hence, the importance of constructing a soundly based public ethic. One of the most pernicious symptoms of this syndrome is mistrust of others. The Latinobarómetro data summarized in Figure 5.5 indicate, however, that distrust of others – and, perhaps, the broader problem posed by the predominance of a private rationale – is no more marked in Colombia than it is in other Latin American countries.

Violence and the Drug Trade

The image of Colombia as having a long history of violence frequently appears in analytical studies on the country, but a number of prominent historical essays[31] have cast some doubt on the accuracy of this depiction. There has, indeed, been recurrent violence, but its nature and intensity have varied significantly over time, and its historical continuity is therefore debatable. The history of the nineteenth century was marked by the difficult task of building a nation out of a disconnected set of regions. This process triggered nine national civil wars and 50 or so regional armed conflicts. However, with the exception of the last of the civil wars – known as the 'War of a Thousand Days' (1899–1902) – these wars were limited in scope, with uprisings overlapping with armistices and elections in what was, in a sense, a collection of alternative and essentially political mechanisms for negotiation in the presence of a chronically weak state.[32] After the outbreak of the War of a Thousand Days and the national trauma caused by the subsequent secession of Panama (1903), the country's regional heterogeneity came to serve as the cornerstone for a strong democratic tradition and – apart from the period during which 'The Violence' broke with that tradition – a civil one as well. Thus, throughout the twentieth century, Colombian democracy was the main institutional mechanism for negotiations among the regional élites represented in the two traditional political parties, Congress and the Cabinet.

The Violence was, of course, the glaring exception to this rule. The country underwent a severe institutional crisis between 1948 and 1957 in which the milestone events were the assassination of the Liberal Party leader, Jorge Eliécer Gaitán, in 1948; the Liberal Party's abstention from the 1950 elections on the grounds that sufficient guarantees were lacking; and the overthrow of President Laureano Gómez in 1953 and of General Gustavo Rojas Pinilla in 1957. The undeclared civil war between the two traditional political parties and its disintegration into what came to be known as 'bandolerismo' immersed the country in levels of violence it had never experienced before except during the War of a Thousand Days. The 1957 plebiscite, which led to the formation of the National Front (1958–74), signalled Colombia's return to its civil tradition. The violence then abated, although it remained at higher levels than those that had existed in the four decades of peace that preceded The Violence.[33]

The Violence brought to light the persistence of other forms of conflict that were very closely linked to regional processes. The most intense conflicts of this sort were land disputes along the agricultural frontier. The occurrence of frequent conflicts in areas where new land is being placed under cultivation is not a characteristic specific to Colombia. What is more specifically Colombian is the existence of an open frontier in many regions, and even in the heartland of the country, as well as the limited presence of the state and military forces in those zones. Given Colombia's complex geography, it is possible for frontier zones to exist just kilometres away from major urban centres. The highly conflictive nature of Colombia's agricultural frontier zones throughout the nineteenth century and in the early decades of the twentieth has been documented in various studies.[34] In the 1930s and again in the 1960s and in the final two decades of the twentieth century, the Colombian state responded to these rural disputes by instituting three agrarian reform programmes. These programmes were notable for their limited scope and lack of continuity, the importance they placed on handing over state land rather than redistributing existing farmland, and their close links to efforts to pacify rural areas. This last feature was particularly noticeable in the third agrarian reform initiative, which began with the National Rehabilitation Plan in the 1980s and then carried over into the 1990s as a formal agrarian reform process.[35]

The map of violence in Colombia since the 1980s has, however, been much more complex due to the presence of shifting combinations of these frontier-zone conflicts with long-standing agrarian disputes (the indigenous population's struggle for land in some regions of the country) and an interwoven maze of guerrilla movements, compounded by the more recent, devastating effects of the drug trade.[36] Some guerrilla movements (FARC, in particular) are a direct outgrowth of these long-standing agrarian disputes, and some of them have survived for decades thanks to the remoteness of many of the country's rural areas, although at times they have certainly come close to annihilation. It should be noted that, with the partial exception of M-19 before its integration into civil affairs in 1990, the country's guerrilla movements have generally been incapable of developing any sizeable urban front apart from a few redoubts manned by radical students and labour unions.

Within this complex framework, however, there is consensus as to the crucial role played by drug trafficking and, in particular, the cocaine trade in recent patterns of violence. The steep increase in violence during the 1980s (see Figure 5.6) coincided with the establishment of the large-scale drug cartels involved in the cocaine trade.[37] The country's location along the transit route between cocaine-producing South American countries and the principal market for cocaine (the United States), coupled with such factors as the existence of a long agrarian frontier over which the state exercises very limited control and an 'informal' sector involved in contraband trade, explain how these illegal business dealings developed so quickly in Colombia. The 1980s boom in the cocaine trade followed a short-lived upsurge in marihuana cultivation and trafficking in the 1970s and was based on the processing of coca paste brought in from Bolivia and Peru, since the cultivation of coca plants was not a traditional farming activity in Colombia. This crop began to increase in the 1980s, however,

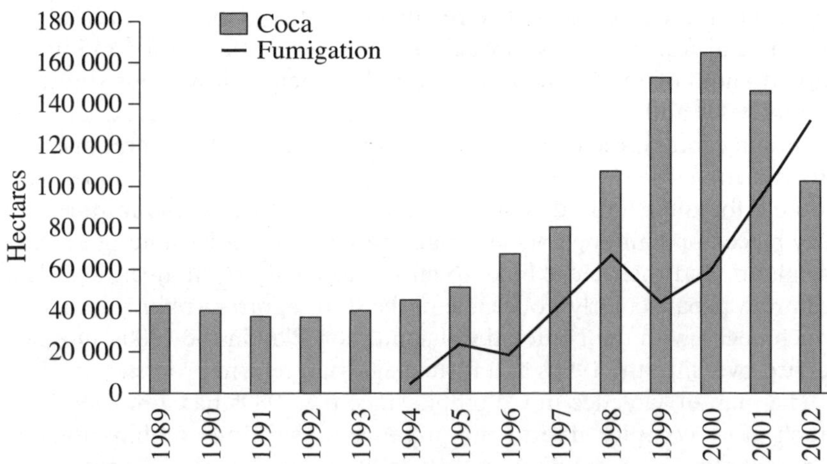

Source: United Nations Office on Drugs and Crime (UNODC), Coca survey for 2002, Bogotá, DC.

Figure 5.6 Coca production area vs sprayed area

and then underwent an extremely rapid expansion in the 1990s as coca farming was successfully reppressed in Bolivia and Peru (see Figure 5.7). The existence of illegal networks already in operation also paved the way for the introduction of poppy cultivation in the 1990s, but the scale of this crop has been limited.

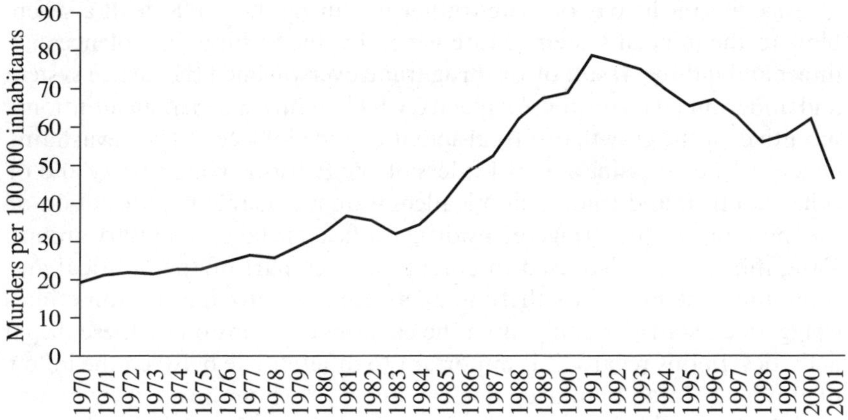

Source: National Police.

Figure 5.7 Murder rate

The drug trade has not only infiltrated the pattern of confrontations found along the agrarian frontier, but has also caused the conflict to spread to what had been fairly peaceful parts of the countryside and has sparked urban violence of the type associated with drug wars and the recruitment of these illegal groups' henchmen.[38] It has also played a central role in the creation and financing of paramilitary organizations. Their coexistence with guerrilla groups in various locations around the country prompted the latter to finance their operations by levying taxes on the drug trade and eventually going into business for themselves, although the extent of their involvement continues to be a subject of debate. More generally, it has helped, both directly and indirectly, to finance the main forms of violence present in Colombia and has had a direct hand in the formation of criminal groups. The practices of these groups have also been a decisive factor in the intensification of all the various forms of violence. The most significant manifestation of this deterioration is the frequency of massacres and kidnappings and the terrorization of the civil population by violent bands or gangs, which is part of the reason for the mass displacement of population groups within the country. Colombia accounts for a large percentage of these problems at the international level. One of the results of the interaction between drug trafficking and acts of violence is the increasing importance, within the context of this conflict, of the possession of control over territories where coca is grown and processed, given the decisive role that such control plays in providing funds for the armed groups.

The corruption fueled by the drug trade and the murder of honest judges by assassins in the pay of drug traffickers during the 1980s dealt a severe blow to the judicial system. More generally, the upsurge in violence as a direct and indirect result of the drug trade overwhelmed the justice system and undermined its response capacity, which in turn acted as an additional incentive for the growth of illegal activities and violence.[39] The devastating effects of the assassination of leaders of the Patriotic Union party and of other political and trade union leaders were a concrete manifestation of the spiraling violence triggered by drug traffickers and paramilitary groups. Drug money was also used to corrupt a large part of the political and economic system. All of these impacts greatly outweigh the sometimes exaggerated statistics concerning the economic dimension of these illegal activities. In this regard, it is important to differentiate between the inflow of funds to Colombian drug dealers, many of whom invest their money outside the country, and the effective inflow of resources brought into the country by these illegal activities, which, according to the best estimates available, may have peaked at 4 to 6 per cent of GDP in the mid-1980s but have generally hovered around 2 to 3 per cent of GDP over the past two decades.[40]

By comparison to the drug trade's impact on the levels of violence, the effects of traditional forms of rural violence and the sharp social inequality characteristic of the country have been less significant. Colombia does, of course, have severe problems with regard to poor income distribution and high poverty levels, and these problems are particularly serious in rural sectors, but these are difficulties that they share with other Latin American countries.[41] The intensification of violence in the 1980s cannot be accounted for by a deterioration of these variables, since they actually improved during those years (Montenegro and Posada 2001). By the same token, an explanation for the considerable decline in the homicide rate registered in the 1990s (see Figure 5.7) cannot be derived from the trends in social indicators, since they were quite mixed, with some improving while others worsened (see section 5.3). In fact, the disbanding of the most violent drug cartel of them all, the Medellín cartel, may be one of the most important reasons for that decrease, given the steep reduction in that indicator posted by Antioquia. In any case, the increase in rural poverty during the 1990s and the upward trend in urban poverty seen during the most recent economic crisis may have set the scene for the expansion of coca cultivation, as well as for common delinquency. More generally, the possibility cannot be ruled out that a combined impact may have been generated by the convergence of the more traditional sorts of social problems with the explosive conditions typical of a country subject to so many different manifestations of violence. In addition, it is important to bear in mind that the improvement in the homicide rate shown in Figure 5.7 has not been mirrored by other indicators of violence, such as the frequency of massacres and kidnappings.

The extensive literature on the subject indicates that violence increases in different parts of the territory when violent agents of drug traffickers or members of paramilitary or guerrilla groups are present in those locations. The presence of such agents is, in turn, associated with access to wealth-generating assets (the drug trade itself, petroleum, emeralds). Social factors of a more traditional sort are also a factor, however. Such factors include an uneven distribution of economic opportunities (measured by inequalities in the quality of life index for the inhabitants of a given area), low educational levels and low rates of political participation.[42]

Apart from the specific costs of the drug trade, acts of violence have also taken a heavy toll. Economic costs include the loss of human capital, added public and private expenditure on security and the distortions generated by illicit transfers of wealth, either by direct means (via kidnappings and extortion) or through indirect channels (for example, via the concentration of rural property in the hands of drug traffickers). Detailed calculations indicate that the net annual costs are around 3 per cent of GDP and the gross costs (net costs plus transfers of wealth) about 4 per cent of GDP.[43] These costs have no doubt impaired economic growth. The strongest argument on this point has been made by Cárdenas (2002), who contends that the increase in violence in the 1980s interrupted the overall rise in productivity and thus slowed the economy's growth. Expressed in these terms, the argument does not seem very convincing, since there are other purely economic explanations for this slowdown and for the economy's poor performance during the 1990s. What is more, Colombia's experiences during that period are fairly similar to those of other Latin American countries in which violence has not been so much of a problem (see sections 5.2 and 5.3). This appears to indicate that, although violence may have influenced economic trends, in the final analysis is has simply reinforced (to an undetermined extent) trends for which an economic explanation exists.

The Nature of the Conflict, the Propensity to Negotiate and the Fragmentation of Power

Analyses of the origin and characteristics of the internal conflict in Colombia have generated an interesting body of literature on its nature, which defies classification in any of the internationally established categories for describing conflicts. One of the points made most often in this connection concerns the inappropriateness of describing it as a 'civil war', given the absence of a large-scale collective division into two bands. Instead, Colombia's internal conflict is characterized by the predominance of a few violent agents or bands that have the capacity to threaten the 'formal' system's hegemony. The citizenry does not identify with those agents. On the contrary, the populace feels threatened and defenceless in the face of violent groups' systematic use of terror to intimidate the civil population. This has prompted a prominent French student of the situation in Colombia to describe the conflict as a 'war against society' (Pécaut 2001) and has moved another scholar to reject not only the concept of 'civil war' but also to rule out 'generalized violence' as a suitable description of the conflict in the country (Posada Carbó 2001b). One of the essential elements in these analyses is an awareness of the fact that, although the state has been threatened and is incapable of guaranteeing social order, it nonetheless does maintain and exercise its legitimacy. Hence, the concept of a 'regime breakdown' cannot be properly applied to Colombia either.

In view of this situation, the 'formal' system's propensity to avoid open confrontation and to rely instead on dialogue and negotiation is somewhat surprising. These traits were reflected in the peace initiatives launched by five presidents, starting with the Betancur administration (1982–86) and ending with the Pastrana Arango administration (1998–2002). These initiatives enjoyed the support of the citizenry, as demonstrated by opinion polls taken at the time, which indicate that a majority of the population systematically preferred negotiation to conflict during the 1980s and 1990s. In fact, Álvaro Uribe is the only president to have achieved a resounding electoral victory and to have maintained his popularity based on a confrontational platform. This, however, can be accounted for by the conspicuous failure of the Pastrana Arango administration's peace initiative. The Turbay administration (1978–82) also adopted a confrontational stance at an earlier stage in the country's contemporary history, when violence had not reached its current proportions. He, however, encountered staunch opposition. Late in his presidency, this opposition led him to design the first peace initiative and then paved the way for the electoral victory of Belisario Betancur, one of whose main campaign promises was to undertake an ambitious effort to make peace with armed groups.

This strategy of offering non-confrontational formulas has been used even in the case of the drug trade.[44] Assassinations of important political leaders drove both President Betancur (1982–86) and President Barco (1986–90) to outright confrontation, but these reactions were invariably part of a cycle which regularly involved a renewed search for alternatives to repression. The most significant of these formulas was the policy of having drug traffickers agree to stand trial in exchange for reduced sentences (and even special privileges while in prison) implemented by the Gaviria administration (1990–94). The provision contained in the 1991 constitution which prohibits the extradition of Colombian nationals was partly a reflection of the widespread intimidation by violence perpetrated by drug traffickers, but it was also partly due to the population's rejection of the idea of using extradition as a means of suppressing the drug trade. It was not until the Samper administration (1994–98) that a sustained, frontal assault was launched against this illegal activity. This effort took the form of the reintroduction of extradition, the curtailment of the policy regarding the use of incentives for standing trial and the increasingly intensive spraying of illegal crops. As shown in Figure 5.6, this policy and the disbanding of the major cartels in the mid-1990s did not really begin to bear fruit in terms of the reduction of illicit crops until 2001 and especially 2002 (UNDCP 2003). This policy of repression has garnered support from the international community and particularly the United States, even during the years of confrontation with the Samper administration. The administration of President Pastrana Arango then formalized the 'Plan Colombia'. After 11 September 2001, this plan increasingly became part of the international offensive against terrorist groups, which now include all the irregular armed groups in Colombia.

This propensity to negotiate is surprising, given the limited success attained by various administrations in this area. The most significant achievements were those of the Barco administration, which succeeded in negotiating the demobilization of two major guerrilla groups – the M-19 and the Popular Liberation Army (ELP) – along with two smaller movements – the Quintin Lame and the Corriente de Renovación Socialista. The reasons for this success have to do with other factors, in addition to Colombia's civil tradition, which, as noted above, until quite recently has been reflected in majority support for negotiation rather than confrontation. This tradition has also, until quite recently, been reflected in a rejection of the idea of having a strong national army. The opposition to this idea dates back to the disputes that arose in the early years of the republic, when the civilist band won out over the militarists, represented by a large number of mainly Venezuelan generals who had taken part in the fight for independence. As a matter of fact, the divergence of Colombia's and Venezuela's historical paths can be attributed to the way in which these initial disputes were resolved. As has been noted, in the nineteenth century this was no obstacle for Colombians wishing to take recourse to uprisings as a means of pursuing political negotiations with a chronically weak national government. The frailty of the state and of its armed forces in many parts of the nation's territory has been a constant feature of the national scene up to and including the present and has facilitated the spread of violence.

Many authors have interpreted this tendency as a sign that the formation of the Colombian nation is not yet complete. While this may be the case, it is equally true that it is a reflection of the Colombian tradition of fragmented power. This phenomenon is rooted in the country's regional heterogeneity, which, ever since the birth of the republic, has led to a rejection of any sort of centralized hegemony or strong national power, even after the promulgation of the constitution of 1886, which spelled the demise of the nineteenth century's federalism. Eventually, this characteristic came to be one of the strongest pillars of the country's democratic tradition. Indeed, democracy has historically been the system of government used in Colombia to permit its regional élites to negotiate with one another. This is the source of its historical fortitude, but it is also the origin of Colombia's tradition of maintaining a weak state.

The powerful centrifugal forces to which the traditional political parties have been exposed in the past decade and the proliferation of new movements which have not managed to form strong, nationwide organizations are more recent expressions of this revealed preference for a fragmented power structure. Another such manifestation is the further fragmentation of power engendered by the 1991 constitution, which provides for more checks and balances of national powers, including some new actors (the Constitutional Court, Banco de la República, the National Television Commission), together with a radical system of decentralized revenue sharing that is similar to systems used in countries of the region having a strong federal tradition (Argentina and Brazil) and that is broader in scope than the systems used by some other federal republics (Mexico and Venezuela).

As new social movements and actors have emerged, the tendency to avoid the formation of a central authority in any sector (manual workers, *campesinos*, civic organizations or even business associations) has remained strong. Furthermore, because of the reproduction of these structures, the violent conflicts that have arisen have continued to be essentially local in nature. This has helped avert the disintegration of the 'formal' system's national structures, but many times (including the present) it has also resulted in a perception of chaos owing to the existence of so many different pockets of disorder. This was an even greater problem in cases where traditional regional power structures' intolerance of new social forces erupted into local conflicts that were so fierce that the adversaries were sometimes annihilated. Just as FARC has its origins in local conflicts, the history of paramilitarism in recent decades and even the destruction of the Patriotic Union in the 1980s reflect processes that have probably been more of a summation of local conflicts than a coordinated nationwide offensive. Even the classic era of violence corresponded, in large part, to conflicts of this sort.

This interpretation of the situation indicates that any solution for the current crisis must necessarily entail a consolidation of democracy that will provide broader opportunities for participation by a wide range of local stakeholders. Today, as in the past, the country's diversity is an expression of its deeply rooted democratic forces. The expansion of democratic channels must, however, be coupled with the development of effective governance, whose core components must be consensus building, respect for differences, an effective justice system capable of overcoming intolerance, and a legitimate monopoly of force.

NOTES

* This chapter was originally prepared for the Project on Economic Policy in the Andean Countries being executed by the Inter American Dialogue and ECLAC with funding from the Ford Foundation. I am grateful to Juan Carlos Ramírez, Joshua Mitroti and María Angela Parra for the collaboration in the preparation of this material, and to Genaro Arriagada, Andrés Solimano and Anthony Tillet for the comments concerning an earlier version of it.

1. In this chapter we will follow the Colombian tendency to use the term 'opening of the economy' (*apertura económica*) to refer to reforms aimed at liberalizing economic activities.
2. See, for example, Dornbusch and Fischer (1992).
3. The Development Plan issued by the Gaviria Administration (see DNP 1991) stated that it was necessary to open up the economy in order to counteract the trend towards economic stagnation. This statement gave rise to a great deal of controversy in the country. A number of authors (including the author of this chapter) questioned the validity of that statement. See, in this regard, the essays presented in Lora (1991).
4. These observations and those made in the following paragraphs are based on various essays on economic history written by this author. See, for example, Ocampo (1994).
5. Export incentives were first created in the late 1950s and early 1960s (the Vallejo Plan in 1957, the establishment of the first tax incentives in 1960 and the introduction of the first preferential credit mechanisms in 1963). Decree-Law 444 of 1967 refined these incentives and supplemented them with the introduction of a crawling peg.
6. For a historical account of these attempts at trade liberalization, see Garay (1991) and Ocampo (1990).
7. For an interesting comparison of changes in Colombian and international production patterns, see Syrquin (1987).
8. See Cepeda Ulloa (1994), who examines the reform package as a whole, and Ocampo (1993) on the more specific topic of trade reform.
9. The main, and most influential, critic of this approach has been Eduardo Sarmiento Palacio. See Sarmiento Palacio (1996 and 1998).
10. See Jaramillo (1998) and Ocampo and Perry (1995).
11. See, in this respect, the essays included in Montenegro (1997).
12. For an analysis of what occurred during those years, see Lora and Ocampo (1986).
13. There is a wealth of literature on this last point. See, among others, Banco de la República (1999), Carrasquilla (1990), Echeverry (2002) and Villar and Rincón (2003).
14. See Ocampo and Tovar (1999 and 2003).
15. See, for example, Fernández (1987).

16. See Palacio Rudas (1995). This interpretation differs from others presented in Steiner (1995).
17. Corte Constitucional, Sentencia C-481/99.
18. See references in note 14 and Villar and Rincón (2003). A less favourable assessment of the effects of the reserve requirement can be found in Cárdenas and Steiner (2000).
19. A few simple calculations can be used to corroborate these statements. Whereas the real interest paid to the national financial system during the 1982–88 adjustment amounted to 3.1 per cent of GDP per year, in 1998–99 the figure was 6.4 per cent. Just the opposite occurred in the case of exchange losses, even though the external debt was larger in the 1990s. Cumulative exchange losses totalled 4.6 per cent of GDP in 1984–86 versus 2.7 per cent in 1997–99. The most prominent critic of this procyclical approach to the management of monetary and exchange-rate policy has been Javier Fernández, who has aired his opinions in his weekly publication *Prospectiva económica y financiera*. See, in particular, Fernández (2000).
20. This is made clear by the development plans of these two Administrations (DNP 1991, 1995). The Samper administration aimed at maintaining more or less balanced consolidated public accounts by covering large deficits of the central government with surpluses generated by the rest of the public sector, including both public-sector enterprises and the social security system.
21. For a detailed analysis of these matters and of the problems regarding the comparability of the fiscal deficit figures, see Ocampo (1997).
22. See DNP/PNUD (2000 and 2003) and DNP (2000).
23. Longer-term income distribution trends are discussed in Londoño (1995). More recent trends are analysed in Ocampo et al. (1998 and 2000) and in Sánchez and Núñez (1999).
24. Colombia shares this peculiarity with Brazil. See, in this regard, Latinobarómetro (2000).
25. See Posada's Carbó's excellent essay (2001a) on this subject, as well as Solimano's comparative analysis of the Andean countries (2003).
26. See, inter alia, García and Uprimny (1999).
27. See the essay by Posada Carbó cited above (2001a).
28. Between 1985 and 1992, the Ombudsman's Office recorded 717 homicides of members of the Patriotic Union, including two presidential candidates, four members of Congress and more than 50 people who had been elected to various public offices.
29. This analysis will continue the convention of using the term 'paramilitary' to refer to right-wing armed groups. It should be noted, however, that the connotation of 'paramilitary' in Colombia is very different from what it is in other Latin American countries where there has been a much closer connection between military and paramilitary groups. In Colombia, it might be more accurate to call these groups 'right-wing guerrillas'.
30. Gómez Buendía (1999). In a similar formulation, this trait has been described as 'rent seeking' or, in other words, the pursuance of individual privileges at the expense of the collective (Garay 1999). A very similar argument is made by Kalmanovitz (2001).
31. These works include the extraordinary essay written by the British historian, Malcom Deas (1995), which begins with a statement that to some extent provides a synthesis of his book: 'Colombia has been, at times, a violent country.'
32. See, in this connection, Sánchez (1991, Chapter 2). For a discussion of mortality rates during these wars and throughout the twentieth century, see Gaitán Daza (1995).
33. See Gaitán Daza (1995).
34. See, in particular, LeGrand (1988).
35. For an overview of these agrarian reform efforts, see Ocampo (1994).
36. The following discussion cannot do justice to the complex issue of violence in Colombia. See, from among the works making up the voluminous literature on the subject in Colombia, the above-cited essays by Deas (1995), Gaitán Daza (1995) and Sánchez (1991); the studies included in Sánchez and Peñaranda (1986), Camacho Guizado and Leal Buitrago (1999) and Deas and Llorente (1999); the report issued by the Comisión de Estudos sobre la Violencia (1987), Pizarro (1996), Montenegro and Posada (2001),

Pécaut (2001) and Palacios and Safford (2002, chapter XV). The study prepared by Reyes and Bejarano (1988) includes maps of violent incidents which illustrate the complex confluence of drug traffickers, guerrilla battles and long-standing disputes about agrarian issues and the rights of indigenous groups.

37. For the history of drug trafficking in Colombia, see Thoumi (1994) and Rocha (2000).
38. This kind of problem, which has been particularly serious in Medellín, has been documented in all its crudity by Salazar (1990).
39. See Montenegro and Posada (2001) and Rubio (1999).
40. On this last point, see Gómez Restrepo (1988), Gómez Restrepo and Santa María (1994) and Rocha (2000). DANE estimates put the coca crop's contribution to the portion of GDP corresponding to the agricultural sector at around 1.25 per cent of GDP in 1994–2002, at a high of 1.48 per cent for 1999 and at 0.89 per cent for 2002.
41. In terms of income concentration, Colombia's level of inequality is exceeded only by Brazil, but it is fairly similar to those found in Bolivia, Chile, Guatemala, Honduras, Nicaragua and Panama, while inequality levels in Argentina and Venezuela are fast approaching those of the group of countries with extremely poor income distribution patterns (ECLAC 2001).
42. See, among many other studies, DNP/PNUD (2000), Montenegro and Posada (2001), Sánchez et al. (2002) and Sarmiento Gómez (1999).
43. See Trujillo and Badel (1997).
44. Regarding the 'negotiations' with drug traffickers, see the interesting essay by Orozco (1990).

REFERENCES

Banco de la República (1999), *Informe de la Junta Directiva al Congreso de la República*, Bogotá, July.

Camacho Guizado, A. and F. Leal Buitrago (comps) (1999), *Armar la paz es desarmar la guerra: herramientas para lograr la paz*, Bogotá: CEREC/IEPRI/FESCOL, Giro Editores.

Cárdenas, M. (2002), 'Economic growth in Colombia: a reversal of "fortune"?', Center for International Development, Harvard University, mimeo, March.

Cárdenas, M. and R. Steiner (2000), 'Private capital flows in Colombia', in Felipe Larraín (ed.), *Capital Flows, Capital Controls, and Currency Crises: Latin America in the 1990s*, Ann Arbor, Michigan: University of Michigan Press.

Carrasquilla, A. (1999), *Estabilidad y gradualismo: ensayos sobre economía colombiana*, Bogotá: Banco de la República/Tercer Mundo Editores.

Cepeda Ulloa, F. (1994), *Dirección política de la reforma económica en Colombia*, Bogotá: Fonade/DNP and Tercer Mundo Editores.

Comisión de Estudios sobre la Violencia (1987), *Colombia: Violencia y Democracia*, Bogotá: Universidad Nacional de Colombia.

Deas, M. (1995), 'Canjes violentos: reflexiones sobre la violencia política en Colombia', in Malcolm Deas and Fernando Gaitán Daza (eds), *Dos ensayos especulativos sobre la violencia en Colombia*, Bogotá: Fonade/DNP and Tercer Mundo Editores.

Deas, M. and María V. Llorente (comps) (1999), *Reconocer la guerra para construir la paz*, Bogotá: CEREC/Ediciones Uniandes/Editorial Norma.

DNP (Departamento Nacional de Planeación) (1991), *La revolución pacífica*, Bogotá.

DNP (Departamento Nacional de Planeación) (1995), *El Salto Social, Plan Nacional de Desarrollo 1994–1998*, Bogotá.

DNP (Departamento Nacional de Planeación) (2000), *Coyuntura económica e indicadores sociales*, Boletín no. 26, SISD, Bogotá, July.

DNP (Departamento Nacional de Planeación) y PNUD (Programa de las Naciones Unidas para el Desarrollo) (2000), *Informe de desarrollo humano para Colombia 1999*, Bogotá: Tercer Mundo Editores, May.

DNP (Departamento Nacional de Planeación) y PNUD (Programa de las Naciones Unidas para el Desarrollo) (2003), *Diez años de desarrollo humano en Colombia*, Bogotá: Alfaomega, January.

Dornbusch, R. and S. Edwards (1989), *Economic Crises and the Macroeconomics of Populism in Latin America: Lessons from Chile and Peru*, Washington, DC: NBER.

Dornbusch, R. and S. Fischer (1992), 'La inflación moderada', *Economía Mexicana*, Nueva Epoca, **1**(1), January–June.

Echeverry, J.C. (2002), *Las claves del futuro: economía y conflicto en Colombia*, Bogotá: Editorial Oveja Negra.

ECLAC (Economic Commission for Latin America and the Caribbean) (2000a), *Equidad, Desarrollo y Ciudadanía*, Santiago de Chile.

ECLAC (Economic Commission for Latin America and the Caribbean) (2000b), *Panorama social de América Latina, 1999–2000*, Santiago de Chile.

ECLAC (Economic Commission for Latin America and the Caribbean) (2001), *Panorama social de América Latina, 2000–2001*, Santiago de Chile.

Fernández, J. (1987), 'Justificación económica del Estatuto Cambiario Colombiano', in *Colombia: 20 años del régimen de cambios y de comercio exterior*, Vol. 2, Bogotá: Banco de la República.

Fernández, J. (2000), 'Recuperación o catástrofe: proyecciones macroeconómicas 2000–2001', *Seminario Prospectiva Económica y Financiera*, **16**, February.

Gaitán Daza, F. (1995), 'Una indagación sobre las causas de la violencia en Colombia', in Malcolm Deas and Fernando Gaitán Daza (eds), *Dos ensayos especulativos sobre la violencia en Colombia*, Bogotá: Fonade/DNP and Tercer Mundo Editores.

Garay, L.J. (1991), *Apertura y protección: evaluación de la política de importaciones*, Bogotá: Tercer Mundo-Universidad Nacional de Colombia.

Garay, L.J. (1999), 'Construcción de una nueva sociedad', *Libros de la Mesa* **2**, Bogotá: Tercer Mundo Editores-Cambio.

García, M. and R. Uprimny (1999), 'El nudo gordiano de la justicia y la guerra en Colombia', in Camacho Giuzado and Leal Buitrago (1999).

Gómez Buendía, H. (1999), 'La hipótesis del almendrón', in Hernando Gómez Buendía (comp.), *¿Para dónde va Colombia?*, Bogotá: Tercer Mundo Editores-Colciencias.

Gómez Restrepo, H.J. (1988), 'La economía ilegal en Colombia: tamaño, evolución, características e impacto económico', *Coyuntura Económica*, September.

Gómez Restrepo, H.J. and M. Santa María Salamanca (1994), 'La economía subterránea en Colombia', in *Gran Enciclopedia de Colombia*, Tomo 8, Bogotá: Círculo de Lectores.

Jaramillo, C.F. (1998), *Liberalization, Crisis, and Change in Colombian Agriculture*, Boulder, Colorado: Westview.

Kalmanovitz, S. (2001), *Las instituciones y el desarrollo económico en Colombia*, Bogotá: Editorial Norma.

Kaufmann, D., A. Kraay and P. Zoido-Lobatón (2002), 'Governance matters II', *Policy Research Working Paper* **2772**, World Bank.

Latinobarómetro (2000), *Informe de Prensa, Latinobarómetro 1999/2000*, Santiago de Chile.

LeGrand, C. (1988), *Colonización y protesta campesina en Colombia (1850–1950)*, Bogotá: Universidad Nacional de Colombia.

Londoño, J.L. (1995), *Distribución del ingreso y desarrollo económico: Colombia en el siglo XX*, Bogotá: Banco de la República/Fedesarrollo/Tercer Mundo Editores.

Lora, E. (ed.) (1991), *Apertura y crecimiento: el reto de los noventa*, Bogotá: Fedesarrollo/Tercer Mundo Editores.

Lora, E. and J.A. Ocampo (1986), 'Política macroeconómica y distribución del ingreso en Colombia: 1980–1990', *Coyuntura Económica*, October; and in Eduardo Lora (ed.) (1988), *Lecturas de macroeconomía colombiana*, Bogotá: Tercer Mundo-FEDESARROLLO.

Montenegro, S. (ed.) (1997), *Los determinantes de la tasa de cambio real en Colombia*, Bogotá: Universidad de los Andes-Facultad de Economía-CEDE, Debates no. 1.

Montenegro, S. and C.E. Posada (2001), *La violencia en Colombia*, Libros de Cambio, Bogotá: Alfaomega-Cambio.

Ocampo, J.A. (1990), 'La apertura externa en perspectiva', in Florángela Gómez (ed.), *Apertura económica y sistema financiero*, Bogotá: Asociación Bancaria de Colombia.

Ocampo, J.A. (1993), 'Economía y economía política de la reforma comercial colombiana', *Serie Reformas de Política Pública*, no. 1, Santiago de Chile: ECLAC, April.

Ocampo, J.A. (1994), 'La formación de la economía moderna desde 1930', in *Gran Enciclopedia de Colombia*, Tomo 8, Bogotá: Círculo de Lectores.

Ocampo, J.A. (1997), 'Flujos de capital, ahorro e inversión en Colombia, 1990–1996', in Ricardo Ffrench-Davis and Helmut Reisen (eds), *Flujos de capital e inversión productiva: lecciones para América Latina*, Santiago de Chile: ECLAC/OECD, McGraw-Hill.

Ocampo, J.A. (1997), 'Una evaluación de la situación fiscal colombiana', *Coyuntura Económica*, **27**(2), Bogotá, June.

Ocampo, J.A. and S. Perry (1995), *El giro de la política agropecuaria*, Bogotá: Tercer Mundo-FONADE-Departamento Nacional de Planeación.

Ocampo, J.A. and C. Tovar (1999), *Price-Based Capital Account Regulations: The Colombian Experience*, ECLAC, Serie Financiamiento del Desarrollo, no. 87, October.

Ocampo, J.A. and C. Tovar (2003), 'Managing the capital account: Columbia's experience with price-based controls on capital inflows', *CEPAL Review*, **81**, December.

Ocampo, J.A., M.J. Pérez, C. Tovar and F.J. Lasso (1998), 'Macroeconomía, ajuste estructural y equidad en Colombia: 1978–1996', in Enrique Ganuza, Lance Taylor and Samuel Morley (eds), *Política macroeconómica y pobreza en América Latina y el Caribe*, PNUD-CEPAL-BID, Madrid: Mundi-Prensa.

Ocampo, J.A., F. Sánchez and C. Tovar (2000), 'Cambio estructural, mercado laboral y distribucion del ingreso: Colombia en la decada de los noventa', *Revista de la CEPAL*, **72**, December.

Orozco, I. (1990), 'Los diálogos con el narcotráfico: historia de la transformación fallida de un delincuente común en un delincuente político', *Análisis Político*, **11**, September–December.

Palacio Rudas, A. (1995), 'Los instrumentos que maneja el Banco de la República como autoridad monetaria, cambiaria y crediticia', in Roberto Steiner (comp.), *La autonomía del Banco de la República: economía política de la reforma*, Bogotá: FEDESARROLLO/Tercer Mundo Editores.

Palacios, M. and F. Safford (2002), *Colombia: país fragmentado, sociedad dividida*, Bogotá: Colección Vitral, Editorial Norma.

Pécaut, D. (2001), *Guerra contra la sociedad*, Colección Espasa Hoy, Bogotá: Editorial Planeta Colombiana.

Pizarro, E. (1996), *Insurgencia sin revolución: la guerrilla en Colombia en una perspectiva comparada*, Bogotá: IEPRI/Tercer Mundo Editores.

Posada Carbó, E. (2001a), 'Reflexiones sobre la cultura política colombiana', *Cátedra Corona*, **2**, Bogotá: Universidad de los Andes.

Posada Carbó, E. (2001b), *¿Guerra civil? El lenguaje del conflicto en Colombia*, Libros de Cambio, Bogotá: Alfaomega-Ideas para la Paz-Cambio.

Reyes, A. and A.M. Bejarano (1988), 'Conflictos agrarios y luchas armadas en la Colombia contemporánea: una visión geográfica', *Análisis Político*, **5**, September–December.

Rocha, R. (2000), *La economía colombiana tras 25 años de narcotráfico*, Bogotá: UNDCP and Siglo del Hombre Editores.

Rubio, M. (1999) *Crimen e impunidad: precisiones sobre la violencia*, Bogotá: CEDE/Tercer Mundo Editores.

Salazar, A. (1990), *No nacimos pa' semilla*, Bogotá: CINEP.

Sánchez, F. and J. Núñez (1999), 'Descentralización, pobreza y acceso a los servicios sociales. ¿Quién se benefició del Gasto Público Social en los noventa?', *Coyuntura Social*, **20**, May.

Sánchez, F., A. Solimano and M. Formisano (2002), 'Conflict, violent crime and criminal activity in Colombia', Research Program of The Economics and Politics of Civil Wars, Yale University, mimeo, November.

Sánchez, G. (1991), *Guerra y política en la sociedad colombiana*, Bogotá: El Áncora Editores.

Sánchez, G. and R. Peñaranda (eds) (1986), *Pasado y presente de la violencia en Colombia*, Bogotá: CEREC.

Sarmiento Gómez, A. (1999), *Violencia y equidad*, in Camacho Guizado and Leal Buitrago (1999).

Sarmiento Palacio, E. (1996), *Apertura y crecimiento económico: de la desilusión al nuevo Estado*, Bogotá: Academia Colombiana de Ciencias Económicas/Escuela Colombiana de Ingeniería/ECOE Ediciones.

Sarmiento Palacio, E. (1998), *Alternativas a la encrucijada neoliberal: mercado, narcotráfico y descentralización*, Bogotá: Academia Colombiana de Ciencias Económicas/Escuela Colombiana de Ingeniería/ECOE Ediciones.

Solimano, A. (2003), 'Governance crises and the Andean region: a political economy analysis', Santiago de Chile: ECLAC, Economic Development Division, *Serie Macroeconomía del Desarrollo*, **23**, February.

Steiner, R. (comp.) (1995), *La autonomía del Banco de la República: economía política de la reforma*, Bogotá: FEDESARROLLO-Tercer Mundo Editores.

Syrquin, M. (1987), 'Crecimiento económico y cambio estructural en Colombia: una comparación internacional', *Coyuntura Económica*, December.

Thoumi, F. (1994), *Economía política y narcotráfico*, Bogotá: Tercer Mundo Editores.

Trujillo, E. and M.E. Badel (1997), 'Los costos económicos de la criminalidad y la violencia en Colombia: 1991–1996', *Planeación y Desarrollo*, **XXVIII**(4), Bogotá, October–December.

UNDCP (United Nations Office on Drugs and Crime) (2003), *Colombia: Coca Survey for 2002*, Preliminary report, New York.

Villar, L. and H. Rincón (2003), 'The Colombian economy in the nineties: capital flows and foreign exchange regimes', in Albert Berry (ed.), *Critical Issues in Financial Reform: A View from the South*, New Brunswick, New Jersey, Transaction.

6. Political economy of Ecuador: the quandary of governance and economic development

Gustavo Arteta and Osvaldo Hurtado*

6.1 INTRODUCTION

Ecuador's social and economic development of the last two decades fell short of what was required to fulfill the needs of its population. Despite arguably abundant natural resource endowments, per capita income has barely grown since 1980. This stagnation is often related to the return to democracy in 1979 by important portions of the constituents. From time to time dictatorship is yearned for, based on the premise of a spurious correlation between this form of government that prevailed in the 1970s and the prosperity afforded by the beginning of oil exploitation in that decade. Despite this simplification of the complex dilemma that economic development poses, it makes evident that many Ecuadorians do not feel that democracy has brought them improved welfare. It is just as troubling that the feeling is partially backed by many indicators of economic and governance performance.

Culprits of the lackluster performance are widely debated. Many blame the political system, regional conflicts, cultural idiosyncrasies, (oil) resource curse, poverty, inequality, corruption and others. While probably each of these contributes to the stagnation to some degree, most corrective efforts have concentrated on economic reform and policies. Often, the latter have ignored political considerations and governance problems. But at the heart of the successes and failures in the efforts to improve conditions most surely lies a combination of both.

The basic problem in Ecuador has been the failure of the democratic system to articulate social demands and channel corrective responses promptly and efficiently. The failure is systemic and cuts through several administrations. Despite limited positive results, economic volatility, political instability and policy disagreement usually derail constructive initiatives. As a consequence, economic growth has been insufficient to reduce poverty, improve income distribution and eradicate other basic socioeconomic ills.

The root cause of the governance and economic troubles lies in the prevailing incentives and institutional structures that exacerbate the problems of the entire chain of principal–agent relations in a representative and indirect democracy. The conditions for interest group influence and concentration of power are overwhelming. Aristocratic and oligarchic legacies, social class divisions, and narrow trade associations are all elements that facilitate political action as a byproduct of their principal motive of association. Further strength of interest group power is derived from asymmetry in firm sizes, products, and high industry concentration that dominates economic organization in Ecuador.

The governance problems of fractionalized political parties, populism and regional conflicts are expressions of interest group influence. What many judge as corruption, a rampant ill in the country, in many cases is a manifestation of extreme rent-seeking activity by interest groups that use legal and illegal means for their benefit.

The reign of interest groups both contribute to and prey upon the weakness of economic and political institutions. In some cases, interest groups capture public institutions or influence their design to serve their purpose. An optimal-policy-seeking economist or a common-good-interested observer would describe a weak institution that doesn't execute policies in the public interest as a failure. Yet, this would not be the perspective of the pressure group that influenced its design. For example, the apparent problem of a banking superintendency that fails to oversee problem banks may in fact be the desired condition for an oligopolistic banking industry. The power of a few bankers can influence the selection of superintendents that serve banks and not the public. At the extreme, the influence can reach the corruption stage when the authority covers-up and protects specific institutions at the cost of general financial stability.[1]

Weak institutions contribute to low policy credibility. Without it, the economy falls vulnerable to shocks because contingent policies that require planning and extended time horizons for implementation are difficult to sustain.

The aim of this chapter is to explore the conundrum of Ecuador's economic underachievement and troubling governance through a political economy perspective. By focusing on both political and economic problems, we strive to gain a better understanding of economic performance under the Ecuadorian political umbrella, and political behavior resulting from the underlying economic conditions. The chapter is organized as follows. Section 6.2 briefly describes the country's political system's performance under the current democratic period. Section 6.3 recounts recent economic performance and conditions. Section 6.4 attempts to analyse the interactions between the economy and politics to explain the governance problems and economic woes.

We wish to recognize at the onset that the chapter does not aim to prove or disprove specific theoretical hypotheses of the political economy literature. Instead, it provides a sort of *tour de force* of applications of various political and economic theories to the governance problems found in Ecuador and its consequences for economic performance. Thus, in some cases the approach bears the cost of providing less than desirable rigor in substantiating some assertions. In spite of this, our principal objective is to document and open the discussion over the governance problems and economic problems from a political economy perspective in Ecuador to stimulate further research.

6.2 POLITICAL PERFORMANCE: RETURN TO DEMOCRACY

Ecuador was the first country in Latin America to re-establish democratic rule in 1977–79 after a prolonged struggle with dictatorships of one form or another. The democratic hiatus began after President José María Velasco Ibarra, in office for the fifth time, in 1970 proclaimed himself dictator with the support of the military. Two years later, General Guillermo Rodríguez, chairman of the Joint Chiefs of the Armed Forces led a coup that toppled Velasco. Toward the end of 1975, the commanders of the three branches of the Armed Forces overthrew Rodríguez. After taking over, they announced their intention to surrender back the power to civilian rule within two years.

During discussions to re-establish democratic rule, the political, economic and social forces divided into three camps. Those with Marxist views asked the military to continue in power until a military-led 'nationalist revolution' (that had been proclaimed earlier) would be completed. 'Right-wing' groups demanded the immediate return to civilian rule through a provisional president who would call for a Constitutional Assembly. A 'progressive faction' proposed a civilian–military agreement that would seek an organized transition toward democracy, which would entail a referendum over the constitutional reforms that would be needed to secure the future of the constitutional system.

In the aftermath of extended discussions, the Military Triumvirate proposed a complex process that they called 'The Legal Restructuring Plan of the State' (Plan de Reestructuración Jurídica del Estado), whose execution called for establishing three commissions composed of political parties, labor union leaders, entrepreneurs and constitutionalists. The commissions had to prepare three proposals: one for a new constitution, another for a new version of the 1945 constitution, and lastly a draft bill with proposals for a set of statutes that would govern the constitutional referendum, elections and political parties. The two constitutional projects were voted upon in a national referendum. Then, a new president was elected according to the new constitution's electoral rules.

Jaime Roldós triumphed in a two-round election that took place in 1978 and 1979, despite conspiracies orchestrated by a sector of the Army connected with the political right and delays of nine months between the first and second rounds. He took office on 10 August 1979. Fourteen Latin American countries later adopted this transition model from dictatorship to democracy, which relied on a civilian–military agreement. Huntington (1968) calls this process the 'third wave of Democratization'.[2]

Ecuador was the first country in Latin America to begin the transition to democracy, and one of the first countries to restore macroeconomic equilibrium (1983) and recover growth (1984). But that momentum was lost as political and economic stagnation has prevailed. What caused the inefficient functioning of the democratic system and poor social and economic performance, to the extent that it is one of the three countries on the continent that lost two decades of economic and social development? This question is challenging and complex. In the following subsections we venture to provide answers for the failures of the political system.

Governance Problems

Political – governance – problems have stalled improvements in citizens' welfare under the current Ecuadorian democratic system. These are expressed through the failure of the system to articulate social demands and channel corrective responses promptly and efficiently. Despite limited positive results, the failure is systemic. Ecuador has not sustained macroeconomic stability as a result. In a few short episodes, stability was briefly obtained through enormous sacrifices, but these were never durable. Promising periods of economic and social growth were halted by crises that not only would lose previous gains but their severity would exacerbate the prevailing social inequities. Moreover, various foretold economic and social conflicts that were carried over from the past snowballed into crises that were unable to find solutions through consensus and negotiation. As a consequence of these series of events, the country was trapped in a vicious crisis-adjustment-crisis cycle.

Political Instability

The major governance problem throughout Ecuador's history has been political instability. However, this problem is not new since it has been a repeated occurrence in the country's history.[3] Until 1996, the current democratic period (the longest in national history), it seemed that the Ecuador had rid itself of presidential turnover. All heads of state until 1996 completed their terms and passed on power to elected successors.[4] However, of the nine presidents in the last democratic period, only two belonged to the same political party (one of them by succession). The rest belonged to different parties.

High turnover of ministers

Highly volatile governments masked presidential stability. Between 1979 and 1996, finance and oil ministers, the most important policy-setting ministries had an average term in office of one year. The high turnover is very similar in the Petroleum Corporation (PETROECUADOR), the most important and largest company, which is responsible for over one-third of fiscal revenues and total export earnings. Although the stability of the education minister was higher, their average time in office was only 16 months.

Averaging these four ministries' terms in office, in the Roldos-Hurtado[5] administration, the average ministerial tenure was 13.3 months, in the Febres Cordero administration 18.6 months. The average tenure of the ministers increased slightly during the Borja government to 21.9 months, but declined again in the Durán government to 16.9 months.[6] One Vice President, Alberto Dahik, was forced to resign in 1995, which was particularly unsettling because he headed economic policy issues in the Duran administration.

Since 1996, political instability has sharply deteriorated. President Abdalá Bucaram, who was elected for a four-year term, held office for only six months after Congress impeached him through a very dubious interpretation of the constitution. He was succeeded by a congressman and not by the Vice President because when codifying a constitutional reform Congress had 'inadvertently' suppressed the text outlining the appropriate legal succession procedures. Congress entrusted the administration to Fabián Alarcón for 18 months as Interim President, a designation not contemplated by the constitution. In 1998 Jamil Mahuad was elected president and all thought that Ecuador was back on the democratic track. However, he was forced to leave office after 17 months because of an indigenous insurrection supported by a group of army officers. Mahuad's Vice President, Gustavo Noboa, took office following the now clearly established succession procedures, and finished the constitutional term on 15 January 2003. Lucio Gutiérrez, one of the colonels that led the insurrection against Mahuad in 2000, took office after winning the second-round elections in 2002.

After receiving a pardon for his participation in the insurrection, Gutiérrez formed his own party (January 21-Patriotic Society Party) and aligned with Pachakutik, the political arm of indigenous groups. He ran an anti-corruption, anti-establishment campaign that yielded him the first place in the first-round elections with 21 per cent of valid votes and 54 per cent in the second round.

The extreme presidential instability we have described between 1996 and 2003 influenced all other levels of public administration, especially for ministers and heads of public companies whose stability is precarious at best. Between 1996 and 2001, the average time of the ministers of economy was 185 days, and oil ministers nine months. These facts explain, in part, why Ecuador is among the 30 per cent of more unstable countries in the world (and certainly in Latin America), in a 155-country sample (Figure 6.1).

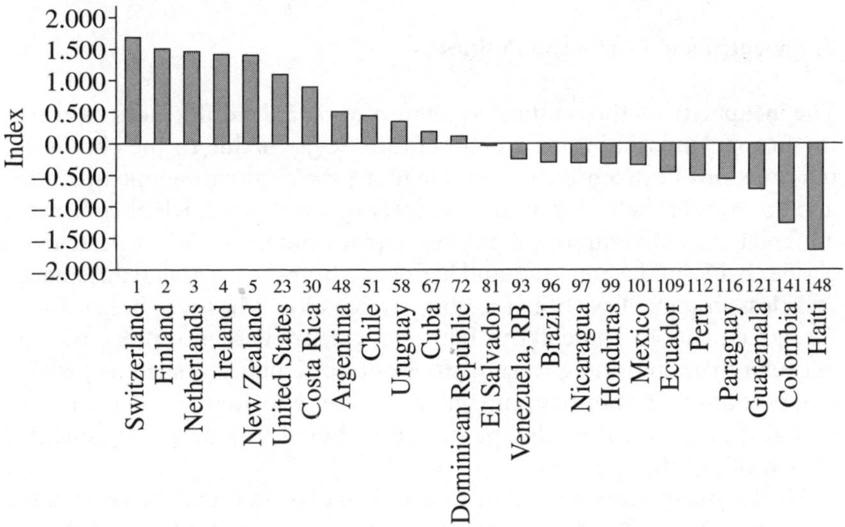

Sources: Del Búfalo and Ríos (2002).

Figure 6.1 Political instability

Volatility of Laws and Reforms

The instability of ministers is mirrored by similar repeated legal changes. Constitutional reforms, economic initiatives and others have experienced permanent changes. For example, the Elections Law of 1978, which established limits on electoral advertising expenditures, was declared unconstitutional in 1984, due to lobbying from a right-wing candidate and the media. It was again re-established 16 years later, in 2001.

During the last 22 years, Ecuador has had two constitutions, one in 1979 and one in 1998. The 1979 constitution suffered continuous amendments, sometimes coming from the executive branch, sometimes through national referendums and other times through legislative action. The reforms were motivated, in the majority of the cases, by partisan interests or ad-hoc demands by politically strong pressure groups. In search of stability of constitutional reforms, the 1998 Constitutional Assembly established that reforms require a one-year period between first and second debate.[7]

The Political Parties Law of 1978 established the requirement that political parties that do not obtain 5 per cent of the total votes in two consecutive elections would disappear. The norm was repealed in 1983, re-established in 1992, repealed in 1996 and re-established in 1997. Between December 1998 and April 2002 Ecuador made six significant fiscal reforms.[8]

Fragmented and Conflictive Politics

The incapacity of the political system to resolve the differences to ensure the proper functioning of a democratic society is due to the conflictive relationships between parties and leaders, the zero-sum-game attitudes, and the populist behavior of the political organizations. Lack of consensus, entrenched conflicts amongst political parties and their leaders, destructive clashes between the executive and legislative branches, regional differences, and class struggles have been the norm in Ecuador. It has even been difficult for agreements to come about between workers and entrepreneurs, and between them and the government about basic policies, such as keeping macroeconomic stability and growth. The conflictive nature of the Ecuadorian political landscape has contributed to a deeply fragmented system of political parties.

The fragmentation is both a cause and an expression of the governance problems. During the current democratic period, Ecuador has had about a dozen political parties, most of them founded after 1977.[9] A large number of political parties would not pose any governance problems to the Ecuadorian democracy if two or three parties could reach majority status in legislative bodies. But none of them have ever reached such representation, and the president has always held minority support in the legislature. In a few cases, the president's party has obtained enough votes to command the largest legislative block; however, even in the best case it didn't represent more than one third of the seats (Table 6.1).

This weak legislative support held by the governments' parties contrasts with other Latin American countries, where the executive branch holds much more congressional control (Table 6.2). The lack of majority political forces is confirmed by the fact that only one party has been in the presidency twice, Popular Democracy (DP); the second coming 14 years after the first one.

Table 6.1 Seats in Congress of government party

Year	President	Government party	Seats in Congress (% of total seats)[1]
1979	Jaime Roldós[2]/Osvaldo Hurtado	CFP/DP	44.9
1984	León Febres Cordero	PSC	12.7
1988	Rodrigo Borja	ID	42.3
1992	Sixto Durán	PUR	15.6
1996	Abdalá Bucaram	PRE	23.2
1998	Jamil Mahuad	DP	27.6
2003	Lucio Gutiérrez	PSP/MUPP-NP	16.0

Notes:
1 At time of election.
2 Passed away while in office in 1981.

Sources: Mejía (1998); for 2003, the authors.

Two factors have contributed to the large number of parties. On one hand, the disposition requiring a minimum threshold of votes needed to remain as a sanctioned party has been revoked several times. Often influenced by minority organizations on the verge of disappearing, the disposition has not been enforced by the Electoral Tribunal, in clear violation of the constitution and election laws. On the other hand, renewed ideologies have emerged, leading new personalities to form new social and political groups to participate in elections. Some have evolved into formal political parties.

The electoral system based on proportional representation used in the country has compounded the fragmentation of political organizations. It prevails because there is a widely held belief that minorities should not be excluded from representation; even those that do not quite surpass the minimum vote count requirement. For this reason, efforts to adopt a system that favors majorities have failed, either because there have not been enough votes in Congress (as was the case in the Constitutional Assembly of 1998), or because citizens have not approved a change in referendums.

Ecuadorian parties also face the constraint of a still maturing political society. That is, one where there is strict adherence by voters to a given set of political ideas and policies. The adherence ought to be expressed by the people's vote for the party's candidates in good times and bad times. This weak constituency relation between political representatives and voters further contributes to political volatility.

The instability of the constituents' vote preferences is more noticeable in presidential elections, where candidates can win or lose the support of 45 per cent of constituents, and it is less noticeable in congressional elections, where preference swings between 1979 and 1996 are 50 per cent lower.[10]

Table 6.2 Congressional seats held by government party, selected Latin American countries

Country	Period	Number of elections	Seats in Congress (% of total seats)[1]
Argentina	1983–93	6	48.3
Bolivia	1980–93	4	33.9
Brazil	1985–90	4	26.9
Chile	1989–93	2	31.7
Colombia	1945–49,1974–94	11	55.2
Costa Rica	1953–94	11	49.6
Dominican Republic	1962,1966–90	8	55.6
Ecuador	1978–94	7	22.0
El Salvador	1985–91	4	47.5
Honduras	1981–93	4	54.2
Mexico	1982–91	4	65.8
Nicaragua	1984–90	2	65.4
Paraguay	1993	1	47.5
Peru	1984–90,1995	3	47.1
Uruguay	1942–71,1984–94	11	45.6
Venezuela, RB	1958–93	8	41.1

Note: [1] House of Representatives only.

Source: Banco Mundial (1998).

Regional interests and differences

Since the nineteenth century, when Ecuador emerged as a nation, marked differences have been evident between the peoples from the Coastal region (Costa) and those of the Highlands (Sierra) in entrepreneurial tendencies, ideologies and *Weltanschauung.*[11]

The regional differences trespass into the political environment. They have hindered the emergence of national parties with countrywide representation. Party constituency is almost completely limited to regional space in the Coast and Highlands. Parties that predominate in one region tend to hold small or minimal voter adhesion in the other. The Social Christian Party

(PSC) and the Ecuadorian Roldosista Party (PRE) have predominated in the Costa, whereas the Popular Democracy (DP), the Democratic Left (ID) and a number of small extreme left and labor parties have prevailed in the Sierra. Despite the supremacy of the four large parties during the current democratic period, none was able to achieve a legislative majority because they could not attract enough votes from regions outside their domain.

Since the early 1980s, the PSC and the PRE have become the majority forces in Congress with populist platforms and clientelistic policies. Their strength has increased as a result of adherence to populist attitudes of other parties on specific issues when approving the government budget, logrolling to increase public spending projects, enacting unpopular but necessary reforms. The populist positions have complicated economic and fiscal management, causing repeated fiscal crises, increasing public debt, chronic high inflation and devaluation, and of course, low growth.

While in office, parties succumb to the need for implementing tough and unpopular policies such as increasing fuel prices (which are set by the government) and taxes to raise revenues or cut subsidies, but when they are out of office, political party leaders adamantly oppose these same policies. The actions of the PSC are one of the clearest and most consistent examples of this, although all parties are guilty of this double standard. The Social Christian Party has successfully opposed raising new taxes or imposing tax increases since the end of its administration in 1988, despite doing those same things when it governed.

Conflicts between a weak executive branch and an obstructing congress

Throughout the current democratic period, the party in office has held minority representation in Congress. This has resulted in weak administrations and antagonistic legislatures. The weakness could have been resolved through permanent alliances or specific agreements to approve certain bills. In both cases, political parties, due to electoral considerations or their populist characteristics, tended to be reluctant to commit to ongoing agreements, and if they did so, the alliances were brief. With the exception of the first two years of the Borja administration (1988–90) when the president managed to assemble a majority through an alliance between his party (the ID) and the DP, alliances tended to breakup quickly, forcing administrations to govern without majority support in Congress.

The minority condition of the administration in office and the transitory nature of alliances contributed to habitual confrontation between the executive and legislative branches in power struggles. Presidents tend to refuse congressional decisions, while opposition blocks obstruct the approval of bills presented by the executive branch. A common practice (until 1998) was for Congress to impeach ministers for mere political considerations.

Presidents, in order to overcome their minority condition in Congress, develop tactics to divide parties by offering individual legislators sinecures if they abandon their parties and change to the administration's side.[12] Through this practice, governments form subordinated groups of congressmen from diverse political parties with whom they can pass legislation or confront the opposition. Often there are also dissidents from political parties due to differences in points of view, but these do not necessarily align with the administration. During 1993, 1997 and 2001, the number of congressmen who had abandoned their parties accounted for nearly 27 per cent of all representatives.[13]

Class and interest group conflicts

Private (that is special) interests have biased policy decisions since the country's founding, but even more so in the last few years. Presidents, ministers, congressmen, judges, superintendents and political leaders either through direct involvement or indirect influence have governed for the benefit of private instead of public interests. The policies, laws and judicial decisions have led to fiscal and financial crises, misappropriation of public funds, and tax and tariff evasion causing large welfare losses. The most significant set of events that exemplify this is the financial crisis of 1999–2000 that cost the country an estimated 4 billion dollars (20 per cent of GDP); partially because the bank superintendent and other authorities covered up bank fraud related to enormous campaign contributions.

At times, special interests hide behind regionalist chatter. Interested parties and their godfathers pressure decisions or criticize measures alleging that these are directed to harming a specific region, province or city. They accuse government policies to correct economic problems, prevent financial crisis, control corruption, and those that are in general in the national interest of being regionally biased and intended to harm the locality. Encased in regionalist talk, special interests, through political parties and leaders, have often obtained support to obstruct sound policies seeking the national interest. A case in point is what happened in 1998–99 when several banks became insolvent due to their bad management and corruption. Repeatedly, the mayor of Guayaquil declared that he would 'rise-up' the Costa against the 'centralism in Quito' if those banks were closed. The threats produced the desired effects temporarily. That is, the banking superintendency delayed interventions and corrective prudential measures were not implemented. Eventually, of course, all the protected institutions failed anyway. However, the actions allowed enough time for outrageous corruption to transfer funds, destroy documentation and for some bankers to flee the country.

With these and other acts of corruption driven by special economic interests – strongly tied to influential political parties – it should not be a surprise that according to Transparency International, Ecuador is perceived as one of the most corrupt countries in Latin America. The country ranks barely better than Bolivia (Figure 6.2).

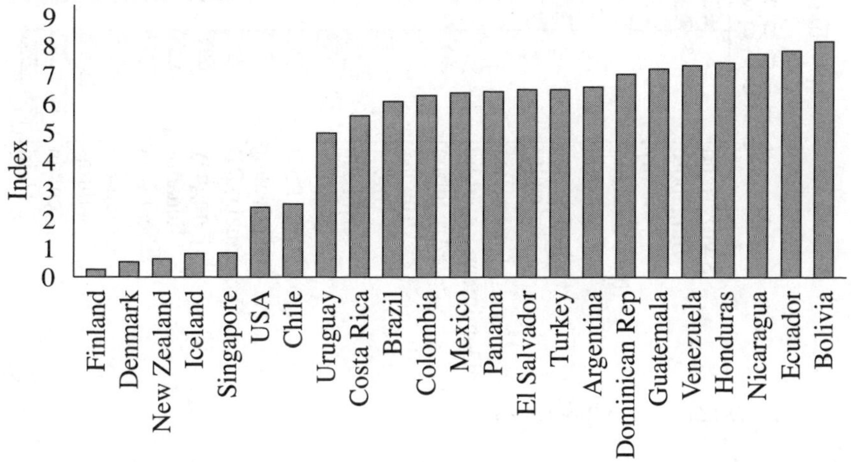

Source: Transparency International (2001).

Figure 6.2 Perception of corruption

Political parties frequently receive fat sums of money for campaigns from a small number of contributors. When in office, or in Congress, elected beneficiaries of the contributions tend to compensate interest groups through public contract adjudication, regulation, permissiveness, approving laws that benefit them and other sorts of boons.

The political and economic network of special interests also operates in the judicial system by obstructing sentences, nominating judges, bribes and other means.[14] The pressure of influential participants often distorts legal rulings. Procedures are complex and obscure to common folk. Cases can take years without end to be resolved. Most Ecuadorians do not have much confidence in the judicial system (see Figure 6.3).

In recent years, the political scene has become ever more complex due to the growing participation of the indigenous communities. The political action by the Confederation of Indigenous People of Ecuador (CONAIE) began in 1990 with mass, and growing, indigenous activism. This marked a renewed use of an old practice used to confront Spanish domination during colonial times. Originally CONAIE came to be and acted as a political force opposed to the democratic system, which it considered foreign to the

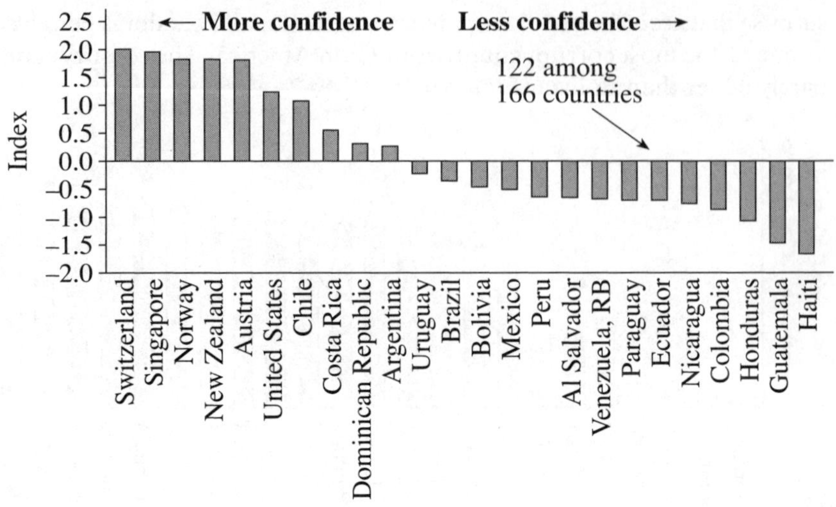

Sources: Del Búfalo and Ríos (2002).

Figure 6.3 Confidence in the judicial system

indigenous communities and even contributed to the problems and was contradictory to their interests.

Later, in 1996, CONAIE abandoned that view and founded Pachakutik, a political party that allowed indigenous people to participate in several elections. Indigenous people have been very successful. They have obtained mayorships in cities where they are the majority of the inhabitants and also in a few where they are not. They have won seats in the legislature. One of their leaders and members of Pachakutik became Vice President of Congress in 1998. Active participation in politics allowed indigenous communities to gain economic and social vindication. One of the most significant achievements came in 1998 when the acknowledgment of collective rights of indigenous people was incorporated in the new constitution, which in fact they participated in drafting.

The accomplishments of the indigenous communities and evolution into a major political group have further added to the already conflictive political environment. CONAIE is now one more effective interest group that influences policy decisions. Their strength was clearly revealed when they orchestrated an insurrection that finally overthrew President Mahuad. CONAIE's president even formed part of the short-lived dictatorship together with a civilian and an army officer.

The latest, and pinnacle, of the indigenous group's political success came after aligning with the new Patriotic Society Party (PSP) to support Lucio

Gutiérrez in his presidential campaign. In 2003, members of Pachakutik formed part of the Cabinet in important ministries (for example, Foreign Affairs) and many middle-level posts in the government's bureaucracy. Thus, it can no longer be said that these social groups are still marginalized from political decisionmaking and process. Despite the success, and as at many times in the past, the weak interlinings of the Ecuadorian system caused a rupture between the PSP and Pachakutik. Just as other parties had done in the past, Gutiérrez and the PSP ran on one policy platform and governed with another. From day one, President Gutiérrez implemented policies 180 degrees opposite to those he promised in his campaign. Fiscal policy followed a conservative path supported by an IMF program that sought Washington Consensus-type reforms. Instead of fighting corruption, he staffed an administration replete with close relatives that gave rise to outcries of nepotism. Guitérrez's military background brought out authoritarian tendencies when, following months of internal and public quarrels with his electoral allies, he forced members of Pachakutik out of the administration.

The 2002 election brought the military back to prominence. Gutirrérez appointed many former military officers to important posts in his administration. Additionally he has already given the military active roles in customs administration and announced their role in economic development projects such as rural roads construction. Even though Gutiérrez won in free elections and democracy continues, time will tell if his military background brings back greater military presence in policy making.

Summary

A political system gains social legitimacy when it has been able to protect civil liberties, human rights, and extends universal social participation through equal opportunities to all its citizens. Put in economic terms, the system – democracy in our case – gains legitimacy when the institutional system is able to resolve many of the principal–agent problems that arise; that is, when the system effectively makes compatible the interests of its citizens with those of representative public officials, limiting the influence of special interests, in an institutional framework that permits effective governance.

Ecuadorian democracy has largely failed to gain legitimacy. Its institutions have conspired against governance; as a result, instead of helping resolve economic and social woes, the poor results have made Ecuadorians distrust their institutions. According to the 1996 Latinobarómetro survey[15] only 34 per cent of the population were pleased with the democratic system, while 16 per cent were totally dissatisfied with the system. In December 2001, after overcoming the 1999 crisis, nine out of ten Ecuadorians still expressed dissatisfaction with congressional actions, and six out of ten were dissatisfied with the government's performance.[16]

6.3 ECONOMIC PERFORMANCE

The Ecuadorian democratic system managed to survive economic crises as well as social and political conflicts. However, the system has not contributed to spawning or facilitating sufficient and sustained growth. During the two decades of democratic rule, illiteracy and mortality dramatically fell, access to schools increased, and life expectancy improved significantly. Nonetheless, GDP per capita is almost the same as that in 1979. In comparison, Chile's per capita GDP in 1979 was 1.5 times higher than Ecuador's; in 2000, the Chilean GDP per capita was 4.2 higher than the Ecuadorian one. Growing unemployment and stagnation of real wages have spawned the emigration of thousands of Ecuadorians.

Given the size and variety of resources, Ecuador's economy has underperformed for many decades. The last 20 years, which coincide with the reign of democratic rule, present particularly troubling stagnation. Between 1950 and 2001 per capita income grew at an average of 2.2 per cent per year but much of it came during the oil-boom era of the 1970s, which allowed a period of very high per capita growth (6.2 per cent). Since 1980, however, the country has barely managed to grow at all. Average GDP growth in this period fell to 2.0 per cent per annum, below population growth.

Sub-par growth has coexisted with high instability. Inflation escalated to an average of 41 per cent between 1980 and 2000, from 12 per cent during the 1970s, and its volatility increased fourfold. The country regularly failed to complete policy reforms and structural adjustment programs sponsored by the IMF. Meanwhile, the 1980s and 1990s presented mixed results for social indicators of development.

Various economic and external factors explain the deteriorating performance of the Ecuadorian economy. The following sections review these factors.

Low Growth

Ecuador's economy was shifted off its growth path by the large-scale exploitation of petroleum in the early 1970s. In this decade gross domestic product (GDP) grew at an average of 8.5 per cent per year, above the 3.8 per cent averaged during the 1960s. The boom experienced, however, lasted only until world oil prices fell, as OPEC was unable to enforce its cartel policies (see Figure 6.4).[17]

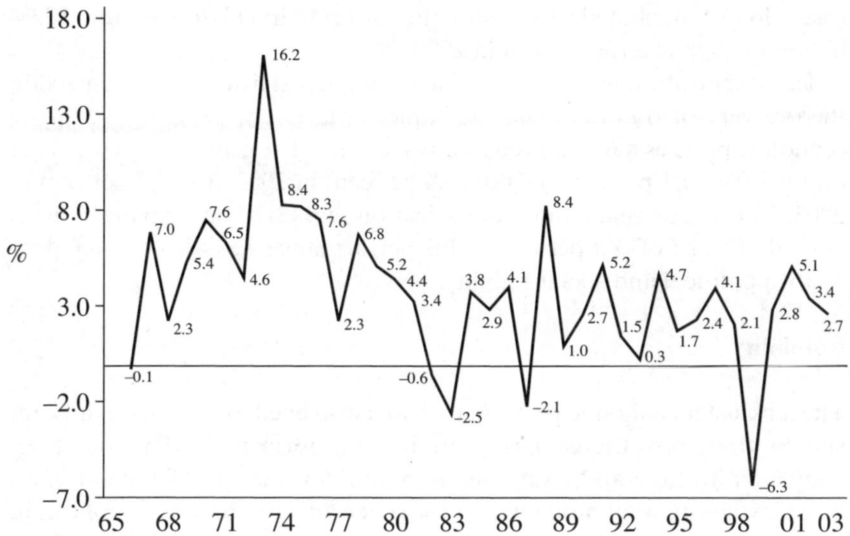

Source: Central Bank of Ecuador, based on revised national accounts in US dollars.

Figure 6.4 Ecuador, GDP growth 1965–2003

In the 1980s, GDP grew 2.1 per cent per year. This average fell further in the 1990s to 1.7 per cent per year. Most of the growth in the 1980s came from traditional agricultural sectors. In the 1990s, the sectorial contribution was more diversified. Oil, manufacturing, commerce and services explain over 60 per cent of GDP growth.

In this 20-year span the economic growth could not keep up with the growth of the population (2.2 per cent) and could not absorb the growing labor force. As result, unemployment rates jumped from single digits in the 1980s to double digits in the 1990s.

In the late 1990s, the economy entered a slow and painful deterioration. Domestic political instability combined with a series of negative external shocks stalled key sectors. The Asian financial crisis halted the small (to international standards) but nevertheless important capital flows that generated a consumption and credit boom.[18] Firms' debt burden began to grow, which caused deterioration of banks' balance sheets. The El Niño weather phenomenon devastated coastal agricultural production and infrastructure. The falling world demand depressed prices of the leading export crops. GDP growth in 1998 fell to 2.1 per cent. In 1999, the accumulation of negative factors pushed the Ecuadorian economy into its deepest recession on record. GDP fell 6.3 per cent. The currency crisis (see below) contributed to a contraction of GDP in US dollars from $23.4 billion in 1998 to $15.6 billion in 2000.[19]

The stabilization induced by dollarization (established in March 2000), the recovery of oil prices and the implementation of generally adequate economic policies have allowed steady recovery. The economy grew 2.8 per cent in 2000; 5.1 per cent in 2001; 3.4 per cent in 2002; and 2.7 per cent in 2003. In the four years under dollarization real GDP has expanded at an annual average of 3.5 per cent. This performance was also bolstered by relative political and social stability.

Instability

The lackluster economic performance was worsened by various significant shocks that took the economy off its long-term path. This has been coupled with high and rising inflation and devaluation of the currency. Price instability went along with a roller coaster of attempts to control it. Policy efforts typically coincided with a new government's initial efforts to implement stabilization programs that were almost never concluded. The whole array of monetary and exchange rate policies were tried, from full fixed regimes to free floating and everything in between. However the fundamental problems that fed inflation were never controlled.

Supply shocks

Pure statistical time series analysis reveals that from 1965:01 to 1998:04, Ecuador's economy was trend stationery.[20] This means that the factors that have caused economic volatility in Ecuador have not altered the long-term economic growth rate. Instead, the economy has been subjected to permanent 'shocks' and transitory or cyclical events (Figure 6.5).

It is possible to identify 11 'shocks' that permanently altered the level of gross domestic product.[21] All of these can be defined as supply shocks. Only four of the shocks were positive and associated with petroleum events in the 1970s. The events in the 1980s and 90s were all negative. These events that have permanently reduced the level of GDP were associated with natural phenomena (El Niño/debt crisis 1982, El Niño 1998, and 1987 earthquake) and the armed conflict in 1995.

Controlling for these shocks, Fernández and Lara (1998) estimate that the long-term economic growth rate under stable conditions was 4.35 per cent between 1965 and 1997.[22] Additionally, the movements in GDP around the long-term trend can be assigned to temporary demand shocks, cyclical variations or pure random elements. Fernández and Lara do not discriminate among these. However, they determine that the transitory

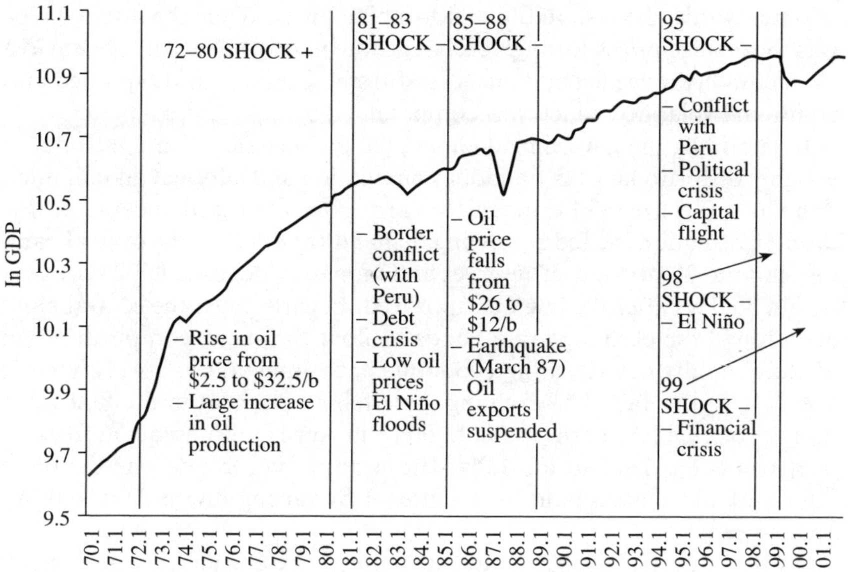

Source: Fernández and Lara (1998).

Figure 6.5 Ecuador, effects of exogenous shocks in GDP (1970.01–2001.03)

shocks fade away (or revert to the long-term trend) within an interlude of eight to ten quarters (2 to 2.5 years).

Comparing the average (compound) growth rate of the last two decades of 2.2 per cent per year to the long-term stable growth rate, we can conclude that the economy severely underperformed as a result of the volatility.

Policy instability

Just as external shocks contributed to economic instability and displacement from potential long-term growth, policy instability has contributed to short-term instability. Aggregate demand policies and deficiencies led to price volatility.

Price instability While Ecuador never experienced hyperinflation in the technical sense,[23] it did present high chronic inflation from the 1980s. Average inflation jumped from 12 per cent per year in the 1970s to 37 per cent and 44 per cent during the 1980s and 1990s, respectively. Beginning in 1996, inflation began an escalating trend that accelerated upon the unfolding of the financial and currency crises in 1999.

Exchange rate policies were just as unstable: between 1995 and 1999, a system of exchange rate bands designed to generate credibility was 'adjusted';

in other words, the system broke down nine times. While the original idea was to stabilize prices through exchange rate management, the system lost the credibility it needed and unsuccessful stabilization efforts spiraled into additional volatility, which was compounded by unwise fiscal policies.

In late 1998, the government eliminated the income tax and introduced a highly distortionary tax on money circulation and adopted an unlimited deposit guarantee. The moral hazard generated and incentives for disintermediation incited a growing demand for dollars. The central bank lost close to 30 per cent of reserves and monetary deposits fell 24 per cent within 30 days after the law was approved. In early 1999, the central bank abandoned the exchange rate bands to float the sucre, complicating an already rapidly deteriorating economic environment. On a weekly basis banks began to fail. The exchange rate fell 80 per cent in the first three months of 1999. After the 'bank holiday' in April and subsequent freezing of deposits the demand for dollars went out of control despite the futile efforts of the central bank to counter it by raising interest rates above 153 per cent.

As 70 per cent of the banking system failed or came under state control, the public liability acquired was monetized. The devaluation of the sucre became a leading indicator of the expected consumer price inflation that lags money creation by about 11 months. Between July 1998 and January 2000 the exchange rate fell 477 per cent. In the last three months alone, the sucre devalued 126 per cent.

In a span of about four months the central bank more than doubled base money to bail out some banks and to pay the deposit guarantee. These factors outweighed the impact of the huge contraction in domestic demand and the bank deposit freeze, leading consumer inflation to rise to 61 per cent by the end of 1999 and cost inflation to 187 per cent (Figures 6.6 and 6.7).

The downward spiral concluded only after the country abandoned its currency to adopt the US dollar in March 2000.[24] Once dollarization was established, prices raced to adjust to purchasing parity levels. Annual inflation reached its peak of 108 per cent in September 2000. But since then it fell steadily to 2.2 per cent by July 2004 and was expected to reach about 2.8 per cent by the end of 2004.

The high rate of inflation that prevailed until 2003 – by international standards – hides greater price stabilization. Inflation of tradable goods inflation has averaged close to zero since the first quarter of 2002. These represent about two-thirds of the goods and services measured by the consumer price index. Additionally, since mid-2002, about 92 per cent of the overall inflation rate has been caused by price increases in five items: rent, electricity, water, education and transportation. With the exception

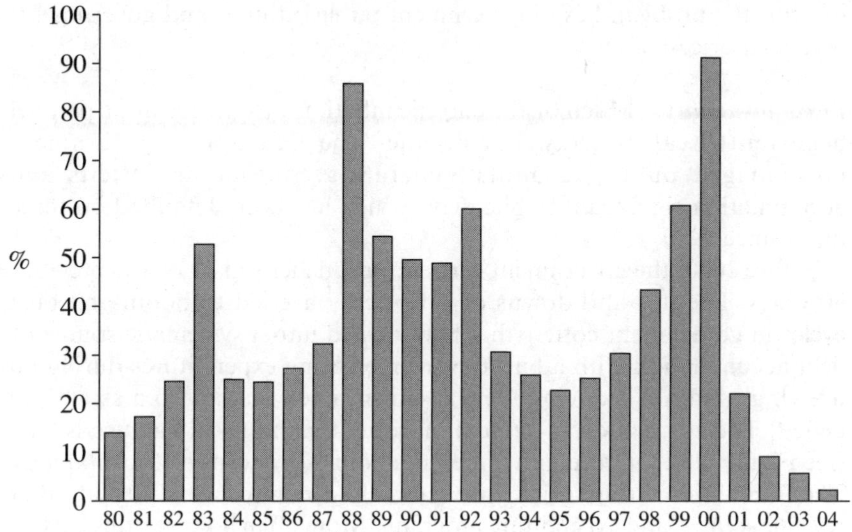

Source: Central Bank of Ecuador.

Figure 6.6 Ecuador, inflation (year-end)

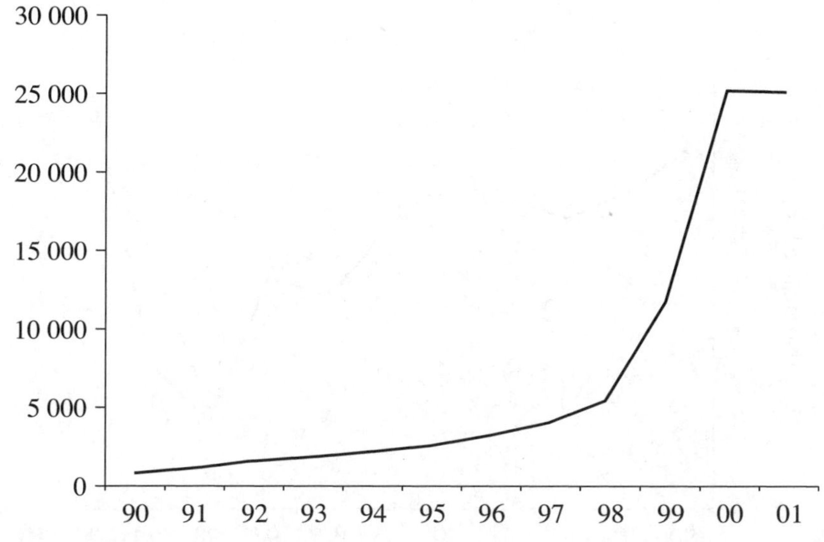

Source: Central Bank of Ecuador.

Figure 6.7 Nominal exchange rates (sucre/US$)

of rent, the problem lies in government public utilities and government-regulated prices.

Fiscal instability Much of the chronic inflation was the result of parallel persistent fiscal disarray. For decades, the Ecuadorian government mismanaged public accounts, generating continuous deficits and accumulating significant public debt, which has been defaulted on three times since 1980.

Before 2000, the government carried fiscal deficits in 21 of the previous 30 years. The ups and downs of oil prices have led to boom and bust cycles in government coffers that have turned into a systematic source of debt accumulation with a bias toward increasing expenditures during oil upswings and not reducing them in down times, leading to a structural deficit. The correlation of annual oil revenues and fiscal balance is 0.87 (see Figure 6.8). Oil revenues represent about 30 per cent of fiscal takings. The fluctuations in its price automatically generated volatility in other revenue sources and expenditure programs. More often however, this led to a tendency to finance the deficits through money creation, with the subsequent inflationary pressure. As a result, the country suffered repeated currency and debt crises. In 1999 and 2000, these were pushed to the limit by a major financial crisis that strained the government finances, generating a severe acceleration of inflation and devaluation.

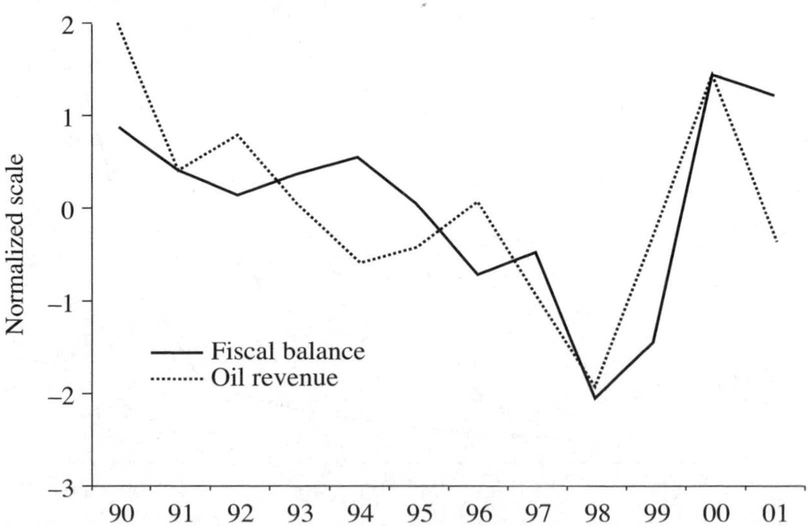

Source: Author.

Figure 6.8 Fiscal volatility and oil revenue volatility

Beginning in the 1980s, various attempts at structural reform were made. However, these created a vicious cycle of austerity packages, devaluations and public protests that were followed by a slackening of fiscal policy and accelerating inflation. In this period, the average fiscal deficit was 7.3 per cent of GDP.[25] Total public debt ballooned from 38.8 per cent of GDP in 1980 to 104.5 per cent in 1989.

In the early 1990s reform efforts were deepened; however they were not sustained. In 1994, the government consolidated the foreign debt and through a Brady Plan, restructured its debt with commercial and official creditors. Lower interest payments, because of partial debt servicing before the renegotiation and because of better terms obtained afterwards, helped maintain a NFPS deficit of 0.4 per cent of GDP on average between 1990 and 1995.

In the mid-90s a cascade of negative external and domestic events contributed to the derailment of the adjustment and stabilization process. A short border conflict with Peru in 1995 and its related military expenditures pushed the fiscal deficit over 1.0 per cent of GDP. Then political instability and the El Niño phenomenon brought to the surface the accumulated structural deficiencies. The average annual deficit jumped to 3.4 per cent, while the accumulated fiscal deficit between 1996 and 1999 was 13.1 per cent of GDP. The plummeting of oil prices exposed a weak and narrow fiscal regime. In 1998 the new government unsuccessfully attempted to reach an agreement with the IMF. The projected deficit in mid-1998 exceeded 10 per cent of GDP. Adjustment measures helped bring it down to 4.8

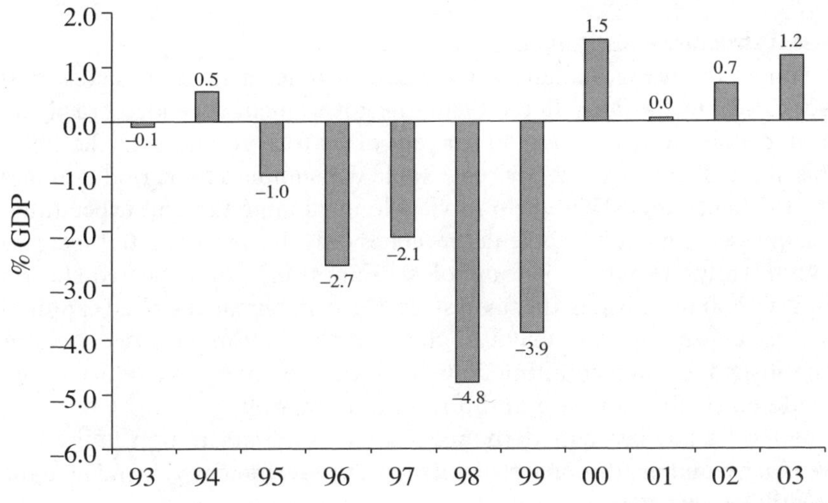

Figure 6.9 Ecuador, non-financial public sector balance, per cent of GDP

per cent. Nonetheless, the economic stagnation, policy errors and halfway reforms had severely deteriorated firms' balance sheets in various sectors. The difficulties were passed onto the banking system, which because of deficient prudential supervision and regulation did not present clear alerts of the underlying problems.

In 1999, the financial crisis was full blown.[26] The unlimited deposit guarantee created new government liabilities of over $2 billion, which later increased to over $4 billion or about 20 per cent of GDP (Figure 6.9).

The fiscal deficit approached 4 per cent of GDP for the second straight year. The government took desperate fiscal measures, some to correct its previous mistakes. Four major tax reforms in 12 months were not enough to prevent defaulting on its foreign and domestic debt in late 1999.

Structural Weaknesses

The heart of the problem lies in the ineffective or inefficient institutions, policies and instruments to counter the volatility. Public expenditures exhibit extreme inflexibility because of generalized earmarking and prefixed programs. The tax regime that prevailed before 2000 was weak, full of loopholes and exemptions and inefficient. The only alternative open to the government was debt accumulation. Between 1990 and 1999, domestic debt ballooned from $213 million to over $3 billion. Foreign debt averaged 69 per cent of GDP in the same period, and following the regularization of payments in 1994, rose from close to $10 billion to $16 billion.

Fiscal structure – institutions

Much of the fiscal volatility is the result of a deficient tax structure and weak fiscal institutions. In the 1980s, the government depended heavily on unstable oil revenues, up to 40 per cent of its total revenues. In the 1990s this share dropped to 32 per cent. Table 6.3 summarizes period averages of fiscal accounts. These help to view long-running tax and expenditure weaknesses. The more stable tax revenues only, however, did not increase significantly. A myriad of loopholes, exemptions, sophisticated elusion and evasion prevailed in the tax system. Corrupt bureaucrats had captured the tax collection department of the Ministry of Finance. It had never established a tax-accounting system. Forms for filing tax returns were outdated. It did not have an information-crossing system. In sum, the country did not have a modern functioning tax administration entity. This weak legal and institutional structure left the government vulnerable to the volatile oil revenues.

Table 6.3 Ecuador, consolidated non-financial public sector 1990–2003, period averages

Category	1990–94	1995–99	2000–03	Average 90–98
In per cent of total revenue				
TOTAL REVENUE	100.00	100.00	100.00	100.00
Oil revenue	35.77	28.4	27.2	32.35
Exports	26.63	15.1	20.5	20.85
Domestic sales of fuels	9.14	13.3	6.8	11.50
Non-oil revenue	52.87	65.0	70.0	58.09
VAT	12.25	16.2	25.7	13.94
Income (personal + corporate)	3.01	2.4	9.6	2.79
Excise	5.53	7.2	2.9	6.64
Import tariffs and surcharges	6.81	8.8	6.2	7.71
Social security contributions	10.44	9.6	10.0	10.41
CTT	0.00	1.9	1.1	0.00
Other	14.84	18.8	14.5	16.59
Operating balance of public enterprises	11.36	6.6	2.7	9.56
In per cent of total expenditure				
TOTAL EXPENDITURE	100.00	100.0	100.0	100.00
Current expenditure	72.95	75.8	75.7	74.07
Interest payments	19.69	20.1	18.6	18.72
Foreign	17.75	14.9	14.6	15.98
Domestic	1.95	5.2	3.9	2.74
Wages and salaries	29.00	29.2	26.8	29.74
Consumption of goods and services	10.44	9.6	12.9	10.11
Other	13.80	16.8	17.5	15.50
Capital expenditure	27.05	24.2	24.3	25.93
Overall balance (in per cent of total revenue)	–1.60	–13.6	3.7	–6.35

Source: Original data Central Bank of Ecuador.

It wasn't until after the crises that the creation of an autonomous Internal Revenue Service (SRI) produced significant improvement in value-added and income tax collections. The series of tax reforms mentioned above between 1999 and 2000 repealed a large part of the exemptions and loopholes and raised the VAT rate from 10 to 12 per cent. These set of reforms added to the institutional changes and good and honest administration have increased tax revenues by more than 6 percentage points of GDP. The SRI has effectively cracked down on evasion and implemented modern invoicing procedures. It set up a sophisticated computer network designed for information crossing. To clean up the inherited bureaucracy, the new administration in the SRI fired and laid off about 1000 tax administration employees within a year. Only two public officials were retained.

These advancements on the revenue side have not been matched on the spending side. Expenditure policy in Ecuador is almost non-existent. After taking out the funds committed to debt service and wages, the government faces about 30 per cent of earmarked or prefixed spending. Only about 10 per cent of revenues are discretionary. This rigid expenditure situation also contributes to fiscal volatility since the margin for countercyclical policy is minimal.

Spending control, ex-post evaluation of projects has generally not been the norm. As a result, there is no accountability over the efficiency and effectiveness of public spending. The budgetary process boils down to making sure that the corresponding transfers to the prefixed spending programs and earmarking are planned and executed (Figure 6.10). Only

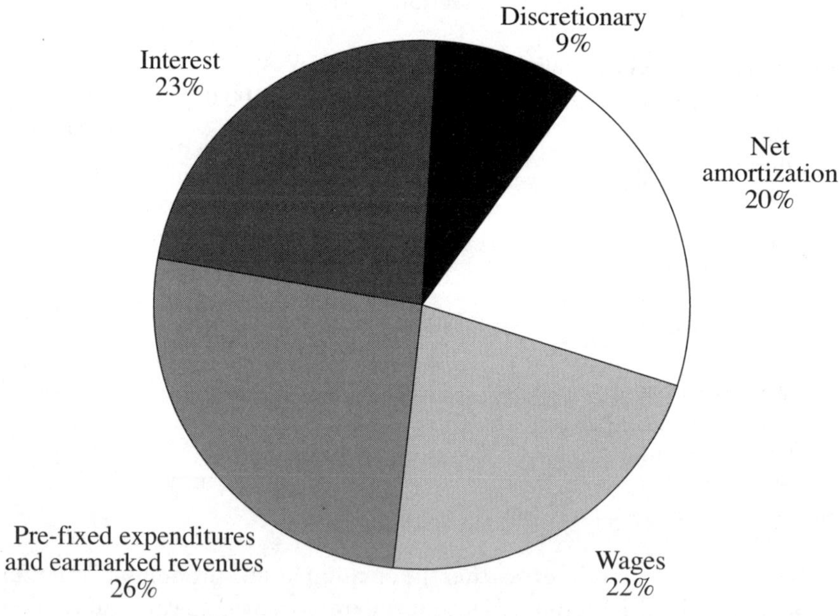

Source: Gallardo (2001).

Figure 6.10 Distribution of expenditures

in 2001, with the support of the World Bank, the government began to implement an information system to track expenditures. However, the results of this are not evident yet.

The constant fiscal ups and downs led to debt accumulation exceeded the fiscal capacity to service it. As a result, and to further finance government growth, governments resorted to central bank financing. The lack of institutional independence of the monetary authorities meant that they succumbed to government demands. A reform in 1992 prohibited credit to the government. However, the ban was circumvented through the banking system.[27] The monetization of the fiscal deficits sustained the chronic inflation and devaluation rates described above.

The recent transformation to a dollarized monetary regime should in part alleviate monetary instability. Between 2000 and 2003, various episodes evidenced the more strict fiscal financing constraint. The government has been forced to make adjustments and produce three consecutive years with fiscal surpluses.

If these trends along with the tax collection efforts are sustained, at least the sort of instability that prevailed in the past should diminish. Of course much more needs to be done to protect the *real* economy from the volatility that it will have to cushion in the absence of nominal adjustment mechanisms. But this is beyond the scope of this chapter.

Low productivity

From a simplified neoclassical growth model it is possible to synthesize the bottom line for the low growth rate of the Ecuadorian economy, which is the absence of productivity in the aggregate economy. Arteta (2000a) estimates the contribution of total factor productivity (TFP) from 1965 to 1997.[72] Table 6.4 presents the contributions of increases in capital, labor and total factor productivity for this period and various subperiods.

Marked by changing trends in economic performance, the decomposition of output growth yields significant differences in the contribution made by total factor productivity (TFP). In the period 1965–97, labor contributed 39 per cent GDP growth during this period, while TFP contributed 33 per cent and capital 28 per cent. Thus, to an overwhelming degree, economic growth in Ecuador has been driven by factor accumulation, in particular labor. Even though for the entire period studied the increased participation of labor is a bit higher than the growth in factor productivity, most of the subperiods demonstrate that labor has played a much larger role. But marked changes are evident when the period is broken down into the three decades. In the 1970s TFP contributed to almost 50 per cent of high output growth (8.4 per cent). This can be explained by the beginning of large-scale petroleum exploitation. Not surprisingly, this period followed a period at the end of

Table 6.4 Sources of growth in Ecuador (in percentage points)

Period	Growth rate of output	Contribution by component[a]			Per cent contribution to growth[b]		
		Labor	Physical capital	Total factor productivity	Labor	Physical capital	Total factor productivity
1965–97	4.64	1.8	1.3	1.54	(–38.8)	(–28.1)	(–33.1)
1965–69	3.11	1.19	1.29	0.63	(–38.3)	(–41.5)	(–20.2)
1970–74	10.16	1.9	1.6	6.65	(–18.8)	(–15.7)	(–65.5)
1975–79	5.49	1.71	2.2	1.58	(–31.2)	(–40.1)	(–28.8)
1980–84	1.27	1.26	0.9	–0.9	(–99.6)	(–71.1)	(–70.7)
1985–89	1.44	1.12	0.37	–0.05	(–77.7)	(–25.6)	(–3.3)
1990–94	2.97	1.4	0.32	1.26	(–47)	(–10.8)	(–42.2)
1970–79	8.38	2.01	2.2	4.18	(–23.9)	(–26.2)	(–49.8)
1980–89	1.79	1.33	0.69	–0.23	(–74.6)	(–38.5)	(–13.1)
1990–97	2.82	1.53	0.45	0.84	(–54.2)	(–16)	(–29.7)

Notes:

[a] The contribution of labor is its compound growth rate for the period multiplied by its share ($1-\alpha = 0.70$) and the contribution of capital is its growth rate multiplied by its share ($\alpha = 0.30$).

[b] Represents the proportional contribution of each factor to the growth rate.

Source: Author's calculations based on Central Bank data.

the 1960s when there was a large accumulation of the capital stock. This trend however reversed in the 1980s when TFP was negative and most of the scant growth (1.8 per cent) on the decade was attributed to ever-higher participation of labor in the economy. Between 1990 and 1997, the growth in productivity rose and explains one third of the economic growth. However, the accumulation of labor still explains over 54 per cent of recovery from the previous decade.

An effort is made to explain the variation of aggregate TFP. Regression analysis suggests that over 47 per cent of the variation in TFP over time is explained by petroleum production that commenced (on a large scale) in 1972. In addition, natural disasters explain another 40 per cent of TFP growth. Taking these factors into consideration and incorporating them into a parametric estimate of TFP reveals that there was no aggregate productivity growth from 1965. The TFP estimates are statistically indifferent from zero.

Overall, these results suggest that the growth in total factor productivity may explain only a small proportion of the economic growth in Ecuador at best. In particular, some sectors such as manufacturing seemed to have benefited from improvements in TFP. However, recognizing that the country has not been able to sustain prolonged periods of high growth rates, it is also possible to conclude instead, that it is the lack of factor productivity that may be the source of the scant growth in Ecuador (Figure 6.11).

An extension of the above mentioned estimates for the period after dollarization shows no significant change in the long-term trend (Arteta and Baus 2003). Although the stability afforded has increased the average contribution of productivity to GDP growth to over 40 per cent since

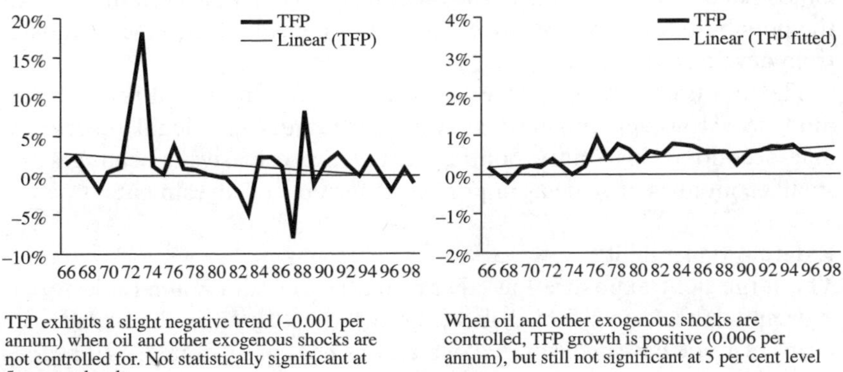

Source: Arteta (2000).

Figure 6.11 Ecuador, total factor productivity (TFP) growth, 1966–98

dollarization was adopted, in 2002 productivity growth fell back to historical levels.

No contingency planning

As demonstrated above, the country is highly susceptible to shocks, particularly those related to oil markets. Nonetheless, the country has never instituted contingency plans or any sort of stabilization fund. The same is true for the El Niño and La Niña phenomena. These occur on average every 3.5 years generating an estimated $400 million in costs.[29] However, the government never built an emergency fund or disaster insurance scheme. Until 1998, and then only on the eve of an imminent financial crisis, the country never set up a deposit guarantee system.

This lack of prudential planning is also expressed in the low domestic savings rates that average 18 per cent. Total investment as a share of GDP averaged 19.2 per cent during 1965–2001. This share decreased in the 1990s to 18.5 per cent. The three-year moving average ICOR (incremental capital-output ratio) over the last ten years has been very volatile. During 1990–94, it was 4.9; during 1995–99 it was –43.5; while during the entire decade it was 11.8. Thus the ICOR, with all its deficiencies as a precise indicator, suggests inefficient investment spending. Arguably, 18.5 per cent annual investment was either 'excessive or inefficient' considering average GDP per capita growth was negative during his period (–0.1 per cent). Most likely what the economy needs is not only higher investment but also better investment.

A probable contributor to the lack of productivity is low technological advancement. Ecuador only manages to attract annually an average of 3.0 per cent of GDP in foreign direct investment. Making matters worse, almost all of it corresponds to the oil industry. This trend certainly retards the possibility of administrative and technological advancement transfer from developed nations.

The unattractiveness of investment in the country would need further analysis. However, business surveys repeatedly cite legal insecurity, macroeconomic instability, political turbulence, excessive tax changes and small economies of scale as important deterrents of investment.

External vulnerability

The large debt exposure has always made Ecuador vulnerable to the exogenous shocks mentioned above. Over the last 30 years, the Ecuadorian terms of trade have deteriorated, which was not compensated, as it needed to be, by productivity growth for the economy to remain competitive. All these factors have led to almost permanent current account deficits, which in the ten years prior to the 1999 crisis sum to 47 per cent of GDP (Figure 6.12). A large aggregate demand and import compression in 1999–2000 led to large surpluses. However, the economic recovery process in 2001–03, appreciation of the real exchange rate and construction of the heavy crude oil pipeline (OCP) inflated the current account deficit. These deficits have been 173 per cent financed by FDI.

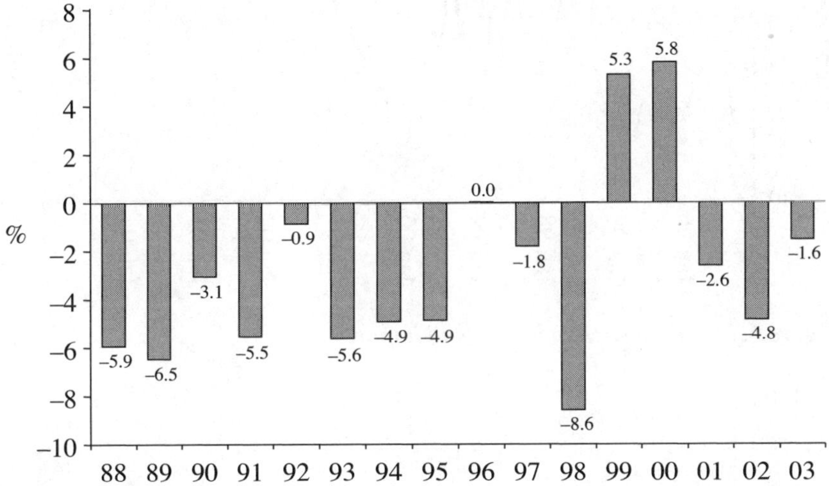

Source: Central Bank of Ecuador.

Figure 6.12 Ecuador, current account balance as per cent of GDP

The economic rebound from the depths of the crisis compounded by the appreciation of the exchange rate fueled import growth (Figure 6.13). However, the rate of growth of imports slowed significantly and by 2003 it was expected that it would approach its equilibrium level as a result of four factors. First, the rate of appreciation is subsiding reaching only about 3 per cent in 2003. Second, the repressed import demand during the crisis years has been satisfied. Third, the imports related to the construction of the OCP have ended. Four, the growth rate of worker remittances that has been financing a good deal of consumer imports and private consumption has declined (Figure 6.14).

Non-competitive domestic markets

A much-unstudied problem in Ecuador is the degree of market competition. However, superficial observation and a few industries that can be analysed suggest a high degree of monopolization, which affects firm conduct and market performance. We present a few examples in Table 6.5.

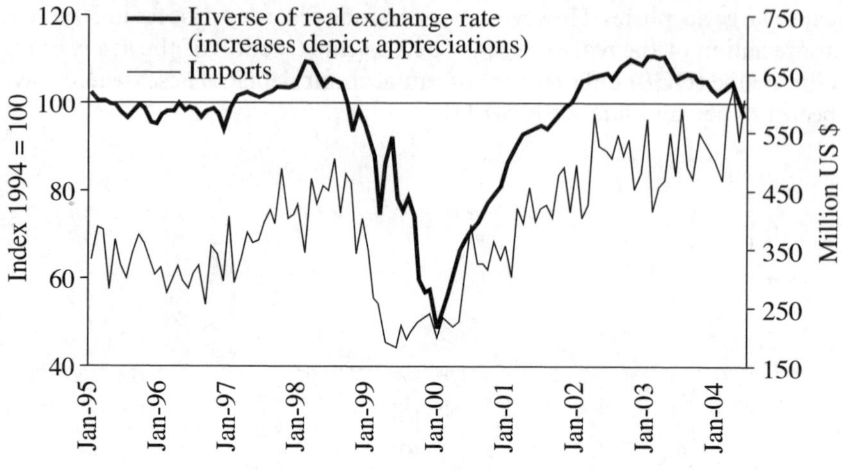

Figure 6.13 Real exchange rate and imports

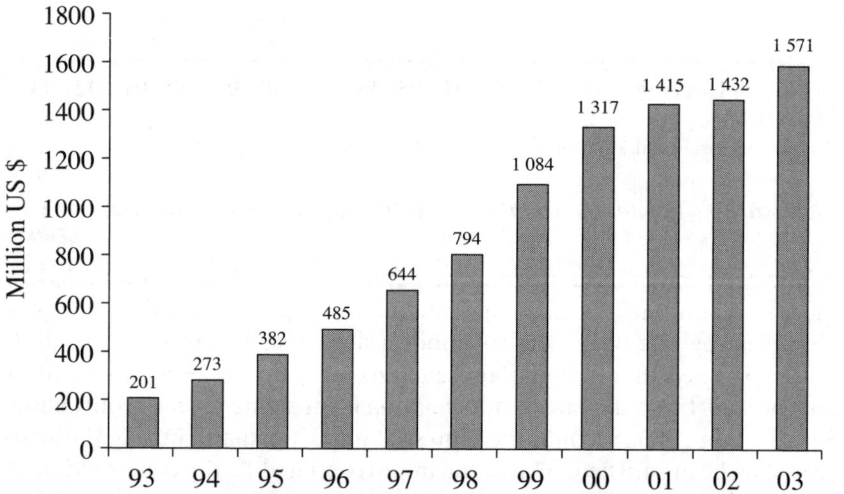

Figure 6.14 Worker remittances

The lack of competition surely hinders the merits and benefits of competition from flourishing. Low growth and high prices, lack of dynamism, limited variety of products and low quality products are all common across Ecuadorian industries. Additionally, government-granted monopolies, protection schemes, price controls, subsidies and others aggravate sub-par economic performance.

Table 6.5 Market concentration

Sector	No. firms	Observation
Electricity generation	9	Seven state–owned. These represent almost all power generation
Telecommunications	3	Divided by three regional markets – state-owned
Cellular providers	2	National market
Wholesale gasoline distribution	1	State-owned
Cement	3	
Automobile builders	3	All under GM and GM–Isuzu partnerships
Banks	24	Top five represent 75% of assets
Beer	2	One holds 89% of sales
Domestic airlines	5	One – Air Force-owned represents 93% of passenger travel
Soda beverages	5	Coca Cola and Pepsi represent 92% of sales
Supermarket chains	4	Two represent 86% of urban sales

Poverty and inequality

Much of Ecuadorians' disenchantment with democracy comes from dissatisfactory economic results. The people expected democratic rule to help reduce the socioeconomic ills of poverty and inequality. However as Figure 6.15 shows, poverty has barely declined. This stagnation is also evident in real per capita income and real wages. In constant prices and in current US dollars, GDP per capita was lower in 2001 than in 1980. The minimum real wage in 2001 was 42 per cent lower than in 1980 and 10 per cent lower than in 1975 (see Table 6.6). These figures are consistent with the insignificant growth in productivity and powerful indicators justifying people's perceptions.

Table 6.7 presents data on the distribution of poverty between rural and urban areas as well as across regions. Poverty in rural areas is 70 per cent higher than in urban areas. What is most striking from the table is the change between 1995 and 1998 in the different regions. While before most of the rural poor were located in the Highland region – where the indigenous population is concentrated – since the crisis the Coastal region surpassed it in the share of its population below the poverty line. However, the same change does not occur for indigence. Urban poverty also changed in similar fashion. The economic crises affected the coastal provinces disproportionately more.

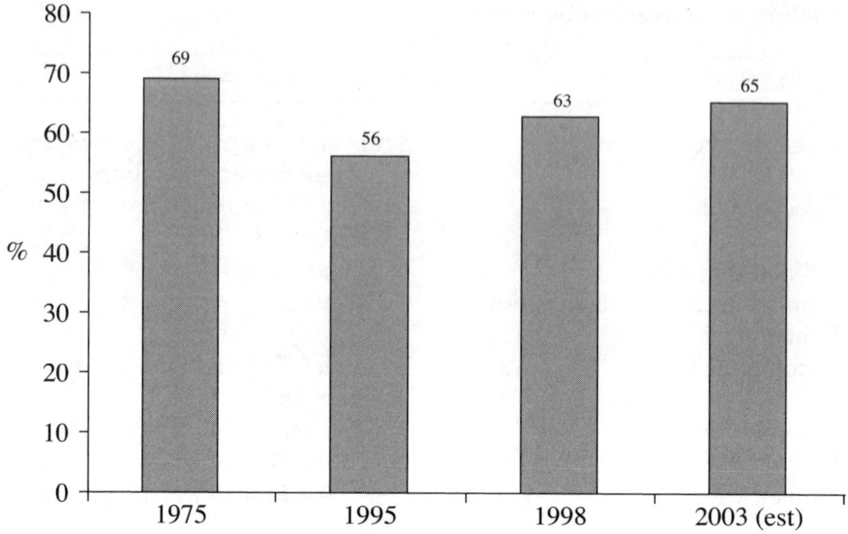

Figure 6.15 *Ecuador, poverty incidence*

Table 6.6 *Per capita income and real wages*

	Per capita income		Minimum monthly wage	
	1975 sucres	US dollars	1975 sucres	US dollars
1970	10 503	272	1344	28
1975	15 598	624	1711	68
1980	19 009	1511	2688	194
1985	18 911	1371	1952	112
1990	18 815	1095	1143	66
1995	20 046	1678	1772	149
1998*	18 700	1619	1631	142
1999*	17 012	1109	1358	98
2001*	17 678	1396	1537	121
2002*	18 643	1642	–	138

Sources:
For 1970–95: Ruíz (1998).
For 1998–01: The author's estimates from data in 'Información Estadística Mensual', Banco Central de Ecuador. These are based on the old National Accounts. For reference, under the new dollar based national accounts released in 2002, GDP per capita for 2002 was $1.92 compared to $1.772 for 1995.

Table 6.7 Ecuador, poverty incidence by region and area 1995–98 (consumption method)

Area	Region	Poverty 1995	Poverty 1998	Indigence 1995	Indigence 1998
Rural	Coast	74.9	83.7	30.5	43.1
	Highlands	77.7	81.5	39.1	49.7
	Amazon	69.9	75.1	23.8	38.7
	Total	75.8	82.0	33.9	46.1
Urban	Coast	42.5	54.4	9.2	15.3
	(Guayaquil)	37.5	45.8	8.0	10.9
	Highlands	42.2	38.9	12.6	9.3
	(Quito)	29.9	29.5	7.8	5.3
	Amazon	47.2	45.3	14.4	9.8
	Total	42.4	48.6	10.6	13.0
Total	Coast	53.9	64.3	16.6	24.7
	Highlands	57.6	59.9	24.1	29.2
	Amazon	65.5	69.3	22.0	33.0
	Total	55.9	62.6	20.0	26.9

Source: Human Development Report, Ecuador 2001, based on INEC Survey on Living Conditions and Standards.

Income distribution

Income distribution presents similar flat trends to poverty. Estimates of distribution of income across households have barely changed in over 25 years. The Gini coefficient estimate in 1979 was 0.575 compared to 0.502 in 1995 and 0.555 in 2000.[30] Households representing the highest 20 per cent of the population earn over 60 per cent of total income. Meanwhile the lowest 20 per cent earn 2.2 per cent of total income.

These facts constrain economic growth by limiting the size of the domestic market for goods and services. Economies of scale are often not achievable. The depth of poverty and large inequality limit the access of most of the population to better education and health services provided by the private sector. This widens further the gap between rich and poor.

Of course, not everything is bad. During the democratic period access to basic services and needs has improved significantly. Table 6.8 presents a sample of the progress in areas such as life expectancy, infant mortality and others. These steps forward however seem to get lost amidst the rest of steps back.

Table 6.8 Ecuador – indicators of social development

Indicator	Value
Life expectancy	
1960	53.1 years
1994	69.3
2001	70.4
Infant mortality rate	
1960	124 /1000
2000	19 /1000
2001	24/1000
Literacy rate	
1970	72%
1999	89.20%
2001	91.00%
School registration rate at each grade – % of population 6–23 years old	
1980	69%
1999	82.10%

Source: CORDES (1999).

6.4 INTERACTION OF ECONOMICS AND POLITICS

The Ecuadorian economy suffers from various ills that contribute to its sub-par performance. It is susceptible to shocks that alter its growth path and suffers from low productivity, which retards growth. Income and opportunities are unequally distributed, which hinders good market functioning. Many key economic policies and institutions are deficient, outdated and replete with incompatible incentives. Meanwhile, the major governance problems are political instability and lack of consensus. A fractionalized party system and polarized political scene produce electoral volatility and cycling of majorities that antagonizes political agents and generates policy instability. The ongoing disagreements prevent compromises, hinder negotiation processes and yield a barren ground for definitive change to occur. Twenty years of reform efforts have not been sustained because of policy discontinuity. For this, the country has paid a high price in the form of low growth, instability and foregone time.

What Explains the Economic and Political Performance?

Sections 6.2 and 6.3 attest to various independent hypotheses of the governance problems and the economic woes. However, the factors present in both are interest group influence and institutional weakness than embed principal–agent problems. These elements translate into lack of transparency and concentration of power that invite rent seeking and rent protection. These hinder efficient economic performance and feed conflictive political action. The end result is an inefficient government averse to change and prone to passing the cost on to the least influential interest group as well as regulation and policy setting susceptible to political and vested interests' influences. We analyse the effects of weak institutions and interest groups in economic issues and political performance in turn.

Economic Effects of Interest Group Influence and Institutional Weakness

Interest group influence marks much rent seeking activity in Ecuador. Protection of special privileges can be traced back for decades in terms of land reform, labor reform, trade reform and others.[31] While in the past these were entrenched in the oligarchic political structure, since the return of democracy interest group activity has become increasingly more evident in the legislative scene and in ministerial and supervisory posts. Much of the political action focuses on limiting economic competition.

Groups that benefited from trade protection under the import substitution umbrella in the 1960s and 70s became open adversaries to opening of the economy in the 1980s. These same groups adamantly opposed the elimination of the fixed exchange rate that prevailed in the 1970s. Some sectors of inefficient domestic industries still lobby to maintain high tariffs. The automobile industry is a case in point. It takes about 30 days for local manufacturers to fit a bus chassis in an Ecuadorian auto body assembly plant, compared to about four days in industrialized nations. Yet, employees and firms are quick to defend 'national industries' when the 27 per cent tariff (plus other taxes and surcharges that add to over 50 per cent of nominal protection) are called upon to be reduced. The protection and inefficiencies are expressed in the high prices of the sheltered industries. For example, the average price of an automobile in Ecuador is 50 per cent higher than in the US market.

Similar cases are present in textiles, plastics, metallurgical, cooking oils, and many other industries. Table 6.5 above sampled the degree of oligopolistic structure in various industries. As Stigler (1971) points out, higher industry concentration provides for higher interest group power. What we have observed in Ecuador over the past 20 years of democratic rule is a wide range of interests, from public sector unions to business trade associations that generate tax policy debates. Each seeks or protects its own interest, while public-interested economic reforms are usually given less importance. Opposition usually succeeds in blocking reforms, allowing only halfway changes, or repealing laws by manipulating legal formalities and the courts.

After a decade of debates, the country is yet to change its obsolete social security system, power and telecommunications infrastructure, seaports and airports mostly due to reform efforts being boycotted by vested interests in public sector unions. The protection from competition, private sector participation and prudential regulation in aggregate contribute to high production costs and low productivity.

Interest groups' interference also contributes to weak institutions. In some cases, they capture public bureaucracies or influence their design to serve their purpose. Of course, often this is the result of an evolutionary process where beneficiaries of a system create a vested interest. This is the case of public sector unions, teachers' associations and the like. The problem is compounded by the incentives inherent in bureaucratic administration (Niskanen 1974). Job perks and benefits are created and protected. Since the checks and balances of the institutional framework are inadequate, and the political incentives are stacked against controlling government growth in public agencies, where the latter exploit the perks through very questionable – and even corrupt – collective bargaining agreements and budget processes. These benefits have reached even the extremes of establishing heir rights to public posts, as is the case in the Social Security Institute. To compound the problem, when proposals are made to reform this fleecing of the state, public sector employees strike or simply engage in rent-protection lobbying campaigns.

But just as common as vested interests are outside groups that influence the operations of an institution. One of the most blatant recent examples of this in Ecuador is the banking superintendency.[32] With very few exemptions, superintendent appointees are usually related to top banks. Independent supervision is compromised. Another very common occurrence is influencing government to fill ministerial posts with personalities tied to interest groups. This is one of the causes of the volatility in policy, since once a minister's policy position is exposed to the public, the struggle amongst interest groups to topple the minister is great.

Weak institutions contribute to low policy credibility, leaving the economy vulnerable to shocks because contingent policies that require planning and extended time horizons for application are not sustained. For its entire history, the Central Bank of Ecuador was widely respected for its technical staff. However, its dependence on the government limited its policy options.

Vulnerable to political influence, it usually succumbed to pressures to monetize fiscal deficits or benefit politically powerful banks or economic sectors. Thus, its policy attempts to control inflation were always doomed. Lack of credibility contributed to time-inconsistent policies and chronic high inflation.

Political machines controlled by interest groups also profit from these weaknesses. Public sector bureaucracy is highly susceptible to political interference. Government agencies have become bloated with political appointees that lack job qualifications. For example, in the mid-1980s, central bank staff were augmented from about 2000 employees to 6000 to comply with electoral promises of jobs.[33] A more extreme case is the Ecuadorian Social Security Institute (IESS). Various administrations have successively increased the number of posts to over 15 000, when it does not need more than about 3000 staff, according to experts.

The political instability brought about by the flux of ministers, lack of legislative consensus and so on, spilled over into economic volatility (Figure 6.15). The high turnover of key ministers (not to mention recent presidential instability) leads to stop-go economic policies, unfinished economic programs and reform efforts that start but are not followed through.

Economic policies have not had continuity from administration to administration, and in many cases not even during the same administration.

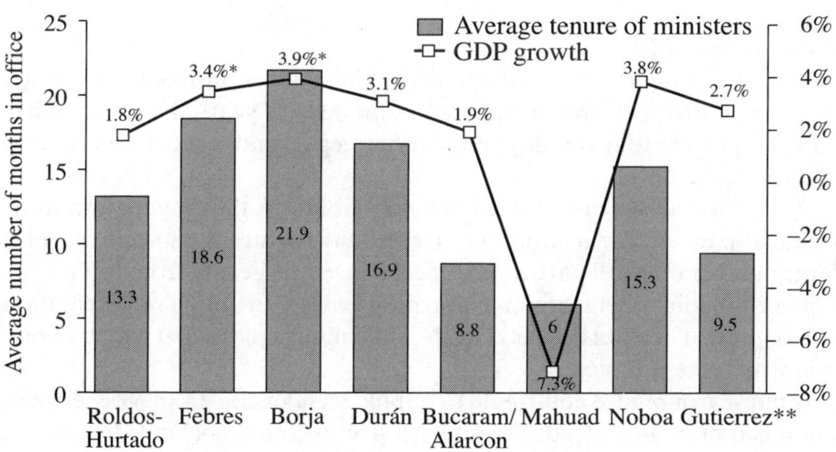

Notes:

* These were adjusted to exclude the distortion from the disruption of oil exports resulting from the 1987 earthquake.

** 2003 only.

Figure 6.16 GDP growth and ministerial instability

As a result, the country has not implemented a long-term program seeking macroeconomic stability, growth and social justice. In fact, during this democratic period, the country negotiated ten letters of intent and reached eight agreements with the International Monetary Fund, but Ecuador has only completed three of them.[34] In the cases when programs were not followed through the economy was managed erratically, without any agenda or direction.

The welfare losses from interest group activities that do not contribute to economic growth but only to transfers from one sector to the other are very difficult to measure. However, if we assume that without all the instability policies that would have corrected the ills of the economy, and GDP would have grown at its potential stable rate of 4.35 per cent per annum, real GDP would be at least 1.6 times higher.

Political Effects of Interest Group Influence and Institutional Weakness

The governance problems of fractionalized political parties, populism and regional conflicts are expressions of interest group influence. Different – competing – groups certainly benefit from the status quo, even though it brings overall negative effects on the political system through weak institutions, political instability, lack of consensus and the inability of the system to resolve society's problems.

Political instability

Interest group influence contributes to the high political instability. Although in general and with the exception of the last six years the country has enjoyed presidential stability, ministerial, legal, and legislative volatility have been the norm.

As argued above, interest groups contribute to the fragmentation of political parties. The institutional framework creates the incentives for a large number of small parties. But special interests benefit from it. They do not need to join other, perhaps competing groups, to obtain representation in Congress. They can do this directly by forming a party that would obtain minority representation.

Interest groups also contribute to populist tendencies. Demagoguery and populism provide a façade for interest groups to hide behind. In essence, special interest free-ride on populist campaigns to get their candidates elected. Then, once in office, they are quick to reap the benefits of complacent public officials.

Another way of looking at party fragmentation is as a diversified representation of interest groups with political labels. This abstract view may be helpful in understanding legislative instability and lack of consensus.

The cycling of majorities or majority coalitions, an important source of the governability problems, and the consequence of the fractionalization of Ecuadorian political representation, constitute a major barrier to carrying out reforms. The cycling of majorities leads to legislation getting approved by one coalition, but soon after it getting modified by another coalition. Sometimes this seesaw occurs through actions across the different branches of government. An exemplary case of this was the value-added tax fiasco in 2001. The government proposed an increase in the tax rate. Congress did not approve it. The government, through the executive veto managed to enact it. The opposition from Congress appealed to their ideologically friendly and 'dependent' constitutional court, which annulled the increase in the tax. This process lasted about four months. Economic agents partially paralysed their activities and partially speculated on the outcome of the tax increase. In the meantime, the IMF program was at stake and falling oil prices seemed to require other fiscal measures to compensate for the lost revenues.

There are two cases where the lack of consensus accumulated insurmountable costs. One is the ten-year delay in building a second oil pipeline, which finally began operating in the fourth quarter of 2003. The other case is the never-ending struggle over the focus of modernization reforms, especially those that call for privatization of government-owned enterprises. Many years of discussion have not been able to find a consensual strategy. According to most public opinion polls about 55 per cent of the population support the privatization and about 30 per cent oppose it. Most of the support is concentrated in the Coastal provinces and business sectors. Under particular conditions, reforms have been approved to allow privatization. However, opposing groups have managed to block privatization attempts by public protests and legal reforms. Other times, political uncertainty, electoral cycles and government turnover have scared off wary investors.

Regional differences in Ecuador also play into policymaking and reform philosophies. The more trade-oriented and business-minded Coastal region repeatedly favors modernization policies and smaller government. But at the same time, business sector rent-seeking and industry protection are influential. On the other hand, the population in the Highland region has tended to be hesitant or incredulous of modernization. Constituents have historically favored more state intervention in the economy, although the recent growth in the non-traditional export sector in this region has somewhat modified the region's attitudes.

Military arbitration

Political instability brought the need for military arbitration on several occasions during the democratic regime. Whilst it is true that the armed forces have contributed towards the stability of the democratic order, especially in circumstances that in early years might have caused the collapse of the democracy, it is also true that the armed forces have become an influential force that have sometimes acted beyond their constitutional mandate. On occasions, some army members have violated the constitutional order. In 1987, the air force commander led an insurrection against President Febres Cordero alleging that the president had trespassed on military norms. In 1995, the army chiefs pushed the administration to remove Vice President Alberto Dahik because the president was weak and could not subordinate the army to his authority. In 1997, the Joint Chiefs of Staff umpired after President Bucaram was removed by a Congress resolution because there were doubts about its legal legitimacy. In 2000, a group of middle-ranking army officers supported an indigenous insurrection and formed a dictatorship because of the social unease of the country during the Mahuad administration. Soon after, they passed power to then Vice President Noboa in a hurried session at the Ministry of Defense.[35] In addition, there have been public statements by army members and hidden pressures aiming to influence decisions that may affect their interests, or what the army believes to be the country's interests. For example, the armed forces opposed the construction of the new oil pipeline. Similarly, they control the Civil Aviation Board that rules over airline licenses. Historically, they have protected the air force's commercial airline, TAME, from competition by limiting entry.

After former Colonel Lucio Gutiérrez was elected president for 2003–07, increased role of the military became evident. His background has led him to appoint numerous former military officials to his ministerial cabinet and other key public offices. Gutiérrez has also announced that he will propose constitutional reforms that would allow military personnel to vote. Time will tell if this greater participation of the military will become a threat to democracy or not. But certainly, recent events have changed the past two decades of diminishing military influence in politics.

The influence of special interests is not limited to the executive and legislative branches. As was argued above, the court system is dependent on the political front. Different parties and influential groups frequently pressure judges and judicial decisions. By interfering even in the courts, the end result is a very high degree of ingovernance. Since the people don't even have a last recourse of reliable action to guarantee their rights, the effective principal–agent relationship lacks the 'end-monitor' to rule over disputes. Thus, the system or institutional framework allows a huge loophole for democratic representatives (that is agents) to shirk without the people (that is principals) having a last option to demand true representation.

The unchecked interference of interest groups in the Ecuadorian democratic system through strong institutions and independent courts, leads to severe misrepresentation. For the most part, voter-citizens are unprotected from even extreme and corrupt rent seeking and protection that are preventing economic and social development. These elements provide an ideal political environment for a democracy to minimize the interests of voter-citizens. Importantly, current generations would have the incentive to pass-on the bill to future – non-voting and not represented – generations. Thus Ecuador's highly indebted economy is the result of the type of incentive structure that Buchanan and Wagner (1977) aptly call 'democracy in deficit' in reference to the tendency of current generations to consume at the expense of future generations.

Feedback of Economic Conditions to Political System

The prevailing susceptibility of the political system to interest group influence and lagging institution building arises from a variety of sources. Some may come from cultural origins inherited from colonial times, others from the socioeconomic conditions. As Crain and Tollison (1993) point out following Olson (1965), unfortunately political science and economics have been unable to provide robust predictive theories of the formation of interest groups. Suggestive hypotheses point to the prevailing incentives and institutional structures. Others, in particular Olson, emphasize pre-existing conditions that may render political activity more effective, for example organizations and groups that form for some other purpose that later find political action to be an effective byproduct to further their interests. This is the case of trade associations, unions, social clubs, and so on. Under this hypothesis, the conditions for interest group influence and concentration of power in Ecuador are overwhelming. Aristocratic and oligarchic legacies, social class divisions, narrow (for example regional) trade associations are all elements that facilitate political action. As a byproduct of their principal motive of association, links of kin, landownership concentration, and special rights handed down from colonial times, evolved from business oligarchies into political oligarchies. Further strength of interest group power is derived from asymmetry in firm sizes, products, and high industry concentration that dominates economic organization in Ecuador, allowing, according to Stigler (1971), more effective collective action.

An important factor that contributes to the political instability is the absence of social consensus. Again, this is the result of a tug of interests. Political analysts have pointed out to exhaustion how the deficiencies in the democratic institutions and players cause political stalemates that block economic reform efforts. Democracy requires equal access and assumes basic freedoms. These however are truncated in Ecuador because of unequal opportunities and endowments. The severely skewed distribution of income, which is correlated with deficient access to good health and education, inhibits smooth democratic participation. Information gaps between those who have it and those that don't play into the lack of consensus and the continuous acceptance of populist policies and candidates.

These factors are magnified as between urban/rural populations and among indigenous and non-indigenous ethnic groups. Poverty and less access to health, education and basic services are more pronounced in rural and indigenous populations.

Reforms towards the Improvement of Governance

The need to overcome some of the governance problems mentioned, as well as to set up sound functioning institutions, has been under discussion and consideration for many years in Ecuador. In the constitution approved in 1978, a disposition limiting the parties' fragmentation was included. According to the norm, if a party was to continue existing, it had to have national organization and receive at least 5 per cent of the national votes in two consecutive multiperson elections. A specific Political Parties Law was passed to regulate the birth, life and extinction of political organizations. The purpose was to establish a group of doctrinaire, democratic and representative parties, and make them appropriate channels of political expression. Additionally, the law provided political organizations with public funding.

The Elections Law approved in the same year established electoral expenditure restrictions, in order to ensure equal access to media appearances by any candidate or political party. Through this restriction, lawmakers intended to avoid the predominance of money in campaigns, and avoid inappropriate advantages of some candidates at the expense of others.

In the constitutional reform of 1983, Congress granted the president's capacity to send a project as economically urgent, in which case it had to be discussed and approved within 15 days. If it was not debated and voted upon, the bill would automatically become law, but Congress retained the capacity to reform it or revoke it in the future. The reform also took away from Congress and gave to the executive the ability to set public sector wages.[36] The reforms were useful for the 1984 and later administrations, since they were allowed to carry out programs and face economic crises, especially in cases when the government did not hold majority support in Congress.

Since Ecuador returned to democracy in 1979, Congress became used to restaffing the Supreme Court of Justice according to the interest of political parties that held a majority in Congress. To avoid this practice that gave rise to corruption and politicized intervention in the judiciary, a constitutional reform in 1997 extended life tenure to Supreme Court judges, and established a transparent selection process based on merit. Vacancies were supposed to be filled by cooption. Also, the National Judiciary Council (Consejo Nacional de la Judicatura) was created, as an institution in charge of governing and managing the judicial branch. The reforms mentioned have not resolved the weaknesses of the justice system, but the changes have helped reduce problems. More time is needed in order to change lower courts in the same fashion as the Supreme Court.

The Constitutional Assembly undertook the most ambitious efforts to resolve governance problems in 1998. It approved norms to strengthen presidential authority, limit legislative intervention in economic issues, promote cabinet members' stability, avoid political intervention in Central Bank policies, eliminate political parties without minimum electoral support, eliminate mid-term congressional elections (usually lost by the political party in office), give the president capacity to increase public spending and taxes, forbid Congress to increase the fiscal budget, establish simultaneous decentralization of income, expenditure and functions, establish independence and stability of tribunals of justice, and bar Congress from removing Supreme Court judges.

Perhaps three crucial issues remained unresolved: (i) substitution of the proportional electoral system by majority rule, which would encourage political party consolidation and promote majority formation in Congress; (ii) transformation of the Constitutional Tribunal into an independent court of constitutional justice, and (iii) elimination of political parties' control over the Electoral Supreme Court. Such control has been a source of electoral fraud and violations of political-electoral laws.

Despite these three shortcomings, the norms set in the new constitution were thought to be able to fix the major governance problems of the Ecuadorian democracy. However, for the most part, this has not been the case so far. The first president under the new constitution, Jamil Mahuad, lasted in office just one third of his term. During his brief 16-month administration, he had three ministers of economy, several oil ministers, even though Congress could not impeach ministers. Although the new constitution granted extensive legal, budgetary and policy independence to the Central Bank, its board had three presidents during the Mahuad administration. Despite enjoying more constitutional power than his predecessors, President Mahuad led the country to an enormous economic and social crisis, almost provoking the collapse of the democratic system.[37] In a last and, many argue, desperate effort to re-establish economic stability, Mahuad abolished the national currency, and declared the US dollar as the official Ecuadorian currency.[38] In doing so, the president trampled on the Central Bank's autonomy and advice.

The reforms approved by the Constitutional Assembly have not had the desired effects on other areas of public life. The Supreme Electoral Tribunal has not obeyed the norm to eliminate political parties without 5 per cent of popular support in the last two elections. All political parties with congressional representatives continue fragmented with personal or local interests, government intervention, and other conflict of interests, regardless of the norms seeking to avoid it. Despite a constitutional prohibition, a provincial autonomy project was almost approved (and the risk of such approval has not disappeared). The autonomy system would have caused large revenue losses to the central government while keeping its spending obligations. Both Presidents Mahuad and Noboa, and Congress violated the constitution, for example, when they abolished the sucre as the national currency. They also infringed the constitution when they sent multiple-issue urgent economic bills to Congress in violation of Article 148 of the constitution. Congress has proposed bills to increase public expenditures against constitutional norms that allow only the president to do so, and neither Mahuad, Noboa or Gutiérrez have complained. Additionally, four years after the new constitution came into effect, Congress is yet to enact a number of laws to adapt legal statutes to the new Magna Carta.

6.5 LIMITS OF LEGAL FORMALITIES[39] AND FINAL THOUGHTS

Constitutional reforms aiming to resolve the main governance problems of the Ecuadorian democracy have proven to be enough to provide the political system with the stability necessary to improve social and economic conditions. The last experience in 1998 – Ecuador has had one constitution every nine years on average – suggests that constitutional engineering is not enough to resolve the governance problems of Ecuadorian democracy, or enough to build the necessary institutions for a well-functioning democracy.

The correct functioning of institutions also depends on the people in charge of running and building them, who in turn depend on the citizens that form a political society. Hence, people's everyday behavior, which is determined by cultural values of society, is also important. In other words, the set of values, feelings, attitudes and customs matter as well.

Some cultural values of several sectors of Ecuadorian society do not seem to be compatible with good functioning democratic institutions. Ecuadorians tend to ignore norms, disobey rules and decisions. People often do not honor agreements; thus, suspicion and distrust instead of confidence are frequently present in social and political relations. Citizens make claims to have their needs satisfied and their problems resolved through government action and public authorities instead of through their own individual effort.

People and organizations do not harmonize special with collective interests in their daily life. It is common for authorities to subordinate the public interest to individual and special interests. Lack of tolerance, a tendency toward conflict, and the misplaced conviction that when one wins the other one loses, block the possibility of rational discussion, interest matching, consensus building, and negotiation of agreements. The notion of possible win-win negotiations is not widely held – perhaps precisely because of a long history of bad experiences resulting from non-democratic manipulation of processes and institutions.

Decisionmakers are often more concerned about the beneficiary of their decisions rather than caring about the merits, needs and rights of those who demand the attention of the authorities. People trust more in political influence and personal relations than in institutions and legal norms. Therefore, democracy is not seen as a political system demanding equal obligations and providing equal opportunities to people. Political relations shape a network of commitments, privileges and sinecures. The network is preference-ranked above national interests, economic growth and social progress. The proclivity to transfer individual responsibilities to the state and its authorities creates the conditions for paternalism and populism. The absence of the long-term view – a consequence of high volatility – drives people to expect immediate results from policies that would otherwise require time, effort and perseverance to develop and reveal the benefits. All these are weaknesses that have retarded the formation of citizens committed to the country's future, one in which they ought to participate with their generosity and effort.[40]

To improve governance in Ecuador, it will be just as necessary to build sound and strong institutions as to work toward building better citizenship. This is not an easy task. The 1998 Constitutional Assembly contributed in this direction by approving Article 97, in which rights and obligations of Ecuadorians were laid down for the first time in the constitutional history of Ecuador. Before, only rights were extensively stated but never obligations. But of course, better citizenship requires much more than proclamations. It requires long education processes in schools, the media, religion, political parties, and organizations of civil society.

The profound governance problems in Ecuador require encompassing changes. The solutions are complex because, as we have argued, the problems involve economic and political issues. Progress has been made in both areas. However, many of the remaining problems correspond to the bidirectionality or synergy between deficiencies of the political system that prevent economic progress and conversely. Concerted efforts will be required to resolve the economic inefficiencies and inequalities that distort the incentives to political agents. But at the same time, governance impasses need to be resolved to find consensual reform programs that can allow sustainable economic policies.

NOTES

* The authors are grateful for the auspices of CEPAL, the Ford Foundation and the Inter American Dialogue. We thank Andrés Solimano for his guidance and comments on earlier versions. Special thanks go to Paul Beckerman and Igor Paunovic for helpful critiques and observations that improved the chapter. We also recognize insightful suggestions made by the participants at a CEPAL conference on the political economy of Andean nations held in Santiago, Chile. Finally, we would like to thank Vicente Albornoz for his input into the final revision. We take full responsibility for any remaining errors or omissions.

1. See CORDES, *Tendencias Económicas y Financieras* (1999), for an account of the Ecuadorian 1999 financial crisis where camping contributions, a connected superintendent and the largest private bank all conspired to obtain special privileges.
2. Huntington (1968).
3. It is possible to trace this back to the period 1925–48 when the country had an average of one president per year, some constitutional, some dictators and even ad-hoc presidents that resulted from chaotic political circumstances.
4. Except in the case of President Jaime Roldós, who died in a plane crash while in office and was replaced by his Vice President.
5. Jaime Roldós and Osvaldo Hurtado are considered a single administration. Roldós was in office for 21 months, and Hurtado for 39 months. At the time, the presidential term lasted five years.
6. Burbano de Lara and Rowland (1998), pp. 99–103.
7. Currently, the proposal to revoke this norm counts on the majority support of Congress and political parties.
8. The income tax was eliminated in 1998 and replaced by a 1 per cent tax on capital transactions, which was eliminated in 2000 after the income tax was restored in 1999. In late 1999, the VAT rate was raised from 10 to 12 per cent. After a long debate in 2001, this tax was raised from 12 to 14 per cent in 2001. Two months later, the Constitutional Tribunal declared it unconstitutional, and was decreased back to 12 per cent.
9. Almost all the parties that existed before that year have disappeared since they did not maintain the minimum vote requirements (Conservative, Liberal, Socialist, Extreme Left Front, Communist, and People's Force Concentration). These vanished parties were important political participants in the early and mid-20th century, especially the Conservative and Liberal parties, which had been very influential since the foundation of the Republic in 1830.
10. Mejía (1998), p. 27.
11. In the Coast region, liberalism, entrepreneurship and big business are common traits. In the Highlands, meanwhile, social and religious conservatism with hacienda-like paternalism are more common. Despite this contrast, both regions have an entrenched bias toward government assistance and rent seeking, but again with differences. In the Coast region the tendency is to seek mercantilist aid to businesses while preaching liberal economic policies and small government. In the Highlands, strong lobbying for rent protection in agriculture, industry and trade dominate along with more predispositions toward a welfare state.
12. This practice is called 'cambio de camiseta' (shirt change) in reference to the change in alliance that the administration's offerings cause.

13. CORDES (1999), p. 167.
14. For example, the once prominent businessman and owner of Banco del Progreso, Fernando Aspiazu, is currently in jail at the time of writing for not paying taxes, and not because of his bank felonies, even though the financial fraud and scams were proven beyond doubt over two years ago. Bankers who have caused bankruptcy of their institutions, and who have swindled the Central Bank and the clients, have obtained beneficial sentences and the right to be reimbursed part of the performing loans portfolio, to the detriment of the clients.
15. PNUD (1998).
16. *Monitor*, December 2001.
17. Ecuador was a full member of OPEC until 1993 when it abandoned the cartel.
18. Arteta (2000).
19. These figures come from the revised national accounts in US dollars issued by the Central Bank of Ecuador in 2002 and differ from earlier versions of this material presented in Chile and New York. The rates of growth are very similar to the old national accounts. The largest difference occurs in 1998. The old accounts reported GDP growth at 0.4 per cent while the new accounts report 2.1 per cent growth. In 1999 the output decline in the old accounts was 7.3 per cent, while in the new ones it was 6.3 per cent. By far the greatest difference between the new and old accounts lay in the levels of GDP in current US dollars. For example, the old accounts reported GDP falling from \$19.7 billion in 1998 to \$13.6 billion in 2000. The new national accounts report GDP at \$23.4 billion and \$15.9 billion for the same years, respectively.
20. Fernández and Lara (1998). The author extended the exercise to 1998.04. In the first quarter of 1999, which coincides with the beginning of the crises a structural break occurs in the series. However, since the economy is still in the recovery phase, it is not possible to determine if GDP will return to its long-term growth rate or if the crises caused a structural trend break of the series. Moreover, the meticulous econometric exercise required is beyond the scope of the present chapter.
21. Fernandez and Lara (1998) identify 11 shocks or structural breaks. We identify one more negative break in 1998.01, which we attribute to El Niño and another in 1999.01 that marks the unfolding of the beginning of the financial and economic crises.
22. This is lower that the simple arithmetic average growth rate of 4.9 per cent during this period. The difference is due to structural changes in the economy.
23. Cagan (1956).
24. Arteta (2001) provides a succinct description of the factors that contributed to dollarization.
25. This is an implicit estimate obtained from the growth of the public debt, which reflects the variation of the consolidated public sector balance. There are no reliable figures for the NFPS until 1988. In the years 1988, 89, and 90 for when there are official statistics, the average deficit was 2.1 per cent of GDP. But this figure excludes central bank losses from the sucretization of private external debts in the early 1980s and later modifications. More importantly in these years, the government did not service its foreign debt completely.
26. See CORDES 1999–2000. Also, a comprehensive account of the institutional deficiencies is given in Comunidad Andina (2001).
27. The independence granted in 1998, during the constitutional reform, was too little too late to prevent interference in the Central Bank board when the fiscal and financial crisis of 1998–2000 unfolded.
28. For this, we decompose the rate of economic growth into its most basic economic factors: capital (k), labor (l) and technological change or productivity (a). $y(t) = a(t)k(t)^{\alpha}l(t)^{\beta}$. Taking time derivatives of the logarithmic transformation of the above neoclassical growth function and assuming constant returns to scale the capital and labor shares add to one ($a + (1 - a) = 1$), the expression relates the growth of output (Y_t) to the growth of the capital stock (K_t), of labor (L_t) and of technology or productivity growth (A_t),

$$Y_t = A_t + a_t K_t + (1-a_t) L_t.$$

The decomposition of this can be done either by applying growth accounting methodology (as suggested by Solow (1957) and followers) of applying fixed factor shares or parametrically. Arteta (1999, 2000) estimates the contribution of these factors to GDP using both.

29. Arteta and Samaniego (2002).
30. CORDES (1999) and PNUD (2001).
31. Hurtado (1997).
32. See supra note 14.
33. There was so much redundancy that even the gardening department had multiple managerial levels.
34. One was by the Hurtado government, another by the Febres Cordero administration and more recently by Noboa.
35. Although in this instance the constitution describes unambiguously the succession of power, the intrigue was the point at which Noboa assumed power. It should have been in Congress not in the Ministry of Defense.
36. Before the reform it was common for Congress to bind administrations by abruptly raising wages without financing. To pay for higher wage bills, the administration would have to propose or implement unpopular adjustment measures that would hurt the political party in office, and during the next election. This exacerbated political cycles, instability and economic policy.
37. To be fair, Mahuad inherited an economy with severe underlying economic and financial problems. Many of these can be traced to irresponsible economic management by previous administrations and political volatility. Before he took office a large portion of the banking system was already insolvent. El Niño was devastating the country's agriculture and infrastructure. Oil prices, at $10 a barrel, had dropped to their lowest levels in over 30 years. However, his administration made significant policy errors that made a foreseeable crisis much worse.
38. This highly controversial policy was, in fact, unconstitutional. Article 264 of the Political Constitution has not been repealed or modified. This article states that the Central Bank has the exclusive responsibility for monetary policy. Moreover, the article still states that the sucre is the official currency. 'La emisión de moneda con poder liberatorio ilimitado será atribución exclusiva del Banco Central. La unidad monetaria es el sucre, cuya relación de cambio con otras monedas será fijada por el Banco Central.'
39. On this issue we would like to refer to important publications such as *Democracy in America* (de Toqueville 2000), *El Subdesarrollo está en la Mente* (Harrison 1989), *Making Democracy Work* (Putnam 1994), *La Sociedad de la Desconfianza* (Peyrefitte 1996) and *Confianza* (Fukuyama 1996).
40. Hurtado (1994), pp. 107–21; Hurtado (2001), pp. 121–8; CORDES (1999).

BIBLIOGRAPHY

Araujo, M.C. (1998), 'Gobernabilidad durante la crisis y políticas de ajuste', Proyecto CORDES – Gobernabilidad, *Documento de Trabajo* no. **6**, Quito: CORDES.

Arcos, C. (1998), 'Demandas y conflictos sociales en el sistema político ecuatoriano', Proyecto CORDES – Gobernabilidad, *Documento de Trabajo* no. **10**, Quito: CORDES.

Arteta, G. (2000), 'Los flujos de capital extranjero en el Ecuador: uso, destino y consecuencias', *Cuestiones Económicas*, Quito: Banco Central del Ecuador.

Arteta, G. (2000a), 'Productivity growth and industrial structure in the Pacific region, Ecuador', *Pacific Economic Outlook Structure Project*, Japan Committee for Pacific Economic Outlook, Osaka, Japan.

Arteta, G. (2001), 'Dollarization in Ecuador: experiences, challenges, and lessons', *American Insights*, September (See also www.iamericas.org).

Arteta, G. and C. Baus (2003), '¿En dolarización ha cambiado la competitividad?', *Carta Económica*, **4**, Quito.

Arteta, G. and P. Samaniego (2002), 'Patrimonio del estado y sustentabilidad fiscal en el Ecuador', in Gustavo Garcia (ed.), *Patrimonio del Estado*, Caracas: IELSA.

Banco Mundial (1998), 'Más allá del consenso de Washington', Washington, DC: World Bank.

Buchanan, J. and R. Wagner (1977), *Democracy in Deficit: The Political Legacy of Lord Keynes*, New York: Academy Press.

Burbano de Lara, F (1997), 'Antecedentes de la nueva democracia, la ilustración de los años 60 y 70', Proyecto CORDES – Gobernabilidad, *Documento de Trabajo* no. **3**, Quito: CORDES.

Burbano de Lara, F. (1998), 'Cultura política y democracia en el Ecuador: una aproximación a nuestros vacíos', Proyecto CORDES – Gobernabilidad, *Documento de Trabajo* no. **10**, Quito: CORDES.

Burbano de Lara, F. and M. Rowland (1998), 'Pugna de poderes, presidencialismo y partidos en el Ecuador: 1979–1997', Proyecto CORDES – Gobernabilidad, *Documento de Trabajo* no. **7**, Quito: CORDES.

Cagan, P. (1956), 'The monetary dynamics of hyperinflation', in Milton Friedman (ed.), *Studies in the Quantitative Theory of Money*, Chicago: University of Chicago Press.

Chávez, A.P. (1998), 'Reforma constitucional ¿Más gobernabilidad?', Quito: FESO.

CORDES (1999), *La Ruta de la Gobernabilidad*, Informe final del Proyecto CORDES – Gobernabilidad, Quito: CORDES.

CORDES (1999, 2000), *Tendencias Económicas, Políticas y Financieras*, Quito: CORDES.

Comunidad Andina (2001), *Los Seguros de Depósitos en los Países Andinos: Propuestas para un Régimen Común*, Lima: Secretaría General Comunidad Andina.

Crain, M. and R. Tollison (1994), 'Toward a positive public choice', in Mark Crain and Robert Tollison (eds), *Predicting Politics: Essays in Empirical Public Choice*, Ann Arbor, Michigan: University of Michigan Press.

de Toqueville, A. (2000), *Democracy in America*, New York: Bantam.

Del Búfalo, E. and G. Ríos (2002), 'Venezuela: from stability to turmoil', mimeo, Santiago de Chile.

Echeverría, J. (1997), 'La democracia bloqueada: teoría y crisis del sistema político ecuatoriano', Quito: Editorial Letras.

Fernández, G. and C. Lara (1998), 'Los shocks exógenos y el crecimiento económico en el Ecuador', *Documento Técnico* no. **48**, Dirección General de Estudios, Quito: Banco Central del Ecuador.

Franco, R. (ed.) Sociología del Dessarrollo, Políticas Sociales y Democratia, Siglo XXI, México.

Freinderberg, F. and M. Alcántara (2001), *Los Dueños del Poder*, Quito: FLACSO.

Fukuyama, F. (1996), *Confianza,* Atlántida, Buenos Aires.

Fundación Futuro Latinoamericano (1998), *Consensos para una Propuesta de Gobernabilidad para el Ecuador*, Grupo de Cousin I, II y III.

Gallardo, J. (2001), *Reforma Fiscal: Garantía para las Nuevas Generaciones*, Quito: Ministerio de Economía y Finanzas, August.
Harrison, L. (1989), *El Subdesarrollo está en la Mente*, México City: Limusa.
Huntington, S. (1968), *Political Order in Changing Societies*, New Haven, Connecticut, Yale University Press.
Hurtado, O. (1994), 'Cultura política', in *Léxico Político Ecuatoriano*, Quito: ILDIS, pp. 107–21.
Hurtado, O. (1996), 'Gobernabilidad Democracia y Pobreza', *Proyecto Mitigación de la Pobreza y Desarrollo Social, Serie de documentos* no. 7, Quito: PNUD.
Hurtado, O. (1997), *El Poder Político del Ecuador*, Quito: Editorial Planeta.
Hurtado, O. (1999), *Deberes y Responsabilidades Para Ser Buenos Ciudadanos*, Quito: CORDES.
Hurtado, O. (2001), 'Cultura y desarrollo', in Franco (2001).
ILDIS (1990), '*El Tribunal de Garantías Constitucionales, Conflictos y Jurisprudencia Período 1980/1990*', Quito: ILDIS.
Mancero, A. (1997), 'Gobernabilidad del desarrollo a través de la democracia: enfoque del problema, documento provisional para discusión', mimeo, Quito.
Mancero, A. (1998), 'Ingobernabilidad y transición de la democracia Ecuatoriana', Proyecto CORDES – Gobernabilidad, *Documento de Trabajo* no. **9**, Quito: CORDES.
Market Consultores (2001), 'Monitor de la opinión nacional', Quito, December.
Mejía, A. (1986), *¿Una Democracia Ingobernable? Arreglos Constitucionales, Partidos Políticos y Elecciones en Ecuador, 1979–1986*, s.e. Mexico DF.
Mejía A. (1998), 'Partidos políticos: el eslabón perdido de la Representación', Proyecto CORDES – Gobernabilidad, *Documento de Trabajo* no. **5**, Quito: CORDES.
Mejía, A. and N. Wray (1997), 'Asamblea nacional para la reforma política, límites y posibilidades', Proyecto CORDES – Gobernabilidad, *Documento de Trabajo* no. **1**, Quito: CORDES.
Niskanen, W. (1971), *Bureaucracy and Representative Government*, Chicago: Aldine-Atherton.
Olson, M. (1965), *The Logic of Collective Action*, Cambridge, Massachusetts: Harvard University Press.
Organización Demócrata Cristiana de América (1996), *Elecciones en América Latina 1995*, Caracas: ODCA.
Peyrefitte, A. (1996), *La Sociedad de la Desconfianza*, Santiago de Chile: Editorial Andrés Bello.
PNUD (1998), *Gobernabilidad y Desarrollo Democrático en América Latina y El Caribe*, Quito.
PNUD (2001), *Human Development Report*, Quito.
Programa de Apoyo al Sistema de Gobernabilidad Democrática (1998), 'La reforma electoral', *Colección Reforma Política* no. **4**, Quito: Universidad Politécnica Salesiana.
Programa de Apoyo al Sistema de Gobernabilidad Democrática (1997), 'Los grandes temas de la reforma constitucional', *Colección Reforma Política* no. **1**, Quito: Universidad Politécnica Salesiana.
Programa de Apoyo al Sistema de Gobernabilidad Democrática (1997), 'Nueva justicia y revocatoria del mandato', *Colección Reforma Política* no. **3**, Quito: Universidad Politécnica Salesiana.

Programa de Apoyo al Sistema de Gobernabilidad Democrática (1997), 'Reforma política y asamblea nacional', Colección *Reforma Política* no. **2**, Universidad Politécnica Salesiana, Quito.

Putnam, R. (1994), *Making Democracy Work,* Caracas: CEDAI.

Ruiz, L. (1998), 'Ecuador: tendencias de la distribución del ingreso; una visión panorámica', Proyecto CORDES – Gobernabilidad, *Documento de Trabajo* no. **9**, Quito: CORDES.

Salgado, G. and others (1997), 'Consulta popular: reflexiones y propuestas', Proyecto CORDES – Gobernabilidad, *Documento de Trabajo* no. **2**, Quito: CORDES.

Salgado, G. and others (1998), 'Temas para la reforma constitucional ecuatoriana', Proyecto CORDES – Gobernabilidad, *Documento de Trabajo* no. **4**, Quito: CORDES.

Salgado, G. and S. Santiago (1998), 'Problemas fiscales y gobernabilidad', Proyecto CORDES – Gobernabilidad, *Documento de Trabajo* no. **8**, Quito: CORDES.

Sánchez Parga, J. (1995), 'Conflicto y democracia en Ecuador', *Serie Diálogos*, Quito: CAAP.

Sánchez Parga, J. (1998), *La Pugna de Poderes: Análisis Crítico del Sistema Político Ecuatoriano*, Quito: Abya Yala.

Sánchez Parga, J. (1999), *Cultura Política en la Sociedad Ecuatoriana*, Quito: Abya Yala.

Solow, R. (1957) 'Technical changes and the aggregate to production function', *Review of Economics and Statistics*, **39**, August, 312–20.

Stigler, G. (1971), 'Theory of economic regulation', *Bell Journal of Economics and Management Science,* **2**(3).

Stigler, G. (1974), 'Free riders and collective action: an appendix to "Theory of economic regulation"', *Bell Journal of Economics and Management Science,* **5**, 359.

Transparency International (2001), *Report*.

Verdesoto, L. (1996), Temas para una sociedad en crisis ¿Es Posible gobernar desde los consensos?', Quito: Fundación Esquel.

7. Governability and economic performance in 1990s Peru

Miguel Jaramillo and Jaime Saavedra[*]

'En el Perú lo único permanente es lo provisional'
'In Peru, only the provisional is permanent.'
Héctor Verlade, architect and writer in Lima

7.1 INTRODUCTION

The decade of the 1990s brought a series of changes to Peru that, it is often argued, altered the direction of the country. Viewed from a broader historical perspective, however, the period is perhaps similar to other eras in Peru's political past. A charismatic leader without a formal organizational structure comes to power with ideas of reform and institutes an authoritarian government that ends in rampant corruption, economic crisis, and in political upheaval. President Leguía's (1919–30) project, 'la Patria Nueva', is perhaps the most recent example in Peruvian history, but there are others.

At least two important characteristics, however, set the 1990s apart from previous decades. In the first place, they were part of a period of democratic rule that had started in 1980 and was characterized by historically unprecedented levels of political participation, at least in terms of people's access to government and exercise of their right to vote. As is shown in Table 7.1, in the last half-century, Peru has changed from being a country where only a small per cent of the population was registered to vote into one where the majority of the population can effectively choose its own authorities. Secondly, this democratic period occurs within an international context in rapid transit towards greater economic integration and, as recent history in Peru demonstrates, stricter standards for individual countries' political behavior.

Both of these characteristics, greater political participation and economic integration, highlight the importance of the connection between governability and economic performance. The first, in terms of sustaining a demand for democratic procedures and institutions whose existence and performance are clearly shaped, however, by phenomena such as terrorism, economic crises, and the fiascoes of Peruvian political parties. The second, because it is the more open economies that are more dependent on international trade and finance markets and that are also then the most sensitive to shocks coming from financial and direct private investment reacting negatively to governability problems.

Table 7.1 Electoral participation 1939–2000

Year	Register votes	Valid votes	Population	Register votes/population
1939	597182	339193	6207967*	9.7
1963	2070718	1814568	9906296**	20.9
1980	6485680	4123776	17031221***	38.1
1995	11974396	7226341	23836867	50.2
2000	14567467	11085870	25662000	56.8

Notes: *1940, **1961, ***1981.
Sources:
Electoral data 1939–1980, Tuesta (1987): 295, 259, 233; 1995, 2000: ONPE.
Population, National Census of Population.
Own elaboration.

In this context, economic reforms cannot be profoundly sustained by governments with autocratic tendencies. Ultimately, the character and institutional scope of these economic reforms are to a large extent contrary to the needs and goals of an authoritarian government. The points of conflict, moreover, are not simply limited to reforms that are specifically democratizing, like those that are aimed at reinforcing access to information or government accountability, but also present themselves even in reforms that, for example, are aimed at introducing better foresight in macroeconomic policies. The extent to which the government's autocratic tendencies shape the political process responsible for the initiation of reform determines both the strength of the reforms and their sustainability.

This new context of democracy also changed the roles of the many mediating actors in Peru's political and economic system, including multilateral organizations (financial and political), investment banks, and risk-evaluation agencies. It is as a result of this change in context that the more traditional roles of the international agencies of the United States, from the State Department, the CIA, and Congress, to the NGOs focused on human rights have all been redefined. Although some of these agencies have a long and complex history in Latin America, their roles have become much more important in the face of the Cold War's end and the new priority of the United States' executive branch to see democracy at the top of its agenda for the region. The interrelation of the interests and agendas of these different actors will directly influence the results of Peru's internal political process. For example, in the case of Peru it has been stressed how the result of a battle waged by the CIA and the State Department have influenced political outcomes regarding certain controversial aspects and people in the Fujimori regime.[1]

From a political economy perspective, there are three clearly distinct periods in Peru's recent history. In the first period (1990–92), the management of the economy was dominated by stabilization policies and a movement away from the vaguely heterodox visions of Fujimori's electoral campaign towards reforms much more in line with the dominating Washington Consensus – monetary control, adjusting the price of public services, commercial opening, and redirecting the economy to be one in which the market is the principal allocator of resources. The administration in this period, meanwhile, succeeded in maintaining alliances with other political forces in Congress that allowed them to push through their reforms without the specter of major obstacles. The economic results included a significant reduction in inflation, but this reduction came at the cost of allowing economic activity to remain stagnant.

The second period (1993–95) is characterized by a more accelerated advance of economic reforms already launched and the initiation of new reforms which focused particularly on the process of privatization, changes in the regulation of the labor market, liberalization of the financial market, the improvement of the tax system, and, once the new resources began to enter the system, on social policy. In the political sphere, constitutional rule, along with the array of other political forces, was overturned in Fujimori's 'auto-golpe' in April of 1992, an event which was supported by the armed forces and an important portion of the population. With help from political manipulations of the judicial branch, the new Congress, which was under the control of the executive branch, gradually eliminated institutional checks and balances, slowly closing off channels of horizontal accountability and offering the regime a free reign in the implementation of its policies.

The motivations behind the acceleration of the liberal economic reforms and the change of the state's role are complex. Three factors seem to be key. First, the disastrous results of the previous decade enormously discredited heterodox economic policies. Second, there was a new legitimacy in Latin America to a combination of reforms that tried to return the central role in the allocation of resources to the market. Third, there was decisive pressure from the multilateral organizations that conditioned their financial assistance to the implementation of reforms. In the case of privatizations, these factors were joined by a precarious fiscal situation, which was in part caused by the large deficits that public companies had incurred in the previous decade. Any alternative route to begin reforms that would make those state-owned businesses efficient could carry political costs that might be greater than the political cost of privatizing them. The reforms were successful in terms of economic performance. At the beginning of 1993, the economy began to grow vigorously, the investment rate recovered, and inflation continued its descent into single digits. This helped promote Fujimori's re-election in 1995, which for many people was an essential requirement for the continuation and consolidation of the new economic model as well as an opportunity to strengthen the institutional normalization of a regime legitimated by a popular vote.

The third period (1996–2000) would show how this perspective was wrong. Not only was there no progress on the initiated reforms – in some cases there were even significant steps backwards, but the government also quickly revealed its absolute disinterest in managing itself within the confines of a democratic regime.[2] The long-awaited reform of the state was never initiated, the privatizations were first decelerated and then suspended, the programs focused on incorporating greater participation of people with little capital in these processes were eliminated in favor of a more arbitrary allocation in public assets, while new businesses tied to the armed forces were created. The trade reforms were converted into just one episode insufficient to put the country at the level of even its neighbors, the autonomy of regulatory and supervisory organizations (such as SUNAT) was cut short, and social spending began to respond increasingly to the political priorities of the executive. In the political sphere, this course had its corollary in an ever-increasing deference to the armed forces, control of the other autonomous branches of government, policies of intimidation, persecution, and buying out of political opponents and the press, and also in the manipulation of mass media. The political strategy was directed towards just one goal: a permanent hold on power. Economic performance in this period was worse compared to the earlier Fujimori period and also in comparison to the average performance in Latin America at the time.

Peru in the 1990s seems to be an excellent case for studying the relationship between governability and economic performance in the new international context, as much for its representative elements as for its extreme ones. This chapter will approach the complex relationship between the economic and the political through an analytical narrative that attempts to define and dissect the links between the two spheres. The sources for this study include existing literature, empirical evidence based on public perceptions of institutions, and interviews with experts in the field.[3] The text is organized as follows: the next section will explain the conceptual framework of the chapter. In the third section we will discuss some structural characteristics that determine both the way the political process unfolds and the nature of its relationship with economic performance. The fourth section addresses the political process of the 1990s, and the fifth analyses the economic reforms and the political economy of those reforms. The sixth section briefly analyses the main macroeconomic variables at work. The seventh section returns to political variables and how they determine economic performance. Finally, the eighth section presents some reflections on the connections between governability and economic performance based on the Peruvian experience.

7.2 GOVERNABILITY AND ECONOMIC PERFORMANCE: A CONCEPTUAL FRAMEWORK

Recently, there has been a tendency to re-evaluate the influence of the political arena on economic processes, and especially the positive influence that the mechanisms of democratic institutions have on economic performance. The dominant perspective in political science used to dictate that a political explanation of economic processes either somehow identified the intervention of 'contingent factors' and the direction of that intervention or, alternatively, to pinpoint the superficial-structural signs of the structural economic factors. Today, however, political forces have an independent explanatory weight. This change came in response, in part, to the testimony of experience, which carries a lot of weight in Latin America and perhaps especially so in Peru.

The strength of this explanation is also owed to the development of an institutionalist vision that successfully established the importance of the political sphere in economic theory. In the institutionalist framework, which takes many of its cues from Douglass North's work, institutions provide a set of rules that create and define opportunity for individuals and groups and also provide the mechanisms to make those rules effective (North 1990). This aspect is important because it determines the stability and predictability that economic actors need to confirm that their decisions will further their goals and that are necessary for smooth economic management. This perspective provides a meeting place between economics and politics by suggesting a better context and a more important role for the effect of the political variables on the economy.[4] The growing interest of economists in political phenomena and their application of analytical instruments of rational choice to political situations has also contributed to this trend.[5]

From the perspective of development economics, the subject of governability is related to the same concern expressed in calls for 'second generation reforms' that tackle critical institutional aspects in the quest for sustained economic growth (Burki and Perry 1998). Different affinities can be seen in the various approaches to this subject. A good part of the literature, particularly in Peru's case, has had a tendency to restrict itself to identifying only the *technical* difficulties of implementation. This literature generally refers to human resources that the state and 'establishment' reformers count upon, and to the competition necessary for the initiation and advancement of all kinds of reform, from reform of institutional design to reform of the structure and execution of the legal system (Ugarte 2000). An alternative approach focuses on the elements of the 'pending agenda' of reform as a confirmation of what still needs to be done, without considering why those pending reforms do not get to the level of reconstruction of the state and without acknowledging the ways in which what is not done, as well as what is done, determines the performance of an economy (Abusada et al. 2000). The logic of this interpretation is that greater economic success has not been achieved because structural reform has not been completed.

In other cases, the focus is on the analytical side of political economy, approaching the subject according to the logic of the structural reforms and acknowledging the inherent difficulties of implementing them.[6] In addition to the technical conditions, the analysis incorporates political elements such as the hindrance of even the special interest groups that are within the coalition that supports the administration, like the actions of those who stand possibly to gain or lose as a result of the reforms, and like the administration's style and political leadership. In this framework, political conditions play an explanatory role in economic performance. Nevertheless, the logic of these elements can be different than the logic found in an economic analysis and takes more from the political science perspective, where it is not expected that political reform will necessarily come from economic reform. From this perspective of an analysis that incorporates the internal turmoil of the reformist alliance, the pressures that come from interest groups, as well as social demands, it seems more 'natural' that reform of the state has not yet occurred. Some analyses have started with the view that the reform *could not* occur and tried to work out why, approaching the question at the level of either reform of a specific policy or area, or reform of the state in general.

The analysis from the political science perspective has generally focused on the issue of democratization. It incorporates the idea of a rational political agent and views institutions as presenting a range of options that guide the behavior of various social actors. The concept of governability is central to analysing post-1980s Latin America and has taken a central role in the crisis of political parties and of the party system itself.[7] The decline of the existing political parties' ability to appeal to the public and to articulate people's concerns are central factors in explaining the rise of non-traditional leaders that were able to push through difficult structural adjustments and broad economic reform. The most obvious cases of this phenomenon are Argentina with Menem, Brazil with Collor de Melo, and Peru with Fujimori. But another important aspect of this trend that becomes clear in these examples is the general weakness of pre-existing political institutions. Included in those political institutions, and of great particular importance, are the justice system and its effectiveness. Like the new results-driven style of government exemplified by Menem and Fujimori, the serious crises of the political party in Latin America in the 1980s are ultimately associated with a very weak institutional system that did not have stable or solid mechanisms of vertical accountability and that could manage the relationship between the governed and the governors – the relationship of representation (O'Donnell 1994). These are the characteristics that O'Donnell refers to as 'delegative democracy', in which the electorate – outside organic channels of participation and support – gives a governor an open commission to govern. 'Government-by-decree' is indicative of this type of political regime.[8]

The notion of horizontal accountability complements the concept of vertical accountability incorporating the whole set of state institutions (O'Donnell 1997). This marks the confines of the 'rule of law', in between the socioeconomic and the political. Truly democratic rule of law is a system of interwoven legally defined accountabilities. The diagnosis is that rule of law in Latin America is largely ineffective, and caught up in obstacles such as: deficient or inadequate application of the law, negligent gaps in the law, discriminatory and abusive behavior of government bureaucracies towards citizens (especially towards the disadvantaged), unequal or non-existent access to the judicial system and to due process, and illegality or irresponsibility in the handling of public affairs by informal mechanisms of operation controlled by private regional, local, or (in the Peruvian case) national powers. This panorama of problems reveals the lack of depth of the state, especially in its legal system. O'Donnell suggests that this situation can be made worse in cases where the democratic transition has been accompanied by anti-state economic policies.[9] As we will discuss later on, in the case of Peru, there was a reconstruction, rather than destruction, of the state that had been financially devastated at the end of the 1980s. This reconstruction, however, did not impede the informal power that grew with the Fujimori regime and that came to control the other powers of the state, eliminating any possibility of horizontal accountability. Reform of the state moved in the opposite direction to the growth of this informal power, and as this power accumulated more control of the government, the passage of real reform became increasingly difficult.

In Peru the relationship between politics and economics seems particularly strong. The analyses, however, often stress very different things. From a focus akin to that of the current neostructuralist approach, the association between neoliberal policies, political authoritarianism, and social exclusion is automatic. The analyses vary from focusing on inadequate macroeconomic policies that ignore the structural inequality of Peruvian society (Figueroa 1999) to policies that both favor a model of primary exports and neglect problems of poverty (Gonzáles de Olarte 1998). One criticism directed to this line of analysis emphasizes 'its exaggerated normative tone and "denunciation", that make it difficult to understand the complex relationships between structural reforms and political processes' (Tanaka 1999, p. 122). The suggestion presented here emphasizes the study of concrete policies and their dynamics and finds the approach of the new political economy to be very useful (for more in this vein, see Ortiz de Zevallos et al. 1999; Tanaka 2001).

Solimano has suggested a framework for the analysis of the political economy of the Andean countries that incorporates two blocks of variables: a block of variables that affect governability, on one hand, and another that affect economic performance, on the other, and explores the connections and interactions between both blocks of variables that jointly produce economic and governability outcomes. This chapter adapts Solimano's framework to incorporate political science perspectives on the problems of governability in the fragile and 'incomplete' Latin American democracies. The following two sections focus, respectively, on the structural variables that condition Peruvian politics, the governability of the country, and the circumstances and actors whose interactions shaped the policies of the 1990s. Then the chapter turns to the economic 'block', emphasizing the characteristics of the reforms that have been undertaken as well as the economic results of those reforms and then coming back to the discussion of interactions between the economy and politics.

In a broad sense, governability has been understood as the capacity of the political authority to organize and direct public affairs in an effective way (Huntington 1968). Because legitimacy is not necessarily inherent to governments, the definition incorporates both legal and de facto regimes equally, while the role of political institutions is not specified. Legitimacy, however, is an element that has been emphasized in more recent definitions. Although 'the exercise of power and authority constitutes the modulating factor of governability' (Brautigan 1994), in democratic regimes it is also involved in the acceptance of a social contract that connects the government with the governed and that incorporates the rules both for the political system (representation, that is vertical accountability) and for the development of the institutions (rule of law, horizontal accountability). Kauffman et al. (1999), for example, incorporate these elements into the definition of governability and include the capacity to design and implement public policies in an effective way. A country is more governable when there are clear rules to the political game that are broadly accepted, when the laws are effectively carried out and are changed through transparent procedures, when mechanisms of representation exist that effectively establish an organic relationship between the state and the citizen, and when the state has the capacity to enact strong and effective policies.

Because it is difficult to establish totally objective indicators of these dimensions, citizens' perceptions of them provide important indicators of the level of confidence in institutions and government – the essence of governability. Indicators of governability, such as approval ratings of the president or of economic policy or of people's perceptions of institutions, are highly correlated with indicators of economic expectations and people's perceptions of the economic situation (see Figure 7.1). Clearly, the relationship between governability and economic performance runs in both

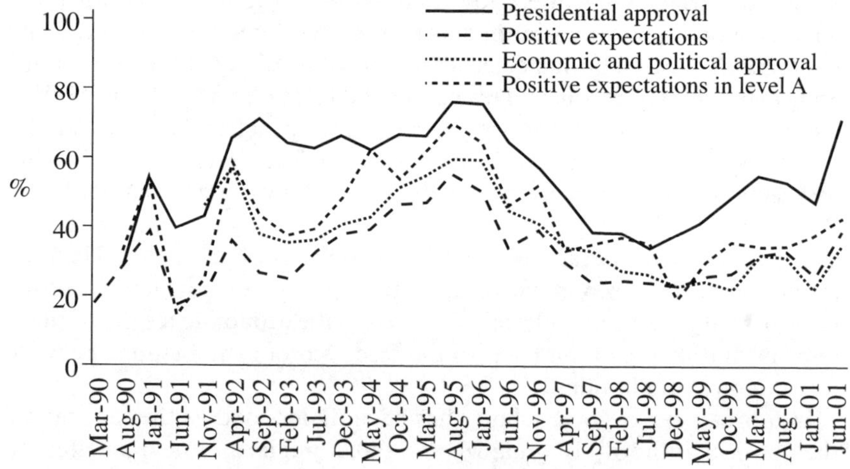

Note: 'Level A' represents a function of levels of income and assets of the section with the highest socioeconomic status. Here we use it as a proxy for the expectations of investors.

Figure 7.1 *Approval ratings for the President, for the political economy, and expectations for the economic situation (five-month moving averages)*

directions. Distinguishing the causality in the relationship is very difficult, both because the interaction bounces back and forth between the variables and because the period of analysis is very limited. This study proposes a relationship that goes from governability to expectations of economic performance and then comes back around with economic performance affecting governability.

7.3 STRUCTURAL FACTORS AND POLITICS IN PERU

The most striking characteristic of Peru's national political history has been instability. During its first 20 years as an independent country, Peru had 30 governments and seven political constitutions. In the twentieth century, after two decades of peaceful transitions of power through regular elections (1895–1914), elected governments began to be pushed out by regimes that took power through coups d'etát at the rate of approximately once every ten years.[10] Political stability, in the sense of predictability of compliance with the stated rules of the political system, rules that are essential to governance, has therefore not been a characteristic of Peruvian political history. This instability comes in part as a result of the initial conditions of Peru's political climate: an elite unconvinced of the convenience of political independence from Spain, of a heavy colonial inheritance of institutions with absolute power, of social fragmentation, and of ethnic exclusion (Bonilla 1972; Domínguez 1980). It also comes in part from certain structural characteristics such as: the complexity of its geography, the slow process of national integration, and the still-serious problem of severe inequality in the distribution of wealth.

The country of Peru encompasses a particularly complicated territory of land. Its landscape includes 84 out of the 104 microclimates and 28 out of the 32 climates that can be found on the planet, a variety of conditions which qualifies it as one of the most geographically diverse countries in the world. Getting a hold of so heterogeneous a space, from barren coastal deserts to a dynamic Amazonian forest, with a high mountain range that crosses the country longitudinally, is an as-yet unfinished task for the Peruvian state, whose presence in much of this territory is merely symbolic. The geographical distribution of physical infrastructure and services is extremely unequal, as is the distribution of income and per capita consumption (Escobal and Torero 2000). The proportion of public spending over which local and regional governments have real decisionmaking power barely reaches 5 per cent of total public spending.[11] Both economic activity and political power are strongly concentrated in Lima, and, despite the presence of regional political movements, the tendency has been towards ever-greater centralization. The enormous growth of public spending that has been considered as part of the definition of a developed state since the 1960s has not helped to change this inclination towards greater centralization.

One consequence of the structural factor in the political sphere has been the weakness of regional movements that have been incapable of articulating a viable decentralist political platform and have tended, instead, to concentrate their efforts on parochial claims.[12] One recent national survey reveals that in spite of a strong conviction that decentralization is important for regional economic development, Peruvians distrust their local leaders and local authorities.[13] The role of regional movements in the political process, therefore, has typically been important mostly in election periods as a mechanism to guarantee a political clientele, but has generally become less important once those periods are over. Additionally, since regional political movements have been practically unable to mediate the relationship between government and citizens, political leaders have opted to communicate directly with local populations. This strategy, as we will discuss later, was used with singular effectiveness by President Fujimori.

The issue of ethnicity, while it has never been at the center of political debate, has always been present in a relatively explicit way. The sweeping advance of urbanization in the last half-century has accentuated the predominantly mestizo character of the population, in spite of the survival of a strong indigenous tradition, particularly in the southern mountain range and of the important presence of a native population made up of diverse ethnic groups in the forest. Table 7.2 reveals that according to the information from the latest available census, only 20 per cent of the population claim Quechua or other native languages as a first language. This percentage is smaller in Lima than in the rest of the country, but is much higher in districts with more rural populations, like Cuzco. The percentage of people whose first language is an indigenous language has dropped dramatically in recent decades. In the 1940 census, the number was as high as 51 per cent, and by 1961, it had already dropped to 36 per cent. This sizeable diminution is not only due to more racial integration, but also to changes in people's self-perceptions about their own ethnic status.

Ethnic factionalism in Peru has been largely mediated by the particularly heterogeneous composition of the mestizo population, which incorporates very diverse and intermingled ethnic origins. This type of dispersion has favored the development of a broad and unique nationalism that has operated as a shock absorber to defuse ethnic conflict.[14] Despite these kinds of mediating qualities that nationalism seems to offer, the categories that Collier (2001) proposes suggest that the apparent domination of the mestizo population that characterizes Peru's ethnic diversity masks a reality of deeper ethnic divisions.[15]

Table 7.2 Population five years old and older, organized by first language, 1993

	Total[1]	Spanish	Foreign language	Quechua	Other native languages	Subtotal native languages	% of total
Perú	19 190 623	15 410 070	383 812	3 166 453	575 719	*3 742 172*	19.50
Lima	5 720 256	5 119 629	228 810	549 145	286 013	*835 157*	15
Cusco	878 973	307 641	8 790	559 906	10 548	*570 453*	65
Resto del País	12 591 394	9 982 801	146 212	2 057 402	279 158	*2 336 561*	19

Note: [1] Excludes the respondents that did not state what language or dialect they first learned to speak.

Source: INEI – National Census of 1993. Elaboration: GRADE.

The issue of ethnicity, nevertheless, has not driven the organization or the workings of Peru's political climate. Supporting this idea is the fact that ethnicity has not had a large role in the political violence of recent decades in Peru. It is also clear that the attempts to introduce the issue of ethnic conflict in the last political campaign backfired. In this vein, it is important to note that the indigenous populations, generally dispersed in rural zones, do not have well-defined organizations that represent them, and have been unable to have a voice in national policy as a result. Historically *indigenismo* has never constituted an alternative policy and the indigenous populations have had a much more important influence culturally than they have politically.

This does not mean that the subject of ethnicity has stopped being important in the more recent political processes, or that a color-blind 'national culture' has been successfully constructed. Recent research instead suggests that the labor market rewards those of lighter skin colors, and, in effect, that ethnic differences have an impact on the incomes of ostensibly similar individuals, even within the heterogeneous mestizo group, in the same job market.[16] In terms of the role it has played in recent politics, in one illustrative example, the electoral campaign of 1990 was distinguished by the xenophobic reactions of the people to the idea of having an Asian president and by the then-candidate Fujimori who astutely took advantage of the issue and managed to position himself as the candidate of 'los chinitos y los cholitos' in opposition to Vargas Llosa, the candidate of 'los blancos'. The effect of the ethnicity issue was also apparent in the recent political campaign, when current (at the time of writing) president Alejandro Toledo manipulated his ethnicity as a political asset and called to unify 'todas las sangres' behind his campaign. Ultimately, the issue of ethnicity is an important factor in Peruvian politics, despite the fact that it is not one that drives political proposals or platforms, nor one that inspires violent conflicts.

Another important structural factor that conditions the unfolding of policy in Peru is the inequality of income and wealth. Even though recent studies show a reduction of the dispersion of income in the last two decades, through periods of recession and growth, inequalities are enormous (Saavedra and Diaz 1999). Behind these inequalities there is the larger inequality in the distribution of opportunities for social advancement. For example, large differences in the quality of education between public and private; urban and rural; and also within public schools, have made the system ineffective in equalizing opportunities. This substantial inequality conditions politics, creating a political culture that cultivates populism. Strong redistributive pressures have shaped a new central role of social policy in government spending. An example of this is the importance of food programs during the 1990s. These pressures also affect the viability of state reforms and the ways in which these reforms attempt to create more efficient public organizations that attract more qualified personnel, have more demanding processes of selection and evaluation, and that offer more competitive salaries. Typically, this is opposed because of its social implications: less qualified workers would have to vacate their positions for other, more qualified, workers that would probably get better salaries.

Finally, it is important to discuss the influence of the larger international context on the political developments of the country. In this vein, two elements have made Peru a matter of international interest and, in recent decades, particularly a place of interest to the United States: the strong presence (if not in numbers of supporters, then in effectiveness of their actions) of the terrorist groups of Partido Comunista Sendero Luminoso (SL) and the Movimiento Revolucionario Tupac Amaru (MRTA), and the presence of narcotraffic. Even though their effects and scopes are different, in both terrorism and narcotrafficking, the central issue for the world becomes hemispheric security. In the case of terrorist group advances, in a fin-de siècle version of the domino theory, the principal fear of the United States has been the possibility of terrorism spilling into neighboring countries. Similarly, there is no doubt that drug trafficking has been the central force driving US foreign policy towards the Andean countries. The major preoccupation of these policies has been containment, or at least apparent containment, of the flow of cocaine into the United States. A large part of the support that Fujimori garnered is explained by his successes in handling both terrorism and narcotrafficking. The rise to power of Montesinos, the controversial adviser to Fujimori, is also attributed to supposed advances in these two areas.

7.4 THE POLITICAL PROCESS OF THE 1990s

Peru began the decade in the midst of its greatest economic and political crisis of the century. In the last three years before 1990, there was an accumulated fall of about a quarter of GDP, and inflation surpassed annual rates of 7000 per cent. In political events, the steady advance of terrorist groups paralleled the ever-increasing ill repute of political parties. The elections of 1990, then, became a confrontation of two outsiders to national politics. On one side was Mario Vargas Llosa, whose intellectual reputation was internationally renowned, and whose youthful leftist militancy had gradually yielded to a liberal radicalism, managed to pull together a group of parties that were center-right. On the other side was a university professor, who was an ex-dean and an ex-President of the National Assembly of Deans, and who, with ambitions of a seat in the Senate, led an independent political group that operated without any kind of established party structure endorsing it.

The campaign was clearly centered on the issue of the economy, and was driven by the conflict between two opposing positions: one candidate was for a shock stabilizer and the other was against it but offered no alternative option that he would support instead.[17] Beyond the campaign issues, it was clear that there were two principal challenges facing the next president. In the economic sphere, the president would somehow have to reduce hyperinflation and reactivate the economy, while in the political sphere, he would have to halt the thus-far unstoppable advance of the terrorist groups SL and MRTA. It was understood that the governability of the country in the near future depended upon success in both of these two spheres.

In a dizzying jump in popularity in the last two weeks of the campaign that was driven by both the state's mass media and by others close to the would-be governing Aprista Party, Fujimori entered the second round and triumphed over his opponent by a wide margin. He was then left with the task of mapping the course of economic policy. Initially associated with rather heterodox economic advisers, some of whom even helped shape his cabinet, it would take Fujimori some time to choose a path of fiscal and monetary orthodoxy and liberalizing reforms. Only with the 1991 appointment of Carlos Boloña as Minister of Economy and Finance, did the direction of macroeconomic policy and the viability of reforms that gave the market a larger role in the allocation of resources become clear. As will be seen, the reasons for this direction have little to do with Fujimori's ideological position, whose political antecedents locate him more in the center left than these economic policies would imply.

In such a complicated context, the alliances that Fujimori created to give his regime stability had two important sources of support: the first came from the Congress and the second came from the armed forces. On the congressional front, lacking his own bench-support, his alliance with the Apra gave Fujimori enough backing to push through his first stabilizing measures that even earned an easy endorsement from his old election-time rivals. They observed the way that Fujimori successfully implemented the substantive part of his economic program, even as he neglected, they argued, a critical component of social protection. In fact, as the liberal tendencies of the economic program grew more pronounced, the support in the Congress began to come more from the Fredmo and less from the Apra. Up until 1992, the Congress was not a significant obstacle to the executive branch's implementation of its economic measures.

The opposition of the Congress to the measures that the executive wanted to put forward began to be concentrated on issues of the anti-subversive struggle and of human rights, and this opposition became a critical factor in the relationship between the administration and its other, eventually principal, source of support – the armed forces. The investigations of human rights abuses in the fight against subversives had, since the late 1980s, been a source of tension with the armed forces and a determining factor in its relationship with various administrations. The official position of the military had been to consider the disappearances and deaths of civilians related to the anti-subversive struggle, if not as unfounded lies, as acts of war that by definition should only be investigated internally and according to military law. Congress's decision to reject norms oriented at giving the armed forces greater autonomy to fight against subversives in November of 1991 aggravated the conflict-ridden relationship between the legisilative power and the army, and served as an alibi for the coup that was already being planned.

The relationship between Fujimori and the armed forces was from the start mediated by Vladimiro Montesinos, who was an ex-collaborator of the CIA, a lawyer for several of the generals involved in cases of drug trafficking and, beginning in 1989, adviser to the National Intelligence Service. Objections over Fujimori's foreign origins were quickly dismissed when he was forced to take up residence in a military compound between the first and second rounds as a result of a supposed threat to his life that, it was later discovered, appears to have been a ruse created by Montesinos to win the trust of the then candidate. Tensions between the President and the military, however, were still present, in part because of the presence of Montesinos, who, despite his expulsion in the 1970s for selling military secrets to the United States, still wielded a powerful influence within the institution. In this context, the 1991 Law of the Military Situation gave the president power to choose the commander-in-chief from all high-ranking officials, eliminating norms and changing the rules to allow officials to retire irrespective of their years of service (Obando 1999). This broke the army's institutional mechanisms of succession, granted the president an enormous amount of personal discretion over the military, and left high-ranking officials virtually at his mercy.

In April of 1992, under the pretext of a crisis of governability allegedly sparked by the obstinacy of the legislative power and the corruption of both the legislative and judicial branches, both were taken apart and Congress was dissolved. These events occurred at the moment when public confidence in the Congress and political parties had fallen to their lowest historical levels.[18] Given this context, the overwhelming support of citizens for the coup is not surprising – many of them identified strongly with the President's critiques of 'traditional politicians' and of Congress's inefficiency. Public opinion perceived a conflict between governability and democracy: it saw democracy as an obstacle to solving the serious economic and political problems of the country (Cotler 2000, p. 22). The international reaction, much stronger than the government had been prepared for, reflected a very different point of view than Peruvian public opinion and forced the government to hastily look for a way out of isolation from the international community. This way out took the form of an election to choose a new Congress, whose first action was to write up a new constitution which would be passed by a very narrow margin in a national plebiscite a year later.

The lack of a Congress that could balance some of the power of the executive facilitated the implementation of the first of Fujimori's economic reforms. It is difficult to think that a set of such broad reforms with such vast implications could have been implemented with the same speed in a political context that was more democratic. Any economic program is easier to implement without institutional balances and fiscalization, but the lack of these mechanisms also makes the sustainability of any success much more uncertain. Perhaps the best case to illustrate this is the issue of privatizations that is discussed later in the chapter. Before going further into this point, it is important to understand exactly what was included in the package of reforms that was described by observers as both the deepest and the broadest set of reforms implemented in Latin America in such a short period of time.

7.5 THE STRUCTURAL ADJUSTMENT: STABILIZATION AND ECONOMIC REFORM

Peru's stabilization program began in August of 1990. The initial objectives of the program were: the elimination of hyperinflation, the reintegration of Peru back into international finance systems, the re-establishment of macroeconomic order, and the resolution of the balance of payments crisis. Along with an orthodox program focused on reducing the macroeconomic imbalances, it was decided to also implement a set of structural reforms inspired by the Washington Consensus. The resounding failure of Alan García's heterodox policies coincided with the hegemony in Latin America of a set of recommendations for reform that, as their central tenet, emphasized placing more trust in the market as the mechanism to allocate resources. The poor performance of state institutions during the previous decades was reinforced by the public sector's terrible management of resources at the end of the 1980s to create a disastrous impression of state control of the allocation of resources that made it easy to justify a drastic change of the government's position towards the market. Multilateral organizations exerted tremendous pressure in favor of the reform movement and made the transfer of new financial resources conditional upon the gradual implementation of many of these reforms.

The 'structural reform' in Peru involved a much broader set of reforms that were directed at, on one hand, restoring a basic macroeconomic balance (macroeconomic policy reform), and, on the other, giving the market more room to allocate resources, rewriting the role of the state in economic activities, and promoting private initiatives. The set of structural reforms included both the liberalization of foreign trade and tax reform. To liberalize foreign trade, the government moved from a complex external tariff structure with high averages and broad dispersion to a much simpler arrangement with very few exceptions. In the case of taxes, reform was focused on simplifying and modernizing the system and on improving the administration of taxes. Other reforms were aimed at making markets more dynamic, beginning a process that made the labor market more flexible, deregulated the financial system, and opened up the capital account and the balance of payments. Simultaneously, an aggressive process of privatization of public companies began. These reforms were principally focused on creating better conditions for private investment and on promoting competitiveness. As we will see, many of these reforms, like the fiscal policy, were strongly influenced by political swings of the government and, towards the end of the decade, the background of serious political instability and a prolonged recession left it very unclear what the direction of the economic model was.

Monetary and Exchange Policy

With the beginning of the stabilization program, monetary policy recovered its independence from the previous fiscal management and became a key part of the struggle against inflation. This was achieved through the restriction of primary financing to the public sector and bank promotion. Unlike the experiences of other Latin American countries, in Peru the money supply was used as the nominal anchor of the program as it simultaneously unified the exchange market and created a floating exchange rate.

As a fundamental part of the economic program, the regime experimented with a series of reforms of the system of exchange between March of 1990 and August of 1991. The first measures affecting exchange rate policy were directed at the implementation of a system with *flotación sucia*, a floating exchange rate within certain controled parameters, (in this case, with the intervention of the BCRP) and a liberalization of the exchange market that eliminated all the restrictions on the buying and selling of foreign currency. The multiple exchange rates were eliminated and exchange rate policy was put in line with the goal of keeping the growth of the money supply consistent with inflation control. The policy of flotation, combined with the important influx of capital and the increase of mining exports, created a reduction in the real exchange rate that would be maintained throughout the decade. In this context, part of the discussion of policy in the first half of the decade was dominated by the debate over an assumed 'slower exchange', while the attempts of the BCR (Central Bank of Reserves) to influence even at a nominal level were not particularly effective. Ultimately, with the exception of a small academic circle, it seemed clear that the monetary authority did not have the instruments to influence the real exchange rate in a context of strong dollarization.

It is clear that the monetary goals on the part of the Central Bank of Reserves allowed inflation to reduce and opened the possibility of a recovery of total production levels. Nevertheless, it is important to note that the descent of inflation towards single-digit levels occurred during a prolonged process that reflected the many initial difficulties of implementing a coherent stabilization plan in the face of the pragmatic skepticism of the President.[19] But, ultimately, it is the institutional reform of monetary policy that has proven to be more important for the long term. This fact was taken into consideration and reflected in the 1993 constitution, which established the autonomy of Peru's Central Bank of Reserves with the purpose of preserving monetary stability in the new Organic Law.[20] The new Organic Law of the BCRP, which is still in use, prohibits the financing of the public sector, the providing of guarantees, the giving of sector credits, and the establishment of systems of multiple exchange rates. It is difficult to imagine that the present stability of prices, even in the face of the political turbulence of the last three years, could have been achieved without this reform.

Fiscal Policy and Tax Reform

In the arena of taxes, the Fujimori administration had inherited a broken system, demoralized and prone to corruption, all of which was reflected in a decline in tax collection. Given the massive tax evasion, the tax burden barely reached 4 per cent of GDP, and the collection was concentrated on just 700 companies.[21] The government's strategy was directed both at altering the tax structure – basing it instead on a smaller quantity of permanent input, a much smaller number of exonerations, a larger base of contributors – and at modernizing the system of tax collection – improving technologies for the control and collection of taxes.

On the institutional level, a process of reform began in 1991 in the SUNAT aimed at its modernization and at the strengthening and consolidation of its management and decisionmaking autonomy. These changes, along with new tax legislation, resulted in a gradual increase in the tax burden and a tarnishing of the image of the institution. Beginning in the middle of the decade the image and levels of public acceptance of the SUNAT (National Superintendency of Tax Administration) gradually eroded, mostly in response to the government's increasing use of intimidation as an instrument against political adversaries. Ultimately, what was a successful administrative reform was transformed into a complex history of capable political manipulation. The SUNAT became part of the distressing history of the last years of the Fujimori government, in which the administration's informal power governed many of the supposedly autonomous institutions, including the Judicial Branch and the Office of Public Prosecution of the Nation.

Although it managed to get fiscal accounts under control around 1993, the proximity of elections would demonstrate the fragility of the discipline the administration had achieved. Public spending rapidly expanded in 1994 and in the first trimester of 1995 in the face of an unusual complacency on the part of the International Monetary Fund. There were pending reforms in this area that would have transformed the effort to restore fiscal discipline into a sustainable process of healthy management of public finances, but then a rash of serious decisions were made 'on the brink of the abyss'. The transition from managing a basic system dictated by the fall in resources to administrating a more complicated structure with growing resources, many of them non-recurring, required a series of institutional reforms, that in a pre-election context, the Fujimori administration had no interest in beginning. Unfortunately, after the election the administration still showed no signs of interest in beginning the difficult reform process. Paradoxically, a part of this reform, the Law of Fiscal Prudence, was passed just towards the end of the second period of Fujimori's presidency, and it was he who violated that same law first. Another part of institutional reform of the fiscal sector, the part that was related to the budgetary process, was advanced very incrementally, in such a way that towards the end of the decade it was still the President who decided the size of the budget and the size of the fiscal deficit.[22]

Financial and Capital Market Reform

The financial reform had as principal objectives the elimination of financial controls, the reduction of transaction costs in financial operations, and, in the medium term, the development of a capital market. Along with the liberalization of the interest rates and the elimination of the use of internal credit for the financing of the public sector,[23] the Fujimori government rescinded the Law of Nationalization of Banks and Insurance that had been promulgated by the previous government. The entire banking and financial legal framework was also renewed with the purpose of improving competition, solidarity, and confidence in the financial system, of stimulating the level of savings, and of promoting the expansion and diversification of financial services.[24] The Supervision of Banks and Securities was strengthened and the role of state institutions in the capital market was redefined, dissolving the bank of promotion, re-envisioning the functions of the national bank and the Financial Corporation of Development (COFIDE). The pension system was also reformed, transforming from a model with a common fund to one in which individual accounts are administered by specialized companies (administrators of the pension fund), following the Chilean model. Finally, a process of restructuring the state financial systems was begun through mergers, liquidation, and privatization.

On the other hand, the opening of the capital market was initiated in the 1990s to stimulate both foreign investments in the country and the repossession of Peruvian capital that had migrated outside the country during previous governments. In this vein, the measures of the 1990s included the total liberalization of capital flows with other countries, the unregulated opening of bank accounts in the country on the part of national and foreign agents, as well as accounts held abroad by domestic agents, and the free possession of accounts in foreign currency.

The opening of the capital market and the commercial market simultaneously has been one of the most criticized elements of the program's sequential reforms. Since the capital market adjusts more rapidly than markets for goods, the high interest rates that were prevalent at the start of the program of stabilization attracted capital in the context of the low interest rates in international markets. This generated strong pressure on the exchange rate, lowering still more the price of imported products, recently liberalized, and increasing the deficit of the commercial balance. Nevertheless, the restrictions on the capital market were not consistent with the government's program of privatization and attraction of foreign investment.

The financial reform, like the reform of the capital market that was carried out in 1996, has been considered successful (Morris 2000), having achieved, for example, an increase in financial intermediation, a diminution of interest rates, and a reinforcement of the regulation and supervision framework. This context permitted the development of new financial instruments that started to deepen – although only very slowly – the capital market. Nevertheless, large segments of the population still exist that are not taken care of by the financial system and that prefer other methods of saving. In spite of the reduction in interest rates, the cost of capital has been persistently high, with unusually high and resistant spreads, producing little or no improvement in the efficiency of the banks. Also, the development of a mortgage market has been limited to houses of very high value and so far financial instruments have not been developed that would permit the market to broaden to other sections of the population. Meanwhile, the bank of consumption faced serious problems because neither the banks nor consumers had developed a culture of savings and debt that would allow them to manage their finances in the volatile Peruvian context.

Commercial Reform

The reform of foreign trade was implemented with more than one objective (Velarde and Rodríguez 1992). On one hand, in the medium term, increasing competition in the sectors that produce tradable goods in the economy is desirable. On the other hand, in the short term, the program attempted to limit the increase of inflation by reducing the inflation of tradable goods. The process, although initiated later than in other countries in Latin America, was unusually aggressive. The principal measures were applied between 1990 and 1992, a period in which the dispersion of nominal tariffs was diminished and parallel tariff barriers were eliminated (Abusada, Illescas, and Taboada 2001). The average tariff (without considering exceptions) was reduced from 43 per cent to 29 per cent. In all sectors with the exception of agriculture, the level of effective protection was dramatically lowered, profoundly changing industries of final consumption, which before had counted on levels of protection that were higher than 100 per cent on many products, including dairy products, nutritional products, and clothing.

The opening of commerce continued in the following years, with additional reductions in tariff levels, the elimination of all types of parallel tariff restrictions on the importation of goods, the simplification of all customs procedures, and the elimination of the state monopolies of the importation of food. It is worth noting that the agriculture sector was treated differently than other sectors. In effect, an over-tariff was created for certain agricultural and derived products (dairy, cereals, and sugar) that although its stated objective was to stabilize internal prices of certain agricultural products, clearly had an underlying protectionist slant that ultimately worked to benefit the retailers of agricultural products much more than to benefit national agriculture (Escobal 1992). This special treatment of agriculture is an example of how on a few issues of particular interest to President Fujimori, national policy moved away from the general trajectory of the political economy and of the structural reforms. In the case of agriculture, protectionist policies remained throughout most of the decade.

The rest of the decade was marked by a heated debate over the expediency of moving towards a flat tariff structure versus establishing a tariff structure that would have several tiers and would protect national industries.[25] Within the private sector, there existed a strong opposition movement against the establishment of a single tariff that objected to the lack of fairness in the government's promotion of competition between Peru and its commercial partners both inside and outside the Andean region. For its part, the Ministry of Economy and Finances argued that past attempts at privileging sectors with no natural comparative advantages had ultimately only generated more corruption and losses in the fiscal income of the country. Although the voice of the Ministry of Economy and Finance (MEF) on this issue was always very clear in favor of a flatter tariff structure, the President's weak conviction on the matter prevented this view from being reflected in policy. It was only in April of 1997 that a new reduction in tariffs, again with the exception of farming goods, established that tariffs of 25 per cent on certain items became 20 per cent and tariffs of 15 per cent became 12 per cent. With these modifications, the average tariff decreased from 16 to 13 per cent.

Despite the fact that initially the reduction in tariff protection was very rapid, towards the end of the decade the average tariff in Peru was higher than other countries in the region, as can be seen in Figure 7.2. Measured in terms of degrees of openness,[26] it is possible to appreciate the significance of the observed increase in the importance of external commerce, that permitted the index to move from 0.25 in 1991 to 0.33 in 1998 and to again achieve recently the level of openness that it had two decades before

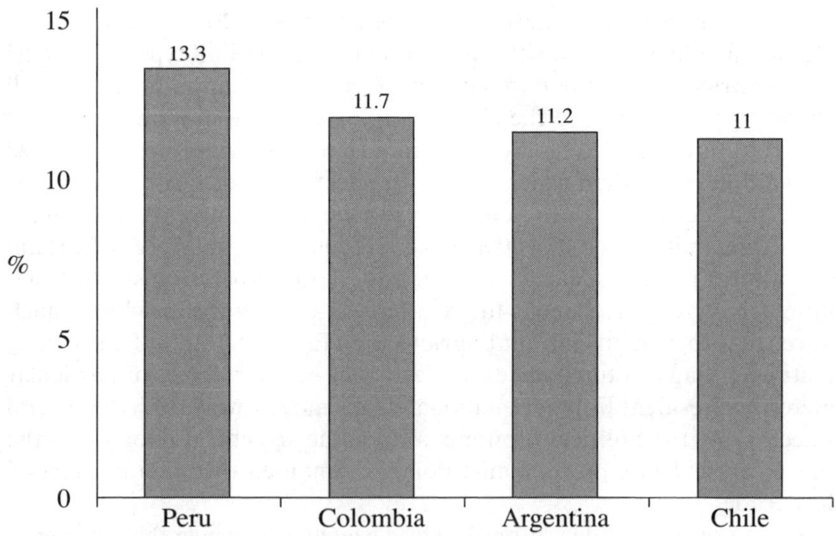

Source: PrompPerú (1999).

Figure 7.2 Average tariffs in 1998 (ad-valorem rates)

(1982), similar to the one that Colombia had at the time (Figure 7.3). It was also clear that while Peru demonstrated a slight tendency towards greater openness, Chile and Colombia were becoming more open much more quickly. Peru's path was much more similar to the pattern exhibited by the economies of countries that, for their respective sizes, were considered to have closed economies, like Brazil.

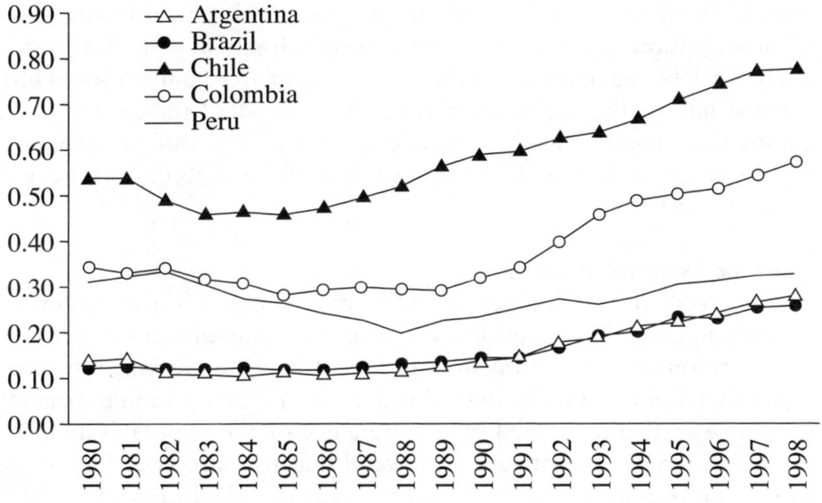

Source: LADB, Integration and Regional Programs Department.

Figure 7.3 Evolution of degrees of openness (exports + imports)/GDP 1980–98, selected countries

Changes in the Role of the State

From the 1970s through to the beginning of the 1990s, the Peruvian government participated in the economy through both entrepreneurial activity and intervention by fixing of prices in different markets. The policies that were implemented as part of the structural adjustment program, however, assumed that there would be a change in the role of state intervention in the economy. In fact the restructuring of the public sector, the elimination of the state monopolies in the commercialization of some foods and fuel, the beginning of an aggressive process of privatization of public companies, the diverse reforms that aimed at making the labor and financial markets and the capital account in the balance of payments more flexible, and so on, all made it clear that the state was aiming to provide a system in which the market was the principal mechanism for the allocation of resources. The state took itself out of many aspects of production activity, in many cases performing the role of the regulator rather than the producer of goods or the provider of services.

These new tendencies on the part of the government were institutionalized as part of the 1993 constitution that defined the state as a subsidiary to the private sector and as a promoter of private initiative. In this context, three parallel processes served to push the state into this new role: the process of privatization of public businesses, the development of an institutional framework of regulation, and the promotion of free competition. During the first half of the 1990s, there was progress in all of these areas, just as, during the second half of the decade, there were also different degrees of regression in all of them. In the next subsection, we will concentrate on the issue of privatization.

The process of privatization

Fiscal problems, the inefficiency of public companies, the existence of strongly interventionist policies, as well as undercapitalization and the lack of new resources for investment, drove the Peruvian government to initiate a privatization program in 1991 (Alvarez 1992). The decision to begin this process was also facilitated by the influence of the multilateral agencies and reinforced by the privatization trend that was also sweeping through other countries in the region. It was also true that the Fujimori regime did not have the political party base that in other circumstances would have pressured him to keep some state enterprises as a mechanism to extract rent. The political base of the regime lay mainly with the armed forces, and it was precisely in businesses related to this sector that not only were there no privatizations, but there was even an expansion in activity levels, particularly towards the end of the decade.

In the middle of 1991, a normative framework began to take shape to stimulate and to regulate private investment in public companies. The Commission of Promotion of Private Investment (COPRI) was created and methods of promotion were established that included selling of actions and assets, borrowing of services, concessions. The Peruvian strategy of privatization demanded that investors not only pay for the transfer of assets, but also for investment commitments: for example, in the case of the telecommunications or electricity sectors, investors would have to pay for the expansion of the services and in the case of the mining industries, they would have to pay for further exploration.[27]

In that same vein, the 'Law of the Promotion of Foreign Investments' was created that established equal treatment for both national and foreign capital, with which foreign investment could establish itself in all sectors of the economy and be used for whatever type of enterprise the law allowed. During the first years of the decade, a set of norms were approved with the purpose of generating a legal framework that was adequate and could guarantee private investment flows. A series of institutions were also created as part of the mission to make good on the commitments taken on by the businesses and, in the case of natural monopolies, to prevent the abuse of dominant market positions.

In 1992, ten companies were privatized through COPRI and the creation of different special privatization committees (CEPRIs), which translated into US$212 million in revenue for the state treasury with US$706 million in a projected investment. Nevertheless, it was not until 1994 that the sale of the natural monopolies in the telecommunications sector (CPT-Entel Peru)[28] and the electricity sector (Edelsur and Edelnor) gave the privatization process real force. That year the amount collected by the sale of actions and assets reached US$2579 million with a projected investment of US$2050 million. During 1995 and 1996 the privatization process entered a stage of acceleration and deepening and then began to slow down around 1997. In total, at the end of 1999 all of the privatizations had generated revenue of US$8917 million and US$8800 million in commitments to invest. Some 40 per cent of the total collection came in the telecommunications sector, followed by the electricity sector, which accounted for 21 per cent, the mining sector with 14 per cent, and the hydrocarbon sector with 11 per cent.

In many different aspects, the privatization process in Peru was successful. The quality and coverage of diverse services improved substantially, and by 2000 the amount of commitments to invest had exceeded 11 000 million dollars, which was more than what the government had obtained for the sale of its assets. Nevertheless, many errors in the implementation of the privatization plan meant that gradually the privatizations lost political support. In the first place, during the development of this normative framework little attention was paid to the issue of transparency of information about the transactions taking place and of the final destination of the resources generated by the process. Without autonomous institutions to control the process and with norms that granted significant discretion to the executive authority, the government and its technocrats were relying on the entry of new investment to silence critics. In this sense, the fact that there were no spaces available for people to discuss or debate the privatization process and that the mechanisms for using the resources obtained were never clarified, both worked to make the process socially illegitimate.

Secondly, it was not taken into account that even when the privatization process had an overall positive social effect, there were still always winners and losers. Despite the improvements in efficiency in those same private sectors that in many cases generated important increases in the well being of consumers (Torero and Pascó-Font 2000) the perception of the social benefits of the privatizations was very negative. In the case of the privatizations in the telephone sector, for example, the principal improvements in well being happened initially, when access to telephone service was improved for segments of the population that before had been marginalized; nevertheless, this change came at the cost of increasing the price of service to the middle classes, usually the most vocal segment of the population, that had in previous decades had a poor, but highly subsidized, service.

Although the one evaluation available to date of the impact of privatizations shows that even in the worst cases, privatizations directly and indirectly created as many jobs as they destroyed, they also had important direct negative effects that were not managed adequately. No systems of social protection were implemented for the displaced workers from the privatized sectors and many of those that lost their jobs could not find a way to regain salaried employment in the formal sector and had to either begin to work independently without any social protection or to simply leave the labor market altogether. The fall in well being of specific groups of workers was painful and severe and their suffering was not alleviated in the short term. This makes it clear that if reforms take place without explicitly taking into account who wins with their implementation and, even more importantly, who loses, both the viability of the reforms and the general well being of the population will be put at risk.

One idea that could have given a new perspective to the privatizations process was the program called Citizen Participation that attempted to expand the participation of the small saver in the process. The program's purpose was to increase the small saver's access to the benefits of privatization through preferential buying of companies' actions and stimulating the development of a market for local capital. The first experiences under this new system (Banco Continetal y Cementos Pacasmayo) worked very well, with even more participation than had been expected. During the Peruvian release of a package of Telefónica assets in 1996, which coincided with an international launching of the company's assets, demand through the system was significantly higher than supply. Faced with the dilemma of whether to sell the shares to these small shareholders or those that could take their demand to the New York stockmarket, the government chose the latter, generating a huge amount of frustration among the former[29]. Subsequent action sales were much lower-profile.

The government was not interested in politically selling the process. Citizen Participation was considered as an option for generating a political constituency in favor of the process. The administration's abandonment of the program meant that it was leaving behind one of the few programs that was aimed at communicating with and making participants of more Peruvians and expanding the number of people who would benefit from the privatizations. This reflected the scorn with which some advisers to the process treated the stated objective of communicating clearly with the population.[30] This mutual distrust between citizens and government meant that even when the processes were transparent in terms of the access that was available to the bidders and the uniformity of the rules that governed all potential investors, the population still did not feel adequately informed.[31] The problem grew even worse when the opposition in Congress demanded an explanation for where the funds generated in the privatizations were going. In response to this congressional questioning, public opinion began to oppose the continuation of the process. The dismantling of Citizen Participation illustrated a change in the administration's governing style towards policy that was increasingly created at the discretion of the executive to further immediate political objectives. This new style explains the creation of the National Public Savings Fund (FONAHPU) that was mandated to finance pay increases for pensioners in the public sector with shares from different public companies.

Towards the end of the 1990s, the state not only stopped privatizing but also even created a state-owned airline, and maintained interests in the real estate and hotel sectors. In all of these cases, the interests were connected to the armed forces, the real political support behind the regime. Despite the government's apparently liberal rhetoric and its promotion of open competition, a variety of businesses linked to the armed forces, like the army press corps, the Industrial Services of the Navy, and the aforementioned airline, TANS, were not forced to compete fairly with private companies. The political power of the armed forces not only allowed them to keep these sources of rent during the privatization process, it also meant that these businesses were maintained even in the face of attempts at control on the part of the civilian authorities, such as the Contraloría.

Labor Reform

For decades, Peruvian labor regulations, developed during a period of import substitution, consolidated in both a marked protectionism and a rigidity in the labor market. At the beginning of the 1990s the OIT (International Labor Office) characterized it as 'probably the most rigid, protectionist, interventionist, and confused in Latin America' (OIT 1994). The labor legislation granted absolute labor stability after a very short period of time (three months) by making the costs of firing employees tremendously high. The extra benefits granted also substantially increased the non-salary-related costs to employers. This framework could be viable in an economy with a heavily protected market at the cost of a growth in informality, and this was, in effect, the experience of Peru the 1980s. The opening of the economy created a new scenario in that formal businesses required more flexibility if only to maintain themselves in the market. It was in this context that, beginning in 1990, the reform of labor regulations was finally undertaken.

The labor reform was implemented to reduce the costs of contracting and dismissal, as well as making the determination of salaries, hours, and types of labor contracts more flexible and in the control of the individual employer. The first measures adopted eliminated the bureaucratic restrictions on the use of temporary contracts and expanded the ways to contract employment for a fixed period of time. To a large extent, these measures didn't do more than legalize a series of practices that had been becoming a habitual response to both the rigid laws and the authority's incapacity to really investigate and control labor practices.

One of the intentions of the legislative reforms was to eliminate absolute labor stability. According to the constitution of 1979, labor stability was a right of all citizens, meaning that the new reform could only be a partial elimination of labor stability that protected against arbitrary dismissal and only affected those people hired after the reform's implementation. The workers contracted before November of 1991 could demand alternatively rehiring or severance pay in cases of unfair dismissal. Absolute labor stability was abolished in the constitution of 1993, and was replaced with laws that protected against arbitrary dismissal of all salaried workers. The costs of dismissal were also reduced with the establishment of mandatory severance pay for every year that the person worked, up to a maximum of 12 years, and, in cases of unfair dismissal, without obligation on the part of the employer to rehire the worker. In the same way, proceedings to qualify for dismissals with 'just cause' were simplified and reduced. Table 7.3 summarizes the principal changes in labor laws.

In 1992 the government permitted the creation of more than one union per business, guild, and economic activity, eliminating the monopoly of the single unions and transferring the negotiation from the sectoral level to the level of the firm. Intervention of the state was limited and the process of arbitration was substantially modified. It was established that workers on strike should receive their salaries until they returned to their jobs.

If the rate of unionization had been falling since 1987, these changes reduced it even more. The growing use of temporary contracts also served to dissuade people from union association. The percentage of salaried workers in the private sector that worked in a company with a union went from 30 per cent in 1987 to 6 per cent in 1997. In the public sector, the unionization

Table 7.3 Changes in Peruvian labor legislation 1991–97

Law	Principal content
D.Leg. 650 (July 1991)	Employers must deposit payment for Compensation for the Served Time (CTS) of their employees in an account of an authorized financial institution
D.Leg. 728 (November 1991)	New flexible contracts for young people Makes work procedures (days and hours) more flexible Eliminates labor stability of contracts after 1991 Makes the use of temporary contracts easier and broadens their use Severance pay for dismissal: a monthly salary for every year worked, for a maximum of 12 years Liberalizes use of temporary and complementary services
Law 26136 (December 1991)	Overtime pay is increased by 25% to 50% of the salary for a normal hour worked
D.S.E. 08-PCM/92 (March 1992)	The employer's contribution to the National Housing Fund is increased from 5% to 8%
Law 25593 (July 1992)	The requirements for unionization are made more flexible, allowing more than one union to form in each company. As part of this, during strikes, the company may suspend salaries until labor activity is re-established
Law 25981 (January 1993)	FONAVI[1] is eliminated as the responsibility of the employer and the employee's responsibility is increased by 9%
Law 25897 (July 1993)	Creation of a system of private pensions
Law 26233 (November 1993)	FONAVI input from employer moves to 6%, the input from the employee moves to 3%
Law 26513 (July 1995)	Protection from arbitrary dismissal replaces absolute labor stability Terms of temporary contracts are expanded The difference between the maximum working day for men and women is eliminated
Law 26504 (August 1995)	FONAVI contribution from the employer moves to 9%, input from the employee goes to 0%
D.Leg. 854 (October 1996)	Overtime pay is reduced from 50% to 25%
D.Leg. 871 (November 1996)	Severance pay for dismissal: a salary and a half per year worked, a maximum of 12 years
D.Leg. 853 and D.Leg. 855 (January 1997)	FONAVI contributions are reduced for the employer from 9% to 7% but this includes allowances for affected tax areas
Law 26851 (August 1997)	FONAVI contributions are reduced for the employer from 7% to 5%

Note: [1] FONAVI = National Housing Fund.

Source: Pascó Font and Saavedra (2001).

rate fell from 75 per cent in 1990 to 13 per cent in 1997 (Saavedra and Torero 2002).

In the second half of the decade, the tendency towards greater flexibility was reversed when the cost of dismissal was raised, increasing severance pay to salary and a half for each year worked. The non-salary labor costs increased during the decade. On one hand, the rate of contribution to the FONAVI (National Housing Fund), that in practice was actually a tax to fill out the form, was increased, and on the other hand, the maximum amount of diverse contributions was increased, especially between 1990 and 1992. As a result, the non-salary costs were substantially higher than they had been in the previous decade. In summary, while there was a loosening in labor laws in the sense that labor stability was eliminated, the incentives that were created for hiring temporary workers, the relatively high cost of labor, and a business atmosphere that was much more competitive, all pushed an important part of the labor opportunities to be given out through alternative contracts, and the percentage of workers with formal employment and social benefits decreased.

Social Policy

The struggle against poverty was a central focus of the government's rhetoric during the 1990s. The government implemented a set of programs aimed at increasing social spending and reducing both poverty and extreme poverty. Many diverse indicators show that there was a real transfer in resources to zones that were poorer and an expansion of the coverage of various social services. Various remote zones of the country were given government attention for the first time and a range of social programs were put into operation in those areas. Nevertheless, the increase in spending and levels of access and quality of social services was insufficient. Ultimately, the increase of social spending was not accompanied by the development of efficient institutions and was instead increasingly tied to the administration's political priorities.

Social spending

The stated objective of Fujimori's administration was to increase public spending in social sectors to total 40 per cent of all public spending. Table 7.4 shows the evolution of public social spending. It's clear that social spending grew considerably between 1993 and 2000, as much in relation to GDP (from 3.2 to 8 per cent) as in relation to total public spending (from 18.4 to 45 per cent). Nevertheless, one must remember that the public social spending includes all of the government spending in the social sector, a definition that incorporates the general spending of the government in education, health, and justice, and therefore includes social spending on the general population as well as benefits limited to the poor populations. The spending related to the struggle against poverty also grew significantly between 1993 and 1998, from 1.2 per cent to 1.9 per cent in relation to GDP, and 7.1 per cent to 11.1 per cent in relation to total public spending.[32]

CEPAL (1999) has shown that Peru was the country in the region that most increased its public social spending per capita, in real terms, between 1990–91 and 1996–97. If this increase was significant, it is largely because the levels of public spending were extremely low at the beginning of the 1990s. In spite of this evolution, social spending as a percentage of total public spending was, in 1997, only the average in Latin America, behind Argentina, Uruguay, Brazil, and Chile, that all had more than 60 per cent of their total public spending set aside for social spending. Around 1997, social spending as a percentage of GDP in Peru was only 6.3 per cent, as compared to the average in Latin America, which was 12.4 per cent.

The struggle against poverty

In 1990 a new institutional framework as part of the struggle against poverty began to be created. In 1991, the National Fund of Compensation and Social Development (FONCODES) was established as a decentralized organization, autonomous from the president of the republic, with the purpose of focusing on the population in extreme poverty through the development of programs of social support, infrastructure, and productive development (see box: 'the FONCODES model'). In 1992, the National Food Assistance Program (PRONAA) was created to provide food rations in rural and marginalized urban zones. The National Institute of Education and Health Infrastructure (INFES) directed its principal investment in the construction and rehabilitation of school buildings. The Ministry of the Presidency (MIPRE) was reactivated to combine almost all of the new social programs of the government.[33] This ministry not only had responsibility for the administration of the majority of the programs of the struggle against poverty, but also took under its care the Transitional Committees of Regional Administration (CTAR), which had been created as a temporary system until regional authorities were elected. The 1993 constitution mandated that these elections be deferred until 1995,[34] but they were postponed indefinitely. Throughout the decade this strategy allowed the president to have more control of spending; given that the ministry came to control between 25 per cent and 30 per cent of the total government budget, the administration had a large margin of discretion over social spending.

In 1996, the Ministry of the Promotion of Women and Human Development (PROMUDEH), was created with a more diffuse mandate and to assume the management of some of the MIPRE programs. Between 1997

Table 7.4 Evolution in social spending

Category	1993	1994	1995	1996	1997	1998	1999	2000
Level (millions of current dollars)								
GDP[1]	34 805	44 801	53 653	55 827	59 056	57 005	52 028	53 880
Total public spending[2]	5 970	8 105	10 044	10 044	9 969	9 727	9 281	9 457
Social spending[3,4]	1 101	1 999	3 575	3 575	3 703	4 042	4 080	4 307
Spending in poverty reduction programs[4]	423	590	546	846	1 089	901	1 005	1 046
%GDP								
Total public spending	17.2	18.1	18.7	18.0	16.9	17.1	17.8	17.6
Social spending	3.2	4.5	6.7	6.4	6.3	7.1	7.8	8.0
Spending in poverty reduction programs	1.2	1.3	1.0	1.5	1.8	1.6	1.9	1.9
%Total spending								
Social spending	18.4	24.7	35.6	37.2	37.1	41.6	44.0	45.5
Spending in poverty reduction programs	7.1	7.3	8.4	7.9	10.9	9.3	10.8	11.1

Notes:
1 The data for 2000 are preliminary.
2 Includes current spending and capital spending of central government. The data for 2000 are preliminary.
3 Includes spending in education, wealth and extreme poverty reduction programs.
4 Executed data, except for 2000 that is estimated.

Source: Central Reserve Bank of Peru, INEI, Instituto Cuánto.

THE FONCODES MODEL

FONCODES was created with the mission of improving the living conditions of the most poor, attending to the basic needs of the population with an emphasis on nutrition, health, education, sanitation, economic infrastructure, and the development of production. Its operating mechanism was the financing of demand-driven projects. In the first trimester of 1998, FONCODES had executed 28 289 projects, of which 70 per cent were in areas of social infrastructure (nutrition, health, education, and sanitation) and the rest were in the areas of economic infrastructure (agriculture, transportation, and energy). The FONCODES used criteria based on an index of problems in particular districts that includes indicators of undernourishment, education, housing, and basic services. According to a World Bank study, FONCODES, along with the PRONAA, had the best performance in its spending, measured by the correlation between the percentage of resources directed at helping the bottom 40 per cent of the population and the rate of coverage of this impoverished group.

and 1999 there were various attempts to improve the coordination between social policy and the allocation of resources to agencies and programs. Given the evidence that there were many duplicated functions and problems with allocation, as well as a lack of both transparency and accountability in institutions, there were initiatives to improve interinstitutional and intersectoral coordination of the programs.[35] In 1999, the government even designed a first Contingency Plan of Social Protection, a plan that had as its objective to protect the zones that were the most vulnerable to any possible recession or economic crisis. Nevertheless, the advance of these initiatives was very slow due to the fact that they started to stop acting with the regime's objectives of controlling the growing movement of the resources for the state's social spending.

One innovation that is important to emphasize is the active incorporation of the population in different phases of some specific social programs. The use of participatory methodologies in this area tried to give those who had historically been marginalized a voice, to improve the quality of the decisions, and to incorporate feedback from the beneficiaries of the program in a way that strengthens the democratization of local-level decisionmaking and increases the transparency in the use of resources. With different emphases and levels of success, the principal executors of FONCODES, the

Committees of Local Health Administration (CLAS), the Local Teams of Priority Actions (ELAP) of the Project for the Implementation of Economic and Social Investment (PROFINES), among others, were all examples of organizations that used these participatory methodologies. Recent research, nevertheless, has underlined the diverse ways that participatory mechanisms can be applied, given the level of complexity of the community, the type of local leadership, the role of intermediaries, the institutional reinforcement that is involved, the public good aspects of the given product, and the characteristics of the 'external agents'. This analysis emphasizes the elements of risk that can turn the process of participation into a process that is both antidemocratic and inefficient.

These social programs were not free of political manipulation on the part of the Fujimori administration. At the same time that the administration was spending more in general and in particular in the zones where the state had never before entered, it also used social policy as a way to legitimize the government, and in particular to legitimize Fujimori (Gonzáles de Olarte 2000). This explains in part the higher levels of approval that he had towards the end of the decade, in spite of that fact that he had been in power for ten years and that the economy had been in recession since 1998. The mere fact of providing daily meals to more than 10 million Peruvians acted as an immense source of political power.[36] Fujimori used that power whenever he could. Aside from the issue of the absolute quantity that was spent, there is the question of the efficiency of the spending – after they had spent the money (more that $5000 million annually) it seemed reasonable to expect to see a sizeable decrease in levels of poverty. In effect, the administrative mechanisms of many of the social programs turned them into welfare programs. One of the most important characteristics of the social institutions that were put into place was the way that they strengthened the dependency of the population on state-controlled resources, a dependency which was exacerbated by the growing use of state resources for the purpose of proselytizing through social assistance programs. This dependency dynamic was reinforced by the dysfunctional public system that attempted to address the problem of poverty, in which diverse institutions literally competed for a clientele by offering the same products or services.

FONCODES, in spite of having been considered one of the most successful social funds in Latin America during the 1990s, became, along with other programs, an effective instrument to proselyze, given the absence of mechanisms of accountability, in a context of the increasing politicization of the budget decisions. Schady (2000) documented this phenomenon, finding a correlation between the progression of spending and the proximity of election periods, and between the selection of provinces to receive funds and the magnitude of expected political returns from each province.

7.6 MACROECONOMIC PERFORMANCE

The stabilization program had strong recessive effects on the economy during the period of 1990–92. As can be seen in Figure 7.4, starting in 1993 there was a sustained growth in total production; GDP registered an average annual growth rate of 6.4 per cent during the period of 1993–97. Only in 1996 did growth slow as a consequence of the important reductions in public spending that were necessary to reduce the fiscal inequalities that had been incurred in the months previous to the 1995 elections.

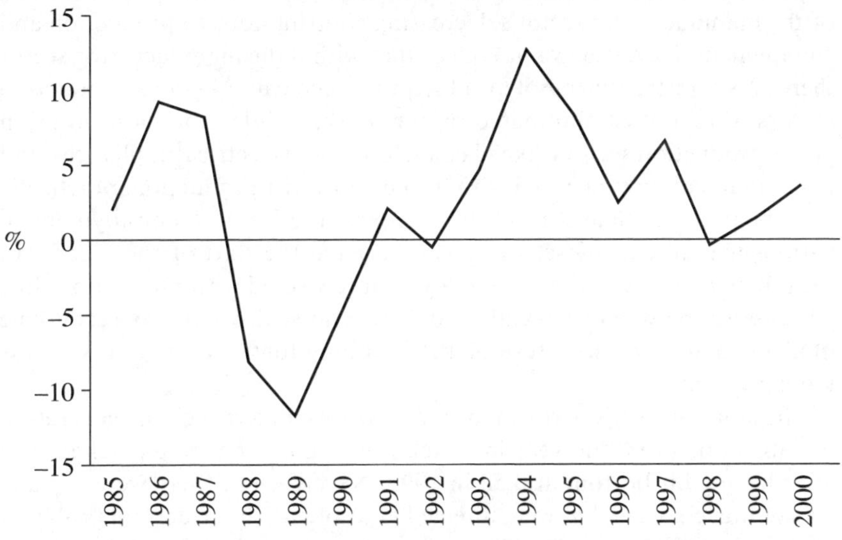

Note: Calculated from a base from 1994 during the period of 1990–2000 and with a base from 1979 for the previous years

Source: Central Reserve Bank of Peru. Website available in February of 2001.

Figure 7.4 Growth rate of GDP 1985–2000 (per cent)

At the start of 1998, a series of climatic financial and political shocks submerged the country in a prolonged period of recession. For two years per capita production reduced, and in 2000, it grew less than 2 per cent. In terms of domestic demand and level of economic activity that was reflected in employment or revenue, there was stagnation for a long period of time. The observed growth during part of the decade could not be sustained in the face of external shocks, of inadequate macroeconomic management of these shocks, of the postponement of reforms – especially those that promoted private investment, and of the serious political crisis.

An important point in terms of the impact of the reforms is that the sector distribution of production has not varied significantly since 1990 (see Table 7.5), despite the disagreements over the way that the chosen path of the political economy was deepening the economy. The manufacturing sector represented 15 per cent of total production followed by commerce and agriculture (approximately 18 per cent) and then by mining (11 per cent). Although there appears to have been only a slight reduction in the importance of manufacturing, this reduction is part of a long-term pattern of the manufacturing sector's decreasing contributions to production and employment. Nevertheless, it is clear that within the manufacturing sector there was a restructuring of production. Some capital goods production sectors were almost eliminated by the market while other consumption goods production sectors, like plastics, household electrical appliances, and paper that had only survived with the help of tariff production, practically disappeared. As Saavedra (1997a) shows, the level of employment in various manufacturing sectors was reduced at the start of the decade. In the following years, however, employment recovered with production. In a broad sense, between 1990 and 2000 there is no evidence that the economic model changed the structure of the economy towards one that was less industrialized.

The labor market's performance was positive in terms of the generation of jobs until 1998, the year in which the employment rate reached 0.60 after having hit bottom at 0.52 in 1992. Nevertheless, there were not any substantial changes that were directed at resolving the structural problems of the labor market, and the little growth in productivity kept real salaries from growing significantly and allowed the informal sector to occupy more than half of the population.

Along other lines, the correction of the distorted relative prices that existed at the end of the 1980s, combined with orthodox fiscal and monetary policy, significantly reduced the inflation rate. After the years of hyperinflation of Alan García, inflation reached 132 per cent in 1991 and 56.7 per cent in 1992. In the following years there was a gradual reduction in inflation along with an increase in economic activity. In 1995, inflation reached 10 per cent and in 1997, the government managed to bring inflation down to single digits (see Figure 7.5). Cuba (2001) attributes the reduction in inflation during the 1990s to monetary policy and to the influx of capital, which also brought the exchange rate down and made it stagnant until at least 1997. The country approached 2000 with inflation that was 3.9 per cent annually – the lowest rate in the last 40 years.

Table 7.5 *Composition of GDP by sector 1990–99 (per cent)*

	1990	1991	1992	1993	1994	1995	1996	1997[1]	1998[1]	1999[1]	2000[1]
Farming[2]	7.8	8	7.3	7.6	7.6	7.6	7.8	7.7	7.9	8.7	8.9
Fishing	0.7	0.5	0.7	0.7	0.7	0.6	0.5	0.5	0.4	0.5	0.6
Mining and Hydrocarbon[3]	4.4	4.4	4.5	4.7	4.7	4.5	4.6	4.7	5	5.5	5.4
Manufacturing	15.6	16.1	15.7	15.5	16	15.5	15.4	15.2	14.7	14.5	14.9
Construction	4.1	4	4.1	4.7	5.6	6	5.7	6.2	6.3	5.5	5.1
Commerce	14.4	14.5	14.4	14.1	14.6	15.1	14.8	15	14.6	14.1	14.4
Other Services[4]	53	52.5	53.4	52.7	50.9	50.7	51.1	50.7	51.2	51.1	50.7
Total[5]	100	100	100	100	100	100	100	100	100	100	100

Notes:

1 Preliminary.
2 Includes the fishing sector.
3 Includes the non-metal mining sector.
4 Includes direct taxes and importing rights.
5 GDP calculated with a base from 1994.

Source: Central Reserve Bank of Peru. Website available in Feburary of 2001.

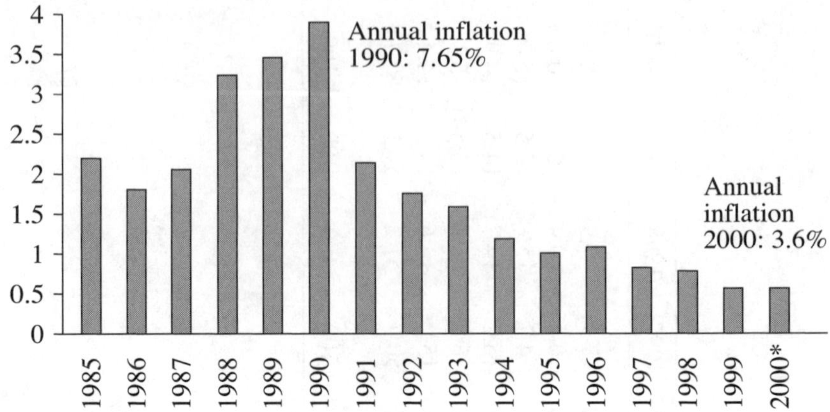

Note: * Accumulated January–December 2000.

Sources: Central Reserve Bank of Peru (1998, 1999) and INEI (2000).

Figure 7.5 Annual inflation 1985–2000 (log base)

Once through the stabilization period, both the country's savings rate and its investment rate began to slowly recuperate. As can be seen in Table 7.6, internal savings grew steadily from the end of 1992 to 1997, with a slight dip in 1992. The composition of these savings also changed significantly, with public sector going from the net spender it had been at the end of the 1980s to having a savings rate of 5.2 per cent of GDP in 1997. On the other hand, external savings also grew until 1995 and during the last decade represented 5.4 percentage points of GDP, decreasing only in recent years.

Investment also showed a new vitality, growing to 16.5 per cent of GDP in 1990 and then reaching up to a peak of nearly 25 per cent in 1995. During the period between 1995 and 1997, private investment rose to the highest levels in the previous 15 years. The accelerated growth of investment during the first few years in the 1990s was much faster than the growth in internal savings, and the natural adjustment mechanism was an increase in the deficit of the current account in the balance of payments until 1998. After 1998, investment again demonstrated a tendency to decrease that both coincided with the economic cycle and was largely due to the political instability at the time.

Part of the increase in the deficit on the current account is explained by the commercial balance. As a consequence of commercial opening and of the reduction of the real exchange rate, imports increased steadily throughout the period of growth between 1993 and 1997. Despite the argument that the export sector would be one of the hardest hit by the stabilization program,

Table 7.6 Macroeconomic flows (as a percentage of GDP, base 1994)

Category	1990	1991	1992	1993	1994	1995	1996	1997	1998	1999	2000
SAVINGS-INVESTMENT											
Internal saving	11.8	12.9	11.5	12.7	16.5	17.1	16.7	18.8	17.2	17.8	17.1
Public sector	–5.5	0.8	0.7	2.2	3.0	2.3	3.9	5.2	4.0	1.8	0.8
Private sector	17.3	12.1	10.8	10.5	13.5	14.8	12.8	13.6	13.2	16.0	16.3
External savings	4.7	4.4	5.8	6.6	5.7	7.7	6.1	5.2	6.4	3.7	3.0
Investment	16.5	17.3	17.3	19.3	22.2	24.8	22.8	24.0	23.6	21.5	20.1
Public sector	3.2	3.5	4.1	4.7	4.8	4.7	4.3	4.4	4.5	4.8	4.0
Private sector[1]	13.3	13.8	13.2	14.6	17.4	20.1	18.5	19.6	19.1	16.7	16.1
BALANCE OF PAYMENTS											
Balance of current account	–4.7	–4.4	–5.8	–6.6	–5.7	–7.7	–6.1	–5.2	–6.4	–3.7	–3.0
Commercial balance	1.3	–0.6	–0.9	–1.7	–2.2	–4.0	–3.6	–2.9	–4.3	–1.2	–0.6
Services	–1.2	–1.2	–1.6	–1.7	–1.1	–1.4	–1.2	–1.3	–1.2	–1.4	–1.5
Income from production factors	–5.8	–4.0	–4.5	–4.7	–4.0	–3.7	–2.9	–2.5	–2.6	–3.1	–2.9
Current transferences	0.9	1.4	1.3	1.5	1.7	1.5	1.6	1.6	1.7	1.9	1.9
Capital account	–2.4	–0.2	2.4	5.3	8.6	5.7	6.3	9.7	3.4	2.1	2.1
Private sector	0.2	0.4	0.6	3.5	8.5	4.8	7.3	4.2	3.8	4.6	2.2
Public sector	–3.6	–0.4	–1.1	–1.4	–0.8	–0.3	–0.8	1.0	–0.1	0.7	0.5
Short-term capital	1.0	–0.2	2.9	0.4	1.0	1.2	–0.3	4.5	–0.3	–3.2	–0.7
Exceptional financing	8.3	4.1	4.1	1.8	3.6	2.8	1.7	–1.4	0.6	0.1	–0.1
Net reserve flows (BCRP) (–)	–0.6	–2.3	–2.0	–1.9	–6.6	–1.7	–3.5	–2.9	1.8	1.5	0.4
Net mistakes and omissions	–0.6	2.8	1.3	1.4	0.9	0.9	1.7	–0.1	0.6	0.0	0.7
NON-FINANCING PUBLIC SECTOR											
Savings in current account	–5.5	0.8	0.7	2.2	3.0	2.3	3.9	5.2	4.0	1.8	0.8
Capital revenue	0.1	0.3	0.3	0.1	0.1	0.0	0.1	0.0	0.1	0.1	0.1
Capital spending	3.3	3.8	4.9	5.3	5.9	5.5	5.0	5.1	4.9	5.0	4.1
Public investment	3.2	3.5	4.1	4.7	4.8	4.7	4.3	4.4	4.5	4.8	4.0
Other capital spending	0.1	0.4	0.8	0.7	1.1	0.8	0.8	0.7	0.4	0.2	0.2
Economic outcome	–8.7	–2.8	–3.9	–3.1	–2.8	–3.1	–1.0	0.2	–0.8	–3.1	–3.2
Financing	8.7	2.8	3.9	3.1	2.8	3.1	1.0	–0.2	0.8	3.1	3.2
External financing	6.3	4.1	3.2	3.0	2.4	2.5	0.8	–0.4	0.4	–0.1	1.2
Internal financing	2.4	–1.4	0.5	–0.4	–4.7	–1.2	–3.6	–0.7	0.0	2.4	1.2
Privatization	0.0	0.0	0.2	0.4	5.1	1.8	3.9	0.9	0.5	0.8	0.8

Note: Includes variation of stock.

Source: Central Reserves Bank of Peru.

a fixed exchange rate, elevated tariffs, and high interest rates all meant that even exports, although still much lower than imports, still demonstrated a certain vitality. The increase in the deficit was also explained by more servicing of external debt and interest and by the growing negative balance of the non-financing service account.

Even though the current account deficit could have been financed adequately before, its continual fluctuations for several years around 6 per cent of GDP continued to worry the authorities until 1998. In the next two years, external crises and the phenomenon of El Niño affected Peru's external accounts, and yet the deficit on the current account managed to be reduced substantially to 3.7 per cent of GDP, largely as a consequence of the reduction of imports in the 1998 recession.[37]

7.7 REGULATED DEMOCRACY OR DICTATORSHIP ON TENDERHOOKS?

Two events that followed the closing of Congress in 1992 dramatically affected the Fujimori regime's political fortunes: the crucial blow to the subversive threat that was represented by the capture of the Senderista leader, Abimael Guzmán, and the beginning of economic recovery. Even though the connection between these two events and the interruption of constitutional rule is in no way clear, they were both used by the administration, its vocal officials and supporters to legitimate the regime. The 1995 elections could not have come at a better time for Fujimori. Aside from the expansion of fiscal spending, Fujimori used the armed forces in political propaganda, as well as the National Intelligence Service (SIN) to spy on his political rivals, both as tools to mastermind his first re-election. More important, however, was that the opposition that Fujimori faced was extremely weak. There is no doubt that this weakness contributed to the effectiveness of Fujimori's anti-political-party and generally anti-politics rhetoric. The principal opposition front, Unión por el Perú (UPP), was effectively a collection of 'traditional' politicians, as Fujimori liked to call them, that crossed the spectrum from right to left. Unable to offer either new political figures or an alternative economic approach, the UPP had difficulty in creating a message that could reach and resound with the public.

Many people's expectations reflected a belief that the re-election would initiate a period of consolidating the reforms that had been begun and of tackling the 'pending agenda' of reform in a context of economic growth and institutional 'normalization'. Not much time went by, however, before these expectations began to be disappointed. On the economic side of things, the price of the excesses in public spending during the election campaign had to be paid, which meant an adjustment that drastically reduced the growth rate in the economy. Politically, the defeat of the pro-government candidate in the Lima mayoral election less than a year after Fujimori's triumph illustrated the difficulty of successfully endorsing candidates. In this context, the preservation of power was quickly confirmed as Fujimori's bottom line when Congress approved the Law of Authentic Interpretation, which opened the doors to a third consecutive term.[38] A television station's divulging of information about the income of Fujimori's adviser, Montesinos, and the subsequent persecution of the owner and his family, as well as the participation of high-up officials in the armed forces in drug trafficking, and the torture and assassination by agents of the then obscure and now suspect SIN, all brought public approval of the president down to its lowest level and resulted in the first public manifestations of rejection of the arbitrariness and authoritarianism of the government. In this context of public disavowal of the regime, the taking of the Japanese embassy by the MRTA at the end of 1996, paradoxically, allowed the regime to sigh with relief.

The erosion of the second Fujimori administration was quick, as can be seen in Figure 7.6. In the face of dwindling public support, the government's response was a combination of more authoritarianism, albeit limited by international conditions, and greater populism. Although 1997 marked an inflection point in the decade in the sense that it was a year of the reinitiation of economic vitality, even this change in economic events did not halt the fall in presidential approval ratings or recover the momentum of reform of Fujimori's early years. Two alternative explanations for this are: (a) the economic growth did not 'trickle down' to people of lower socioeconomic status, and (b) the political decisions of the government were undermining its own capacity to govern. The policies during the rest of his time in office and his public statements suggest that President Fujimori believed in the first of these hypotheses. Nevertheless, public perception did not seem to respond to Fujimori's efforts and between the middle of 1996 and the beginning of 1998, approval of the political leader of the government, President Fujimori, had fallen close to 25 points, much more than that of the economic policy (see Figure 7.1). Intuition suggests that there was a general dissatisfaction with the political situation that was dampening people's enthusiasm over economic recovery.

Indicators of the public's perceptions over what was one of the pillars of the reformist agenda, increasing the importance of the market in the allocation of resources, reflect a slight decrease in approval in the first few years of the decade, that nevertheless in all cases stayed above 50 per cent and, for some indicators, even hovered close to 80 per cent (see Figure

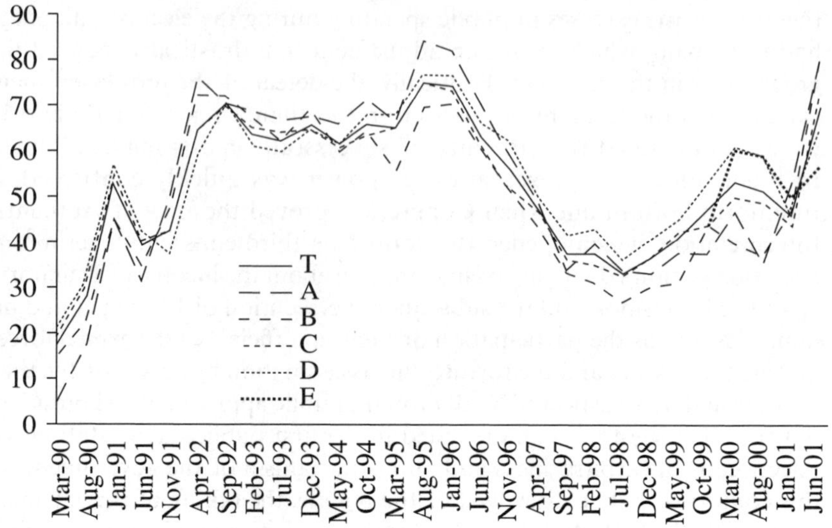

Note: A–E indicate socioeconomic level according to the classification created by Apoyo Opinión y Mercado (1997), where A indicates the population with the most resources and E with the least resources. T represents the total.

Figure 7.6 Approval of the President's management of the Republic by socioeconomic segment (five-month moving averages)

7.7). With respect to whether the state needed to reduce in size, however, the percentage of people that agreed that it did, in fact, need to be smaller, declined significantly. Attuned as he was to public opinion surveys, the President understood that the reform of the state, associated in the public's mind with a reduction in size, would have a high political cost. Even the Minister of Economy, who liked to call himself a liberal, declared in 1996 that the reform of the state had to be postponed for reasons 'of the political moment'.

Soon the President became an open critic of the 'neoliberal' economic policies of his own government, an attitude he exhibited at the major meeting of Peruvian companies. The international crises that followed, combined with the President's populist demands, complicated macroeconomic management, and rendered the government incapable of successfully working against the recession that would stretch through the rest of the decade.

In the political sphere, the government's hardening reflected a new strategy that combined intimidation, blackmail, and cooption. According to the evidence revealed in the videos of meetings of adviser-to-the-president Montesinos with businessmen (particularly those from the communications

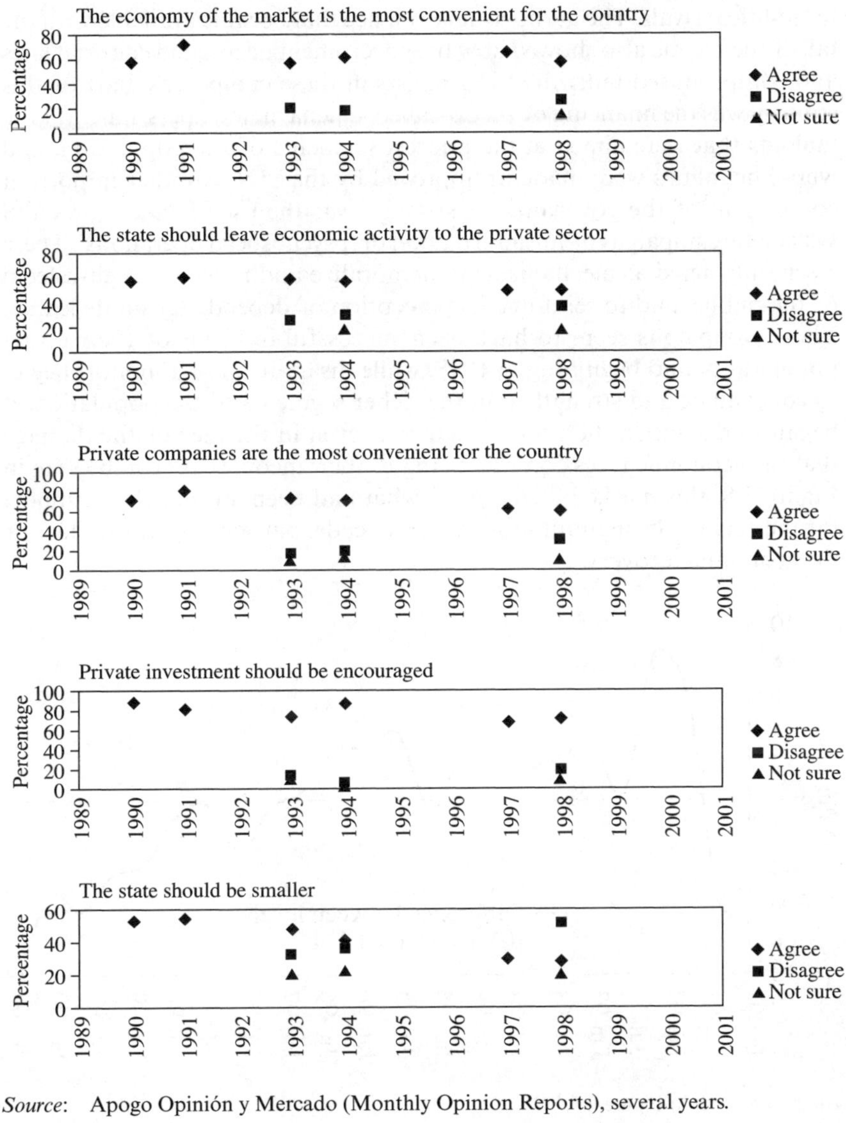

Source: Apogo Opinión y Mercado (Monthly Opinion Reports), several years.

Figure 7.7 Public perception of economic issues

sector), the government seems to have used the recession to control employers and, especially at the end, used the police power of SUNAT and the judicial branch to control civilians. Most of the important mass media were used to uphold the image of the President and to carry out smear campaigns against his political rivals. The audiovisual evidence that became available with the fall of the regime also showed how the government negotiated editorial lines and compromised individual journalists in these campaigns. Part of this strategy was the financing of the so-called 'chicha' newspapers, muckraking tabloids that were aimed at the poorest segments of the population, and whose headlines were made or approved by the SIN. Another important component of the government's strategy was the use of talk shows and systematic campaigns of misinformation or 'psychosocial operations'. These essentially acted as mechanisms to demoralize and reduce the self-esteem of the public, and to reinforce its perception of dependency on its leader. These campaigns seem to have been successful in terms of their target populations, and beginning in 1998, while disapproval of Fujimori began to consolidate and strengthen in the richer segments of the population, it began to decline in the poorer segments, even in the face of the damage that the economic recession was doing to their incomes. As can be seen in Figure 7.8, this marked a change in what had been an interclass support for the regime throughout most of the decade, particularly at the start of the economic recovery.

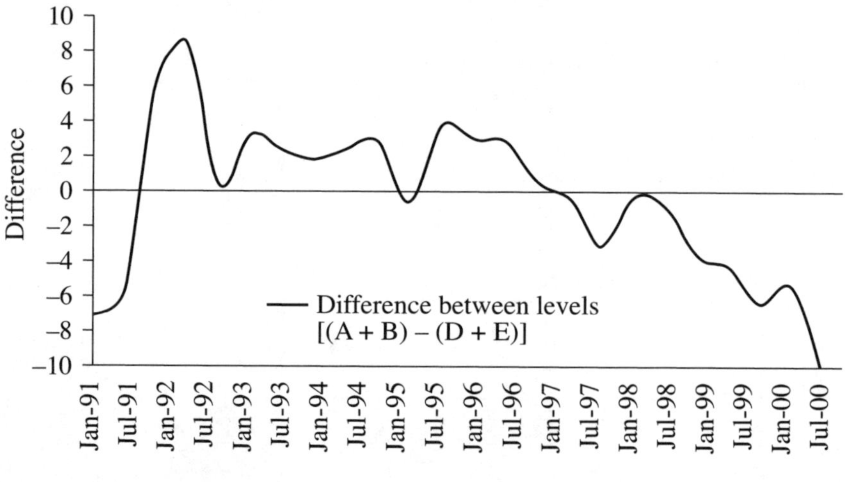

Note: See note to Figure 7.6.

Figure 7.8 Difference in presidential approval between socioeconomic levels

In effect, in spite of the evident achievements, like peace with Ecuador, Fujimori would not reach the same levels of approval that he had had throughout most of the decade. His final comeback comes in the context of an electoral campaign and is largely driven by popular sectors. This is partly explained by the 'campaigns of annihilation' of his political rivals, like the mayor of Lima, Alberto Andrade, and the ex-President of the Peruvian Institute of Social Security, Luis Castañeda, in the mass media, that generated a sensation of inevitability around Fujimori's third term. In part this was also related to the display of propaganda that included a distinct change of color of the movement that Fujimori led and the massive appearance of the motto of his group in public places, particularly in zones like the hills overlooking the city of Lima, under the control of the armed forces. The figure of Alejandro Toledo, that now seems so important with only two months until the elections, would come to fill the void of the leader of the opposition in the new context of the discovery of the fabrication of false signatures for Fujimori. This discovery tainted Fujimori, in spite of the attempts to mediate its effect by the Jury of National Elections and the Public Prosecutor's Office that, to the surprise of few, found only the accusers guilty.[39] The time to implement a 'campaign of annihilation' proved to be too short on the one hand, and, on the other, the strategy seemed to be reaching a stage of diminishing returns. At the end of the campaign, the people in the street and the pressure of international governments forced the head of the National Office of the Electoral Process to ignore the elementary arithmetic of the questionable numbers that emerged, that indicated that Fujimori could still win in the first round, and declared that there would be a second round.

7.8 FINAL REFLECTIONS

In the 1990s, Peru went from reform to counterreform in three stages. The first period (1990–92) is marked by the stabilization policies and the beginning of reforms in line with the so-called Washington Consensus, all under a democratic regime and without a parliamentary majority. The second period (1993–95) was characterized by an acceleration of the reforms and a strong economic recovery, under a political regime that gradually closed channels of horizontal accountability by eliminating institutional checks on the power of the executive. During the third period (1996–2000) the administration's unconstitutional political objective to stay in power after 2000 was soon revealed, and the management of the economy and public policy were soon subordinated to this political goal. In this context, the reforms were first frozen and then reversed, reinforcing the authoritarian and populist characteristics of the regime. Peru's economic performance in this time was much worse than it had been in the middle of the decade and than the average performance in the region. This history is consistent with the two characteristics that stand among the indicators of the dimensions of governability in Peru from 1997 to 1998, gathered from Kauffman, et al. (2002): the administration ranks low in terms of giving people a voice, of accountability of officials, of political stability, and of a government that abides by the law, but ranks high in terms of governmental effectiveness and quality of regulation (Kauffman, et al. 2002).

Two central questions in analysis of Peru's economic policy throughout the decade are why the reforms were begun and then why they were postponed or reversed. In terms of the first question, the spectacular failure of Alan García's heterodox policies left the country in an economic and political chaos that forced the government to look for other economic and political alternatives. It was this context of an enormous crisis among the political parties that permitted a virtual unknown to rise to the presidency, whose very obscurity and separation from the more established political machine granted him an unusual autonomy in the face of traditional interest groups. The range of options for Latin America at that time was dominated by the Washington Consensus, which looked to recast the market in the role of main allocator of resources. A particularly attractive virtue of a more active market for a pragmatic president like Fujimori was that it opened the possibility of getting new financial resources in a context in which the public finances were virtually bankrupt and international reserves were negative. Multilateral organizations also put pressure on the government to open the market and allowed the administration to establish a minimal technocracy that the Ministry of Economy and Finance could use to push through reform.

While this answers the question of why reforms were started, the reasons that the reforms were stopped are equally important. One hypothesis is that the President agreed with many of the critics of the government that argued that the economic model did not 'trickle down' to the poorer sectors of society. The solution for that problem lay in less market control over resources and more government control. The President's opinion on economic issues that were the most directly related to sectors that he had a personal affinity with or interest in, certainly support this hypothesis. Nevertheless, the growing impatience of the President with the economic policies of his government is largely explained by the deterioration of the political situation, which at its core stemmed from Fujimori's determination to remain in power after 2000. The reasons for the abrupt end to the reform process now seem very clear: Fujimori himself, as well as those followers that were most closely related to the armed forces (his main source of political support), had much to hide. Because of these illicit activities, beginning reforms that had democratizing content, or even reforms that would have put a limit on the arbitrariness of the decisions of the government, was not part of his agenda. It was also true that a populist management of public resources did seem to offer the possibility of getting him in a better position for the 2000 election.

Particularly important to Fujimori's political agenda was maintaining an institutional setting in which he could continue to freely develop the informal power that governed supposedly autonomous organizations such as the judicial branch, the nation's public prosecutor, the censored Constitutional Tribunal, and the SUNAT. These informal powers were even reflected in the very actions of the executive. These are abundant: from his use of emergency decrees to hide illegal or awkward transactions, the use of the presidential plane to transport cocaine, the lack of public information about the use of resources from the privatizations in spite of the continued demands from Congress, to the transfer of regulatory agencies from the MEF to the Ministry of the Presidency (PCM) due to a friendship between both ministers and then the subsequent return of the organisms to MEF when the minister of PCM was set free (*Semana Económica*, August 1998), and including the payment of millions of dollars to Montesinos to leave the country in September 2001. The rule of law demanded one major area of reform: accountability. This type of reform meant horizontal accountability, as well as transparency of the government accounts to Peruvian citizens, included vertical accountability, and directly collided with the informal powers that constituted an important part of the regime. There was no intention of advancing a reform of public service that would increase transparency in the use of public resources, advance a process of decentralization that would gradually grant more administrative and financial autonomy to regional authorities, or that would begin the much-demanded reform of the judicial branch.

At the same time, the first-generation economic reforms began to lose support and were seen by the government as a political liability. The process of privatization, for example, began to be perceived negatively in terms of its impact on the overall well being of Peruvians. As has been shown, evidence existed that suggested that there was not a net loss in jobs, and there was rather an increase in the well being of the very poor, even if it came at the cost of the middle classes. The privatization was also used with the objective of eliminating the fiscal deficit and with it, inflation. Nevertheless, the process of privatization became so unpopular that the government effectively froze it, making the administration's lack of conviction on the usefulness of the reforms clear and prioritizing short-term political needs above the long-term economic health of the country. The unpopularity of the reforms can be explained by various reasons. Largely, it was due to the fact that the government did not implement systems of social protection for workers that were displaced by the entry of private companies. Many of those that lost their jobs could not manage to adequately reinsert themselves into the job market and had to either conform to unstable independent work or simply leave the job market altogether. The fall in the well being of specific groups of workers was large and painful and was not alleviated in the short term. Also contributing to the reforms' unpopularity was the fact that decisions about whether to privatize and about how to use the resources that came from the privatizations were not made in a public and transparent way. Even more importantly, there was never any policy of explaining the nature of the reforms to the public and convincing them of the advantages of the process.

Another example of the erratic course of the reforms is in foreign trade. Although the opening of Peru happened very quickly, at the end of the decade, the average tariff level of many other countries in the region was much lower than Peru's, and the tariffs in Peru stopped decreasing just as the government began to increasingly use quantitative restrictions. Similarly, the regulatory agencies for public services began to lose autonomy and the independence of INDECOPI, the entity in charge of consumer protection and open competition, also began to be questioned. Towards the end of the decade, there was not a clear ideological orientation in the administration's management of the economy. Although the basic management of fiscal and monetary policy continued to be orthodox in the government's rhetoric, underlying was the change in the government's orientation towards a growing arbitrariness and ad-hoc management of sectoral policies.

After Fujimori's fall, an important set of reforms has been questioned by many public sectors. As has been argued, in many cases the reforms were postponed, reversed, or simply badly implemented. But to this must be added the fact that whatever political measure was implemented during the 1990s runs the risk of being questioned at its margin of convenience, for the simple fact that it was implemented by the Fujimori government. This constant questioning and re-evaluation brings its own risk of returning to the destructive pendulum swings in policy which go from one extreme to the other, with serious damage in the long term to the country's political and economic well being.

Some maintain that it was the very lack of political opposition to the reforms that is explained in part by the lack of alternative options and in part by the actions of the government to take over whatever institution could oppose its initiatives, that ultimately served to erode the initial political support of the reforms. According to this logic, in a more democratic system, the reforms might have been implemented more gradually, but they would also have been implemented better and would have had greater sustainability. The Peruvian experience in the last 40 years, characterized by the pendulum movements of its policy and economy, nevertheless denies this presumption. Indicators of governability for 2001 reveal significant improvements in terms of giving citizens a voice and accountability, but also show a backward slide in the effectiveness of government and the quality of regulation. An important challenge facing a government as concerned as the current administration is with governability is how to assure the public and the world that institutional reform eliminates the possibility of 'violent lurches' and generates a climate of sound policy that, in turn, makes the government more effective. This requires not only much stronger institutions, a public service that attracts qualified professionals, transparency and solid systems of horizontal accountability, but also the establishment of mechanisms that allow the policies that are eventually implemented to be the result of long-term political agreements. In this vein, the debate over the constitutional reform that began in the last few years will be an important indicator of how much of this challenge the Peruvian political class can successfully confront.

NOTES

* The authors are grateful for the comments of Andrés Solimano, Hubert Escaith, and Carol Wise. Also, they wish to thank Elsa Bardelez for excellent research assistance. This chapter was prepared for the project 'Political Economy of the Andean Countries', under the auspices of the Ford Foundation.

1. One reading of the Peruvian political process that emphasizes the role of this battle and presents it as a decisive factor can be found in Cotler (2000).
2. President Fujimori did not lose the opportunity in international forums to present his peculiar, and to other Peruvians even embarrassing, concept of democracy: a regime that offers economic development to its citizens.
3. The evidence includes a time series of indicators of the perception of public opinion on aspects of governance, expectations, and economic performance. These indicators are regularly publicized in monthly reports written by Apoyo Opinión y Mercados S.A. and are frequently used in analysis of the political situation. The time series has not been subjected to a systematic study. The type of information is similar to that used by Kaufmann, Kraay, and Zoido-Lobatón (1999) to construct indices, although in their case it is presented in conjunction with data from expert opinion.
4. In the political science camp the 'autonomy of the political' has been long accepted, being, for many in the camp, a premise of the discipline.
5. For more on the effects of this in contemporary political science, see Miller's (1997) survey.
6. For example, Naím (1995); for a macro-vision of Peru along these lines see Kisic (1999). At a more feasible level of the public sector, there are also discussions of the political dynamic in structural adjustment (Guerra-García 1999) and of institutional reforms (Ortiz de Zevallos et al. 1999).
7. The work of Guillermo O'Donnell and Adam Przeworksi has been perhaps the most inspirational in the field, functioning as important 'nuclei' in the academic work Latin America.
8. For analyses of Peru that incorporate some of these elements see those of Cotler (2000) and Grompone (2000).
9. O'Donnell (1997).

10. Estimation is based on the chronology by Tuesta (1987), pp. 22–4.
11. During a large part of the 1990s, while more than half of the current public spending was channelled through the CTAR (Transitional Advisory Board of Regional Administration), it had no decision making power over the spending. The spending that they could control at that level was financed only with their own meager resources. The provinces and district municipalities, on the other hand, received their own income and resources from the Municipal Compensation Fund (FONCOMUN). The resources of this fund are distributed from the Ministry of the Presidency using a standard of allocation based on the municipality's population size and poverty level.
12. One recent example is the Macro Región Sur movement, which was maintained by the political and economic elite from southern Peru, and, until the end of the decade, was focused on obtaining preferential tributary treatment for the region. Similarly, regional movements of the rain forest seem to have the defense of the system that the law has established for them as their principal objective.
13. Instituto de Estudios Permanoz (Institute of Peruvian Studies, 2001).
14. Nationalism is a complex subject that the more recent national historiographies have depicted as a process that, even from the most optimistic of outlooks, was still largely incomplete until the end of the nineteenth century. See the illustrative debate over the role of the indigenous population in the war with Chile (Bonilla 1990; Mallon 1990; Manrique 1990). For the rest, the development of this national identity, of Anderson's (1983) 'imagined community', has followed a singular process, that, unlike western Europe (Weber 1976), was for the most part independent of the state's limited capacity to drive the process.
15. Collier (2001) finds that ethnic politics can produce diverging results if the ethnic diversity of the group implies the domination of one specific group or if it implies general divisions in the population. Ñopo, Saavedra, and Torero (2002) document the existence of differences in income between ostensibly similar individuals of different ethnicities.
16. Ñopo, Saavedra, and Torero (2002) document the existence of different income levels between ostensibly similar individuals that differ in their ethnicity. Mestizos that have lighter skin earn more than other mestizos, but less than individuals considered to be white.
17. For more on the determinants of the shock, see Guerra-García (1999).
18. In March of 1992, only 15 per cent of the population approved of Congress's performance, the percentage that said they trusted Congress had fallen to 16 per cent, and the percentage that said they had confidence in political parties came to 12 per cent 'Apoyo Opinión y Mercado 1992'.
19. In 1993, three years after the initial implementation of a stabilization policy, the rate of inflation was still at levels of around 40 per cent annually. While there was certainly an important decrease, it is in sharp contrast to the rapid end of hyperinflation in Bolivia in the 1980s.
20. Unlike the monetary authorities of other countries, the BCRP does not have any purpose related to the level of economic activity of the country.
21. In the middle of the 1980s, the tax burden had been more than 15 per cent of GDP (Baca 2000).
22. Interview with advisers of the Ministry of Economy and Finance.
23. In practice, the high interest rates of 1990 were maintained, that being so elevated actually allowed the interest rates to be determined by supply and demand.
24. The capital requirements for a banking operation rose, a Center of Risks was created, and, with the support of the Central Bank of Reserves and financial institutions, a Fund of Securities and Deposits was created, which covered a maximum amount of the individiuals' deposits.
25. This debate was revisited in 2000, by a manufacturing lobby that defended the convenience of the several-tiered system.
26. Defined as the proportion of the sum of imports and exports with respect to the internal gross product.

27. As Gonzáles de Olarte (2000) explains, the influence of capital from the privatizations doesn't only impact direct investment and additional commitments, but also, affects the creation of a 'state of confidence' that attracts investment to distinct sectors of the economy.
28. The companies CPT-Entel Peru obtained a surprising value of US$1391 million and a projected investment of US$1565 million.
29. The campaign of diffusion had not made it clear that there was a serious possibility that not all of the demand would be met, probably because such a strong response from the local market came as a surprise.
30. Interview with a general manager that advised several privatization processes.
31. In fact, with the exception of a few specific processes, there were no further questions or requests for information on the part of investors.
32. This includes some of the programs whose actions attempt to focus on the most poor, according to the classification system of the INEI.
33. The Ministry of Labor and Social Promotion developed a few programs linked to the labor market, the most important of which is the Labor Youth Training Program. Its budget nevertheless was very small and it depended heavily on external resources. The Ministery of Agriculture, on the other hand, administered programs of supposedly productive promotion with a largely rural clientele and that developed a strong slant towards welfare, particularly in the atmosphere of the election.
34. Political Constitution of Peru, 8th Temporary Disposition.
35. Numerous anecdotes exist about funds that were directed at schools before the actual school existed that could use them. In other cases, the speed of the allocation of funds meant that they constructed the same kind of school in all of the country, ignoring the particular differences of geography and climate in each region.
36. This number comes from Vásquez and Riesco (2000), p. 89.
37. It is important to mention here that the official numbers of the current account can hide various problems of information that come from the revenue in foreign currencies from the illegal exporting of narcotics and uncertainty over other accounts (like the net revenue of tourism or problems in the registering of transfers of Peruvians' payments abroad). The 'account errors and omissions' of the balance of payments registers a net positive revenue of US$3794 million between 1991 and 1997 – the equivalent of almost 50 per cent of the commercial deficit accumulated during that same period and almost 20 per cent of the deficit on the current account. In other words, a net positive revenue of foreign currency exists that has been the equivalent of a fifth of the current account deficit and that is part of the explanation of why, in spite of the current account deficit, the country has still continued to accumulate reserves. This revenue, nevertheless, fluctuated greatly and it is unclear how stable it was.
38. This law decreed that because of the way the article of the constitution that only admitted one immediate re-election had been applied, Fujimori had not been re-elected in 1995.
39. Forms were discovered with more than a million false signatures that had been used to register the party that Fujimori led, Peru 2000. The possibility that this could have disqualified the official group was never even considered by the electoral institutions.

REFERENCES

Abusada, R., M.E. Fritz du Bois and J. Valderrama (eds) (2000), *La Reforma Incompleta*, Lima: Universidad del Pacífico-Instituto Peruano de Economía.

Abusada, R., J. Illescas and S. Taboada (2001), *Integrando el Perú al Mundo*, Lima: IPE-Universidad del Pacífico.

Álvarez, A. (1992), 'Situación y perspectivas de la privatización en el Perú', in *Proceso de Privatización en el Perú*, Foro Económico no. 5, Lima.

Anderson, B. (1983), *Imagined Communities: Reflections on the Origin and Spread of Nationalism*, London: Verso.
Apoyo Opinión y Mercado (1992), *Informe de Opinión*, Lima, March.
Apoyo Opinión y Mercado (1997), *Niveles Socioeconómicos en la Gran Lima*, Lima.
Baca, J. (2000), 'El ancla fiscal: la reforma tributaria', in Roberto Abusada (ed.), *La Reforma Incompleta*, Lima: CIUP-Instituto Peruano de Economía.
Boloña, C. and J. Illescas (1997), *Políticas Arancelarias en el Perú 1980–1997*, Lima: Instituto de Economía de Libre Mercado – Universidad San Ignacio de Loyola.
Bonilla, H. (1972), 'La independencia en el Perú: las palabras y los hechos', in *La Independencia en el Perú*, Lima: IEP.
Bonilla, H. (1990), 'El campesinado indígena y el Perú en el contexto de la guerra con Chile', in Steve J. Stern (comp.), *Resistencia, Rebelión y Conciencia Campesina en los Andes: Siglos XVIII al XX*, Lima: IEP.
Brautigan, D. (1994), *Gobernabilidad y Economía: Una Revisión*, Lima: Instituto de Investigación para el Desarrollo y la Defensa Nacional.
Burki, S. and G.E. Perry (1998), *Beyond the Washington Consensus: Institutions Matter*, Washington, DC: World Bank.
Central Reserve Bank (1998), *Memoria Anual*, Central Reserve Bank, Lima, Peru.
Central Reserve Bank (1999), *Memoria Anual*, Central Reserve Bank, Lima, Peru.
CEPAL (1999), *Panorama Social de América Latina 1998*, Santiago: UN-CEPAL.
Collier, P. (2001), 'Ethnic diversity: an economic analysis', *Economic Policy*, **32**, April.
Cotler, J. (2000), *El Fujimorismo: Ascenso y Caída de un Régimen Autoritario*, Lima: IEP.
Crabtree, J. and T. Jim (eds) (1999), *El Perú de Fujimori: 1990–1998*, Lima: Universidad del Pacífico-IEP.
Cuba, E. (2001). *Perú en los 90's: Una Visión desde la Macroeconomía*, manuscrito, Lima.
Domínguez, J. (1980), *Insurrection or Loyalty: The Breakdown of the Spanish American Empire*, Cambridge, Massachusetts: Harvard University Press.
Escobal, J. (1992), 'Marzo de 1991, el mes de las reformas estructurales en el Perú', in Joaquín Vial (comp.), *¿Adónde va América Latina? Balance de las Reformas Económicas,* Santiago de Chile: CIEPLAN, pp. 233–60.
Escobal, J. and M. Torero (2000), '¿Cómo enfrentar una geografia adversa? El rol de los activos públicos y privados', *Documento de Trabajo*, 29, Lima: GRADE.
Figueroa, A. (1999), 'Distribución de ingresos y pobreza en el Perú', in J. Crabtree and J. Thomas (eds), *El Perú de Fujimori: 1990–1998*, Lima: IEP.
Gonzales de Olarte, E. (1998), *El Neoliberalismo a la Peruana. Economía Política del Ajuste Estructural 1990–1997*, Lima: Instituto de Estudios Peruanos/Consorcio de Investigación Económica.
Gonzales de Olarte, E. (2000), *Neocentralismo y Neoliberalismo en el Perú*, Lima: CIE and IEP.
Grompone, R. (2000), 'El Fujimorismo', in J. Cotler and R. Grompone (eds), *El Fujimorismo: Ascenso y Caída de un Régimen Autoritario*, Lima: IEP.
Guerra-García, G. (1999), 'La dimensión política del ajuste económico del Perú', in Elas Bardález, Martín Tanaka and Antonio Zapata (eds), *Repensando la Política en el Perú*, Lima: IEP.

Huntington, S.P. (1968), *Political Order in Changing Societies,* New Haven, Connecticut: Yale University Press.
INEI, *Censo Nacional de 1993*, Lima.
INEI (2000), *Compendio Estadístico 2000*, INEI, Lima.
Instituto de Estudios Peruanos (2001), *Encuesta sobre Descentralización*, Lima, December.
Kaufmann, D., A. Kraay and P. Zoido-Lobatón (1999), 'Governance Matters', World Bank Development Research Group Macroeconomics and Growth and World Bank Institute Governance, Regulation, and Finance, *Working Paper* no. **2196**, October.
Kaufmann, D., A. Kraay, and P. Zoido-Lobatón (2002), *Governance Matters II: Updated Governance Indicators for 2000–2001,* Washington, DC: World Bank.
Kisic, D. (1999), 'Privatizaciones, inversiones y sostenibilidad de la economia peruana', in Crabtree and Jim (1999).
Mallon, F. (1990), 'El campesinado indígena y el Perú en el contexto de la guerra con Chile', in Steve J. Stern (comp.), *Resistencia, Rebelión y Conciencia Campesina en los Andes: Siglos XVIII al XX* , Lima: IEP.
Manrique, N. (1990), 'El campesinado indígena y el Perú en el contexto de la guerra con Chile', in Steve J. Stern (comp.), *Resistencia, Rebelión y Conciencia Campesina en los Andes: Siglos XVIII al XX* , Lima: IEP.
Miller, J.G. (1997), 'The impact of economics on contemporary political science', *Journal of Economics Literature*, **XXXV**, September.
Naím, M. (1995), *Latin America's Journey to the Market: from Macroeconomic Shocks to Institutional Theory, Occasional Paper* **62**, San Francisco: International Center for Economic Growth.
Ñopo, H., J. Saavedra, M. Torero and J. Escobal (2002), 'The economics of social exclusion in Peru: An invisible wall?', Lima: GRADE, www.grade.org.pe/asp/brw_publ1.asp
North, D. (1990), *Institutions, Institutional Change and Economic Performance*, New York: Cambridge University Press.
O'Donnell, G. (1994), 'Delegative democracy', *Journal of Democracy*, **5**(1).
O'Donnell, G. (1997), 'Polyarchies and the (un)rule of law in Latin America', in Juan Mendez, Guillerno O'Donnell and Paulo Sergio Pinheiro (eds), *The Rule of Law and the Underprivileged in Latin America*, Notre Dame, Indiana: University of Notre Dame Press.
Obando, E. (1999), 'Las relaciones civiles-militares en el Perú 1980–1996: sobre como controlar, cooptar y utilizar a los militares (y las consecuencias de hacerlo)', in S. Stein (ed.), *Los Senderos Insólitos del Perú*, Lima: IEP-Universidad de Huamanga.
OIT (1994), 'El desafio del empleo en América Latina y el Caribe', *Documento de Trabajo*, 7, Lima: OIT.
Ortiz de Zevallos, G., H. Eyzaguirre, R.M. Palacios and P. Polarrollo (1999), 'La economía política de las reformas institucionales en el Perú: los casos de educación, salud, y pensiones', *Documento de trabajo* **R-348**, Washington, DC: BID.
Pandolfi, H. and C. Sanborn (1997), 'Fujimori y las raices del neopopulismo', in Fernando Tuesta Soldevilla (ed.), *Los Enigmas del Poder: Fujimori 1990–1996*, 2nd edn, Lima: Fundación Friedrich Ebert.
Pascó-Font, A. and J. Saavedra (2001), *Reformas Estructurales y Bienestar, una Mirada al Perú de los Noventas*, Lima, GRADE-CEPAL.

PromPerú (1999), *Perú país en marcha*, Lima: Peru Roadshow.
Przeworksi, A. and associates (1995), *Sustainable Democracy*, New York: Cambridge University Press.
Saavedra, J. (1997a), 'Liberalización comercial e industria manufacturera en el Perú', *Investigaciones Breves* **2**, Consorcio de Investigación Económica.
Saavedra, J. (1997b), 'Quiénes ganan y quiénes pierden con una reforma estructural: cambios en la dispersión de ingresos según educación, experiencia y género en el Perú urbano', *Notas para el Debate* no. 14, Lima: Grupo de Análisis para el Desarrollo (GRADE).
Saavedra, J. (1998), 'Crisis real o crisis de expectativas? El empleo en el Perú antes y después de las reformas estructurales', *Documento de Trabajo* **26**, Lima: Grupo de Análisis para el Desarrollo (GRADE).
Saavedra, J. and J. Díaz (1999), 'Distribución del ingreso en el Perú antes y después de las reformas estructurales', *Seri Reformas Económicas*, 32, Santiago: CEPAL.
Saavedra, J. and M. Torero (2002), 'Union density changes and union effects on firm performance in Peru', Research Network Working Paper, R-465, Washington, DC: IADB.
Schady, N. (2000). 'Seeking Votes: The Political Economy of Expenditures by the Peruvian Social Fund (Foncodes), 1991–95', *American Political Science Review* **94**(2), June, 289–304.
Tanaka, M. (1999), 'La economía política del ajuste y la reforma estructural en el Perú: el estado de la cuestión y la agenda pendiente', in Elsa Bardález, Martín Tanaka and Antonio Zapata Antonio (eds), *Repensando la Política en el Perú,* Lima: IEP.
Tanaka, M. (2001), *Participación Popular en Políticas Sociales: Cuando Puede Ser Democrática y Eficiente y Cuando Todo lo Contrario*, Lima: IEP.
Torero, M. and A. Pascó-Font (2000), *The Social Impact of Privatization and Regulation of Utilities in Peru*, mimeo, Lima: Grupo de Análisis para el Desarrollo (GRADE).
Tuesta, F. (1987), *Perú Político en Cifras, Elite Política y Elecciones,* Lima: Fundación Friedrich Ebert, August.
Ugarte, M. (2000), 'La reforma de Estado: alcances y perspectivas', in Abusada et al. (2000).
Vásquez, E. and G. Riesco (2000), 'Los programas sociales que "alimentan" a medio Perú', in F. Portocarrero (ed), *Politicas sociales en el Perú: muevos aportes*, Lima: Red para el desarrollo de las Ciencias Sociales en el Perú.
Velarde, J. and M. Rodríguez (1992), *El Programa Económico de Agosto de 1990: Evaluación del Primer Año*, Lima: Universidad del Pacífico, Centro de Investigación.
Weber, E. (1976), *Peasants into Frenchmen: The Modernization of Rural France, 1870–1914,* Stanford, California: Stanford University Press.

8. Venezuela: from stability to turmoil

Enzo Del Bufalo*

8.1 THE END OF AN ERA

A failed military coup lead by Hugo Chávez on 4 February 1992 marked the beginning of a new period of political instability and institutional changes in a country that was until then a model of governance in Latin America. The coup attempt had been preceded by three days of street looting in February 1989. It happened two weeks after the new administration of Carlos Andrés Pérez announced a stabilization and liberalization package supported by a standby agreement with the International Monetary Fund (IMF). This popular upheaval cannot be considered a reaction to the usual negative effects of orthodox stabilization programs, since there was not enough time for these effects to work out. It was rather due to the psychological effects of the announcement itself that caused a sudden disappointment of people's high expectations of a quick return to the better days previous to the 1983 devaluation. A return that people felt had been too many times postponed just because of the inefficiency and corruption of governments.

The addition of a new disappointment to the accumulated burden of a long series of frustrations unleashed the social reaction that signaled the end of an era of stability. The new government had been elected because it had promised a return to the boom days of the 1970s, when the first administration led by Carlos Andrés Pérez enjoyed the huge oil revenue. The stabilization program meant exactly the opposite of what the people were expecting from the new government. But more than that, the government's stabilization program meant the end of the social pact that made possible the stable democracy, enjoyed by Venezuela for several decades in a region dominated by military dictatorships and authoritarian regimes.

Since 1958, the county had been able to build solid democratic institutions. After an initial period of proliferation of parties and conspiracy threats from right-wing groups and a more impelling menace by left-wing guerrilla movements, the Venezuelan political system evolved rapidly into a two-party system with a fairly regular alternation in power. The two major parties commanded around 90 per cent of the electoral votes and the rest went to left-wing parties and other minor political organizations. One of these parties, Acción Democrática, had a social-democratic orientation, while the other, COPEI, had a Christian-democratic ideology; both parties were members of their respective international movements. Initially, only Acción Democrática had a wide popular basis, gained during the 1940s, when it helped to overthrow the last government elected on a restricted electoral basis, and opened up the way for the rising new middle classes to seize power. After the interlude of the Pérez Jiménez dictatorship during the 1950s, Acción Democrática's candidates won the first two free elections and lost a third one to Rafael Caldera of COPEI. By that time, this party had undergone a big transformation from a small urban middle-class party to a mass party that had successfully competed with Acción Democrática for the vote of workers, peasants, and the urban poor as well as the middle classes.

Besides the state institutions, the country also developed a fairly well organized civil society with business chambers gathered in a loose federation called FEDECAMARAS and widely spread trade unions united in the Confederación de Trabajadores de Venezuela (CTV), with strong links to both major parties. Professional associations were also very active and in the late 1970s, neighbors' associations and NGOs for the defense of specific interest started to appear as a clear sign of a dynamic civil society.

This political system and social organization were made possible by a sustained economic growth with low inflation during a period of several decades that started before the establishment of the democratic system. The non-oil GDP grew at an average annual rate of 8.5 per cent during the 1950s, 6.5 per cent in the 1960s and 6.8 per cent in 1970s; while the inflation average rate was 1.3 per cent during the period 1950–60, 6.6 per cent during the 1970s (Hausman 1990). The average wages increased at 2.4 per cent for the whole period 1950–70 (Baptista 1997), while the rate of unemployment was kept around 6 per cent during the same period. The national currency was convertible at a fixed rate at 3.33 bolívares per dollar until 1961, and then, after a brief period of exchange control, the free convertibility was again re-established at a fixed and freely convertible rate of 4.30 per dollar until 1983. Trade balances were persistently positive except for very brief periods and fiscal deficits and public debt were very small and manageable. In such an economic environment income distribution improved considerably. The Gini coefficient steadily decreased from 0.69 in 1944 to 0.40 in 1981 (Baptista 1991). The health programs, the enhancement of educational facilities and a considerable flow of European immigrants initiated in the late 1940s greatly increased the human capital.

It was this institutional framework that was compromised in 1992, mainly because the economic conditions that made it possible were fading away.

But before entering into the analysis of the crisis of governance of the 90s, we should get a better insight into how the Venezuelan democracy really worked by taking into account three major factors:

a) the social composition of the country;
b) the nature of the economic model based on the oil rent perceived by the state;
c) the international context of the 1960s.

Human Geography

Four main regions are distinguishable in the Venezuelan geography that have had some incidence in the formation of regional differences that are relatively minor compared with other Latin American countries. Although they have played some role in Venezuela's historical conflicts, they never consolidated in lasting political differences that could have threatened the unity of the country, even during the nineteenth century when Venezuela was just a loose confederation of regional political caudillos.

The coastal region is where the capital city and the more important industrial and commercial complexes are located, mainly along the axis between the ports of La Guaira and of Puerto Cabello. To the east lie the traditional cocoa plantation lands of Barlovento with an important population of African descent. During the eighteenth century, cocoa was the main export crop that made the fortunes of the more important families of nearby Caracas and therefore played a determining role in the final political configuration of the colony that later gave birth to the Republic of Venezuela. Further to the east lies a less developed area with important oil fields and great tourism potential that has played an important role in Venezuelan history since the arrival of the first Spaniards in the early sixteenth century. To the west the poor and undeveloped Falcon State separates the central axis from the oil-rich Maracaibo area. The population character of the coastal region is akin to the rest of the Spanish Caribbean.

The Andean region stretches from the west part of the coastal region to the southwest up to the Colombian border. It has a very traditional agrarian society that earns its livelihood from high mountain crops raised on small plots of land and it is structured around the family unit and the small town. Culturally, the people of this region have some similarities with their Colombian neighbors and it is the only part of the country that can be considered properly as part of the more extended Andean region of South America. Historically, the region has had a strong influence on Venezuelan politics and before the oil era was responsible for one of the main export items: coffee.

The plains region lies to the east of the Andean region and south of the coastal region along the plains north of the Orinoco River up to the Atlantic Ocean. It has very few urban centers and its western population gravitated around the Andean region, while those living in the central plains are more integrated into the cities of the central coastal region and the rest are linked to cities of the eastern coastal region. The traditional social structure of this region used to be very loose, conditioned by a presence of the so-called extended family and a production organization that rested upon the large cattle ranch (hato) and the small plot of land (conuco) cultivated by poor peasants. This has been a traditional cattle country, home of the llaneros, a mixed-blood race of horsemen that played an important role in the war for independence and during the subsequent civil wars. Their seminomadic lifestyle made then naturally inclined toward a free and egalitarian type of society that tends to reject hierarchical institutional relations in favor of more horizontal personal relations.

The forest region lies on the right bank of the Orinoco river and is made up of two main territories. The first is the south that goes deep into the Amazon basin and is mainly populated by indigenous people belonging to the traditional Amazon cultures. It has very few small towns scattered along the river. It is a frontier territory and has traditionally little bearing on Venezuela's social and political events. But it has a great economic potential as one of the greatest reserves of the planet's biosphere. The second territory is the Guayana region that runs east of the south region to the Atlantic Ocean and for its main part is also scarcely populated with the exception of the area around Ciudad Bolívar. Settled since early colonial times at the narrowest stretch of the Orinoco River, this city had played an important role in Venezuela's history. More recently, since the 1950s, heavy industries had been developed at Ciudad Guayana on the conjunction of the Caroní River with the Orinoco. It is a very rich mineral territory and is becoming increasingly connected with the northern Brazilian state of Roraima.

Ethnic diversity

The Venezuelan ethnic composition inherited from colonial times was a typical mestizo society with considerable clusters of black population partially mixed with the other races and a white minority at the top of the social ladder. A strong European immigration especially after World War II partially changed such a composition, but Venezuela remained a multiracial society where ethnic conflicts are practically non-existent. Social conflicts take place in a relatively homogeneous national environment that did not particularly emphasize ethnic differences, but rather took the form of disputes among different interest groups. Naturally the different ethnic groups are not equally distributed along the different layers of society and subtle forms of discrimination are still present, but in general Venezuela is a fairly homogeneous national state.

In other parts of Latin America, ethnic diversity implies mainly a differentiation along cultural lines in order to exclude certain groups from political power and to link them to the modern labor market in a peculiarly exogenous manner clearly singled out by Arthur Lewis in the 1950s (Lewis 1953). Since ethnic groups are very seldom of pure blood or have an untainted traditional culture, the concept refers more to a particular type of power relation than to some sort of anthropological entity. What really defines the alleged ethnic character is the type of exclusion that characterizes its relationship with the rest of society. Ethnic exclusion is typical of countries where a national state has not being able to create a homogeneous society, by which we mean a society where each person is a sovereign individual formally equal to any other. In such a society racial and cultural differences are no more than personal peculiarities that are part of their own individuality and do not constitute patterns of collective identification. This is the reason why there are no ethnic conflicts in Switzerland.

Venezuela is probably one of the countries in Latin America that has the most advanced social democracy and this has been a major factor in the country's long governance stability within a political democratic setup. Such a social democracy has been the result of a long historical process that started in the second half of the nineteenth century with the so-called Guerra Federal, a civil war that almost entirely destroyed the old colonial social organization and set in motion a dynamic process, and, as a result of which, social democracy advanced much more rapidly than political democracy. Venezuelan history was then marked by a violent succession of caudillos that were an offspring of regional segments acquiring more power from the traditional elite based in Caracas. Thus these dictators were more the expression of the dissolution of the colonial segmentations and despotic personal relations than the political arms of a social elite trying to cling to the old colonial order. This was an asymmetrical process with respect to what was going on in neighboring countries where a Montesquieusque type of political institution were being consolidated for a very small minority, while the rest of the population remained trapped in the ancient colonial segmentations.

The Oil Rental Model

During the late 1920s Venezuela became one of the world's largest oil producers and by the end of the following decade was the first world exporter. Multinational corporations ran the oil industry until 1975 when it was nationalized. But they could only do so by obtaining concessions to exploit the oilfields, while the state retained the ownership of the subsoil and therefore the right to claim the rent originating from such exploitation. This arrangement set in motion a complex interaction process between oil production, state institutional consolidation and social development that made possible an increasing governance of the country that eventually allowed for a stable democratic regime. This peculiar multidimensional arragement of economic, political and social relations is called: the oil rental model.

The expansion of oil production increased fiscal revenue, that enabled a considerable enhancement of government spending that was used to modernize the country. In the 1920s Venezuela was a small and very backward country of less than 3 million inhabitants with a rural population reaching 80 per cent of the total, almost the same rate of illiteracy and a third of the people afflicted by endemic diseases. Four decades later in the early 1960s, the country had 10 million inhabitants with 80 per cent of its population living in cities and having the highest per capita income and one of the best social indicators of Latin America. Such an amazing transformation was possible thanks to the oil revenue accruing to the state and being recycled to private citizens through government spending, subsidies and other less legitimate forms. The latter became a particularly effective mechanism of trickling down of the state wealth to a growing middle class, an improving working class and a fading-away peasantry.

Since there was no meaningful private exploitation by nationals and the multinational corporations operated in the country under the enclave system, legitimate government policies and corruption were the only ways to inject the oil rent into a very poor and undeveloped society. In its early stages up to the completion of the first phase of industrialization in the late 1970s, this mechanism fostered the creation of private entrepreneurial capacity that was previously non-existent. It also helped to improve the human capital of the middle and working classes that dramatically changed the composition of Venezuelan society. Those who were in control of the state institutions were able to direct the distribution process in their favor. This incited the new rising middle classes to seize power in 1945, through a military coup that ended the oligarchic regime of the posgomecista[1] era, by establishing universal voting rights and a program of modernization based on industrialization and land reform, universal education and health improvements. Since then, the two main objectives of Venezuelan politics had been:

1) to get an ever-increasing share of the oil revenue accruing to state; and
2) to try to secure the control of the state through a wining political alliance, organized in political parties that could seize power through elections.

The first one was a consensus objective, since it was considered as the natural way to finance a modernization program shared by almost all sectors of the political spectrum. This sort of national project, synthesized in the motto: *Sembrar el petrolio* (sow the oil), was the basis for the high degree of governance that the country enjoyed for five decades. This is true in spite of the two coups d'état that took place: one in 1948 that established military rule and one in 1958 that ended it. The military dictatorship that ruled during this period shared the same modernization program and did not disrupt the process that was creating those new social practices that, in the end, made possible the establishment of democratic institutions.

It was only a transitory episode caused by some errors committed by the parties led by an inexperienced new political class that were magnified by an international context determined by the Cold War, as we shall show presently. The important fact was that the goal of using an increasing share of the oil rent to finance the development of the country was the basis for the underlying political consensus that, in different occasions during 50 years, helped to renew the social pact among all segments of Venezuelan society. From the political and juridical point of view, the institutional changes brought about by switching back and forth from a democratic regime to a military dictatorship were certainly important; but from the point of view of governance, they were minor modifications in the way the social consensus was realized.

The second objective was responsible for a process of natural selection of political parties that helped to build the two-party system. The change from the oligarchic regime to democracy meant the enhancement of the electoral basis to cover all sectors of society and therefore the need of broad alliances among different sectors of society in order to have a chance to win power. The parties that were more capable of building an alliance among middle classes, workers and peasants had better chances to win elections. Initially two parties, Acción Democrática (AD) and Union Republican Democrática (URD) with social democrat and populist ideologies competed successfully for mainstream votes, followed by the Communist Party (PCV) and other parties like COPEI that did not have widespread support. A better leadership gave AD an advantage over URD and the first democratic Government (1945–48) was an AD government and this fact established it as the majority party that could guarantee sure access to the control of the oil rent. It seemed that AD was on the verge of becoming another PRI and established a regime similar to the Mexican one. But the 1948 coup got in the way and AD was the main target of the following military government repression and was declared illegal. URD was then left as the main legal party, and in fact won the election in 1952, held under the supervision of the military regime, that refused to yield to the government.

By 1958, when democracy was restored, AD had grown stronger after years of underground activities and was perceived as a party with a real chance to win even by those less interested in improvement of society than in their own personal gains. This perception did in fact help the party to win the election and its victory made it the sure way to maintain access to the oil rent. The tendency towards a sort of Mexicanization of Venezuelan politics was again set in motion. But this time it was aborted by the split of the left wing of the party that wanted to push towards a Cuban type of social transformation. The prompt reply of Betancourt outlawing the dissidents made them go underground and start a guerrilla movement, followed shortly by the Communist Party. This caused a crisis of governance for a newly elected government that was already under siege by the far right that was trying to restore the military dictatorship. The crisis was solved by a governance agreement with the other two major parties left: URD and COPEI; this agreement was called *Pacto de Punto Fijo* and lasted for the following 37 years. The other two parties were too small to have a real option to win elections and AD won the second election in 1963.

Being in control of the state, AD was able to implement strong populist policies and to foster patronage as a way to create allegiance to the democratic system and, at the same time, adhesion to the will of the party machinery. The rule of the game was as follows: A strong party was needed to win the election and to gain access to the oil rent distribution process. At the same time, the control of the oil rent distribution process gave the party in power the necessary financial means to command the allegiance it needed to win the next election. All sectors that wanted to have a fair share of the state revenue distribution should establish some sort of connection with the party in power. In the Venezuelan case, the economy of the vote really meant a vote economy where a winning vote was the best way of tapping the oil revenue. But in the early stages of this democratic game, the fact that AD was only a relative majority party posed some problems. A considerable sector of the middle classes, that were not connected to the party machinery, would have been left outside the distribution process with a high risk of breaking the social pact underpinning the democratic process and in fact the very basic consensus on the modernization process. The Pacto de Punto Fijo was the solution.

Officially, the Pacto referred only to institutional post sharing such as the presidency of the House of Representatives that should be given always to a member of one of the opposition parties, a fair distribution in the appointment of justices to the Supreme Court and other judicial posts and so on. In exchange, the opposition parties were to give legislative support for passing crucial laws and should rally behind the government on special issues deemed of national interest such as the defense of democratic institutions and so on. Unofficially, the Pacto set up an informal consultation mechanism among the parties' leaders to decide on the most relevant issues that were afterward ratified formally in the Congress. These informal decision mechanisms were extended to negotiate procurement issues as part of the political bargaining process. State-financed projects were allocated among contractors with connections with parties which were members of the Pacto on a prorata basis. Exemptions, subsidies, permits, grants, financial support by state-owned investment agencies under the framework of import substitution policies were also negotiated in these informal meetings in favor of parties' sympathizers.

This patronage system together with populist policies that trickled down a part of the oil rent to workers, peasants and even the urban marginal population, helped the democratic system by maintaining the necessary macroeconomic equilibria that made possible economic growth and a rapidly stabilizing political system. But these very same conditions helped to consolidate the privileged position of AD as the government party that could become the permanent winner of the elections and the danger of a Mexicanization of Venezuelan politics and institutions was increased by the Pacto. In order to avoid this outcome, a conscious decision was made by the AD leadership to create an opposition party that could be an alternative to AD.

After two victories in a row by AD, its leader, Rómulo Betancourt, intentionally split the party just before the third election, in order to get rid of the left wing, deemed too radical, whose candidate was about to win the nomination of the party. This division allowed the candidate of COPEI to win the election by a small margin. COPEI then became a government party in control of the oil revenue distribution process and could consolidate itself as an equal option to access to the state-controlled oil revenue. In this way the Pacto underwent a refinement, since now all the discontent, normally generated by the exercise of power, could be capitalized on by the opposition party that was a winning option. A new mechanism of pendulous shifting allegiances was set in place that could efficiently help to defuse social pressure and further stabilize the system. Only a tiny minority could not be integrated into this system and expressed itself through other parties of little political significance. The system, supported by relatively abundant oil revenue, worked very well. In a few years, the drive not to waste one's own vote induced almost 90 per cent of the electorate to vote for one of the two major parties, while leftist guerrilla movements lost momentum and gradually returned to legal political life.

By the end of the 1960s and early 1970s, the governance system loomed very stable, fueled by a distribution of the state oil rent that financed the social pact by reaching all sectors of Venezuelan society although in an uneven way. The oil rent was by far the most important exogenous variable that sustained a very high degree of governance. At this stage, patronage, illegal commissions paid to government officials, embezzlements, collusion between private businessmen and government officials, intentional deficits run by state enterprises, subsidies and other manifestation of corruption of this sort, were not a hindrance to governance but rather were essential to it. A proper understanding of the interrelation between the oil rent distribution and the development of democratic institutions is needed to understand Venezuela's governance success until the end of the 1980s and her governance difficulties in the 1990s as well.

International Context

In order to understand why the democracy was finally established precisely in 1958, we should look at the international situation. As mentioned earlier, the development of middle classes induced by the new oil wealth was already well advanced in the 1940s, when the old *posgomecista* regime was toppled and replaced with the first government elected through universal voting rights.

This government did not last more than three years because of its inefficient administrative performance and because it had certain political inclinations that were deemed incompatible with the security of the Free World. In those days, military dictatorship was a preferred option to any democratic elected government that might have or be believed to have some communist leaning. In such a Cold War climate it was easy for the former military allies of AD to topple Rómulo Gallegos' inefficient government and try to pursue the same modernization program under an authoritarian government with impeccable anticommunist credentials. Venezuela's democratic development was stifled by an international adverse atmosphere that helped the spread of military dictatorships all over Latin America and the Third World as an effective measure to fight Soviet expansion.

Customarily after prolonged economic prosperity, an authoritarian government will sooner or later start having a decreasing marginal political utility. This is so mainly because, as their living standard goes up, middle classes will put a greater value on their personal freedom and the satisfaction of such needs as political participation, free expression, development of new patterns of behavior, and so on. In such a case the benefits of the governance provided by an authoritarian regime do not compensate any longer the rising social costs caused by the lack of freedom. This was precisely what happened in Venezuela, where people finally forgot the reasons for having allowed the military to take power and Marco Pérez Jiménez was ousted in January 1958.

The overthrow of Pérez Jiménez was followed shortly by Batista's in Cuba. These events were harbingers of new times for the whole region. The evolution toward communism of the Cuban Revolution and the strong challenge represented by the left-wing guerrilla movements to the democratic regime in Venezuela and elsewhere prompted a new response from the United States. In order to thwart the spread of Cuban-type revolutions in the region, a new set of policies were implemented to foster economically successful democratic regimes in the region that should offer a better option than the Cuban way to development. In this context, it became of vital importance to ensure the development of democracy in Venezuela whose relatively good economic performance offered the potential for making the country a model of development and democracy for the entire region. Thus during the 1960s, Venezuela enjoyed a favorably active international environment that helped the country to consolidate her democratic institutions that successfully survived during the 1970s when practically the whole region plunged into a long period of ruthless military regimes.

For more than two decades, Venezuela remained insulated from the general crisis of the region with no significant contentious issues with its neighbors, from which it received huge numbers of immigrants and entertained a lot of formal agreements of economic cooperation with very few practical effects. The country engaged in an active policy of promoting democracy in the region that gave it some leadership in international fora such as the North–South conference in Paris in 1976, but also caused it great diplomatic tensions with the military rulers of the region. This situation lasted until the 1980s, when the domestic crisis, on one hand, and the return of Latin American countries to democracy, on the other, brought some changes in the international position of the country. As the domestic conflict in Colombia grew in intensity, it became a serious threat to the security of Venezuela's border areas, jeopardizing production and igniting old territorial disputes that caused some diplomatic friction between the two countries, sometimes demagogically manipulated by both governments with no real significant effects. During the 1990s, the Colombian guerrilla activities penetrated even deeper into Venezuelan territory with further damaging effects on the economy of those areas. But on the other hand, after the commercial reform of those years, the trade between both countries has increased considerably and each country has become the other's second major partner.

With the rest of the South American countries, Venezuela has maintained cordial but very loose ties. Its participation in the Andean Pact has had no relevant consequences beyond the above-mentioned increase in trade with Colombia in the 1990s. For a long time the relations with bordering Brazil have been ones of reciprocal indifference as should be the case with two countries separated by the same rain forest. Nonetheless in recent years there has been a promising intensification of economic relations and some integration at the only active border point between the two countries. Venezuelan foreign policy has been more active in Central America and the Caribbean countries, motivated mainly by political reasons with no meaningful consequences for the economic development of the country.

This must not be taken to mean that Venezuela has been a sort of isolationist country. On the contrary, it is a very outward society. But being an oil-exporting country, its ties with the United States and with OPEC have been by far the most important foreign factors in determining its governance and economic performance. Outside them, it may be said that the international context has played no important role in the evolution of Venezuela's governance with the possible exception of the early years of the establishment of the democratic regime. The situation started to deteriorate at the end of the 1980s when the economic and political model based on the oil rent distribution became dysfunctional due to two main causes:

(1) The oil rent was no longer sufficient to finance an adequate income distribution to a society that had grown bigger and more sophisticated. In other words the economic costs of the system began to increase at a faster speed than the oil revenue.
(2) The accumulation of collateral negative effects of the model started to take their toll making the model increasingly dysfunctional and a hindrance to further development.

8.2 THE CRISES OF GOVERNANCE

If governance means the ability to carry on policies with a certain degree of efficiency (as shown by social and economic indicators) with none or a low level of social conflict; we can say that the second oil crisis of 1979–81 signaled a turning point in Venezuela's quality of governance. Until then the latter was probably one of the best in the region with very high participation and political stability with low violence, and good government efficiency. Regulations were important within the import substitution framework, but not particularly heavy, although corruption was increasing and supervision began to relax. The second oil boom ended in early 1983 with the first devaluation of the bolívar in 20 years, a consequence of the mismanagement initiated with the Carlos Andrés Pérez (CAP) government (1974–79) that reached an unusual peak during the following administration of Luis Herrera Campins (LHC). See Table 8.1 for a list of presidents since 1958.

During these two administrations, Venezuela contracted a huge foreign debt, while imports skyrocketed and productivity lagged and investment came to a halt. Under CAP, the debt was contracted mainly to finance huge industrial projects at an accelerated pace to boost a more advanced phase of the industrial substitution process. But during the following administration of LHC, most of the new debt was used to finance current expenditure and to cover public enterprises' deficits. A considerable part of the debt was contracted in order to solve short-run cash problems by many public institutions outside any control of the central government. During this administration government efficiency in providing public services declined sharply and the striking lack of coherent macroeconomic policies accelerated the trend to serious imbalances in this area.

Table 8.1 Presidents of Venezuela since 1958

President	Years
Rómulo Betancourt	1958–1963
Raúl Leoni	1963–1968
Rafael Caldera	1968–1973
Carlos Andrés Pérez	1973–1978
Luís Herrera Campins	1978–1983
Jaime Lusinchi	1983–1989
Carlos Andrés Pérez	1989–1993
Octavio Lepage	1993
Ramón J. Velásquez	1993–1994
Rafael Caldera	1994–1999
Hugo Chávez Frías	1999–(2006)

The LHC government established a new level of inefficiency, corruption, mismanagement and political patronage that swerved away from the county's historical pattern; and a new trend of increasing degradation of the social order and disruption of state institutions set in. It was the administration that had received the greatest oil revenue and became the worst government that Venezuela had had in the twentieth century, only to be surpassed by that of Chávez on both counts: the greater oil revenue and the worst management performance. But the Chávez phenomenon cannot be properly understood without a clear evaluation of this disruptive trend set in place by the LHC government. The refusal to renegotiate the foreign debt in 1981, well before the beginning of the crisis; the insane policy to foster capital exports to drain domestic liquidity and the absolute disregard for any type of bureaucratic efficiency, are just a few of the features of this administration. The decline of oil prices in 1982 and the international debt crisis of that same year abruptly cut the easy access to foreign financing at the same time that the oil revenue shrank. After having depleted the state-owned oil holding (PDVSA) of its foreign reserves, the government was forced, in February 1983, to devalue the bolívar by almost 50 per cent after 20 years of a fixed and free convertible foreign exchange.

Neither can the deterioration of governance during the LHC administration be imputed to mismanagement and unsound policies alone, nor was the election of LHC due to a stroke of bad luck. After all, the people that ran that government belonged to the same political culture as the others before them and were elected under the same system. A better team would not have made much difference in sorting out the new trend that had deeper causes than just bad policy orientation. Any society and economy need good governance and a steady productivity increase in order to function well and although both aspects are interrelated they also have some specific determinants of their own. It is significant that the foreign reserve shortage came about at the end of a period in which the country received a huge amount of oil revenue and it was precisely in this period that the economy suffered a very prolonged recession.

During the period spanning between the first and the second oil crisis (1973–82) the Venezuelan model was considerably altered by the inflows of huge financial resources that could not be absorbed by the expansion of domestic production capacity. This windfall revenue deflected the country's economy from a steady development pattern that it had been following since the 1930s. In the midst of a financial bonanza, private investment was reduced drastically and productivity started to lag, as reflected by the decline in GDP growth and the appearance of inflation as can be seen in Figure 8.1. In spite of the efforts made by the CAP government to expand the productive capacity of the Venezuelan economy, the huge financial resources did not find an efficient absorption in the non-oil real economy because of market restrictions, lack of entrepreneurial capacity, and inadequate social behavior. Such resources were either recycled to the foreign markets in the way of capital exports or were used to boost consumption.

The efforts to complete the industrialization of the country were abandoned by LHC's government altogether. When the second oil boom dried up, the country was left with a bloated non-oil economy and a society with a series of enhanced revenue claims that had no relation whatsoever to the productivity performance of the economy. The very fundamental conditions of the Venezuelan social pact were strained in an effort to ward off the menace of social conflicts, induced by the increasing disappointment of such claims. The government stretched the fiscal and monetary policies over and above the constraints imposed by the new debt service and the diminished oil revenues. Macroeconomic mismanagement became politically correct, a tool to sustain Venezuela's governance model that had made it an

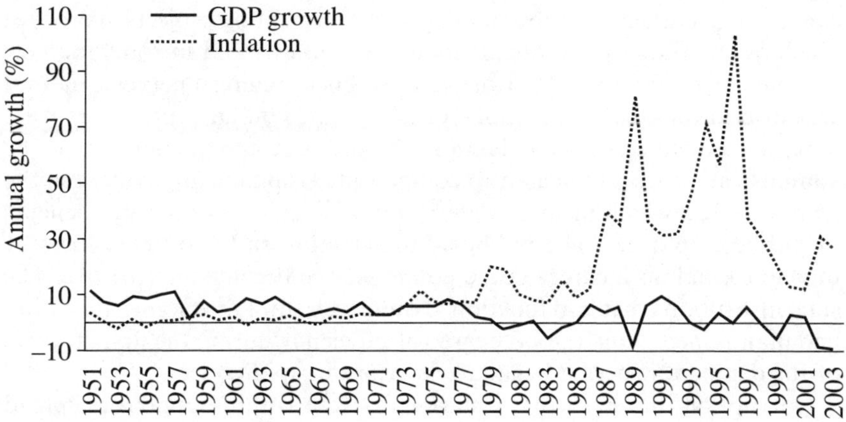

Source: BCV

Figure 8.1 Inflation and growth in Venezuela

island of stability and prosperity. From this moment on Venezuela was on the road to becoming just another Latin American country.

From this point on, the economy became more sensitive than ever before to a political cycle that had been in place since the beginning of the democratic period. In fact, it had become customary for any new government to try to implement a restrictive policy during the first two years of its term and then revert to expansionary policies in the last three years as a means to help the winning of the next election by its candidate. But after 1982, the expansionary phase became more difficult to finance and the LHC administration had to resort to imposition of price controls, multiple foreign exchange rates and import prohibitions. This was thought to be the only way to handle the increasing fiscal and balance problems and avoid, at the same time, any economic measure that would imperil the social pact. None of the necessary adjustments were undertaken. Tax reform was strenuously opposed by the middle classes. Businessmen and lower classes fought the elimination or reduction of subsidies. Inefficient industrialists abhorred reduction of protection. The financial sector resisted independent supervision. Public employees strove to keep their real salaries up, while postponing any organizational and institutional reform that might have affected their jobs.

In this new environment, sound economic decisions were taken only when it became inevitable. Fiscal adjustments were usually done through the very unhealthy method of cutting a fixed percentage across all budget items in order to avoid pressure from powerful stakeholders. This practice caused great damage to public management, disrupting projects in process, blocking ongoing operations of many institutions and introducing new elements of dysfunctional performance by encouraging a perverse natural selection in the quality of public officials. The cuts in expenditure were never accompanied by job reductions; on the contrary, positions in public administration were increased to compensate rising unemployment in the private sector, which meant a deterioration in salaries and other benefits of public employees. The public administration suffered heavy loses of human capital, as a career in the public service became unattractive. The state institutions that had functioned quite well since the Gómez times and had maintained a fairly good degree of efficiency during the first 20 years of the democratic period began to deteriorate rapidly.

Corruption that in the early stages was kept within boundaries spread out as institutions deteriorated, and became all-out graft with no relation to the needs of the maintenance of the social pact. During this period, the two-party system reached its full development commanding almost 90 per cent of the preference of an electorate that participated in the electoral process almost at the same rate. But after 1983, the dissatisfaction of the middle classes began to increase at the same pace as the decline of their real income. The old enthusiasm for the vote and party politics declined with the increasing inability of the state to satisfy the claims of different stakeholders.

The traditional practice of state contract allocation by the shadow committee of senior members of the two parties benefited a lesser number of sympathizers, fostering an increasing sensation of unfairness among the unsatisfied claimants. Among the wider population, the use of political connections to make personal economic gains was no longer seen as an acceptable way to personal success and began to be stigmatized. Finally, the shocking abuses in the allocation of preferential foreign currency during the Lusinchi administration were quite helpful in inducing more and more people to relate their present deteriorating personal economic situation to government mismanagement and political corruption. The *corrupto* became the new villain of the Venezuelan drama and, from the end of the 1980s on, he was considered by public opinion the only cause of all the evils that the people had to endure. Personal unethical behavior of government officials and politicians became also a proxy for the more difficult to understand real causes of the decreasing returns of the model based on oil rent.

The common naïve interpretation associates corruption with bribes, embezzlement, theft and misuse of public funds and other personal mischief; a conception often shared by multilateral institutions and other experts in these matters with a Protestant ethical heritage. But in the more rigorous sense of classical political theory, corruption means above all a stage of *degradation* of the proper organization of a body politic. In the Aristotelian-Polibian tradition a tyranny is the corrupted stage of monarchy, oligarchy is the result of a corrupted aristocratic regime and so on. And it is this concept of corruption that must be emphasized in the case of Venezuela, because the crisis that started in the early 1980s is above all the expression of the corruption of the oil rent model of governance. It is because this model was corrupted that the economic and social indicators started to deteriorate and, as a consequence of this, the governance indicators as well, not the other way around.

The corruption of the system was due to the overgrowth of the social and economic structure far beyond any feasible way of continuing financing it with a steady flow of oil revenue. The oil revenue enabled Venezuela to develop a non-oil economy that depended for its imports upon the foreign currency generated mainly by the oil industry, and to build a large public services sector. The oil revenue was sufficient to finance its foreign exchange requirement properly while this non-oil economy remained relatively small. But the huge inflow of resources during the oil crises of the 1970s and early 1980s overextended the Venezuelan economy and the society reached a new dimension and complexity that were far beyond the natural limits of the model. By the early 1980s, it became clear that the non-oil sector of the economy had to become self-sustainable and this means primarily two things:

(1) It had to generate most of the foreign currency it needed for its continuing development.
(2) It had to finance its social externalities necessary for its growth by paying taxes to the state.

In other words, the flow of resources from the state to civil society had to be reversed and a more natural flow should be established, like in any normal economy and society. In order to do that, a truly productive non-oil economy should be developed and most of the social claimants to the oil revenue should be transformed into active agents in the non-oil economy. In other words, they should be transformed from non-productive claimants of the national rent into suppliers of some factor of production that could be efficiently used in the non-oil economy. This implies drastic changes in the social pattern of behaviors such as:

(1) converting crony capitalists into real entrepreneurs by creating competitive conditions;
(2) turning unqualified workers into skilled workers through intensive human capital investment;

(3) integrating the marginalized population into the modern economy by providing its members with some capacity that make them the suppliers of some factor of production recognized as such by the market;
(4) reshaping state institutions in order to make them instances of social coordination able to replace the system of informal personal alliances that frequently constitute the true ruling mechanism.

These changes require much more than consistent and efficient policy proposals, even if they go beyond macroeconomic policy, structural and institutional reforms. All these proposals address technical aspects that must be complemented with the formation of adequate political subjects that can bring about such changes. The latter dimension is usually obviated by modern analysis. It tends easily to forget that policy proposals are always the expression of a political will and not merely an exercise in technocratic ingenuity. Governance problems stem from two different, although related, sources:

(a) the disruption of organizations and the perversion of institutions in such a way that the political and social system becomes dysfunctional and is no longer able to achieve its legitimate objectives as intended by the subjects that give cohesion to the body politic;
(b) the inability of the political subjects to carry out the necessary reforms for the renewal of the social pact on a consensual basis.

We can distinguish two phases of the Venezuelan crises, each characterized by the pre-eminence of one of these two aspects. During the first years, there was a progressive degradation of social organizations and state institutions with a complete lack of political will for any kind of reforms. The ruling parties and major social stakeholders stuck to the traditional patterns of behavior implementing and supporting economic policies that aggravated the situation. Such was the main feature of the LHC and Lusinchi administrations. At the end of the 1980s, a new consciousness of the need for drastic changes in the economic model began to win over an increasing number of people. But, at the same time, there was a strong resistance to political and social reforms that were necessarily implied in the economic changes.

The failure of the second CAP administration was due to the fact that it was not supported by any meaningful political subject. The reform proposal was improvised under the duress of a critical situation of the balance of payments and amounted to nothing more than the usual IMF recipe. Some of these measures were certainly needed to correct the abuses of years of mismanagement; others were aimed at the replacement of some of the institutions and usual practices of the import substitution model with no clear vision of what would follow. That was left to the market to decide. Far beyond the obvious technical shortcomings of this type of proposals that emphasize the market without understanding how a modern money production market economy really works, the proposals were a first step in the right direction to change the oil rent model. But their main shortcoming was that they were not the expression of a political will of some social subject capable of carrying out the reforms by generating the necessary consensus and alliances.

No matter how good a proposal may seem from a technical point of view, if it is not the genuine expression of meaningful social players' political will, it will always be a *bad* policy. Technocrats with too narrow a training keep forgetting that *policy* is not only wisdom and prudence in the management of affairs or a definite course or method of action selected from among alternatives and in the light of given conditions to guide and determine present and futures decisions. In a more original meaning *policy* is *Politia*, *politeia*: the art of assuring social coherence through the management of power relations that make up the thread of the body politic. Therefore, policy is in itself governance. It is not that a good policy needs good governance to be implemented; on the contrary, a good policy is only such if it makes possible good governance. There is no such thing as a good policy that cannot be implemented because of lack of governance. The lack of governance is rather due to the lack of policies that can effectively build the coherence of the body politic through the management of the material interest of different social subjects.

This was the lesson that CAP, and his team, had to learn in his second administration. A lesson, by the way, that is now being taught to a broader audience by the Argentine case. Instead of initiating a new era of transformation of the Venezuelan economic model that would support a steady path of growth and development, the package of reforms brought about the final collapse of the old system. Being based, as we said, on a poor comprehension of how the modern market economy works, the only partially correct reforms, sponsored by the IMF, were insufficient to address the problems of development. Nonetheless, they were very effective in signaling the end of the traditional parties' role as viable instruments for the distribution the oil revenue among the different national stakeholders. Party defections were then accelerated and those former powerful organizations that commanded citizens' participation were reduced to shabby electoral machineries, disavowed by the general public as mere clubs of corrupted politicians.

The 4th of February coup attempt revealed the new situation quite clearly. That day, people supported democracy against any outdated return to military government, but rejected the old system of governance of which

CAP's reforms were seen to be the latest expression. In fact, contrary to what is commonly believed, such reforms were not perceived to be part of a modernization program. This is certainly the way the Washington Consensus viewed the reforms, but to most Venezuelans it was just another effort to further concentrate the oil rent distribution in favor of privileged minorities and against the impoverished majority of the population. The institutional crises that followed the two coup attempts of 1992 ended up with the ousting of CAP from power through a legal procedure. He was accused of embezzlement and his trial became much more than one person's trial. It became the trial of the corrupted oil rent model that he personified so well.

People identify, in a somewhat simple manner, the corruption of the regime, based on the oil rent distribution, with the unethical behavior of politicians. By doing so, they lump together graft with ineptitude and inefficiency. This lack of awareness that ineptitude and inefficiency could be just as bad as graft is still a major problem in determining the electoral choice and was a major factor in Chávez' election. The aversion to the corrupt politician fueled the search for honest persons, even if they were inept and unable to perform properly. With these shortcomings, it became clear to everybody that radical changes were needed.

Rafael Caldera, an almost retired old politician, was one of the very few that captured the new mood of the people, that had finally accepted the need for drastic reforms, but were hostile to a modernization program that spelled more concentration of wealth. Caldera's first administration was the last government to run fairly equilibrated macroeconomic policies and to keep the economy on a path of growth with no fiscal deficit and no foreign debt. Being one of the founders of the democracy, having cut his ties to the COPEI party, his diagnosis of Venezuela's troubles made him, so it seemed at that time, a viable figure that could lead the democratic transition to a new economic and social order. A mixed alliance of heterogeneous political movements, some of them representing modernizing forces and others being just old interest groups, united by their common contempt for the traditional parties, won the elections. Caldera became the first democratic president to be elected without the support of one of the two major traditional parties; a clear signal that something was changing.

The bipartisan system had ended but was not yet dead. After a few months of tension and internal strife, the modernizing current within the government was expelled and Caldera made a political deal with the AD party boss in order to ensure majority support in the Congress. Meanwhile the serious mismanagement of the inherited financial crisis forced him to enter into an ill-fated policy of foreign exchange control that stalled all possibilities to bring about any kind of reforms. After almost two years of an agonizing economic situation that began with a big devaluation and ended with another even bigger, Caldera went to the IMF, where he had pledged never to go. He then went back to basically the same CAP policies, but with more moderation and a certain social concern, shared by the multilateral organizations that by that time, so it seemed, were beginning to learn their lesson too. The fundamental economic and social changes were postponed sine die and the government tried to administer the old model the best it could, until the next elections.

At the end of the Caldera administration, Venezuela, instead of being the tropical version of a Montesquieusque society, had become just another Latin American country. In a region known for its institutional fragility, Venezuela's political stability since 1958 had been noticed by the literature on the subject (Roberts, 2001). Now the collapse of the traditional parties has become a sort of a puzzle for this institutionalist literature. In fact, Venezuelan parties had stable electoral bases, deep roots in civil society, legitimate political functions and strong internal organization. In other words they comply with those features that, according to this theoretical approach, should assure them a permanent stability (Mainwaring and Scully 1995). In all these studies, the connection between the institutionalist fundamental features and the oil rent distribution process is always missing. Nonetheless, this connection is the true nature of the Venezuelan anomaly: an underdeveloped oil producer democracy. As the political and institutional crises unraveled, the economic system steadily increased its already high inefficiency and vulnerability to fluctuations of oil prices. The state institutions began to fall apart to the point of total inefficiency. Social behavior changed drastically and governance was completely disrupted. By 1997–98, the situation in Venezuela was no different to that of the rest of the region, at least according to the perception of the people, as shown by indicators of cross-section measurements made at that time, to be analysed in the next section.

8.3 AGGREGATED GOVERNANCE INDICATORS

Kaufmann, Kraay and Zoido-Lobaton (1999) had developed certain governance indices to measure the relative performance of each country in six main aspects that define governance: graft, rule of law, regulatory burden, government effectiveness, political instability and violence, and voice and participation. Some of the results cast doubts on the soundness of the criteria selected. Nevertheless, we think they give an idea of the degree of deterioration of Venezuela's governance during the crucial period of the election of Hugo Chávez.

It is unfortunate that we do not have values of these indicators for the early 1980s that would allow us to compare how people perceived the country at that time when expectations were very optimistic. It is not unwarranted to say that probably, most of the indicators would have placed the country in the upper quintiles and very far from the rest of the region. But in Figure 8.2, that shows the 1997–98 results, it appears that except for voice and participation, where Venezuela scores among the upper 50 per cent of the whole sample, in all the other indicators it shows a very poor performance. Particularly disturbing are the results in government effectiveness and graft, where the country is placed among the worst quarter. But after what we have said about the nature of the Venezuela oil rent model, it should not come as a surprise. What once was a fairly good mechanism of distributing the state oil revenue among a backward population had degenerated into wholehearted graft. The effectiveness of the government was so dependent upon the abundance of oil financial resources that it almost disappeared completely when these started to drain.

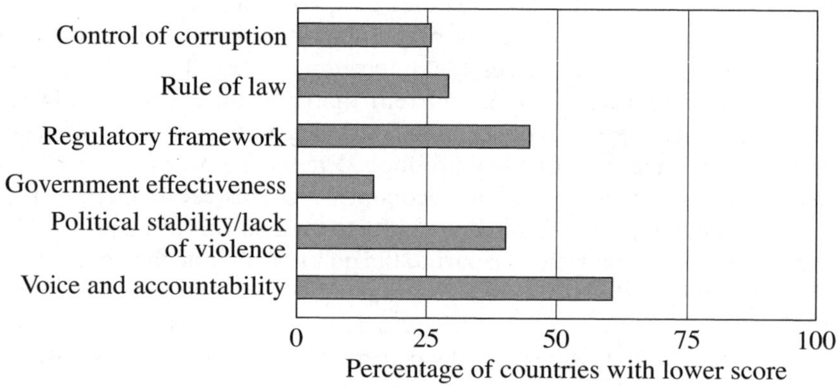

Note: Grey bars represent mean estimate for the percentile rank on each of the governance indicators. The thin vertical lines represent standard errors around these estimates.

Sources: Kauffman, Kraay and Zoido-Lobiton (1999).

Figure 8.2 Aggregate governance indicators for Venezuela

Voice and Participation

This index comprises a series of variables that measure different aspects of the political process such as civil liberties and political rights (Figure 8.3). They purport to determine: the degree of citizens' participation in the selection of government, the independence of mass media, government threatening pressures on private citizens, police ability to make unlawful arrests of citizens, freedom of expression, and of association. They also take into account the possibility for citizens to stand freely for public office and to win elections in a fair and transparent manner. Somewhat surprisingly Venezuela scores worse than Bolivia and Ecuador and better than Colombia and Peru among the Andean group and within the whole region her performance is inferior to that of Argentina, Chile, Brazil and Costa Rica, but superior to Mexico's.

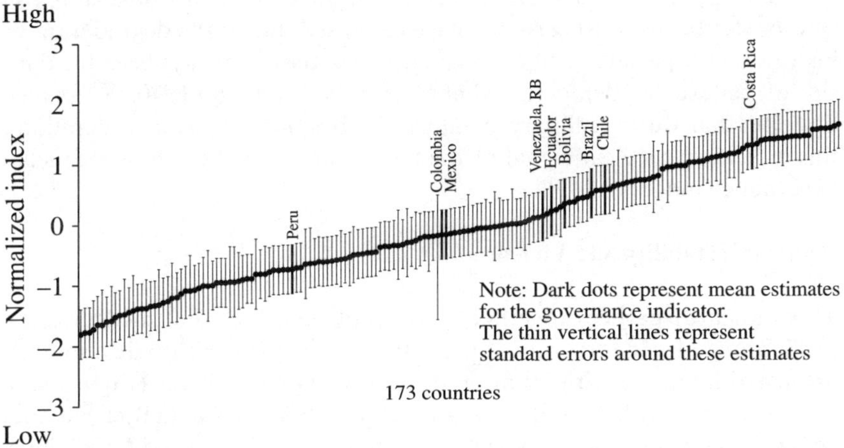

Sources: Kaufmann, Kraay and Zoido-Lobaton (1999).

Figure 8.3 Voice and participation

These results are difficult to explain. They certainly indicate a strong deterioration of the citizens' participation especially after the failure of the CAP administration and the subsequent events. But they probably reflect much more an increasingly pessimistic mood of the general population than a factual curtailment in traditional liberties. In fact, with the loosening of the power of traditional parties, some liberties such as freedom of association and possibility for citizens to freely stand for public office and to win elections in a fair and transparent manner may have actually increased. The lagged effects of an unfinished decentralization process have enhanced others, such as citizens' participation in the selection of government. Locally elected officials such as provincial governors and local mayors have been a counterbalancing power to the deterioration of the central government especially after 1992 and in some cases have been perceived as fundamental features of a new governance model.

The independence of the press has clearly increased with the weakening of the central government. During every democratic administration there have always been a few major incidents of government harassment of the press. But those that occurred in the 1990s were fewer and minor compared with previous periods. Furthermore the independence of the press increased during the Caldera administration period. And by the time these measurements were taken, it was about to become the major political factor in the incoming elections. The press was on its way to become the principal opposition factor to Chávez' regime, as we shall see later on. Government threatening pressures on private citizens and police ability to make unlawful arrests of citizens must certainly have increased due to the degradation of institutions, especially of the judiciary. The latter has always been the dark side of Venezuelan democracy that even in the 1960s and 1970s performed no better than during military dictatorships. In spite of these considerations, this indicator is a clear signal of the low point reached by the Venezuelan governance model in 1998.

Political Instability and Violence

This indicator gathers together a group of variables that measures the probability of a democratically elected government being destabilized or ousted by unconstitutional procedures or violent means (Figure 8.4). Venezuela appears behind Bolivia, Argentina, Chile and Costa Rica but does better than the rest of the Andean group countries, Mexico and Brazil. Now these results were simply laughable before 1992, but in 1998 were puzzling. On the political instability side, the events after Chávez' coup demonstrate the solid foundations of Venezuelan democracy. The fact that Carlos Andrés Pérez was ousted through a legal procedure proved to be a step forward in the consolidation of democracy. Another equally important case of a further consolidation of a democratic culture was the fact that Chávez was elected president with broad popular support and with the votes of many people that opposed his coup attempt. Although political instability unquestionably increased during the 1990s, democracy has certainly deepened in Venezuela, up to the point that we can say that democratic institutions started to permeate deeply into the social fabric in this period. In the previous decades, the country enjoyed great political stability with a very shallow democracy; in the 1990s the situation was reversed.

Probably this indicator continues a confusion between *political instability* and *imperilment of democracy*. It is true that often both situations go together, but this is not necessarily always the case. Political instability could endanger democracy only when it is the consequence of an acute social conflict that cannot be alleviated by economic means and within truly egalitarian institutions; only then does political repression become the means to re-establish social cohesion. Normally, well-established and authentic democratic institutions can survive a period of strong political instability on condition that they are in fact true democratic institutions that allow the contending political subjects to properly convey their political will. When this is not so, then successful coups d'état or endemic guerilla movements are set in place. In Venezuela since 1958, both phenomena have been fleeting events and this is its outstanding feature, almost unique in the region with the only exception being Costa Rica. Coups d'état and guerrilla movements are two forms of political violence that stem from the same source of social inequality mediated by restrictive institutions that do not allow for proper participation in the political power of social subjects. Where coups d'état are recurrent and guerrilla movements are of long standing, democracy is just a juridical fiction or a minority's privilege. In most part of Latin America this has been the case for too long.

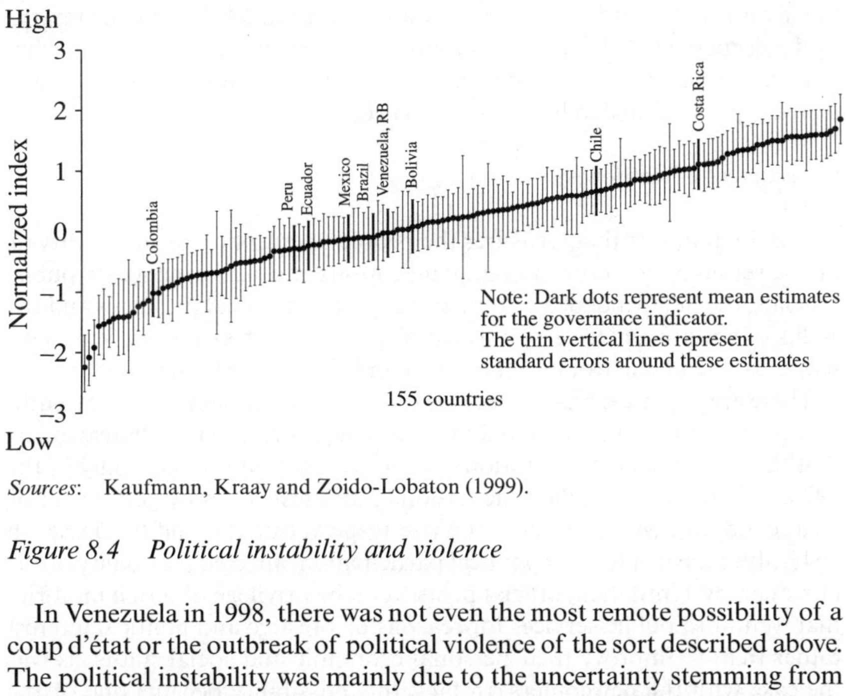

Sources: Kaufmann, Kraay and Zoido-Lobaton (1999).

Figure 8.4 Political instability and violence

In Venezuela in 1998, there was not even the most remote possibility of a coup d'état or the outbreak of political violence of the sort described above. The political instability was mainly due to the uncertainty stemming from the fact that the two traditional parties were no longer viable options, and, as the elections approached, there was no clear definition of new political forces with clear government programs, all the attention being concentrated in two figures created by the mass media that were as politically shallow as their images on the screen. Behind them, there lay a frantic regrouping of political forces that cut across all social strata with no clear political will but to bring about radical changes, those radical changes that Caldera had failed to accomplish. Their main contention with each other was a point of style: the bleak political proposal of the *beauty queen* against the harsh rhetoric of the *warrior*. Like in many developed societies, a strange paradox appeared here: the deepening of democratic institutions in the social fabric seemed to go pari passu with a widespread infantilization of personal and collective behavior.

Therefore, it was all too natural that expectations were determined by the apprehension over an uncertain future. But we should notice that the whole situation developed with no violence. A drastic sentiment of deep frustration and anger against a deeply corrupt system was conveyed through democratic channels in a highly civic manner. We found no other instance in Latin America of such a deep change in the political forces developed within the democratic institutions. Therefore, the electoral process of 1998, like the institutional ousting of Carlos Andrés Pérez in 1993, are benchmarks of the deepening of the democratic culture in Venezuela, in spite of the fact that their immediate outcomes may be disagreeable and unquestionably increase political instability in the short run.

Government Effectiveness

This is an indicator that measures the people's perception of the quality of public services, the professional qualifications and performance of public officials, the independence of bureaucracy from political pressures and the ability of government to carry out credible policies. In this category, Venezuela scores as one of the worst in the world and rightly so (Figure 8.5).

There are historical reasons for this result such as the fact that nineteenth-century civil wars never allowed for the consolidation of a stable bureaucracy; that the national state institutions began to function properly only in the 1920s, when Gómez unified the national administration by getting rid of local caudillos. More recently, the rise to power of the middle classes in 1945, although it enhanced political participation, affected the quality of the bureaucracy. Until then, official posts were the privilege of a rich minority that went into public services for reasons of prestige and political interest rather than to improve their personal economic and social status, as was the case with the newcomers. In fact, this possibility became one of the main features of the oil rent distribution process. A certain bureaucratic inefficiency was a need and, at the same time, a consequence of such a distribution. Its negative effects of poor public management were usually compensated by bigger expenditures made possible by abundance of financial resources. The oil rent model did not foster efficiency in the public sector, on the contrary it made it worse even by Latin American standards.

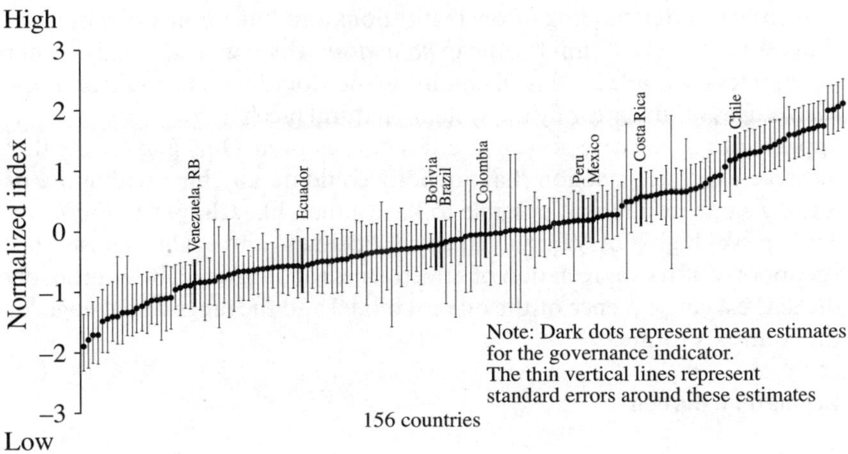

Sources: Kaufmann, Kraay and Zoido-Lobaton (1999).

Figure 8.5 Government effectiveness

In other countries of the region, the lack of fiscal resources imposed a minimum of efficient management that was dispensable in Venezuela.

Having said that, we must recognize that, within the narrow Venezuelan boundaries in this matter, the effectiveness of government was kept at acceptable levels until the end of the 1970s. It was only with the Luis Herrera Campins government that the trend of deterioration set in and afterward was accelerated by the deepening of the crises until the entire public administration collapsed in the early 1990s. This widespread inefficiency of the public administration is an important element in understanding the victory of Chávez in the 1998 election. For one thing, this state of collapse of public institutions with very few islands of efficiency, especially in the local administrations, helped to exasperate the reaction against a corrupt system and increased the willingness to see radical changes. For another, people got so used to such a state of ubiquitous inefficiency and ineptitude, where anybody could perform any task with more or less the same results, that personal qualifications became totally irrelevant in most cases.

This is the most striking characteristic of the Venezuelan anomaly and only in such an environment is it possible for a man like Chávez to become a serious candidate and even win the election for president. What is relevant here is not that Chávez had no previous political training or experience in state affairs, since such a person reaching public office is neither an undesirable nor an uncommon fact in a democracy; but the fact that Chávez has a sort of *cultural* handicap that barred him from even the most elementary understanding of the institutions and functioning of a modern state. We call this cultural handicap *nomadism* which we shall analyse later on. In a less degraded political condition, he would have been sifted at the early stages of his career by the system's natural mechanism of selection, as appeared to be the case at even as late a date as 1996. Only in a society that has reached the conviction that anybody could do anything with more or less the same results, is it possible to have a man like Chávez as *President*. This speaks highly of Venezuelan social openness and egalitarianism, but very poorly of its appreciation of effectiveness at all levels. This is probably the darkest consequence of the oil rent model and the biggest challenge for the country's future.

Regulatory Burden

The indicator in Figure 8.6 measures the impact of regulatory policies that may interfere with the market mechanism or do not provide sufficient institutional support for its normal functioning. Price controls, excessive legal requirements, cumbersome permit procedures may considerably affect investment plans and place an unnecessary burden on the everyday business operations that foster bribery and other corrupt practices. On the other hand, lack of adequate supervision and proper regulation of the financial system may increase the financial fragility and the risk of crises. Here Venezuela's performance is inferior to the rest of the Andean group countries and to other countries of the region such as Brazil, Mexico, Argentina, Costa Rica and Chile. But these results should not be surprising after what we have just said on the collapse of the public administration.

It is worth noticing that one of the very few positive effects of the reforms initiated in 1989 was the general reduction of the regulatory burden caused by price control, import and export permits and the like. On the other hand, the cumbersome bureaucratic procedures worsened even more with the progress of institutional collapse. One of the biggest flaws of that reform program was that it left out the financial system. Moreover, the Carlos Andrés Pérez government increased cronyism in this sector and did nothing to improve its supervision. During this period, insider trading and other unlawful and risky practices increased and traditional poor banking management became even poorer, while almost every major business group tried to establish its own bank. This, together with the high interest rates that became even higher during the institutional crises was conducive to the financial crises that began in December of 1993 until July 1994. It was only then that efforts were made to set in place an adequate system of supervision.

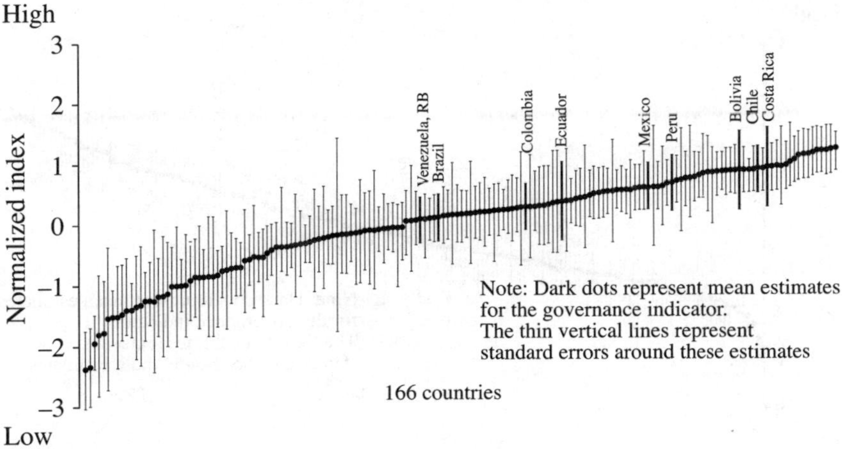

Sources: Kaufmann, Kraay and Zoido-Lobiton (1999).

Figure 8.6 Regulatory burden

Rule of Law

The purpose of this indicator is to measure the degree of people's confidence in the existing rules and laws. The estimation is made by surveying a sample of opinions on the effectiveness of existing institutions in enforcing the law and in solving conflicts and disputes. In particular, it is the judicial system that comes under scrutiny and other law enforcement agencies as well. All the Andean countries are below the average of the whole sample and Venezuela is better placed than Ecuador and Colombia (Figure 8.7).

The weakness of the judicial system is a common feature of all Third World and non-democratic countries, and even highly developed societies show serious shortcoming in the quality of justice they deliver. But generally speaking, citizens of developed countries feel confidence in their justice system and law enforcement agencies. The justice system is the Achilles' heel of modern democracy because it implies a level of citizens' consciousness and political freedom yet to be achieved anywhere. In the case of developing countries, this set of institutions is the most difficult to coat with the formalities of a nominal democracy. It is here where the most serious limitations to the existence of a truly democratic society are blatantly revealed. Venezuela is no exception to this. But the oil rent model gave an additional reason for failure in this area. The ruling agreement between the two major parties provided for a sharing in the nomination of judges on political sympathy lines. Therefore even in the best phase of the model, the

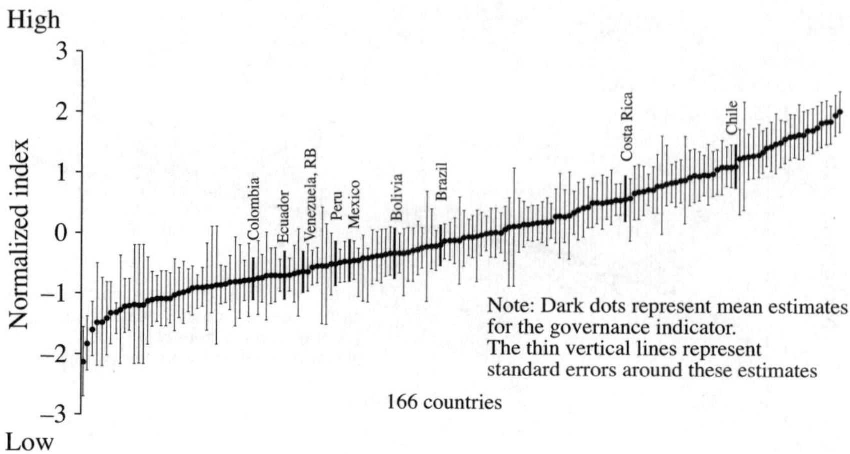

Sources: Kaufmann, Kraay and Zoido-Lobiton (1999).

Figure 8.7 Rule of law

judicial system was highly inefficient and arbitrary. Much more efficient, but equally arbitrary has been the police's performance, while the Venezuelan prison system remains absolutely unacceptable: a true scandal for a civilized society. It is here and not in the other more ideologized issues, comprised in these indicators, that the otherwise almost 'perfect' democracy model reveals its true barbarian nature and its deep underdevelopment.

8.4 A BRIEF REVIEW OF THE VENEZUELAN ECONOMY

As was already mentioned, it is not possible to analyse the Venezuelan economy without understanding the deep impact that oil has had in the main areas of the economy. For example, in 1990–99, a period in which average real oil prices reached $16.9 per barrel for the Venezuelan mix, oil contributed about 25 per cent of total GDP, and accounted for more than 70 per cent of total exports, while government oil revenues represented 59 per cent of total fiscal revenues. The unpredictability and volatility of oil prices make the tasks of policymakers in Venezuela very difficult, and traditionally the economy has been ill-equipped to deal with oil shocks. Table 8.2 shows the impact of oil in the external, fiscal and real sectors during the periods 1970–79, 1980–89 and 1990–99. It is interesting to notice that although oil continues to be very important in all areas of the economy, its share in the fiscal and the external sectors has declined since the 1970s. This is confirmed by the deterioration of oil exports per capita which reached a historical maximum of $2795 per person in 1974 and declined to $635 per inhabitant in 1999.

Table 8.2 Oil impact on the Venezuelan economy

Indicator (average)	1970–79	1980–89	1990–99
Oil fiscal revenues/GDP	15.1	13.2	11.4
Oil fiscal revenues/Total revenues	70.1	60.7	59.0
Oil exports/Total exports	87.4	82.2	71.1
Oil exports/GDP	23.0	21.2	20.5
Oil GDP/Total GDP	31.3	20.0	24.5

Therefore, in periods of oil booms, the economy grows faster, the fiscal accounts usually reach surpluses or manageable deficits, and the external position is strong. On the other hand, when oil prices are low, the economy is usually stagnant, the current account is in deficit and the fiscal accounts become a serious problem for the government. In 1998, a Macroeconomic Stabilization Fund (FIEM) was established to smooth out the fiscal effects of oil shocks. Unfortunately, the new authorities almost immediately modified this mechanism to accommodate the government's fiscal and investment needs, making it less useful as a stabilization tool.

As it can be seen in Table 8.3, the problems for the Venezuelan economy started in the 1980s. From the 1950s and until the 1970s the country enjoyed high GDP growth rates with low inflation, and in general current account and fiscal surpluses. However, during the 1980s GDP growth began to slow down and became very volatile, inflation surpassed double digits and the fiscal situation began to deteriorate rapidly. Also, unemployment and exchange rates showed higher volatility than in previous periods. The main explanation for the change from economic stability to economic volatility were the huge positive oil shocks that hit the economy in the 1970s. During the 1980s the oil shocks were mostly negative which caused a marked deterioration in the macroeconomic conditions and ended with the first failed attempt at stabilization in 1989. As was mentioned earlier, neither the institutions nor the society were ready or equipped to deal with the volatility caused by the succesive oil shocks of the 1970s and 1980s. Of course, the economic policies that worked so well during stable times were unable to cope with a new reality of instability and volatility.

Table 8.3 Summary of macroeconomic indicators

Indicator (average)	1951–60	1961–70	1971–80	1981–90	1991–2000
Real GDP growth (%)	7.9	6.0	4.2	0.7	2.1
Consumer prices (% of period)	1.9	1.0	8.5	25.0	44.8
Current account balance (% of GDP)	–0.7	2.6	2.0	1.9	2.9
Central government fiscal balance (% of GDP)	n.a.	0.2	1.2	–1.3	–1.7
Venezuelan real oil price mix ($ per barrel)	13.3	9.4	28.1	32.3	16.8

Sources: International Monetary Fund (IMF) and Central Bank of Venezuela (BCV).

During the 1991–95 period, several shocks continued to affect the economy and the policy responses to those shocks only exacerbated the period's volatility. Declining oil prices, political instability and a massive banking crisis in 1994 were some of the features that characterized the first part of the decade. In 1996, the government started a stabilization and reforms program called Agenda Venezuela which was supported by the IMF and which enjoyed some short-lived successes. But in 1997 following the political cycle, the government decided to implement expansionary fiscal and income policies and later on eased monetary policy. This did not help to reduce inflation, but economic activity expanded as a consequence of the increase in public expenditure. A negative oil shock, caused by a sharp drop in prices at the end of 1997 and the beginning of 1998, produced a change in expectations for the worse, and the pressure on the bolívar mounted.

The years 1998 and 1999 were very disappointing in terms of economic growth due to low oil prices. The negative conditions in oil markets also caused important fiscal deficits for the central government. The external position worsened in 1998 when the average oil export price was $10.6 per barrel, and improved in 1999 when oil prices started to rise and reached an average of $16.1. However, oil prices skyrocketed in 2000, reaching $25.9 per barrel for the Venezuelan oil mix and the economy started to grow, although moderately given the magnitude of the positive oil shock. As was expected, the external accounts turned around and a considerable current account surplus was attained together with an important accumulation of international reserves. In 2001, oil prices started to decline, negatively affecting growth and fiscal and the external accounts as well. It is interesting to note that, during most of the decade, inflation was high due to a loose monetary policy and backward-looking indexation. However, starting in 1999, and thanks to a very strong external position, the government began to use the exchange rate as a nominal anchor, reducing inflation to less than 20 per cent in 1999 and 2000.

The Real Sector of the Economy

As we should expect of an economy based on oil rent, we find a close correlation between oil prices and GDP growth (Figure 8.8), especially oil GDP, which represents around 25 per cent of total GDP. But in recent years the nature of this correlation has changed radically. The evidence shows that oil prices and GDP growth have a weaker correlation now than in the past, suggesting that positive oil shocks do not contribute to GDP expansion as they used to do. This clearly shows the exhaustion of the oil rent model. That is not to say that oil prices have no effect on the economy. We can clearly see that the drastic drop in prices in 1998 accelerated the downturn, as the subsequent rise helped the country to come out of the deep recession. But this was due primarily to the magnitude of the price variation.

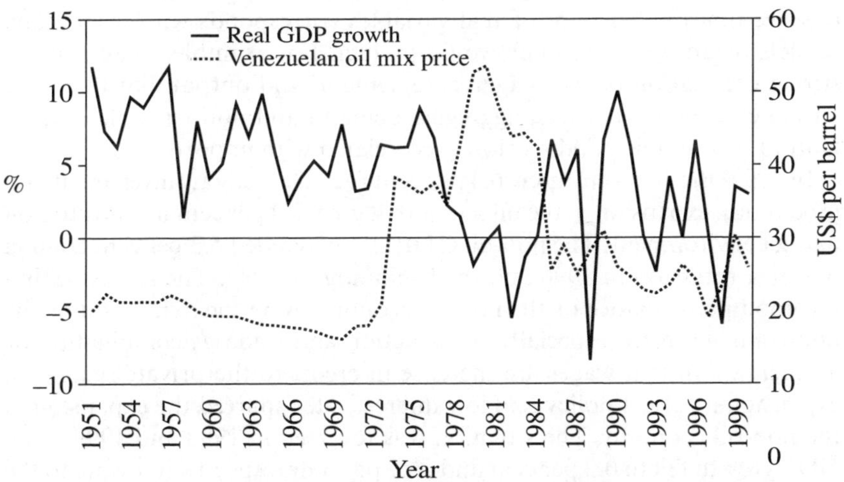

Source: BCV.

Figure 8.8 Oil prices and GDP growth

This reduction of the impact of oil revenue on growth began, as we have already said, at the end of the 1970s when private investment practically stopped and total factor productivity, GDP per worker and capital per worker have been declining steadily since then (Baptista 1997). The consequence of this has been a tendency to stagnation of the tradable sector of the economy, with a short-lived period of recovery depending on the government's economic policy.

GDP growth has been declining decade after decade. In the period 1951–60 GDP grew at an average of 7.9 per cent annually, while in the period 1961–70 grew at 6.0 per cent. In spite of two huge positive oils shocks during the 1970s, average GDP growth reduced to 4.2 per cent in the period 1971–80, in part due to the incapacity of the economy to absorb the huge amount of resources, and the beginning of great volatility in the main macroeconomic variables. More recently, the economy has grown even less, reaching an average of 0.7 per cent in the period 1981–90, although there was a timid recovery in the period 1991–2000 when the economy grew on average at 2.1 per cent annually. Due to the strong correlation between output and employment in the case of Venezuela, unemployment has been low in periods of GDP expansion and has increased during recessions. Lately, unemploymnet rates have been higher than the historic mean, which could suggest increasing rigidities in the labor market or some kind of hysteresis behavior. Because Venezuela is a small open economy, we also observe that the behavior of real variables corresponds with what many models of an open economy would predict. For example, there is not a strong correlation between aggregate demand and output, but there is a strong correlation between aggregate demand and non-tradable output. Output of tradable goods is closely correlated with imports.

In 1997, the economy grew 6.4 per cent fueled mostly by investment and production expansion in the oil sector that grew 9.4 per cent in a positive oil market environment. The non-oil GDP also expanded 5.3 per cent coming out of a recession in 1996 and the beginning of 1997. The forces behind the good performance of the non-oil economy were the dynamism of the non-tradable sector especially construction and trade. A combination of an increase in real wages, an increase in credit to the private sector, an expansionary fiscal policy and low interest rates spurred the expansion in the non-oil economy. The situation was reversed in 1998 and 1999 when GDP growth fell to 0.2 per cent and –6,1 per cent respectively, owing to the deterioration in oil prices and the uncertainty caused by the election that, as we shall see later, this time implied the collapse of the old political system. In 1999, the lack of private sector confidence in the new administration of President Chávez, the rise of real interest rates during most of 1998, and cuts in oil production caused GDP to decrease 6.1 per cent and unemployment to increase to 15 per cent.

During 2000, the Venezuelan economy grew modestly at 3.2 per cent, driven mostly by an increase in public expenditure made possible by the hike in oil prices. It is important to note that unlike other positive oil shocks, this time private expectations did not show a boost as they usually did in previous booms, insulating the private sector from the oil bonanza. This explains why the economy did not grow faster. The extremely poor reaction from the private sector was due to two main factors. First of all, we have already mentioned the reduction of the efficiency of the oil revenue impact on the economy. This is mainly due to the fact that fiscal expansion has an extremely low public investment component and additionally this time did not spur private sector investment either. Most of the fiscal expansion fueled the use of available production capacity and imports. Secondly, this time there was another factor the tended to thwart even this minor response from the private sector: Chávez' mass media performance, of which we shall speak later.

Oil prices started to decline in 2001, and OPEC decided to implement several production cuts. This situation worsened after the incident of September 11 in New York. As a result, economic activity decelerated to a growth rate of only 2.7 per cent. Again, the poor result in terms of economic performance was explained mainly by the loss of dynamism of the oil sector which decreased 0.9 per cent. On the other hand, the non-oil economy grew 3.8 per cent, driven by construction activities associated with increasing public expenditures, the communication sector and manufacturing. Unemployment has declined slightly, yet remains at very high levels compared with the recent historical average. There is some evidence that the high unemployment experienced in the last five years is related to the failure of hundreds of small and medium businesses caused primarily by the overvaluation of the exchange rate and high interest rates. As a result, the proportion of the labor force employed in the informal sector has risen dramatically, reaching more than 50 per cent of the labor force.

The Exchange Rate, Inflation and Monetary Policy

Traditionally more than 90 per cent of foreign exchange comes from the oil and other state-owned enterprises, that are obliged to sell their foreign exchange receipts from their operations abroad to the Central Bank. Therefore, Venezuela seemed to be a natural case for fixed parity. At least this has been the prevalent view on the subject and it was quite consistent with the oil rent model. Since oil exports are not sensitive to the exchange rate, a fixed parity covering a moderate real appreciation of the real rate was thought to be beneficial for the import of capital goods and an efficient way to protect personal real income. Both targets were consistent with the goals of the import substitution that needed cheap capital goods and a relative high demand for consumer goods. In fact, Venezuela had long periods of fixed exchange rates until 1983, when the country started to experiment with multiple exchange rates, floating, crawling pegs and bands.

Until oil revenue was stable, the domestic demand for foreign goods was small in relation to this revenue and the domestic production was little diversified; this seemed to be a sound policy. But in the 1980s when the oil market became highly unstable, the domestic demand for foreign goods outgrew the oil revenue inflows and domestic production could not diversify its supply of export goods, which made the fixed parity policy increasingly costly. On the other hand, the experiment with a freely floating rate in the early 1990s proved to be even more costly. It forced an unusually high rate of interest that had a very negative effect on the real economy and was a major factor in the outbreak of the financial crisis in 1993, while the benefits of the export of non-traditional goods did not compensate for this shortcoming.

So after the ill-fated foreign exchange control established in July 1994 to cope with the financial crises, in 1996 there was put in place a system of bands around a central parity that is adjusted daily. Starting in 2002, the rate of annual devaluation was set to 10 per cent and the width of the band to 7.5 per cent on each side of the central parity. Since this system was implemented, the Central Bank policy has been to keep a smooth path for the exchange rate and a depreciation rate below the one originally announced. As a result, there has been an important appreciation of the real exchange rate in the last five years. This can be seen in Figure 8.9.

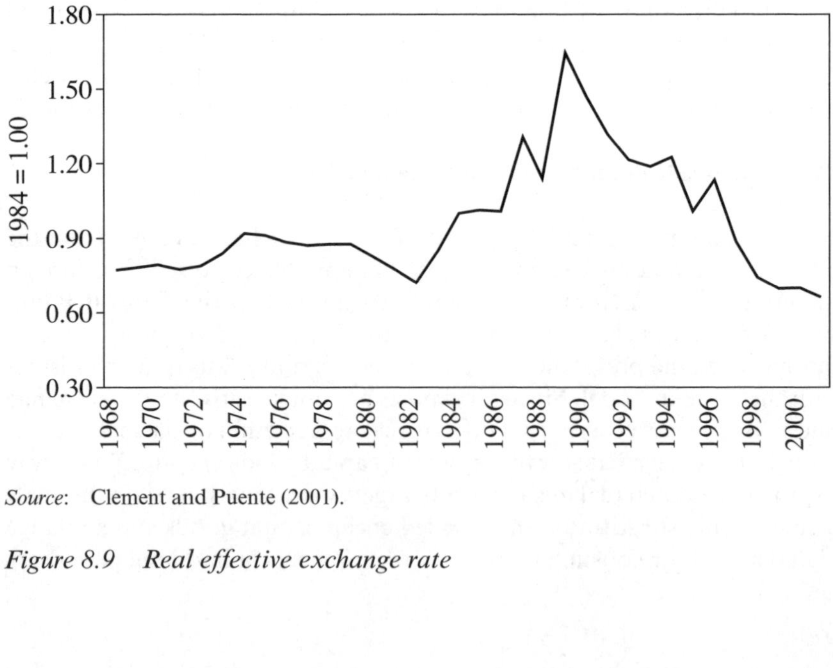

Source: Clement and Puente (2001).

Figure 8.9 Real effective exchange rate

The use of the exchange rate as a nominal anchor has helped to reduce inflation, but at the cost of losing competitiveness in the tradable sector of the economy, especially in the manufacturing sector. The consumer price index (CPI) annual change dropped to 12.3 per cent in 2001, an improvement compared to the average annual level of more than 44 per cent that existed in the period 1991–2000. Inflation was more volatile in those years following the devaluation of the bolívar, for example in 1996 it reached 103.2 per cent. Even though in years of fiscal expansion there have been domestic demand pressures on prices, the appreciation of the exchange rate has been more than enough to compensate for them. Due to the way the Central Bank has administered the band system and the limited scope for monetary policy, interest rates are relatively independent of Central Bank policies and monetary variables have been, for the most part, endogenous.

In general previous to 1992, real interest rates were low and even negative when the external position was strong and there were not excessive pressures on the bolívar. But whenever oil prices declined and the fiscal and external positions deteriorated, as happened in 1993–94 and more recently in the last part of 2001, real interest rates tended to increase at very high levels, negatively affecting private economic activity. For example in 2000, a year of high oil prices and a comfortable external position, the average real deposit rate was –1.8 per cent while in 2001 it was 3.2 per cent. Regarding money, as measured by M2, it is interesting to note the sharp reduction in 2001. In Table 8.4, which shows the main monetary indicators in the five years 1997–2001, we can observe that M2 decreased 5 per cent in 2001. The main explanation for this outcome has been the massive capital outflows that occurred in 2001 as a result of lack of confidence in the government policies undermined mainly by President Chávez' inflammatory political rhetoric. At the end of 2001, as the oil price decreased and foreign reserves deteriorated, increasingly higher expectations of a sharp depreciation of the bolívar started to develop, adding even more pressure to capital outflows.

In addition, the Central Bank kept a very tight monetary policy during 2001 through open market operations, which reduced money in circulation and pushed interest rates upward. In this scenario, the banking system may face problems if high real interest rates and important capital outflows persist as they did under a similar situation in 1993. Nonetheless, the financial system has grown stronger after the banking crisis in 1994. It has gone through a process of capitalization, mergers and acquisitions, with a better supervision that has improved the health of the system. However, demonetization of the economy due to increasing fears of devaluation and/or capital controls and prospects of low growth in the near future may pose serious risks to the system. At this time, the banking system is adequately capitalized, but non-performing loans have started to rise and may signal a gradual deterioration of the banking system. Indeed, the capital adequacy ratio increased from 12.5 per cent in 2000 to 13.6 while non-performing loans as a percentage of the total loan portfolio went from 16.8 per cent in 2000 to 19.8 per cent in 2001.

Table 8.4 Summary of monetary and banking indicators

Indicator	1997	1998	1999	2000	2001[a]
M2/GDP (%)	20.1	19.4	20.4	21.1	18.5
M2 (annual variation %)	62.5	18.6	19.8	27.8	–5.1
Average nominal deposit rate (%)	13.1	35.7	19.7	14.9	14.2
Average nominal lending rate (%)	24.4	47.8	32.5	24.5	24.6
Domestic credit (annual variation %)	23.3	26.1	12.1	15.8	7.2
Capital adequacy ratio (%)	12.4	14.2	13.2	12.5	13.6
Non-performing loans (% of total loans)	9.0	14.9	20.4	16.8	19.8

Note: ([a]) Preliminary.

Sources: International Monetary Fund (IMF) and Central Bank of Venezuela (BCV).

The External Sector

Venezuela's dependence on oil exports has made it possible for the country to enjoy a positive balance on current account for long periods of time, contrary to what is the usual feature for an underdeveloped economy. This fact was certainly a major factor contributing to a stable free exchange rate. But starting with the first oil boom the sensitivity of the current account balance to oil price fluctuations increased substantially. The main reason for this was that the sudden hike in oil prices boosted imports at an accelerated rate that reduced the surplus drastically even before prices began to decline. Both booms, of the 1970s and early 1980s, ended in a huge deficit when prices declined moderately.

After the second boom, the devaluation of 1983, the implementation of multiple exchange rates and import regulations helped to eliminate the deficit. But even with these drastic measures the government was unable to maintain a current account surplus for more than three years. After that, the new Lusinchi administration's expansionary policy, according to the rule of the political cycle, caused a strong deficit during 1986–88, in spite of all the restrictions and regulations, that drained all the foreign reserves at the end of 1988. The subsequent liberalization revealed an economy with an underdeveloped non-oil export base due to low diversification.

This basically means that in times of oil bonanza, there is a substantial increase in oil exports and, as a result, a surplus on the current account. In times of negative oil shocks, the opposite happens. Figure 8.10 shows the evolution of the current account balance as a percentage of GDP for the period 1951–91.

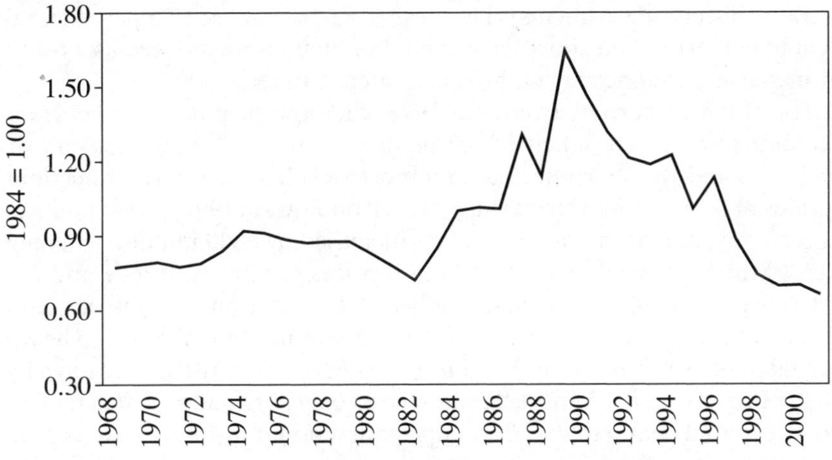

Source: BCV.

Figure 8.10 Current account balance

Venezuela's external vulnerability is also reflected in its dependence on the US market. Exports to the US in the recent past represent more than 50 per cent of total exports and Colombia is a distant second with around 6 per cent of total exports. Most of the exports to the US are oil-related which make Venezuela highly sensitive to American economic cycles. As for the other aspects of the balance of payments, it is important to notice the the capital account reflects the degree of confidence in Venezuela that goes far beyond mere distrust of short-run government policies. It is a known fact that capital outflows are a long established trend of the Venezuelan economy, but in recent years this trend has been aggravated by the uncertainty generated by the political instability. Fortunately Venezuela's external debt is relatively low as compared with international standards, reaching 28 per cent of GDP in 2000. It is a debt that can be managed from the point of view of foreign exchange availability. Its negative effects are much more serious as far as the budget is concerned.

The negative effects of the political instability and governance deficiencies during the five years to 2001 were partially neutralized by the oil revenue as reflected in balance of payments results. Table 8.5 shows that in 1996, a very large increase in oil exports, caused by high oil prices and production expansions coupled with sluggish imports due to weak domestic demand, resulted in a current account surplus of 13.5 per cent of GDP compared with a deficit of 3.5 per cent of GDP in 1995. Meanwhile, the capital account deficit declined owing to higher flows of FDI (related to privatizations and private oil sector investments). The government continued to repay external debt in net terms, and short-term capital outflows were reduced as a result of increasing confidence and high real interest rates.

The situation turned around in 1998 when the surplus on the current account shifted to a deficit of 3.4 per cent, but in 1999 the recovery of oil prices and the sharp decline in imports resulted in a current account surplus of 3.5 per cent. Despite huge capital outflows in 1999, due to political uncertainty, net international reserves increased by $800 million, reaching $14.4 billion at year's end. In 2000, oil prices continued to rise and the external position of Venezuela strengthened. Despite a huge current account surplus, net international reserves did not accumulate further due to heavy capital outflows. This was mainly due to the high country risk as measured by Brady Bonds spreads. Venezuela was second only to Ecuador that defaulted on its external debt. However, an important amount of foreign assets were accumulated in the Macroeconomic Stabilization Fund (FIEM) which together with the net external reserves reached more than $20 billion.

During 2001, the current account surplus was markedly reduced due to a drop of oil exports of around 22 per cent and an increase of imports of more than 17 per cent. As we can see in Table 8.5, oil exports fell to $21 710 million in 2001 from $27 885. This was the result of the price of the Venezuelan oil mix reduction that reached an average of $25.9 per barrel in 2000 and 20.3 in 2001. On the other hand, the combination of an appreciated real exchange rate and the moderated growth of the economy caused imports to increase by almost $2 billion. As in 2000, during several times in 2001 there were important speculative attacks against the bolívar that resulted in an important decline of net international reserves, which fell to $11.8 billion in 2001 from $15.8 billion in 2000. Preliminary data from the Central Bank indicate that capital outflows reached around $9.7 billion. The massive capital outflows were the result of uncertainty with respect to the economic strategy of the government, especially on the fiscal front. It is worth noting that in 2001 foreign direct investment (FDI) flows fell to $2.6 billion from $4.4 billion in 2000. Most of the FDI flows that entered the country in these two years were associated with investments in the telecommunications and oil sectors. The important reduction in FDI flows is related to political noise and the uncertainty regarding recently approved laws.

Table 8.5 Summary balance of payments (US$ million)

Category	1997	1998	1999	2000	2001
Merchandise exports	23 703.0	17 576.0	20 819.0	33 035.0	27 056.0
Merchandise imports	–13 678.0	–15 105.0	–13 213.0	–15 491.0	–17 282.0
Trade balance	10 025.0	2 471.0	7 606.0	17 544.0	9 774.0
Balance on services, income and transfers	–6 558.0	–5 724.0	–3 917.0	–4 433.0	–5 379.0
Current account balance	3 467.0	–3 253.0	3 689.0	13 111.0	4 395.0
Equity investment, net	5 542.0	5 551.0	4 128.0	1 939.0	2 924.0
Direct investment	5 036.0	4 262.0	2 669.0	4 357.0	2 595.0
Portfolio flows	506.0	1 289.0	1 459.0	–2 418.0	329.0
Long and short-term capital, net	–4 957.0	–3 825.0	–6 512.0	–4 729.0	–4 871.0
Capital account balance	585.0	1 726.0	–2 384.0	–2 790.0	–1 947.0
Errors and omissions, net	–1 462.0	–1 442.0	–990.0	–4 503.0	–4 882.0
Reserves excluding gold (– = increase)	–2 590.0	2 969.0	–315.0	–5 818.0	2 434.0

Sources: IMF, BCV and IIF.

The Fiscal Accounts

As in the case of the external sector and given that the state is the owner and administrator of the oil rent, the fiscal result is basically determined by the oil market performance. This means that in times of high oil prices there will be observed, in general, a fiscal surplus, while when prices are low a deficit probably emerges. One of the characteristics of the oil rent model is that most of the distribution of revenues is done through the budget. Before the oil shocks of the 1970s, it was a fairly simple process to distribute oil revenues among different groups. However, as the oil rent faded and society became increasingly complex, the distribution process started to break down either for lack of resources or for failure to reach important parts of the population. Also, 'white elephant investment projects' and the use of public institutions as a means of generating employment drained an important amount of resources and made the budget even more inflexible. Figure 8.11 shows the evolution of the central government fiscal balance as a percentage of GDP for the period 1961–91.

Fiscal management is probably the hardest task for Venezuelan policymakers. As already mentioned, fiscal revenues depend heavily on oil prices and production. Non-oil tax revenues, although they have increased in

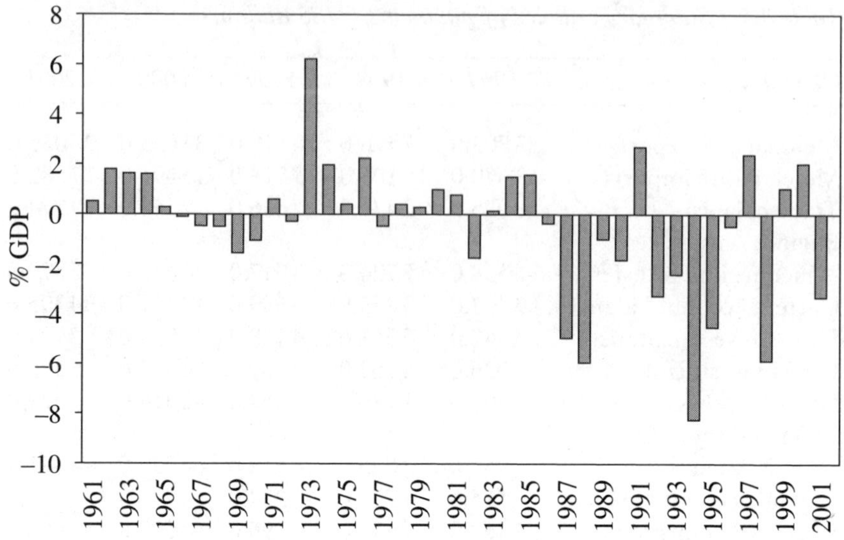

Figure 8.11 Central government fiscal balance

the last few years as a proportion of GDP, continue to be one of the lowest in Latin America. There is also widespread income tax and VAT evasion. In addition, the budget is extremely rigid with many revenues earmarked for specific purposes. On the expenditure side, most of the budget allocations are to pay wages and salaries and public investment has been reduced to very low levels. However, as can be seen in Figure 8.12, public expenditures are of the order of 20 per cent GDP, which is below the average for Latin America. There have been several unsuccessful attempts to reform the fiscal institutions, which are among the less developed of Latin America. Recently, a set of new laws aimed at diversifying revenues and adding more flexibility to the budget have been approved and other measures are still under discussion in Congress. Table 8.6 shows the main fiscal accounts of the central government. Tax collection has improved considerably since 2003.

A key feature of the Venezuelan budgetary process is its lack of credibility. In many cases, assumptions regarding revenues are overly optimistic and expenditures are underestimated, which in turn causes a misleading impression of the fiscal stance. For example, the National Assembly approved the 2002 budget in November 2001. Key budgetary assumptions are: (i) 4.1 per cent economic growth; (ii) 2.87 million b/d oil production; (iii) $18.5 a barrel average oil price; and, (iv) 4.3 per cent fiscal deficit. These assumptions appear to be overly optimistic given that economic growth during 2001 was 2.7 per cent and it is expected to be close to zero

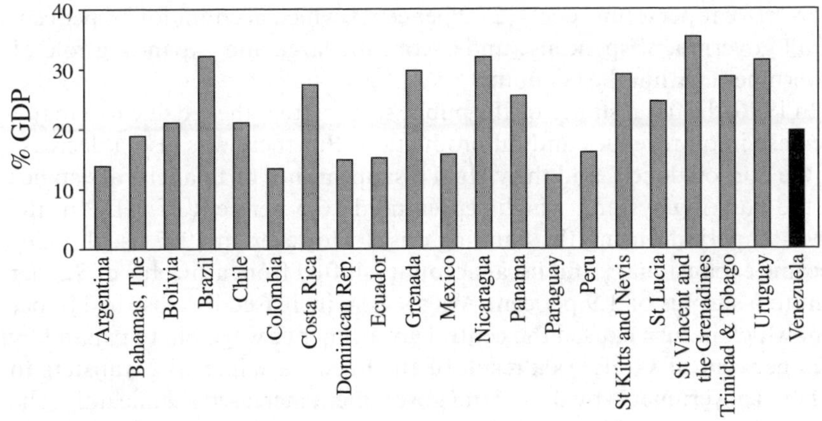

Source: OAEF.

Figure 8.12 Government expenditure

in 2002. Furthermore, the budget assumes that oil production will exceed, by 300,000 b/d, the OPEC quota reduction agreed to by Venezuela, and the price of oil will trade significantly higher than current levels. The 2002 budget also exemplified the rigidity of public expenditures. Approximately half of the budget is composed of non-discretionary spending, primarily mandatory federal, state and municipal transfers such as education (14.8 per cent), social security (10.1 per cent), health (6.6 per cent), defense (6.5 per cent), housing (3.5 per cent) and government (3.2 per cent). Rising

Table 8.6 Central government financial operations (per cent of GDP)

	1997	1998	1999	2000	2001
Total revenue	23.0	16.4	16.6	19.6	20.4
Current revenue	23.0	16.4	16.6	19.6	20.4
Oil revenue	13.3	6.2	6.3	10.0	9.8
Income tax	7.3	1.9	2.1	4.3	2.8
Royalties	3.7	2.3	2.6	4.2	3.2
PDVSA dividends	2.3	2.0	1.6	1.4	3.8
Non-oil revenue	9.8	10.2	10.3	9.6	10.6
Capital revenue	0.0	0.0	0.0	0.0	0.0
Total expenditure	21.1	20.5	19.1	21.2	24.5
o/w interest payments	2.4	2.4	2.7	2.5	2.9
Overall surplus or deficit (–)	1.9	–4.1	–2.5	–1.6	–4.0

Sources: IMF, BCV and IIF.

year-on-year personnel costs (27.2 per cent), which account for 16 per cent of all government spending, underscore the large and expanding role of government within the economy.

In 1996, the fiscal stance of the public sector strengthened due to a major increase in oil revenues and oil production. But there was also a decrease of the non-oil deficit, and the virtual disappearance of financial assistance to the banking system, which represented 16.5 per cent of GDP in the 1994–95 period during the banking crises. However, in 1997 fiscal policy became expansionary and fiscal accounts shifted from a surplus of 7.2 per cent to a surplus of 1.9 per cent. Wages were increased by close to 117 per cent which in turn caused the central government's wage bill to expand by 1.25 per cent of GDP. As a result of the huge wage increase, transfers to regional governments by the central government increased significantly. The sharp reduction of oil prices in 1998 caused a swing from a small surplus in 1997 to a considerable deficit of 4.1 per cent in 1998. In 1999, an increase in oil revenue and the effort by the government to cut expenditure, principally during the first half of the year, improved the overall fiscal position of the consolidated public sector.

The fiscal situation was relatively solid in 2000 when oil prices skyrocketed, but expenditure increased markedly. The consolidated public sector reached a surplus of 2 per cent of GDP. Nonetheless, 2001 was characterized by lower oil prices and oil production cuts to comply with OPEC agreements. In addition, public expenditures rose to 24.5 per cent of GDP in 2001 form 21.2 per cent in 2000 mainly due to salary increases, higher interest payments and higher expenditures associated to welfare programs. Lower oil revenues coupled with higher expenditures resulted in a central government deficit of 4 per cent of GDP in 2001. A recent trend has been increasing interest payments related to a rising domestic public debt. Therefore revenues declined, but preliminary data shows that public expenditures remained at levels similar to 2000, which caused an important deficit for the consolidated public sector. Given that the main pro-growth strategy of the current administration has been the use of expansionary public expenditures, further fiscal deterioration was to be expected in 2002.

The administration's current strategy at the time of writing tends to prefer more emphasis on internal financing and less on external financing. As a consequence, the external public debt has decreased steadily and the internal debt has increased keeping total debt relatively unchanged. In Figure 8.13, it can bee seen how although the total public debt as a percentage of GDP has been around 29 per cent in 1997–2001, the composition has changed. In 1997 domestic debt as a percentage of GDP was 4.5 per cent while in 2001 it reached 10 per cent of GDP.

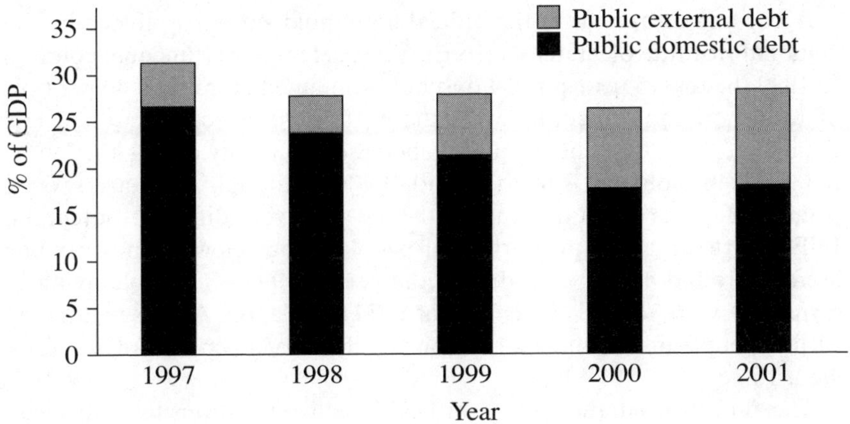

Source: BCV and IIF

Figure 8.13 Public debt

Rising debt service costs, which account for 24.6 per cent of all expenses, increased by 24.1 per cent year-on-year to $8.4 billion, a strong signal that current and recurring expenditures were being financed primarily through the 'rolling over' of public debt. This, in combination with the fiscal deficit of 8 to 9 per cent, could potentially propel Venezuela into a vicious downward spiral, whereby debt issued to finance expenditures results in larger debt payments, which in turn, forces the government to issue increasingly larger amounts of debt. In addition, the increasing amount of domestic debt could have caused higher interest rates, given that the market is not willing to take risky government paper.

Poverty and Income Distribution

Perhaps the most dramatic effect of the collapse of the oil rental model has been the gradual empoverishment of the Venezuelan people. In 1970, exports per capita were $594, and in 1974 they reached $1844 due to the first oil shock. In 1997, exports per capita were even lower than in 1979 when they totaled $527. However, the oil resources helped to finance important improvments to the health and the education sectors. For example, the infant mortality rate (under 5, per 1000 live births) was 61 in 1970 and reduced to 25 in 1998, while the illiteracy rate (percentage of people aged 15 and above) went from 23.5 in 1970 to 8.0 in 1998. More recently, poverty and income distribution indicators have been worsening steadily.

According to data from the official household survey produced by the National Institute of Statistics (INE), Venezuela is a very unequal country. In 1999 the top 15 per cent of households obtained more than 40 per cent of total household income, while the bottom 70 per cent acquired less than 40 per cent. Income inequality increased markedly during the 1980s, but has kept constant since the mid-1990s. Although there are several sources of poverty data, many of them report very different outcomes. INE reported that the proportion of people living below the poverty line average around 46 per cent during the period 1995–98. People living in extreme poverty totaled 22 per cent of total population. As was mentioned earlier, people in the informal sector are around 50 per cent of the total labor force.

The allocations in the budget for health, education, housing, and social programs (which comprise social expenditures) increased to 9 per cent of GDP in 2000 from an average of 6.8 per cent during the 1996–98 period due mainly to increases in the education budget. The anti-poverty strategy of the government in the last several years has been centered on the Unified Social Fund (FUS) which manages several anti-poverty programs and the Plan Bolívar 2000 administrated by the military, which pursues generation of employment through small infrastructure projects. It seems that these programs have not been sufficient to reduce poverty because preliminary data shows that total poverty and extreme poverty might have increased recently (see Figure 8.14).

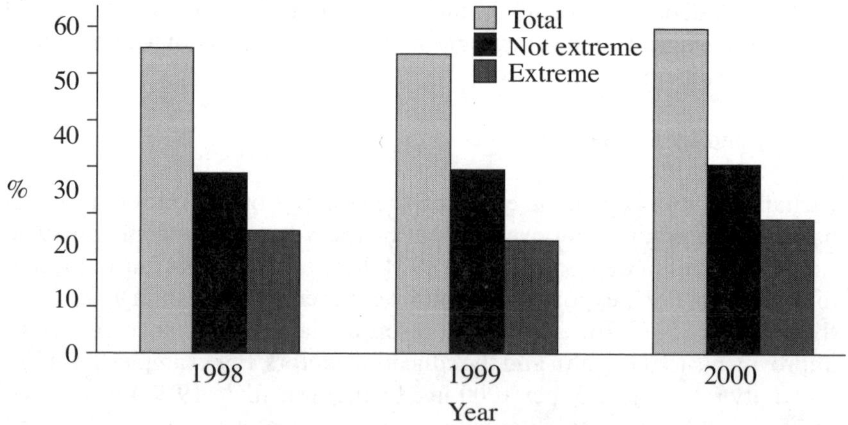

Source: UCAB.

Figure 8.14 Poverty in Venezuela (per cent of population)

8.5 GOVERNANCE AND ECONOMICS: THE MAIN LINKS IN THE VENEZUELAN CASE

Governance affects in many ways the performance of a country's economy. Venezuela is no exception, and previous sections have highlighted some of the negative consequences caused by poor governance in the case of Venezuela. For example, the fragmentation of the political system, shown by the voice and participation indicator, has made it much more difficult to implement reforms. After 1992, the bipartisan control of the Congress majority was lost and it became increasingly difficult to pass new laws without considerable delays. In addition, in those cases where reform projects were able to pass through, they were subjected to so many amendments to satisfy different interest groups that they failed to accomplish their objective. In such an environment it is very difficult to maintain a steady and coherent economic policy. The uncertainty that derives from this situation induces investors to prefer to take an approach of wait-and-see, causing important delays for new projects.

An example of the negative effects of high political fragmentation has been fiscal reform in Venezuela. Despite the fact that there appears to be agreement on the need for diversification of oil revenues, several tax reforms have been insufficient to solve the fiscal gap and the budget still depends heavily on oil prices. And what is even worse, given the decreasing returns of the oil rental model, the budget has become very difficult to manage even with high oil prices, as shown by the present situation. At the time of writing, Venezuela faces one of the deepest fiscal imbalances in recent history. However there have been important delays in approving key fiscal reforms such as the reduction of exceptions to VAT, the approval of a fiscal responsibility law which defines better tax responsibilities between the central government and the local states, and social security reform.

With regard to political instability and violence, until 1989 Venezuela did not have any significant problems. As was mentioned, the country has not had a history of political violence and guerrilla movements as in other Latin American countries. However, with the deterioration of institutions and the impoverishment of the country, common crime has grown substantially and is more important than political violence. This has caused larger transaction costs for the private sector due to increasing security expenditures. Many companies have to spend heavily on security in order to keep their operations going. In fact, there is evidence of foreign firms that have decided to leave the country due to safety concerns and probably many investments have been postponed for the same reason. The inefficiency of the government and the deterioration of the judiciary have contributed to making this cost even higher. It is important to notice that public protests by unions and professional associations to claim better working conditions are common and have become a favorite tool of political pressure.

Perhaps the main governance element that affects economic performance the most in Venezuela is government ineffectiveness. The provision of public goods and services is extremely poor. In addition, civil servants are poorly trained and highly linked to political parties. This causes high rotation of personnel, which disrupts the implementation of public policies. Another problem of public administration in Venezuela is its lack of transparency and credibility. For example, fiscal data is usually not available and sometimes is several months delayed. Macroeconomic policies are extremely dependent on oil prices and are usually neither credible nor sustainable. These problems have become more acute in recent years and they threaten the establishment of a favorable environment for investment and production. Despite important achievements regarding the reduction of the regulatory burden, there are still important sources of excessive regulation in areas such as international trade and business development. Red tape is rampant and widespread through all government levels causing important obstacles to new business and the expansion of existing ones. Unnecessary regulation is closely linked to corruption. Often, firms have to pay important amounts of money to avoid red tape. This could prevent new projects taking place or simply cause foreign firms to go somewhere else.

The deterioration of institutions due to the collapse of the oil rent model described so far implies that the rule of law in Venezuela is among the worst in the region. Citizens do not trust most institutions, especially the judicial system. Of course this represents a source of important costs, not only to people, but also to firms. Businesses would try to avoid at all costs going through the judicial system, trying to reach agreements outside of the legal system. If contracts cannot be enforced in an effective way by the parties through public institutions, then it becomes more difficult to development productive activities.

In summary, governance is of great importance in the case of Venezuela's poor economic performance. It's recent history shows clearly that there are important economic costs associated with political fragmentation, political instability, violence, government ineffectiveness, graft, excessive regulation and lack of credibility and transparency. And these governance problems have deteriorated even further during the last several years in accordance with the increased political turmoil, as we shall see in the remaining sections of this chapter.

8.6 CHÁVEZ'S REGIME

It has been traditional in each Venezuelan election to have a sort of anti-system candidate. At the early stages of the democratic period, when there was still great support for the system, it was usually a burlesque figure that gathered a few votes from people that wanted to express their dissatisfaction in a very irrational manner. These were people that used their vote more as an insult than a way to make a positive statement. But later on, when disillusion began to grow among the better-educated middle classes, especially in the capital city, this place was taken over by a prestigious figure independent from the ruling parties and distant from the political left. A respected diplomat, a great writer, a famous television anchorman played this role, but never reaching more than 5 per cent of the votes. They were essentially public images that express a vague discontent rather than the aims of a well-established political subject. They were one-time phenomena that faded away as soon as the election was over to be replaced by another figure in the next election.

This changed in 1988, when a leader of an independent trade union took this place, showing that the once occasional rage was now becoming a stable desire for reforms. In fact, this movement did not disappear as did all the others, but grew stronger during the events that followed and became a serious option in the 1993 elections, when the two old parties' predominance was finally broken. Those fleeting images of discontent at the fringe of the political spectrum dominated by two main parties were now gaining the central stage, as became obvious during the Caldera administration. As the election approached, the traditional parties' images continued to deteriorate and the polls showed that a leading figure was a former beauty queen: Irene Saez, mayor of one of the richest sections of Caracas, renowned for having done what any mayor usually does anywhere else in the world. A politically shallow figure, in the line of those early burlesque candidates, had now become a serious mainstream political option.

It is difficult to imagine a stronger graphic representation of the governance crises than this one. A mute, beautiful face that could be filled up with anybody's wishes, ideas and hopes. In a far distant second place there was another face, not so beautiful but less shallow: that of Hugo Chávez; rendered famous by a few crucial seconds on the television screen the day of the coup attempt, when he said: 'I take responsibility for what has happened.' In a country used to a political class that never took responsibility for anything, this was the most important anti-system political statement in many years. Enough to make him a serious political candidate; were it not for the fact that, once out of jail, he began to speak his mind and people became rapidly disenchanted with his primitive and confused utterances.

This was the starting situation in 1997, when the crisis of governance reached bottom as shown by indicators previously analysed. It is important to remark that these faces were not the visible representations of new emerging political subjects, but just icons of discontent in the same tradition as the previous ones, but with a fundamental difference: they took leverage directly from the crumbling of the old political parties. At each step of the electoral campaign the corruption and ineptitude of a political class, completely out of touch with reality, increased the anger and disappointment of larger sectors of the population. This mounting rage favored Chávez who offered a more aggressive image than the lollipop, cold face of Irene Saez. As Chávez rose in the polls, the mute beauty was forced to speak out and it was no longer possible to maintain the fiction of her being a serious political option. So she started to fall at the same vertiginous pace as the old parties. One of them, COPEI, had nominated her as the party's candidate, while AD had chosen its secretary general, a figure as old and worn out as the corrupted system itself. As election day approached, in the midst of desperation, both parties withdrew their support for the lady and the old leader in a very shameful spectacle of political opportunism that could only stir public rage even more. They gave their last minute support to a third more serious candidate, but this maneuver was too obvious and too late. Chávez was now the man that many people across all social classes wanted to clean up all that political trash.

We have indulged in this sequence of events to show that Chávez' victory was more the ugly face of the collapse of the old system than the expression of a new political subject. There was not a formal *chavista* movement until the last minute when the Movimiento Quinta República (MVR) was organized, mainly to comply with the electoral law. Behind Chávez' face rallied a heterogeneous multiplicity of dissatisfied people coming mainly from the popular classes, but also from a considerable sector of the impoverished middle class; and even some members of the upper class voted for Chávez. People of different ideological backgrounds, ranging from the old *perejimenista* right to certain fringes of the old left mixed in the common cause to get rid of the old system through democratic means. From this point of view, Chávez' face was also the symbol of the willingness to do by democratic means what in Latin America is usually done by barbarian coup d'état. Once again, a moment of high political instability coincides with the deepening of the democratic spirit.

The *chavista* movement wanted to implement radical reforms. But not being a political subject, it did not have a clear objective and a viable program; and its proposal, in the end, was nothing more than a radical form of classical Latin American political nominalism: a new constitution in a country that already had more than 20. This is an all too Latin American vice of always substituting real changes in social practices and personal behavior for formal legal changes. Certainly, the exhaustion of the oil rent model called for a radical change of social practices and personal behavior and legal changes were justified as a mean to help these changes. But the *chavista* answer to this need concentrated solely on a new constitution and a new set of laws that only added more instability to the already fragile governance, while reinforcing old behavior and social practices. On this point, the *chavista* movement behaved like a nomadic force unable to function within the framework of democratic institutions, increasing the disruption of the social order and having nothing to replace it with. Very soon the new government exhausted itself in bringing about legal changes that purported to be an enhancement of democracy, while its practical behavior increased the degree of arbitrariness. Chávez himself represents very well this dichotomy between a desire for more and better democracy on one side, and a clumsy authoritarian behavior on the other, that more than a political strategy, rests on an original incapacity to understand the nature of democratic institutions.

Since it is not a true political subject but a nomadic assemblage of heterogeneous forces, *chavismo* does not have an articulated intention of building a new despotic social order. In this sense, it is not an ideological movement, as those that have determined the history of the twentieth century. But it implements a permanent harassment of anything that it is perceived as an obstacle to the legitimate aspiration of the people. After three years of Chávez' administration, the feeling that a growing number of people were beginning to have of the country sliding toward a dictatorship originated in this generalized arbitrariness.

This movement is a strange blend of democratic desire trapped by a network of intolerant behaviors at a micro level of the social fabric. Instead of an ideology, it has a sort of *imagery* made out of pieces drawn from elementary school nineteenth-century republican heroes, romanticized twentieth-century revolutionary events, retrieved portions of traditional religious piety and native cultural expressions. It incorporates ideological pieces taken from any known political discourse and social theory to build an indigestible political delirium that fills up the entire mass media space in a society without social subjects and made exclusively of audiences. It is less a traditional political movement than a mass media representation of a social malaise that run deep across Venezuelan society and that can only be captured on the television set. That is what Chávez really is: a TV image that raves incessantly through the mass media in order to exist and by so doing keeps reminding people of the unsolved problems.

In a sense, *chavismo*, like many other 'isms' that have emerged since the 1980s around the world, it is a true *neoarchaism*, that is a bunch of twisted old ideological representations mixed in a new functional context. By the same token, it generates its own foe on the same plane of images. The mass media are the true political opposition to Chávez, not the political parties, not civil society organizations, not business or labor associations. This is further proof that behind this theatre of simulacra there are not political subjects, but only fragmented pieces left by the crumbling of the old model. A society of scattered interest groups cut off from their traditional channels of rent acquisition and political power, unable to recompose around new organizations and new institutions, with no opinion but the one that the mass media have made up for them. Beneath the surface, there is a sort of underground Somalia or Afghanistan-type society, ravaged by semiotic warlords, unable to establish any connection but through the common cause against Chávez who is just another semiotic warlord like them. That is why the political struggle has become a fight for *audiences* rather than for followers. This explains why the mass media feel so endangered at the finest hour of their power and unfettered activity. Chávez' contention that, during his administration, there has not been one single incident of government harassment of the press, as usually was the case in previous governments, has been so far certainly true. Nonetheless, it is also true that no other president had ever before subjected journalists and the mass media to such verbal abuses as they are subjected to now, although they are answering in kind.

Recent Constitutional Changes and Governance Style

The true nature of *chavismo* is that of a nomadic movement led by a raving image that plays the role of chief of government in a sort of permanent mass media drama. At times and only at times, the image becomes a real person, like those movies where cartoon figures mingle with real actors. The so-called Chávez revolution (*revolución chavista*) is nothing more than an effort to make strong social aspirations come true, not in reality but in a cheap TV drama with a neoarchaic script. This mass media performance is a surrogate for true governance and signals the extreme point reached by the crisis of governance.

This drastic reduction of governance to an almost exclusively mass media performance is due mainly to three factors. In the first place, we have the disruption of the public administration system that the Chávez government inherited. In the second place, the lack of a government strategy to cope with this problem beyond the simplistic electoral offers to change the constitution and the legal framework. Finally, the third factor are the very low qualifications of the appointed public officials, for the most part with no previous administrative experience. This has accelerated the traditional high rotation of public officials up to an unprecedented rate. As an example, let us take a look at what has happened with some of the highest posts closely related to the economy. During the first three years of the Chávez administration, there were five finance ministers, three ministers of industry, commerce and agriculture, an equal number of ministers of infrastructure and also of urban development, two ministers of oil and energy and five presidents of PDVSA. When we consider lower posts, things get even worse: technical teams in charge of housing planning, disaster areas, social development programs are frequently replaced and each change means a total disregard for the previous work and a new start from scratch. The end result is that most of the public administration is almost stuck at a never-ending initial stage. This relentless flow of people through key decisionmaking posts is one of the two main features of these political nomads, the other being the lack of understanding of the functioning of modern state institutions.

Therefore, it would be wrong to confuse it with the old populism that was a more or less coherent ideology associated with well-organized parties having precise government programs and with a well-defined ideological framework. Chavez' movement shows little concern with party organization. It has been pointed out (López-Naya 2000; Ramos 2001) that this feature connects this movement with the so-called *neopopulism* such as Fujimori's. This political orientation has, among its main features, the disavowal of party organization and the overcoming of democratic institutions when they are deemed useless or an obstacle (Kenney 1998). The Constituent Assembly and the series of elections and referenda to approve the institutional changes sponsored by Chávez do not seem compatible with the second main feature of the neopopulism.

The main feature of Chávez's electoral program was indeed a new constitution that was to be the new legal base for a long-run transformation of the country. After a few months in power, Chávez called a referendum to approve a new election for a Constitutional Assembly that would elaborate the new constitution. He won the referendum and in the subsequent election for the Constituent Assembly all but five of the elected candidates were his followers. After three months, a new constitution was ready and submitted to the people for the approval in a national referendum held on 15 December 1999. The people came out overwhelmingly in favor of it. After that, a new election for mayors, governors, deputies to the new National Assembly, and for the presidency took place in which once again Chávez won and his movement got a wide majority. Chávez' candidates did very well in one more election, for city council members. Therefore, in a two-year span,

Chávez won six elections overwhelmingly. From this point of view, Chávez's democratic record is impeccable and places him at a great distance from people like Fujimori.

Now the tendency to resort to constitutional and legal reforms as a way of solving social and political conflicts has been a constant feature in Latin American history that has been labeled *nominalism*. And this tradition fits quite well with Chávez' verbal revolution. But Chávez' constitutional reform has also had a real effect. It helped to wipe out the remaining pockets of old parties' political control. And this is certainly the positive side of its nomadism that was so appealing to so many Venezuelans. At the beginning of the year 2000, 80 per cent of the population supported the President. Beyond this cleansing effect, the constitutional reform has had no meaningful impact on the real economic issues, especially in the direction of changing the oil rental model. If anything, some of the reforms, such as the new constitutional article that assures the state property of PDVSA, tend to reinforce the old model. This is another outstanding aspect of the neoarchaic nature of *chavismo*; an example of its radical misunderstanding of the nature of the Venezuelan crisis and of its lack of a viable strategy to respond properly to it. The main constitutional changes are:

(1) The new constitution adds to the three traditional branches of the sovereign power – the executive, the legislative, the judicial – two more: the electoral branch and Citizen Power body made up of the Fiscal General, Defensor del Pueblo, and the Contralor. These high officials ought to be elected by the National Assembly with the active participation of civil society that should propose candidates.
(2) Although the new constitution asserts the federal character of the Republic, an unicameral National Assembly replaces the old two-chamber Congress.
(3) The presidential period is extended to a six-year term with the possibility of immediate re-election instead of the previous five-year term with the possibility of re-election only after two subsequent terms have elapsed.
(4) As a step forward to a more participatory democracy, the new constitution allows for the possibility to call for a referendum to revoke the mandate to the President, governors and mayors, once half of their term in office has elapsed.
(5) The chapter on human rights has also been enhanced and in general the constitution provides for more participation by the citizen in the different levels of the decisionmaking process.
(6) International treaties and agreements on human rights are considered part of the constitutional framework.

(7) Members of the army have now the right to vote and can participate in political debate.
(8) Members of the indigenous minority have three permanent seats in the National Assembly.
(9) Private property is guaranteed, but its social function has been stressed, although for all practical purposes it remains as before.

These are the major changes and in general they constitute an enhancement of democracy. But this participatory spirit is somehow countervailed by an increase of the prerogative of the executive branch. The promotion of high-ranking military officers no longer needs the approval of Congress that has been replaced by that of the President. For the rest, the constitution follows the old one. In general, given that the constitution, at least in principle, improves the participation of civil society in many levels of the decisionmaking process, one would say that the changes do not have any significant bearing on the design and implementation of economic policies.

At the nominal level, the Chávez movement shows a great democratic sensibility. But a serious problem arises when we compare this drive for democratic formalities with the actual behavior of public officials and the President himself. Here a clear tendency to skip proper procedure and to disregard the autonomy of the different levels of responsibility comes out strongly. This dichotomy between nominal democratic drive and practical disruptive behavior of democratic institutions and rules is the most striking feature of the regime. As soon as the new constitution was approved, there were new elections for president, governors and mayors in order to legitimize authority according to the new rules. This was certainly a show of democratic sensibility. But on the other hand, the justices to the Supreme Court (Tribunal Supremo de Justicia) were chosen in the most old fashioned patronage style, taking advantage of the majority of votes in the National Assembly. As for the other high officials such as the Fiscal General, Contralor, and Defensor del Pueblo that made up the new Citizen Power body, the new constitution requires the participation of civil society in proposing candidates from which the National Assembly ought to choose. In spite of this, they were elected directly by the National Assembly. Needless to say, all these justices and officials were drawn from the rank of Chávez sympathizers.

It is not only that the regime has show no sensibility for allowing the opposition to have some institutional participation to ensure countervailing powers and the proper democratic balance, but what is worse, the whole institutional setup seems to collapse into a mess of personal relations and in this mess, the will of the President becomes predominant. Therefore, it is in the realm of practical behavior that the nomadic character of this Chávez movement looms more strongly. A total lack of disposition for consensus building, through negotiations with legitimate stakeholders, gives the government's behavior a strong sectarian tilt that has alienated an increasing number of people and has created a feeling of total exclusion among the middle classes. For example, although the new constitution stresses the participatory character of Venezuelan democracy, the government asked and obtained from the National Assembly the authorization to make important economic laws by decree (Ley habilitante). This has been a practice that every president before Chávez has used at a certain point. The difference this time was that the power given to the President was over a too broad range of issues. Besides, Chávez used this prerogative to issue 42 laws related mainly to economic issues, without that widespread consultation process that the new constitution requires. Most of these laws are just remakes of the old ones, but some of them have important changes and incongruent dispositions that may negatively affect the economy.

This is another good example of the incapacity to understand the functioning of modern institutions. In fact, the lack of disposition by the government to built consensus around these laws was due to its tendency to confuse the legitimate claims for participation in the decisionmaking process with the old practices of cronyism and patronage. Thus not knowing how to establish a proper consultation mechanism with the civil society, the government cut off all lines of communication. If we link this general behavior of high officials with Chávez' speeches in which he gives verbal orders to authorities that are supposed to be autonomous in different matters, a general sensation of utmost arbitrariness in public administration is created. And if we add to this permanent verbal abuse with which the President responds to any issue or claim raised by the civil society, we have a clear explanation for the contention by the opposition that Chávez' governance style is an authoritarian one. But in our judgement this is so not so much because of an authoritarian intention, but because of its nomadic character, which fundamentally does not understand the proper meaning of modern institutions and therefore does not know how to make them function properly.

Be that as it may, these circumstances have caused an increasing hostility among the middle classes that has affected economic behavior, neutralizing all the positive effects of the recent oil boom. Although the macroeconomic conditions were favorable, the domestic propensity to invest has practically collapsed under the heavy political stress. Chávez' arbitrary style gives the impression that there are no clear and transparent rules and this has neutralized all the effects of a very conservative economic policy. This same arbitrariness has shattered his ministers' earlier efforts to achieve a fiscal discipline and has fed sustained capital outflows financed mainly by the high oil revenue. This situation has forced the government to lift the foreign exchange anchor that was its means to fight inflation and represented half of its economic policy, the other half being the high oil prices. With the first objective of its economic strategy having crumbled and the second one shaken by recent events in the oil market, the regime has been left with no strategy. The government needs to negotiate a new strategy to divert the path that is leading the country to a very deep crisis. But from this it is barred not only by its confrontational style but also by the fact that since it has no strategy of its own it does not know what to negotiate. Therefore, in spite of the constitutional intention to enhance civil society participation in governance affairs, the nomadic behavior of the government and the sectarian attitude of the political majority have set the country on a confrontational track, while the population splits in two halves very hostile to each other. Nothing could be further from a participatory society. And no situation can be worse than this to keep a minimun of governance.

For these reasons we should not try to fit this politcal movement into some of the boxes of political science. *Chavismo* should be seen as a new phenomenon partially linked to the globalization process (Medina 2001). In fact, as we have said before, Chávez' regime is indeed the end stage of the oil rental model, because of the persistence of all the old practices that no longer allow for a minimum of governance. In this sense, it is just Venezuela's anomaly. But from the point of view of its ideas, its imagery, it is a neoarchaism bred by a reaction to another previous neoarchaism that has been thrust upon this region since the 1980s. This is what in Latin America and in other parts of the world has been called: neoliberalism.[2]

Therefore, it should not be surprising that its policy proposals are a potpourri of pragmatic approaches and ideological prejudices drawn from almost every known theory or doctrine. At least for the time being, *chavismo* believes that the best economic policy is to reduce inflation by anchoring the foreign exchange rate, no matter what may happen to the employment and growth rates. Moreover, it believes, as some radical neoclassical economists do, that this fight against inflation is the only meaningful policy. It pays lipservice to the need for diversifying the economy, but it concentrates all its efforts on keeping the oil price as high as possible to maximize fiscal revenue for as long as possible, while it does not seem to feel any drive for a coherent program of state reforms. It is convinced that privatization is evil and thunders against wild neoliberalism, but considers hostile takeovers by foreign capital to be all right. It abhors graft but doesn't see the need for competitive bidding and proper procedures. It has the conviction that poor people have the right to encroach on private property to survive, but it does not care for social and poverty alleviation programs. It deeply believes in people's participation in the decisionmaking process, but gladly surrenders to Chávez' whims. In short, *chavismo* is like one of those religious syncretisms, so common in Latin America, and in this sense is the true ideology of a marginal and depauperated population. It is not the expression of a true political subject.

8.7 A NEW POLITICAL ECONOMY FOR VENEZUELA

At this point and time in Venezuela, the governance crisis is much more than a simple set of technical and institutional problems that can be solved by such reforms as capacity-building programs, judicial reforms, ethical and skill improvement of the bureaucracy and the like. All these are important shortcomings that, in Venezuela, are not due primarily to a lack of knowhow, human capital or economic resources. They are caused by an adverse political will that is the expression of the institutional crisis of the old political and social model based on the oil rent distribution through the state. The absence of the proper power relations among well-constituted political subjects is at the bottom of the Venezuelan governance crisis. The reconstruction of these political subjects would only be possible if based on a viable development strategy proposal.

This is a condition all too often set aside by a functionalist perspective, always too simple, too elementary, too technocratic, too limited. Recommendations coming from this approach can be of some use in a very backward society jumping into the world of modern national states from a very far removed and different historical experience. But in a complex society, as most Latin America countries are, they can, at best, be of partial help in solving some specific problems. It is worthwhile to remind ourselves, once more, that a technically sound policy that is not politically viable is as bad as the most unsound technical policy. To differentiate between the technical and the political aspects of a given policy, as if they were independent of each other, is an unhealthy technocratic delusion that has already produced too much suffering in this region.

We have tried to show that at the present stage there are no political subjects in Venezuela; only audiences participating in a sort of mass media charade under which lies a fragmented society where everybody is guessing the other's intentions covered under a pile of meaningless words. The way out of this situation is the formation of new political subjects that can agree on the general lines for a new model of economic growth and social development that does not depend on the oil rent. Only then could a coherent and consensual development policy package be implemented and an institution-building program established.

For the time being, the country will remain in the limbo of a state oil rent model that can provide enough resources to keep the economy running at a low performance level, without reaching the critical situation that we can see in other parts of the region. At least until drastic changes are made in world energy consumption, Venezuela will enjoy a floor superior to other countries to manage a sort of permanent crisis. But although from the economic point of view a long period of mediocre performance is conceivable, such a state does not seem tenable from the social point of view. Should the present state persist, two possible roads are open to Venezuela. The first one will lead to a sort of permanent re-editing of an unfinished *chavista* revolution, interrupted by periods of anti-*chavista* government – a dynamic that, in the end, will permanently disrupt Venezuelan society much on the lines of what happened in Argentina during most of the twentieth century. The other possible outcome is the institutionalization of the present fragmentation that will permanently exclude large sectors of Venezuelan society and will breed endemic guerrilla movements as in Colombia.

As far as the ongoing governance is concerned it reflects the true nature of the present regime. We have characterized the *chavista* movement as a nomadic force that has completely disrupted the old institutions without being able to replace them with new ones. Therefore, the former inefficient governance has degenerated into plain chaos and pure incapacity. It would be just nonsense to try to discern patterns of governance in an increasingly chaotic situation in which governance has become a theater, a sheer representation. Every economic, social, juridical, institutional policy has no longer a rationality of its own, but it is dependent upon the dynamic of a phantasmagoric revolution that in the *chavista* jargon means nothing more than a nomadic drive to nowhere. Whether it would be possible to rebuild political subjects around a new model of open market industrialization fast enough to avoid such a gruesome prospect, is a question that actual events in the making will answer soon.

8.8 POSTSCRIPT

As we were going through the final draft correction of this chapter, some of those events in the making have gathered new momentum, putting the democratic institutions at high risk. An ill-conducted dispute over the newly appointed president and directors to the board of PDVSA unleashed the middle classes' anger that had been simmering since 10 December 2001. That day, all activities stopped following the call by Fedecamaras for a *paro nacional* that essentially required everybody to stay at home. It was a major success for the opposition, especially for the President of Fedecamaras,

Mr Carmona. Later, on 23 January, there were street demonstrations commemorating the end of the dictatorship in 1958: a huge one against the government and another not that big, but big enough, in favor of the government. For the first time the opposition was able to show its strength on the streets. But the only response by the government was the usual verbal abuse and an intensification of its policy of confrontation, especially with the mass media.

Although the verbal battle between the government and a group of journalists went on fiercely, and a few active members of the military came out asking for the President to resign, after a few weeks the tension eased, partially soothed by the comic aspects of such a charade. When the PDVSA employees took to the streets to protest about the new members of the board of directors, the confrontation gathered a new momentum fueled by the violent speech of the President. An active and non-innocent involvement of the main television channels, that suspended their regular programs to focus exclusively on the PDVSA issue, helped to gather the nations attention on the issue. From Thursday 9 April, thousands of people spent their time alternating as viewers in front of the television set and as street protesters in front of PDVSA buildings. The opposition-controlled trade unions confederation (Confederación Nacional de Trabajadores) called a general strike, immediately supported by Fedecamaras. The strike was not as successful as was that on 10 December, but was extended for 24 hours more and then indefinitely. On 11 April, a huge march of protesters that initially should have ended in front of the PDVSA building was detoured by their leaders to the presidential palace, where there was a concentration of Chávez' supporters. As they approached the palace, shooting started and several people died and many more were wounded. For the first time since Chávez took office, there was bloodshed in a demonstration.

After that, events became quite confusing. In the evening several chief commanders of the army appeared on television saying that they were refusing to obey the presidential order to take the troops out into the streets to confront the protesters, and asking instead for the resignation of the President. Later on, the joint staff commander appeared saying that Chávez had resigned. At dawn, Mr Carmona showed up, backed by some of the generals, announcing that he had accepted an invitation to head the new transitional government. The next morning people, mainly middle-class, rejoiced at the news that Chávez had resigned and been taken into custody by the army, while in the *barrios* people in dismay kept silence. Everything seemed to be rushing back to normal, but at five o'clock in the afternoon, on all television screens, appeared the ugly spectacle of Mr Carmona taking the oath as President and signing a decree dissolving the National Assembly and all elected authority, and announcing new elections in a year. To most of the people who had not realized it until then, it was now clear that what had happened was not rebellion by civil society, legally protected by the constitution, but a blunt coup d'état by a bunch of people who had taken advantage of the protesters. The exclusion from the new government of the trade unions, most of the political groups and civil society organizations that had participated in the protest, made clear the sectarian tilt of the new government. The quick and unjustified witch-hunt unleashed by the new 'authorities', and the first policy measures taken, left no doubt as to the leaning of the new regime, labeled by an outspoken anti-Chávez journalist as 'light Pinochetism'.

Then, more and more people started asking for some proof that Chávez had indeed resigned, and so did most of the local military commanders. Meanwhile, after seeing the usurpation act on television, people from the *barrios* started to take to the streets demanding the return of Chávez. Pretty soon it became clear that no such resignation ever existed. All the private television networks put a blackout on what was going on (the public television had been closed down the first night). While there were intense discussions among the military, street fights and looting was happening in many areas of Caracas and other cities, and TV channels transmitted old movies only interrupted by images of angry Chávez supporters at their gates. In 24 hours Chávez was back in Miraflores Palace.

At the time of writing it was too early to make a final evaluation of these events. But we can highlight a few points. It is clear that there was a massive upheaval by large sectors of Venezuelan society, mainly middle classes and workers, demanding the resignation of Chávez. This upheaval was the final outcome of an intransigent policy of a very inefficient government. It was an expression of outrage with no political objective beyond the desire of getting rid of Chávez. It was not planned, but was skillfully manipulated by certain mass media totally out of line. It is also clear that the protesters were goaded into a situation where it was easy to camouflage a coup d'état with a civil society legal disobedience act.

All in all, the democratic institutions of the country responded quite well as soon as the charade was unveiled, leaving many protesters with the sad feeling of having been used by a small group of the adventurers. If the civil society has given Chávez a lesson, the country as a whole did the same to the extreme right and their friends. The majority in both contending groups is fighting over the proper rules of governance, as a way to deepen democracy in Venezuela, not to destroy it. The episode also made clear that the last 20 years of economic and social decline have created a deep division in Venezuelan society catalyzed by Chávez' behavior. His speeches that so much enraged the middle classes make the marginalized population dream of a better future. Until 11 April, it was clear that the only thing that the opposition wanted was to get rid of the nightmare and after that day it was all too clear that what the poor people wanted was their dream back.

Now the country is enjoying a wave of reconciliation. Chávez says that he has learned his lesson and is calling for a national dialogue. The mass media and other leaders of civil society, whose commitment to democracy has been seriously compromised by their behavior during the crisis, are doing the same. But we cannot end this story with the usual fairy tale finale, because all the problems are still there, while the economic situation is deteriorating.

After the Indefinite General Strike (Second Postscript)

The above postscript was written in the aftermath of the failed coup of 11 April 2002. The spirit of reconciliation lasted only a few months and by the beginning of the last quarter of the year the tension rose once more to a high level. In the early days of December 2002, the opposition decided to try to bring down the government through a general strike and a business lockout, which initially was not very successful, and by the end of the third day was fading away. Then the oil industry management and a considerable part of the workers joined the strike in a move unprecedented since 1936. This situation lasted until the end of February 2003, but had no significant effect in weakening the government's position. However, it caused considerable damage to the economy that was already in a bad shape.

Since the end of 2001, President Chávez' popularity has stabilized at around 28–29 per cent approval which is close to the figure with which he was elected the first time (Figure 8.15). This means that he has lost all the popularity that he has won in the aftermath of his first election that rose to 80 per cent approval, but he retains the hard core of his followers coming mainly from the lower classes. However, the intensity of rejection increased enormously during the year 2002 creating a political polarization that has no precedent in twentieth-century Venezuelan politics. The political confrontation had no significant effect on the economy until the coup d'état of 11 April 2002, but after that has been causing significant damage to it.

In our opinion, the bizarre political events that started with the first general strike in December 2000 can only be explained by taking into account the extreme inefficiency of the government in delivering on its promises, that we have analysed in the chapter, but also by the nature of the opposition that has emerged in the recent confrontation. The bulk of the opposition is made up of the disenchanted middle-class and working-class elements that had been hard hit by the economic crisis and irritated by Chávez' rhetoric. Chávez' government is an interesting case of how neoarchaic symbolism can have an intense effect on the economy and social behavior even without any

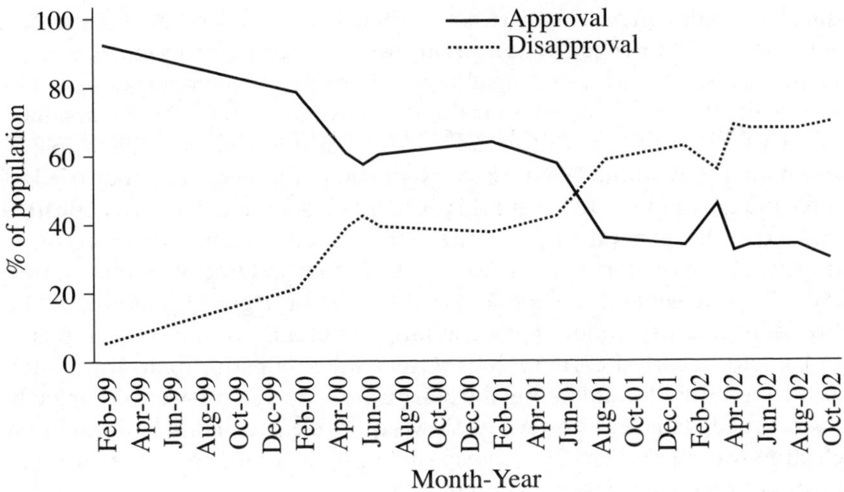

Source: Datanalisis

Figure 8.15 President Chávez' approval rating

specific policy implementation. This mass opposition has no other cohesive factor than the disapproval of Chávez' government. It cut across the entire ideological and political spectrum from the far right to the far left. But the leadership has been provided mainly by figures of the old parties and the old trade union organization. More recently, some of the figures of the rebel oil management had been incorporated into the leadership. Such leadership, identified as the Coordinadora Democrática, has no organic relation with the bulk of opposition masses and no alternative proposal to offer. Their relation with those they purport to represent is only through the mass media, which play a central role in motivating opposition protests and in providing the necessary fora for the opposition leadership to emerge.

This fact is quite important for understanding recent events. In fact contrary to what was explicitly stated, the opposition leadership did not want a solution through election and implemented a strategy that sought to oust Chávez by forcing him to resign, first by a coup d'état that was intended to be camouflaged by voluntary resignation brought about by a huge mass demonstration and bloody reaction of the government that forced the generals to disobey an unlawful order. It is impossible not to recognize the neoconservative flavor of this plan that fits quite well the new international environment where old fashioned coups d'état are no longer acceptable to topple democratically elected governments. But this manner of regime change failed for a lack of proper coordination, probably because there were different actors interfering with each other. The second act of this strategy was the intent to cheat by tampering with the constitutional system of referenda, which allows for consultative referenda and referenda designed to revoke the tenure of elected officials after they have completed the first half of their period. The opposition collected signatures to consult the people as to whether they wanted Chávez to resign and at the same time they tried to force the government to accept this exercise of democracy by street protest and a one-day general strike on the 11th of each month to commemorate those who lost their lives on 11 April 2002. Finally in December, they started the indefinite general strike that asked for the outright resignation of the President irrespective of the consultative referendum that was supposed to be held in early February 2003. Other ways, constitutional ways, such as a referendum for amending the constitution and so on, were completely disregarded. This series of events shows quite clearly that the appeal of an election was mere rhetoric – Chávez-style – to cover for some sort of rapid ousting of Chávez. The question is: why?

The answer is that the loose bunch of people constituting the opposition leaderships were afraid to confront Chávez in a free election. First of all, they represent only small groups and were unwilling to yield their claim to the presidency and other posts in order to form a broader alliance strong enough to defeat Chávez' 30 per cent electoral strength. Second, in a situation of 'power void' created by an abrupt resignation by Chávez, they would be in a better position to negotiate a power distribution to their personal benefit. Third, they know that most of them have been unwillingly accepted as leaders of the opposition due to the strong rejection of Chávez, but most of the opposition people have not forgotten these leaders' past behavior. Now after the tremendous failure of the indefinite general strike that has weakened the economic base of the opposition and has made possible the ousting of more than 25 000 employees of PDVSA, finally the opposition leadership seems resigned to following the road of the electoral solution according to the constitution.

After 19 August 2003, it became possible to hold a referendum to revoke Chávez' mandate and that of other elected officials. Since this is a 'yes' or 'no' decision it was quite probable that Chávez would lose. Then the true problem would show itself in the election afterwards to choose the new authorities. Once again, a divided opposition with no effective organizations, a viable government program and a consensus candidate would have to face a *chavista* movement, without Chávez but with a solid quarter of the voters. Would it be possible for the non-*chavista* Venezuela to do what it has not been able to do in many years? We do not know. Sometimes historical situations change rapidly, but then again sometimes they do not.

What, in our opinion, comes out of this short briefing on recent events, is that, as argued in this chapter, Chávez is not the problem, but a symptom of Venezuela's structural malaise that will remain unchanged even if his government were to end soon. The reshaping of political actors capable of putting in place a roadmap to sustained development, poverty reduction, elimination of exclusion and a more beneficial integration into the world economy is not an easy task. It requires the transformation of Venezuelan social practices in order to breed a new kind of citizenship as the base for better economic and political agents. This true revolution should be opposed to the caricaturesque neoarchaic revolutionary rhetoric of *chavismo*. After all, *chavistas* dream of a new Venezuela with the mind and feeling of the oil-rented Venezuela and as in the old times they long for results without the proper effort.

This being said, it is also true that the actual impasse is taking an increasing toll on the economy, since there cannot be imagined a worst scenario for investment and spending. The year 2002 was a difficult one for the Venezuelan economy due mainly to the negative expectations generated by the political turmoil and lack of confidence in the ability of the government to manage the fiscal deficit. In spite of the stable flow of oil revenue, there was a huge amount of capital outflow and the floating of the foreign exchange rate within certain pre-established limits (+7 and –7 per cent) was abandoned. The GDP dropped 8.9 per cent in 2002 and at least a similar decrease was expected for 2003. Consumption fell 5.5 per cent due mainly to private consumption contraction, gross investment decreased by 22 per cent, the unemployment rate soared to 20 per cent, while 51.5 per cent of the work force is in the informal sector.

The fiscal deficit of the central government for the year 2002 was 3 per cent of GDP, lower than the 4.7 per cent in 2001. This reduction was caused by the difficulty confronted in the international loan market. Actually foreign financing for the year was negative at around 1.7 per cent of GDP. Chavez' administration was then forced to adjust by reducing public spending from 24.5 per cent of GDP in 2001 to 23.1 per cent in 2002. Fiscal revenue was kept at a steady rate 20 per cent of GDP, so that most of the resources to finance the deficit, around 1.6 per cent of GDP, came from FIEM. Borrowing heavily on the domestic market covered the rest.

A 46 per cent devaluation in 2002 spurred inflation up to 31.2 per cent from the 12.3 per cent level in 2001. Prices were also affected by adjustments in certain administered prices, the increase in VAT and the elimination of exemptions. On the other hand, the main monetary variables experienced an important decrease in real terms due to severe economic contraction and capital outflows. The monetary base decreased 9.4 per cent in real terms whereas liquidity (M2) fell 8.8 per cent during the same period. This is the greatest fall since 1996.

During the first quarter of the year, the strong pressure on the bolívar that caused the devaluation raised interest rates. However, after the modification of the exchange regime they started to fall during the second and the third quarter. Then again, they rose once more during the last quarter of the year. The crisis also had an effect on the financial system. The private sector portfolio dropped 25.6 per cent in real terms. Non-collectable outstanding loans rose from 5.1 per cent in 2001 to 6.8 per cent in 2002. The persistence of IDB (Impuesto al Débito Bancario) and the preference for foreign currency as a shield for further devaluation caused a contraction of deposits of 21 per cent in 2002.

The external sector enjoyed the benefit of sustained oil prices in 2002. Imports dropped considerably due to the recession from \$17 391 million in 2001 to \$12 280 million in 2002. Exports showed a small decline from \$26 726 million in 2001 to \$26 219 million. The fall of oil exports at the beginning of December caused by the strike had little impact on revenue. In fact, current account surplus was \$7643 millions in 2002, while in 2001 it was \$3932 million. However, the deficit on the capital account was \$8883, greater than the current account surplus, and the total payments balance was negative causing the international reserves to shrink.

The capital account deficit was ten times bigger than that of the previous year. The factors that contributed to such a huge change were: the collapse of foreign direct investment that fell from a level of \$3300 million in 2001 to \$496 million in 2002; and the outflow of capital showed by the item 'errors and omissions' that increased from \$9899 million to \$10 547 million.

The outflow of capital has been one of the items most sensitive to the political turmoil. However, the change of the foreign exchange regime in March 2002 was also due to an unsustainable economic policy. However, the oil industry strike, initiated in December, had a devastating impact on the external sector of the economy and forced the government to suspend all operations on the foreign exchange market, and to announce a temporary exchange rate control. After almost three month, the market was still closed. It is hard to tell if this situation was due to mere administrative inefficiency or some sort of political retaliation on the part of the private sector. Be that as it may, the consequences for economic activity will be considerable.

This peculiar situation has shown another side of the inefficiency of the Venezuelan economy. Up until the time of writing (the end of April 2003) there had been no shortages of any kind, which may be taken as a signal of the fact that the economy works with extremely great amounts of inventories. Another sign of the inefficiency of the Venezuelan economy was the general strike that lasted for more than two months with few visible effects. One may wonder if a highly developed and efficient economy could stand such a prolonged strike without undergoing a major catastrophe. What has happened in Venezuela hints at the conclusion that people working or not working is of little significance for the economy and this conclusion fits quite well with the nature of an economy fueled mainly by oil rent and not by labor effort.

NOTES

* The author appreciates the contribution of Germán Ríos in the preparation of the economic part of this chapter.

1. After the death of Juan Vicente Gómez in 1935, the political class that was formed under his long regime continued in power with two administrations led by López Contreras and Medina Angarita, both of whom were generals of the ancien régime, that ruled with a mild authoritarian style and with a Congress elected on a restrictive basis.
2. This is not the place to analyse neoliberalism. Suffice it to say that it is also a mix of old liberal ideas, oversimplified views of how a modern market economy functions, and despotic principles that has little to do with the old classical liberalism that sponsored a society of free and equal men. Islamic fundamentalism is another neoarchaism insofar as it is local nationalism.

REFERENCES

Baptista, A. (ed.) (1991), *Bases cuantitativas de la economía venezolana 1830–1989, Communicaciones Corporativas*, Caracas.

Baptista, A. (1997), *Teoría económica del capitalismo rentístico*, Ediciones IESA, Caracas.

Clemente, L. and A. Puente (2001), *Choques externos y volatilidad en Venezuela*, Venezuela Competitiva, Caracas.

Hausman, R. (1990), *Shocks Externos y Ajuste Macroeconómico*, Banco Central de Venezuela, Caracas.

Kaufmann, D., A. Kraay and P. Zoido-Lobaton (1999), *Governance Matters*, The World Bank.

Kenney, C. (1998), 'Anti-politicos intrusos y política democrática', *Politike* **2** (3).

Lewis, A. (1953), 'Economic development with unlimited supply of labor', *Manchester Journal*, May.

López-Naya, M. (2000), 'Organización y discurso en el MVR y el PPT', paper presented at workshop on 'Venezuela: logros, problemas y desafios del actual sistema político, Instituto de Estudios de Iberoamérica y Portugal, Universidad de Salamanca.

Mainwaring, S. and T.R. Scully (eds) (1995), *Building Democratic Institutions: Parties Systems in Latin America*, Stanford University Press.

Medina, M. (2001), 'Chávez y la globalización', *Revista Venezolana de Economía y Ciencias Sociales*, **2** (7), May–August.

Ramos, M. (2001), 'Partidos y grupos políticos en Venezuela (1998–2000) dimensiones ideológicas y cohesión pragmática', *Revista Venezolana de Economía y Ciencias Sociales*, **2** (7), May–August.

Roberts, K. (2001), 'La descomposicion del sistema de partidos políticos en Venezuela vista desde un análisis comparativo', *Revista Venezolana de Economía y Ciencias Sociales*, **2** (7), May–August.

Index